Thomas Francis Meagher

The commercial agency

Thomas Francis Meagher

The commercial agency

ISBN/EAN: 9783337185817

Printed in Europe, USA, Canada, Australia, Japan

Cover: Foto ©Suzi / pixelio.de

More available books at **www.hansebooks.com**

THE COMMERCIAL AGENCY

"SYSTEM"

OF THE

UNITED STATES AND CANADA

EXPOSED.

IS THE SECRET INQUISITION A CURSE OR A BENEFIT?

THE

COMMERCIAL AGENCY

"SYSTEM"

OF THE

UNITED STATES AND CANADA

EXPOSED.

IS THE SECRET INQUISITION A CURSE OR A BENEFIT?

BY

THOMAS F. MEAGHER.

"I love agitation; the fire-bell which alarms the inhabitants of a city saves them from being burned in their beds."—EDMUND BURKE.

NEW-YORK.

1876.

TO

The Merchants, Bankers, Manufacturers, and Traders

OF THE

United States and Canada,

WHOSE CHARACTERS AND COMMERCIAL CREDIT HAVE BEEN SO
LONG AND SO UNSPARINGLY TRAFFICKED IN, AND SO MANY
OF WHOM HAVE BEEN FINANCIALLY CRIPPLED OR
RUINED BY THE SYSTEM HEREIN EXPOSED,

THIS BOOK,

WRITTEN IN THEIR INTEREST, DESIGNED FOR THEIR IN-
FORMATION, AND INTENDED TO PREVENT GREATER IN-
JURY TO HONEST COMMERCE IN THE FUTURE,
IS RESPECTFULLY DEDICATED

BY THE AUTHOR.

TO MY READERS.

An intelligent examination of the claims of the Commercial Agency system, now seeking permanent incorporation into the business life of the United States and Canada, and refused hospitality or encouragement everywhere else, has been a want long felt by the business men of both countries. Up to the present moment, no one, whether from lack of facilities or deficiency of information, or a prudent disinclination to engage in a labor so certain to be onerous and so sure to be followed by bitter controversy, has seen fit to satisfy the general desire; and the writer, consequently, is not alone the first in an untried field of investigation, but has had to undergo the treble work of exploration, classification, and commentary. As he progressed, the dimensions of his subject seemed to expand, and he found himself quite as much embarrassed in choosing what he should exclude as in selecting what he should publish. This difficulty, inseparable from the topic, is relied on to explain and excuse any defects of style or method. For the rest, he believes he has kept within the limits of legitimate controversy, and prevented his unpleasant task of exposure from taking the objectionable and customary form of a rancorous criticism or a splenetic pasquinade. In essaying to set forth clearly the cardinal tricks and devices of a scheme of business of elaborate pretension and ramification, three conditions are essential : practical knowledge, a painstaking collation of evidence, and a disposition to draw just conclusions from proved facts. The author submits his work with confidence as an illustration of the first two. The reader must determine whether or not he has kept within the scope of fair discussion or substituted sophistry for reasoning. From the men who find their profit in the Agency system, favorable opinions are not expected. Indeed, their bitter opposition is desired, and, so far as possible, anticipated. The silversmiths of Ephesus naturally favored image-worship; and the iconoclast need not look for reward or commendation from the devotees and beneficiaries of imposture. But just in proportion to the violence and unreason of deeply and selfishly interested persons should be the desire of the press and the general public to assure the writer a fair and full hearing on the merits.

The author would be unjust to his own feelings if he omitted to acknowledge the many kindnesses of the press and leading merchants when the work was first announced. His hearty thanks are due to over a hundred daily newspapers published in English, German, and French, and over

five hundred weeklies, literary, religious, and polemical — several being
addressed, in the vernacular, to small constituencies of Welsh, Bohe-
mians, Scandinavians, etc., etc. Their considerate and elaborate encouragement, following quickly and spontaneously after the publication
of our Prospectus, in addition to private letters from editors, convinced us, more than any thing else, that our purpose would be fairly
judged, and induced us to enlarge our original plan from a mere collection of evidences of wrong-doing into a ready handbook of means
for reparation.   We felt it was not enough to put the trading public
on its guard, and that we should go farther and place it in a position to
retrieve loss and assert the rights of reputation.   Beside the facts given in
the text, a first instalment of the names of merchants depreciated in capital or character will be found in the Appendix.   This list will be increased
in future editions.   A complete one would entail the publication of a book
ten times the size of the present one, and place it at a price which would
greatly curtail the circulation (for the present, at least) of the more important part of the publication.   To the trading public, more than to any
special efforts of our own, the results of the agitation inaugurated herein
will be mainly due.   The individual merchant who discovers in the following pages, for the first time, his best defence against attempted or successful
libel, will naturally assist in circulating the book in self-defence; but it is
respectfully submitted that what would be a wise self-interest in the instance
of such a person is a just precaution or a judicious preventive for every
one who expects to lead a successful commercial career, and to enjoy the un-
impaired confidence and esteem of his fellow-citizens.

THE AUTHOR.

NEW-YORK, January 3, 1876.

NOTICE

TO THE VOLUNTEER CORRESPONDENTS

OF

THE MERCANTILE AND COMMERCIAL AGENCIES.

WHEN he commenced the publication of this work, the writer proposed to insert in the Appendix the names of the known correspondents of the several Agencies. Whilst it was passing through the press, he learned that large numbers of these persons were already ashamed of the business, fearful of exposure, and, for other reasons, dropping out of association with the Agencies. It occurred to him that great injustice might be done and needless annoyance given to these *converts to self-respect* by a publication of their names *after their withdrawal*, and that some more time should be given to permit the remaining libellers of neighbors to reflect, repent, and sever their connection also.

As his purpose is reformation rather than exposure—the permanent destruction of the detestable habit rather than the punishment of its dupes and accessories—he has finally determined to withhold the names of correspondents for the press or a future edition. Whoever desires to drop his connection with the system meantime, can inform me by letter, and his name will be taken off the list. The incorrigible or negligent can not complain if they find themselves duly announced as in the active exercise of a disreputable practice.

THOMAS F. MEAGHER.

Post-Office Box 4309, New-York City.

TABLE OF CONTENTS.

SECRET BLACK LISTS.

PART I.

THE COMMERCIAL AGENCIES.

———•◦•———

CHAPTER I.

PRELIMINARY.

"BUSINESS SOCIETY"—in the largest sense, the inter-communication of civilized man for admitted purposes of protection, profit, and culture—is a phrase representing an infinitely complex activity; but its definition, for the purposes of this work, may be properly expressed by calling it "that body of men who live by traffic in each other's goods, and profit or lose by reliance on each other's integrity."

The earliest recorded commercial transaction, involving money, is that in the Book of Genesis, 33 : 19, where Jacob is reported to have bought "a part of a field from the children of Hamor for a hundred pieces of money." Barter, exchange of commodity, must have been general, however, during the lifetime of Adam, and, either toward the close of his life, or very soon after it, must have reached a condition of fixed values suited to the wants of his immediate descendants; for we begin to find the word *hesitah*—which means, indifferently, "a lamb" or a "portion"—used as a standard among them: so many lambs, so much land. When the purely shepherd character changed into the more fixed patriarchal form, "flocks" came to be a means of comparison with "herds," and cattle and oxen signified relative values. From the thing itself to the symbol was the next step. One piece of money was marked with an ox; and thus money, as a representative and medium of exchange, took its names and devices from the first subjects of commerce.

A circulating medium may be anything, provided it be a current representative of value. In the Birman Empire, tin; on the coast of Africa, shells; in the interior of the continent, salt; within the territory of the oldest Asiatic and European monarchies, gold and silver—each became a medium; but since Jeremiah bought the field of Hanameel, his uncle's son, that was in Anathoth, and "weighed him the money, seventeen shekels of silver," or the later time when David bought "the threshing-floor, cattle, and agricultural implements of Ornan the Jebusite, for six hundred shekels of gold," silver and gold have been the principal media of trade for the far-scattered descendants of Shem and Japheth.

The modern trader, unlike the ancient, or even the mediæval one, need not bring gold or silver with him to effect purchases. All he requires is to have the reputation of possessing enough, and of being willing and able to discharge his obligations punctually. This reputation is called Commercial Credit.

As the first act of monetary trading was an Exchange, the latest one is neither more nor less. An *executed* exchange leaves undetermined merely questions of False Representation, Guaranty, Warranty, etc., as to the things exchanged. An *executory* exchange, bargain and sale, etc., turn almost wholly on the reputation of the persons proposing it, either in the sense of means to respond in damages, or, wanting adequate means, their assisting reputation for honor and integrity.

In ordinary dealings between men, executory traffic proceeds on a belief in the sufficiency of the means of the buyer; in exceptional cases, on their personal character, *cum* their means; but it is safe to say that society, in the commercial and trading sense, is constantly enlarging its demand for the security of tangible and executable goods, and relying, less and less daily, on the mere moral character of the owner. Whether this tendency be wise or unwise—whether it indicate a lowering of public morality, or a mere extension of relations incompatible with opportunities of personal knowledge of men's characters for honest dealing—is nothing to our purpose. It shows that a just estimate of the trading resources of individuals, firms, or corporations is a first condition of traffic, and that a false one endangers, limits, or destroys the opportunities of traffic, and either suspends, or causes to be withheld from business effort, the chance of honorable competition and the meed of appropriate success.

Since a correct estimate of men's means to fulfil their business

obligations is a first condition of successful business, a false estimate, either because of its being a wrong conclusioh from true
data, or the result of reasoning on an insufficient collection of *data*,
is, to persons engaged in traffic, an injury and wrong of prime importance, which can only result in restricted trading, or inadequate profit, or final ruin. Either consequence is to be avoided
and dreaded. For what do men work, from year to year, if not
for the probability of greater growth in confidence and multiplied
profits? And, even if their capital be so large and assured as to
render criticism or misrepresentation comparatively non-destruc-
tive or non-ruinous, is the escape from failure to be solely regarded,
and not the unjust and exacting struggle which they have been
compelled to wage when fully entitled to a prosperous peace?

In the United States and Canada the trading public, for the
first quarter of this century, had no settled terms of credit, as
now understood, which they applied *indifferently* to all whom
they credited; and none which depended, in any noteworthy degree, on what we may call extrinsic knowledge. Men trusted on
the basis of their own estimate of purchasers, whether as to morals
or means, assisted, perhaps, by the friendly advice of some local
trader who had experience of the habits of the particular applicant for credit. Where their knowledge was insufficient to justify
dealings, or they could not quickly get reliable corroboration, they
contented themselves with their stock, and allowed the proposed
trader to go elsewhere. A secret inquiry was a wound; and while
the seller felt "above it," the buyer was too high-mettled to purchase from the inquirer. Such a state of business was, of course,
a healthy and safe one, but it was also restricted. It was not
suited to a homogeneous political society like that of the United
States, where some States of the Confederation produced rice,
sugar, tobacco, and cotton, and others wheat, wool, iron, and lead—
natural exchanges—and the citizens required the facile substitution
of products to attain and enjoy the benefits of their climatic advantages, their inter-State free-trade, and liberal political institutions. The steamboat, the railroad train, the telegraph, the tide-
water canals, all conspired to quicken enterprise, to enlarge commercial relations, to make one seat of special activity promptly respond to the excitements and fluctuations of other seats of energy
or capital : and hence arose the necessity, with increased population

and production, for more extended markets, for more intimate acquaintance with the resources of traders and the character of go-betweens; and with these came the want of some authentic, or approximately authentic, substitute for the old-time restricted and personal inquiry of the individual merchant into the integrity and means of his proposed customers.

When Astor's agents bartered for peltries with the Indian and French *habitans*, he drove a cash business, and his agents had no occasion to inquire into the existence of a capital which they could see and touch whenever they chose; but when checks, bills of exchange, and promissory notes passed into general vogue as commercial substitutes for the issues of the First National Bank, and indicated the expanding energies of invested capital in forcing a market, it became the interest of producers to acquire a knowledge of the resources of the makers, drawers, and indorsers.

The earliest effort in this direction was by means of what are now known as Commercial Travellers—persons in the employment of a particular house, and accustomed to give the result of their investigation to the particular merchant for whom they worked. This method was expensive. It compelled two or more business firms in the same city to pay twice within a year for practically the same information. It had a further drawback in the eagerness of these travellers to sell under a risk, and so deserve either an increase of salary or an increased commission on sales. These allowances made, the device was sufficient for the occasion. While the American Hercules was yet engaged in his earliest feats of conscious power and beneficence; while the internal seas, lakes, and rivers of the country were throbbing with new forces, and distant communities coming together to traffic in the long and slowly-accumulated wealth of the Arcadian age; when to go or to be in debt, except for a brief period, or without resources treble its amount, was accounted madness or dishonesty,—a post-office address was as assuring as a deed of trust, and a man's full Christian name almost the business equivalent of a chattel mortgage. In such a state of society the casual traveller served his purpose well enough; and what he failed in was amply compensated for by the strict old-time determination to pay the last penny in satisfaction of an obligation. Even the law was rather a reserved than a used corrector and collector of unsettled accounts.

The East (there was, properly speaking, no West then) sold and the South bought; and the year's end found the balances adjusted and the temporary debtor a desired customer for the next year. What has more recently come to be called "Southern honor" had its origin in these justified confidences, and the commercial traveller was quite sufficient for all the demands arising out of them.

But the spirit of change entered into the people with the new discoveries. It soon seemed barbarous to imprison for misfortune in business, when speculation and energy, in tossing the dice of desperate chances, came to be regarded an individual honor and a national characteristic. The statutes in reference to arrest and imprisonment sensibly relaxed in several States. A bankrupt law followed. The introduction, outside of cities, of double-bolted doors, of burglar-proof safes, of a more general carrying of arms on the person, typified the growing sense of insecurity and the recedence of confidence. Some new contrivance had to be improvised to meet the new conditions of society. The formation of an association of merchants in New-York was the first step; the next was the joint appointment of a common agent, S. P. Church, to secure and forward weekly reports of the condition and business relations of merchants dealing or proposing to deal with the metropolis. His letters were copied and distributed among the members; were afterward printed, for greater expedition; and, finally, were bound and preserved under the title of "Church's Reports." Mr. Church was succeeded in the business by his brother, John R. Church. Lewis Tappan followed John R. Woodward and Dusenberry next entered the field; and in 1842 the feeble voices of two competing bureaux of Business Intelligence might be heard in New-York, only to be increased, some years later, by the addition of Bradstreet's, piped for a time on the banks of the Ohio, and transferred to the Hudson in the faith and trust of attaining a lustier pitch and more profitable perfection.

We have traced the need, and introduced the applied remedy. We admit the need. We deny the efficacy of the remedy.

CHAPTER II.

THE PRIMA-FACIE DIFFICULTIES OF SAFE INQUIRY—THE SPE-
CIAL DEFECTS OF INVESTIGATION BY BUREAUX OR IN MASS.

LIFE insurance is based on the certainty of death to a particular number of men in a particular period. The Northampton
tables are found, by long experience, to be equivalent to a mathematical demonstration of this number. But who can formulate
solvencies or insolvencies? or, if this can not be done in the
mass, who could affix the term of either to any particular man or
firm?

Quetelet, in his *Sur l'homme*, has shown a recurring series of
crimes, preserving a close approximation to uniformity of number
in a given period, but he reaches the result by considering crimes
as deeds of violence and, of course, the effective cause of death,
and not as mere breaches of moral or statutory law. In other
words, he takes the same known certainty of death as the Northampton tables, and merely differentiates, with the aid of census
and prison reports, from the result of violence to the variety of
methods of its illustration.

But there never can be a Table of Fraud compiled or logarithms of insolvency perfected. In its very essence the former is
elusive, and, resting in *intent* more than in consequences, human
ingenuity would be taxed in vain to seize it, in any stage of progress or development, in the individual or in the community;
whilst the latter, as it may be the result of a single. bad bargain,
as well as of a succession of bad bargains, or the incalculable acts
of others, is no less incapable of calculation. No system can be
devised, therefore, to overcome, or accurately anticipate, conditions and circumstances so complex and variable. In life insurance, besides, the insurer proceeds not only on the proved
average of deaths in a community, but he secures a scientific opinion of the state of health of the applicant *at the time of his ap-*

plication. Constitutional maladies are readily discovered. Aptitudes, or conditions specially favorable to the acquisition of contagious diseases, are noted; and a simulated health, or a fraudulent withholding of indicative symptoms or facts, is made sufficient to avoid the policy. The insurer, too, is in receipt of benefits long before he is called on to discharge obligations; and during the running of the policy, as well as afterwards, he has opportunities of detecting whatever might be used to defeat his liability. The merchant, on the other hand, must act at once, and give or refuse credit within a brief period. He must judge of appearances without scientific assistance. If he inquire personally and at the moment, he may either receive correct or false information, the value of which can only be truly determined when the time of credit shall have expired; and if he inquire through third parties—like the Agencies—he is only substituting their presumption for his own. Anything approaching a basis for a credit *formula* is plainly out of the question in commercial transactions, however recent may be the examination or however thorough the examiner. Wanting a basis of certainty, or method of averages, all attempts to define what are and what are not judicious estimates of credit must drop from the pretence of system to the plane of guess-work, with less or more chances in favor of or against the guesser. Whoever can best acquire the greatest amount of proximate truth in reference to the condition of a trader can (other things being equal) best determine whether credit should be given or withheld; and as the most recent and thorough investigator is most likely to arrive at a wise conclusion by procuring the latest information attainable, the individual who is incited by the greatest pressing interest is more apt than any one else to guess with less hazard of being every time, or in the majority of cases, mistaken. All men do not fail in business; the majority of traders prosper; few of the prosperous become fraudulent to become more prosperous temporarily: these are the rules for guidance possible, in all events; and these leave the whole inquiry of the application of credit to particular individuals to be only safely prosecuted by the person who might suffer personally through negligence, or by some one who bears an almost identical relation to the credit-giver.

In a later chapter we shall apply agency estimates to individuals, compare agency estimates with each other, and demonstrate, from the comparison, the infinite superiority of individual over agency guesses; but, meantime, we proceed to notice the salient elements of business life on which both must proceed to form and express opinions. The prime causes of business failures are, besides overtrading or illegitimate speculation, personal and family extravagance, gambling, and harlotry. We do not mention drinking; for it is, as a rule, the effect of failing fortunes, and not the efficient cause of them; whereas the other operative vices usually spring from excessive hopefulness or a luxury begotten of success. It might even be doubted whether or not indulgence in ardent spirits—short of habitual incapacity to do business—has ever, of itself, produced a business failure. Commercial honor never stood higher in this country than when the act of trading was opened and closed by a social glass in the very temple of Juno-Moneta. This habit led to intimacies and offices of hospitality and friendship. The fact of barter was only one incident of a social intercourse which the veriest cheat could not bring himself to disregard with impunity. Individual honor was pledged as well as commercial fidelity; and if reverses followed and the latter was not redeemed, the seller had no occasion to expect the pretended unfortunate had only passed from foraging on friends to an opulent privacy. The shamefacedness which now drives the professional gambler, and almost him alone, out of a society in which his word has been broken, was then so potent with all classes of men that our oldest merchants cannot recall an instance of one of their craft flaunting the profits of a fraudulent failure in the faces of his victims. Suicide or exile removed the dishonored; and public opinion enforced the alternative with greater vigor and remorselessness than courts or juries have since been able to exercise.

The far-reaching and secret habit of speculation with business capital in gold and stocks—"operating," as it is called in the language of the street—presents, in itself, an obstacle so great to the attainment of any sort of average certainty in calculating business risks, as to be practically impossible for the Agencies. It is no longer confined to the avowed brokers and speculators of our money centres. The artisan, the farmer, the merchant classes, all contribute their quota of enthusiasm and supply their share of margins, and the merchant class, notably and naturally, more than all the rest. With a broker in Wall street and a stock indicator at his elbow, the trader has every opportunity of taking a hand in that immense traffic in gold and stocks whose annual sale by means of the Gold Room and New-York Stock Exchange alone is computed at $22,000,000,000. A fortune may be made or lost in a day. A third, one half, all the capital and credit of a firm may be risked and swamped in less time than it would take to remove the shutters or open the safe.

The temptation afforded by this kind of speculation is not limited to any class of persons or any kind of business. It reaches everywhere. The clerk and his employer, the confidential manager and the senior capitalist, the company's secretary and the banking-house cashier, feel the insidious influence of the rise and fall of gold and stock in Wall and Broad streets. It has become so universal that its results can no longer be separated, with any accuracy, from such heretofore controlling processes as the procession of the Seasons, the growth or failure of Crops, or Peace or War at home or abroad. Outside speculation is no longer an exceptional fact in the lives of our business men—a Tulip-Fever or a Cochin-China madness; a "put," a "call," or a "turn" have become a general language and express a general activity. In the era of knee-breeches and silver buckles, people pointed at a wagerer in the few stocks then in vogue as a man apart from the ways of men. To-day the difficulty would be to show a man who is not a wagerer on the possibility of a possibility—a secret thrower of the dice of chance—a tossing Bull or a squeezing Bear of some State or municipal security, preferred railroad, mining or manufacturing stocks. There may be no account of his transactions in the ledger. They may be—generally are—kept secret from his business friends. But they write themselves in his care-worn face, and either lift him to sudden affluence or precipitate him into as wondrous poverty.

How can a mercantile or commercial Agency learn, calculate, or approximate the extent of this universal habit on business men's capital and credit? How can it foretell by an hour, a month, or a year, whether an unknown investment shall prove fortunate or unfortunate, when the investor himself is so often mistaken and deceived? Many times the whole available floating capital of the country is turned over in Wall and Broad streets within a year. Who can predicate of any particular part of it that the places which knew it once shall know it any more forever ?

We do not ask how it is possible for the Agencies to anticipate a Black Friday or some lesser calamity at any time—for prescience like this could not be pretended ; but we inquire, what can they know of the ordinary daily dealings of any single man in the Stock Board or in the Street? Absolutely nothing. The reader versed in the names and fortunes of Wall and Broad streets need only look at the ratings of any dozen of his acquaintances to learn the consequence. A more perfect *bal masqué* cannot be conceived. Every one will be found to have a different character from what the reader knows him to possess, and one just as different from his " street" character as it is possible to be variant. Relations find poorer relations, who could not control one thousand dollars over and above the value of their seat, rated in the hundreds of thousands ; others, with hundreds of thousands, not rated, or despitefully used. It would occupy too much space to give instances which must be at the finger-ends of every banker, broker, and operator. While we pay from $150 to $5000 yearly subscription, we must not be surprised to find Henry Clews & Co. standing as high in credit as A. T. Stewart & Co. when the firm was not worth one tenth of its liabilities, and Jay Cooke & Co. exalted to the skies in credit and capital at the very moment when courts of Common Law and Bankruptcy were contending, preliminarily, which should dole out his shrunken values and appease the cries of speculating widows and investing orphans.

Harlotry and concubinage are just as difficult of estimate as secret speculations. They are mainly modern in our commercial classes. The leman and the kept-mistress were, forty years ago, the luxuries of the professional classes and the hereditary capitalist in lands or slaves. The growth of great commercial fortunes, and the decreasing horror of libertinism, transferred the custom of two households to the sons of trade, proper; and investments of this kind are now, very generally, elements of disturbance and doubt in the computation of business risks.

Whilst we think the moderate use of ardent spirits should not be weighed, if it could, in credit ratings, we concede that the dual family establishment is of prime significance to the creditor class.

Its progeny are recklessness, desperation, shame, and ruin. Indulged in, at first, as a contrast to the even tenor of conjugal love; persisted in afterwards from a sense of choosing between the evil of loss and the disgrace of exposure, but always a source of present prodigality, and an inducement to hazardous ventures promising large returns, the meretricious relationship affects the business community more than all other causes combined. The expenses of the admitted home may be estimated by the careful creditor at all times, and curtailed by the debtor in emergencies. The exactions of the hidden hospice of lust are under the direction of the imps of whim and caprice, and are only certain to be uncertain, sure to be selfish and profligately persistent. Worse than wine, worse than faro, the hidden *liaison* corrodes and crushes the man of business. Faro may select one from thousands to load with a special luck; wine may make friends who shall prove of service in the day of trouble; but Lais, never compensative, hastens to plant the poppy of forgetfulness over her latest victim, and celebrates his ruin by advertising it to his successor.

Personal and family extravagance in dress and living is another subject of consideration in estimating business risks. It is undoubtedly carried to great excess, but it is under the restraint of publicity, and therefore subject to approximate computation. It is not always voluntary or a proof of poor business habits, the thriftiest and most prudent often submitting to it from necessity, and making up for prodigality at the house by parsimony at the store. Again, is not this the era of show? and how can we always be positive that the front pew at the church, for a fabulous price, or the sumptuous entertainment, or the costly equipage, are not so many judicious advertising tricks, and well calculated to lead to business advantages in extremity, or even go far to compensate for restricted capital?

All these subjects must, in one form or another, enter into the calculations of the circumspect seller. They should be considered carefully by the agencies, if agencies are to attempt supplanting individual investigation. In this connection, inquiry, to be efficient, must be impersonal, dispassionate, direct as possible, and thorough. Is it? Not at all. The chance phrase of some chance acquaintance is picked up by the readiest or most attentive ear.

It may mean a fast life with abundant means, a fast life without means, or a fast tendency, with the highest commercial standing and integrity. To Deacon Sniveller, of the basement, a Park outfit is proof of coming bankruptcy in the case of Solomon Lightheart, of the first floor front. An equal expenditure for the support of "The Home for able-bodied Pharisees" would insure a very different interpretation. What is mere energy and dash to the critic of forty years is dare-devilism and recklessness of the worst kind to the eye of sixty or seventy years. Weston, without explanation, is only a "tramp," and Bennett unexplained, with his yachts and wagers and walking matches, is only a younger Jim Mace, with the *Herald* newspaper thrown in. So controlling and important are these shallower judgments of the tattlers of trade, which the agencies represent, that the heartiest, the purest, and the financially strongest men are obliged to resort to a self-protecting hypocrisy and make-believe in their exterior life and bearings. From these persons, too, rather than from the straight-laced, churches receive their best aids and charity finds her most munificent benefactors. By a further and parallel necessity, almost every great business scandal and fraud recently broached and practised has had a religious phase to it. Howard's Washington Steeple rested on the empty vaults of the Freedman's Savings Bank. The Clergyman's Retreat in Lake Erie prefigured the bankrupt glories of Ogontz. And almost all the wildest or least-principled of the disciples of Mammon, from Fisk and Gould to Cooke and Clews, raised temples to Christ in veriest mockery of the Nazarene.

We have indicated a few of the obstacles to any kind of accuracy in business estimates; we proceed to notice the one above all others which produces inaccuracy and injustice. Any one who has read the reports of the agencies knows that they are suffused with the essential essence of the spirit of Cant. Liquorish praise or deadly ichor distinguishes them. That set of men who may be classed as the old maids of the sex, whose spleen is greater than their judgment, and their active malice greater than both, are the fact and surmise gatherers and the true authors of these undermining commentaries. Their test is a simple one : Is he a church member in good standing? Does he subscribe to the Tract Society, direct a Sunday-school, help in a choir? In either event a cheery certificate passes. Lesser claims to piety are also recognized, but in a descending scale. An " A 1 " heathen will generally be found to bear, in the private archives, a worse financial character than the struggling " brother."

It is not alone the tendency of the shrewdest and most politic business men to anticipate hostile cant by acquiring a church membership. The owners and city and country reporters of the agencies affect the same judicious show of moral pretence. McKillop, of McKillop & Sprague Co., acts as pastor to a congregation at Flatbush, L. I., in a church partially erected and wholly supported by him. The admitted reason of his ministration is to save the expenses of a regular clergyman. The profane allege that it is to preserve, in fullest opportunity of weekly iteration, the standing advertisement of his own godliness and contributions. Tupper, of Dun, Barlow & Co., carries his mortified body—attenuated by many fasts and vigils—across the rapt visions of the Seventh Avenue United Presbyterian congregation. Anderson, of the same agency, is an active Methodist and hot revivalist. Wiman was a rigid Presbyterian in Toronto, a Baptist in Montreal, and is now an Episcopalian on Staten Island. It used to be the pride and boast of Tappan, the foster-father of the system, that he retained no man in his employment who was not a church member, and who could not give the text of the Sunday sermon.

The device is a natural one. In all ages the shrines of piety possessed a special attraction to the most adventurous spirits. Silly nobles, weak kings, here and there, attempted to escape oblivion by a stained window, a tapestry-lined chancel, or an enduring sculpture ; but the most lavish givers have always been the boldest getters, from the Borgias of Florence to the church-building Plantagenets and Tudors of England. The comment holds good in our own time. The church not raised on the profit of adulterated food, watered stocks, or a well-timed " corner" seldom or never rises outside the granger districts of our God-fearing society. Science is the beneficiary of the successful literary or professional man. Humanity or philanthropy attracts the ingots of the honest and humane. The religion of rewards and punishments secures the greater portion of the deceitful favors of the profitably time-serving and advantageously corrupt of every trade and calling.

In these church associations, mainly, the agencies procure their private history of business men.   You may live long next door to a city merchant without knowing his private history.   Belong to the same church with him, or know a brother who belongs to it, and your greatest difficulty will soon be to cut off or lessen the flow of scandal which the connection pours by unknown processes out of his home and into yours, and *vice versa.*

The agencies dabble in these waters of bitterness for want of better.   They must accept the measures in which they are meted out or go unrefreshed.   The blind, the halt, and the lame, in the outside world's opinion, here drop their defects and crutches and go forth new men.   The hearty, and upright, and straightforward, in the outside world's opinion, are admonished and soon made to feel their unworthiness.   The results to character are astounding judged from a non-church standard ; but they are certain, and contribute more to the tone and temper of agency opinion and litera-ture than the inquisitiveness of the press, the disclosures of the courts, or the loquacity of traders, combined.

Let us not be misunderstood : we make no war on the grand inquisition of the churches.   We merely inquire of the business men of the country if they are content to be judged by the knaves and hypocrites who may enter into these leagues for the purpose of more recondite fraud or the more facile satisfaction of malice.

The truly good members are not the tale-bearers and slanderers. They are too busy serving God to injure their fellows.   But the splenetic, the suspicious, the sore-headed press forward in the work of slander and detraction, and assume and hold the places fitted for modest merit and true piety.   The narrow-minded zealot; the addle-pated professor of some pet social fanaticism; the knave who fawns on the prosperous only to assail the aspiring with more successful malignity : who would, who should, be content to be judged by these? or, being judged, who would submit to have these horned beetles and stinging wasps of the social hive pass current for the correct in conduct, the best in manners, and the highest in business dealings?   Into these church reservoirs of news, backbitings, profitable malice, and passionate phariseeism the agencies go for material for opinion.   They contribute the " facts" often, the " tone" always ; and the agencies, from necessity or design, receive the darkest pigments in their reports, and the most bleaching lotions as well, from the dripping of the sanctuaries.

The reader can estimate the chances of accuracy in the presence of these complex difficulties resting in the very nature of the agencies' investigations, or arising out of the initial efforts to prosecute them. He can, we think, already agree with us in our first proposition, that the agency pretence of aiding trade by correct estimates of credit and capital is sadly marred at the very threshold of our criticism; and that between elements which would embarrass and deceive the very best individual examination into a man's circumstances, and others which go merely *to disturb the transmitting medium*, the agencies are powerless to intelligently advise risks or to regulate credits.

CHAPTER III.

FURTHER DIFFICULTIES OF THE SYSTEM CONSIDERED : THE AGENCIES CREATING THEM.

GIVEN a perfectly honorable management, a mercantile or commercial agency such as McKillop & Sprague Co., Dun, Barlow & Co., and J. M. Bradstreet & Sons possesses certain *inherent* defects. No man can serve two masters. An agency cannot, in the nature of the thing, take pay from the buying and selling classes and do full justice to both. It must be two-faced, under the operation of its conflicting purpose. The Western subscriber who purchases imported goods on credit in New-York finds the seller a subscriber here. The New-York subscriber who goes to Boston, Lowell, Philadelphia, or Cincinnati for particular lines of manufacture, finds the seller a subscriber in those cities. Vendor or vendee, both pay the agency, and the agency must strike *an accommodating mean* to secure their support, or, to be fully just to one, must take the other's pay while it depreciates or destroys his responsibility. The first consequence is a natural and inevitable one. To get and keep subscribers the agencies must approximate their opinions of themselves (when it reports them as they really are) ; and, efficiently for others, it must depart from what they conceive themselves entitled to, and incur the loss of patronage. Between the caution of the seller, which always exacts a large allowance of surplus assured assets, and the halcyon opinion of the buyer, who always places a flattering rating on his own resources, the agency finds its first difficulty, and enters, in self-defence, on its first deception. As it takes pay from both it endeavors to satisfy both. To cater to the seller's sense of caution it indulges in cheap generalities and crams of business wisdom. To a grain of even hypothetical statement it adds a pound of flimsy phrases which may mean anything or nothing to the eager and suspicious inquirer. The ratings dance up or down like colored balls in a toy fountain, as the

stream of drivel rises from " good for a *reasonable* credit" up to " good for all engagements, but of little reputation in the trade, and worth watching," and falls again to " the man has capital to *some* amount, which cannot be ascertained," or " pays promptly, but the money is presumed to come from his father, who failed in business last year and is *supposed* to work on a salary."

To add to the Delphic doubtfulness and wary inconsequence and attenuated meanings of these reports, a language of symbols is adopted, where the Arabian Alphabet and Roman Numerals do service in affording lurking-places for ignorant guessing; labyrinths of inference where the seeker of information may wander in endless mazes, lost; covered ways where character and credit may be " knocked in the head " or not with sublime indifference and benign impartiality—the end and object of all the *finesse* being simply to shield and shroud in a twilight haze the tricks and devices by which wholesalers and retailers, buyers and sellers, are all exploited, and neither benefited, intelligently rated, nor intelligently advised.

This is not merely an intermittent vice of the system of attempting to reconcile two irreconcilable interests ; to extend and preserve a clientage in practically antagonistic classes : it is the first and insurmountable consequence of the enlargement of the system beyond the service of the selling classes, and its perversion, for the simple purpose of clear gain, to every one who will buy a reference-book and advance a subscription.

A second intrinsic and insurmountable difficulty of the system is the remoteness of the persons affected, whether as seekers or givers of credit, from the information giving and receiving centres. We do not mean remoteness in space—for the telegraph, if parsimony did not prevent its use, might be made to overcome that element of inconvenience—but remoteness, in degree, from the original sources of information. The chief office or district one, or the manager of either, has never personally *met* five hundred of the hundreds of thousands of persons who figure in the agency pages and reports ; of this five hundred the *true* financial position of a *single one* has never been *personally* inquired into and determined by the person in charge of the chief office or district offices. The collection of names and pretended data in the agency books is simply the result of chance contributions of intelligence from, generally,

the least self-respecting and least-liked man in his own community :
self-reporting, which is taken for granted, if joined with any
professed interest in or service for the agency, or is accepted with
thanks because costless, and merely toned down with a judicious
respect for the benefactor ; or the reprinted and revamped accumulated odds and ends of business directories and former or
other agency reports, of ten to thirty years' standing. Not a par-
ticle of this agglomerate of names, figures, guesses, self-praise, dis-
praise, malice has been subjected to critical examination by the
agency managers, in the first instance. They collect it in New-
York from the country, receive and dump it into print, and trust
to luck whether it shall ever be inquired into ; or, if inquired
about, shall be powerless for good or evil because of its vagueness;
or, if erroneous and harmful, that it will be viewed as an attempt
in the interest of trade to be commended or overlooked.

Now, while it is manifest local sources of information are the
very best and the only reliable means of *data*, persons in the vici-
nage, even if in high standing, are the most likely to be passionate
and prejudiced estimators of its value and importance ; and the
reader can readily judge of the original value of *data* furnished by
unpaid *volunteer* censors, inquisitors invited to judicial functions
by haphazard selections from a lawyer's directory and their own
reference-books, or the eager witnessing of some competitor in the
same line of business " over the way." The volunteer informer is
sure to have a reason of his own in meddling with his neighbor's
affairs. Human experience disqualifies him as an unsupervised
collector of facts or opinions. The substantial men in a community never sink to this work. It can only be performed or tendered, therefore, by the ill-at-ease, struggling, acrid spirits of the place
—the meddlesome, mischief-making busy-bodies, whose moving-
springs are envy, greed, uncharitableness, or disappointed ambition.

The requested legal inquisitor generally bears the same relation
to his profession that the volunteer informer bears to society at
large. He is never the leading man, never among the leading men
of the local bar, if the town have three thousand or over inhabitants. In small places, he may be among the least engaged of the
two or three who can survive in such restricted pasturage. But
he is sure to be asked, either because he is *not* engaged in lucrative
litigated practice (for such a man would be too much related to

and associated with the business men, and too self-respectful to speak), or because he *is* engaged in some accessory employment, like that of a notary, commissioner, etc., which indicates in itself, to the legal profession, a struggle for life on the stray planks and spars where some higher purpose, some nobler ambition, went down in storm or darkness; or, finally, because some satisfactorily rated subscriber engages him for cheap collection work, at low prices, knows him best, relies on his friendly obsequiousness, and refers to him in furtherance of his own ends, and, perhaps, for better injury to his most hated competitors. Postmasters, postmistresses, and medical doctors, whose names are readily found in the post-office or town directories, are also picked out at random, and transferred by the agencies to what they term their "Correspondents' List," which is drawn upon when necessary. As these persons act without pay, their punctuality is the only qualification regarded. *These are the only sources of supply possessed or used by the agencies outside of New-York and the larger cities.* Their only recommendation is their cheapness, for they cost the agency nothing; and it is from these sources, and long accumulations of their tinged, muddy, and credit-destroying contributions, that the agencies pretend to dole out, at from $150 to $5000 yearly, the elixir of a lusty business life, and the healing water of business salvation!

The agencies, in fact, do not know the people inquired about; they do not know the persons from whom they inquire about them; they do not know, and can never learn, except through the intelligence of a libel-suit or the crash of a bankruptcy, whether or not these persons report falsely or only a tittle of the truth; and it is this unrevised, unauthenticated hearsay of hearsay, this secret *cloaca* of the most distressed and desperate of the community— unfiltered, undeodorized, and infected—that the agencies pretend to be the product of their paid *attachés*, examination of original records, and the impartial judicial result of a process of searching examination pursued under their own painstaking and dispassionate supervision. Judged by every personal test, it is just the antithesis of their representations. Indeed, it may be conceded that the agencies could not do otherwise; the expense of becoming acquainted by record, and keeping acquainted weekly, even with the fluctuations of business men in the city of New-York alone, would exhaust the resources of the strongest agency. It is not attempt-

ed; it could not be effected, if attempted, by less than a million of
capital, confined to a single city; and hence the second radical and
insurmountable difficulty results, as we have noted, in not alone a
necessarily vague and indefinite, but a prejudiced, passionate, and
purely haphazard expression of what one person, with motives all
unknown to the agencies, says of one or more other persons, with
means or character unknown to the agency or its office employees,
who cook the books and dish up the reports. The work of revis-
ing the financial standing and credit of the business men of the
United States and Canada, which Dun, Barlow & Co. claim to be
done by their own travellers *four times a year*, so as to render their
quarterly reference-book of some value, would require the aid of
1424 men *constantly employed as travelling reporters only*. If their
entire staff of paid employees (numbering less than 500), from errand-
boys to managers, in all their branches in America, worked in that
capacity twelve months in the year, *a period of not less than three
consecutive years must elapse* before the affairs of each trader could
undergo a single personal investigation! During all this time their
offices should be deserted and closed, and the work of soliciting
subscriptions wholly abandoned. The same argument is relatively
true of the other agencies. Besides these inherent difficulties, the
avarice of the proprietors of the agencies, assisted and encouraged
by the indifference or gullibility of the trading public, has fastened
several additional causes of difficulty and embarrassment on the
original project. The *publication and sale*, for profit, of yearly,
half-yearly, and quarterly reference-books, is one of the first and
worst of these. This is a plain temptation to the dishonest or
doubtful trader to secure the agency for his own purposes, *since
he is apprised of what he is rated at*, and is naturally anxious to
propitiate the critic of his solvency, or actively mislead the impugn-
er of his integrity. When the rating is an agreeable surprise,
the trader naturally encourages the enterprise. When it is not
favorable, he sets to work to make it so by propitiating the pretended arbiters. Failing in this, by oversight or otherwise, in one
year, he turns to the publications of some of the competing agencies for the next. The consequence is seen in the contradictory
ratings given of the same person or firm by two or more agencies
for the same year or a series of years. When the ratings are not
copied from each other by the rival companies, the fluctuations of

reported standing and credit are largely produced by these active methods of interference. The observer sees one needle violently recording changes of direction, while the other is fixedly pointing to a settled course of prosperous voyaging; while one pilot shouts "all's well," the other shrieks "breakers ahead;" and while the interested inquirer watches the whirling indicator, and listens in doubt and amazement to the confusing assurances, he becomes only certain of one thing—that he has learned nothing more valuable than his conviction that "all hands," except himself and others financially interested in the outcome of the venture, are busily and profitably occupied in trading on its purely speculative features. As a prudent man he will trust to neither; as a cautious man he will treasure his experience in his own breast; as both, he will take care not to attract attention to his discovery, but leave the public to find out the secret for themselves by a saddening realization of the assault on their judgment and pockets. He may be pleased to read the truth in these pages; but if he be wanting in public spirit and a leek-eater, he will renew his subscription and buy the next reference-book; and the agencies will go on making money by the yearly traffic in the fears or credulity of the trading public.

Another indication of the determined greed of the agencies, and one also largely injurious and destructive to any policy of learning the true standing of business men, is the development of Collection bureaux in connection with them, and owned and controlled by them. J. M. Bradstreet & Son, alone, have not yet adopted this specialty. The subscriber who entrusts his claims to the agency for collection *advertises, by so much, his doubtful or valueless credits;* suffers from having them placed in the hands of the cheapest, least expert and self-respectful lawyer, such as we have indicated; and in very many instances, in the hands of the attorney recommended to the agency by the creditor's debtor, or only self-introduced to the agencies by his own necessities and want of responsibility. Friendly delays, inefficient prosecution, the need of employing additional counsel in case of litigation, are a few of the earlier consequences to the creditor. The later ones are: compromises, cooked up by a man capable of becoming an eavesdropper on his neighbor for the mere love of the employment, and, therefore, capable of being bribed to produce them; bankruptcies precipitated, in which the attorney, as attorney for the moving creditor, will be paid out of the *debtor's* estate three or five times as much as he could have collected from his client, the creditor, in case of collecting the full amount of the claim; or a return of the claims, particularly if unliquidated, with the purchased assurance that they would cost more than they are worth. The scheme of collection, however, although of no value to creditors, except in cases where the debtor is eager to pay, and the laughing-stock of the bar in every other case, serves one purpose for the agency. It enables them to call on the attorney, who hopes to secure any chance patronage which they may have to dispense, for his opinion of any citizen in his vicinity, suddenly inquired about, and, as it costs nothing, this is reason enough with the agencies for its introduction and existence. Its damaging influence to the selling classes is easily traced. Whom this incompetent and always uninfluential limb of the law is acquainted with personally or through the medium of a *douceur* are discovered to be rated far above their means; whom he dislikes or is not on profitable relations with, are marked down; and the business public have to bear the consequences of the latest devices of the agencies to secure the opinion of the only man in the community who sets no value on his pretended knowledge *except what he can make out of it by indirection.* "Like master like man." Why should he trouble himself, for a possibility of patronage, to acquire by a laborious search the true resources of a merchant, when he knows that the agency, which receives immense remuneration, does not condescend to pay out any portion in securing it? He forwards his gratuitous guess, or his bribed opinion; finds satisfaction in gratifying a spite or making a point for a crony; and turns to negotiate for some fire or life insurance company, which might occupy the talents or reward the industry not illustrated so much in contests in court as in applications to the Governor for vacant notaryships, or in wire-pullings for some justice-of-the-peace nomination.

We have sketched the intrinsic difficulties in the way of the usefulness of any mercantile or commercial agencies whatever; indicated the accidental impediments to usefulness added by the avarice of their managers; and cleared the road for that detailed and more searching analysis of their interior workings which it will be the province of the following chapters to enforce by precept and example.

CHAPTER IV.

WHAT THE AGENCIES RECEIVE : WHAT THEY DO FOR IT, AND HOW IT IS DONE. HOW THEY THRIVE WITHOUT DESERVING. "THE HEALTH-LIFT," AND "MOTH-EXTERMINATOR."

THE three agencies, J. M. Bradstreet & Son, McKillop & Sprague Co., and Dun, Barlow & Co., having their principal offices in New-York, claim, together, some 150 branch offices in the United States and Canada. Each endeavors to start as many self-supporting and paying branches as it can; neither ever continues a losing branch "for the promotion of trade," that is, the advantage of subscribers in other places. In all the principal cities the agencies are found competing for local subscriptions; in those of small population they sometimes try the experiment, but desist when the receipts fail to justify the expense. The three institutions extract nearly $8,000,000 yearly from the merchants, manufacturers, and traders of both countries.

This enormous drain on the resources of the business community has not been going on for more than a few years; but it is safe to say that since 1841 more than $60,000,000 have been collected by the present agencies or their predecessors in the same line of effort. Allowing for the payment of salaries, printing reports, rents, etc., a net profit of between $20,000,000 and $30,000,-000 must have been received and divided among the proprietors !

One would expect to find some very heavy items of disbursement for procuring the information which produces this royal revenue. Surprise will become wonder when we assert that, outside of the city of New-York, where reporting and subscription-getting go hand-in-hand, the agencies, together, have not spent $50,000 for collecting information which they dispense with such magnificent profit, and that even this sum was largely spent in the effort to get subscribers, and not a dollar of it, purely and simply, to learn the business standing of business men ! In other words, the

whole aim and object of the agencies are to expend only to profit
themselves, and they care nothing for the acquisition of true and
useful information, if it must be costly, for its own sake.   Their ·
expenses are incidental to the receipt and disbursement of their
revenue ; nothing, or next to nothing, is applied, outside of New-
York and the principal cities, to earning or deserving it.   If a
subscriber wants definite intelligence, he must pay for telegraphing : the agencies will only pay for postage if the applicant can
afford to wait from *five* to *thirty* days for an answer by mail.
Whatever they can get for nothing they sell ; what they would
be required to pay for is never purchased.

For instance, if H. H. Shufeldt & Co., of Chicago, or Smith,
Angus & Co., of Milwaukee, desire to inquire about the credit and
standing of M. J. Cummings or Irwin & Sloan, grain merchants
in Oswego, N. Y., the agency's part in supplying the information
entails an expenditure of exactly 12 cents.   The application is
first made to the Chicago or Milwaukee offices, which pay each
from $50,000 to $70,000 yearly profit on subscriptions alone ; either
office posts a letter to the Syracuse branch, which office either replies by returning the information on its record (which may be one
or more years old), or mails a query to E. M. Fort, the unpaid Oswego
correspondent, whose particular qualification for answering is that
he is a coal dealer, doing business only as agent, having recently
no business of his own, for reasons currently understood.   If the
letter is sent to Fort, he replies at his leisure to the Syracuse
office, which, in turn, mails its opinion of Mr. Fort's opinion, concealing his name, to the Chicago or Milwaukee branch, as the case
may have been.   After this pilgrim's progress the *wise* result is
communicated to the original inquirer, who meantime may have
had the luck to either have lost a good customer or to have escaped
the possibility of being deceived into trusting a bad one.   In this
process, it must be apparent to the reader, that the agency would not
presume to inquire from a person or firm of first-class business
principles, and only imposes the loss of time on one whom they
have already favored beyond his deserts, or who expects they will
do so.   This illustrates the role of the commercial Volunteer correspondent.

Now let us take the course pursued in the instance of the At-
torney-detective-correspondent, whose sole compensation is the

hope of having claims sent to him for collection, and being represented by the agency as the most reliable and brightest legal luminary of that neighborhood. Suppose Richardson & Co., of St. Louis, or A. Thomson & Co., of New-Orleans, or Drexel, Morgan & Co., Eaton & Cole, and J. M. Thorburn & Co., of New-York, inquire in the New-York or local offices for the antecedents of Martin F. Braisted & Co., bankers, New-York City, and it transpires that one of that firm formerly lived in Westchester County, N. Y., the agency drops a letter (return postage, 6 cents) to James P. Sanders, of Yonkers, N. Y., *their* reliable attorney and legal luminary aforesaid, who, in reply, retails whatever the glibbest tongue may tell him or the least laborious investigation may result in. Of course, an examination of the county records is not thought of, nor is any other source than rumor consulted; for remitted claims are few and far between in Yonkers, and shoe-leather must be saved for respectable intermittent appearances in justice courts.

Just here it is proper to add that the agencies' habit of recommendation cuts both ways. No attorney is recommended to subscribers or others who is not a correspondent, although the agency will unblushingly deny the fact, and the inquirer is refused the opportunity of choosing the generally better and abler men at the local bar, who will not condescend to resort to such an association for a practice.

It may be said this course is not in accordance with a true economy, for they must expect to be found out some time, or become generally discredited, and business men are not apt to continue paying for nothing. The suggestion would have force if applied as a test to any business involving an exchange of a real commodity whose defects could and would be discovered by every buyer in every place; but it has no analogy to the case of an enterprise which *possesses the coercive power of rating every man in the community as its managers or clerks may see fit.*

To fully understand the agencies we must always bear this fact in mind:—that they practice an exceptional business, with exceptional means of affecting the purse or the pride of every man whose name they choose to put into print. To appreciate the consequences we must remember that human nature is a limited quantity, and that whoever can do what the agencies can do by rating and printing—to say nothing of private reports—will always find more dupes or sycophants than assailants.

If a dozen palpable errors are discovered in the reports by a business man in an interior town, he concludes that they occur through the partiality or cupidity of the local correspondent—objects to apply the experience to the whole field of agency reporting—and determines that, since error and falsehood are so easily passed for truth and accuracy, he had better join the enterprise, and purchase a favorable rating or guard against an arrantly false one. He does not buy or sell on the agency *dicta;* but he determines to join the vast array of approved souls whom he finds translated by a subscription into the higher heaven of business beatification, and to avoid the fate of the less thoughtful and prudent, who are sent to the limbo of mercantile discredit.

The errors of the agencies in this manner, far from being deterrents to patronage, are most urgent and active inducements to patronage. Thousands of honest and reliable men subscribe in self-defence; other thousands subscribe for utilizing the aids which such a system supplies to contemplated fraud. Between both classes, the lists increase with a growing rapidity, and the example is only lost on the strongest minds or the strongest capitalists. Suppose a business man is convinced of the inutility of the institutions, and carefully avoids contributing to them. They rate him notwithstanding. They rate his competitors. At some point his interests will be found to conflict with his opinions. The agencies have an additional subscriber, if not a convert.

Another consideration is also operative. As business fraud is best effected by means of a credit-giving agency which *pretends* to be indifferent, and circulates largely where applicants are otherwise unknown, the knave and swindler know where to find an ally under the mask of an enemy. Their own opinion of themselves would not go far or yield fruitfully. A single false representation might cut short a career of roguery by giving occasion and justification for an order of arrest and putting in of bail. If the rogue can keep his tongue quiet, and have an agency to do his talking, the danger is averted; opportunities are multiplied; and a scheme, which might otherwise be rendered futile after a single effort, in a single city or town, is enabled to achieve an elaborate and far-reaching failure with comparative immunity.

It may well be doubted whether any plan was ever devised

appealing to so many of the worst and lowest human motives at once. The quack-medicine business proceeds on one principal national weakness : the known peculiarity that almost every one considers himself or herself ailing, in some way, in a country whose prevailing sickness is dyspepsia and the attendant hypochondriacal affections. The patent-right fever appeals to the well-known traditions of suddenly acquired wealth, by means of even simple inventions in an era of inventions. The New-England Genealogical Bureau was never a real success, although it flattered family pride in a particularly sensitive portion of the country, anxious, somewhat, to compete with the untabulated pedigrees of the Southern chivalries. But the agencies touch the weak, the vindictive, the unscrupulous, in their greeds, their fears, their rivalries, their passions, their hopes of betterment, their anxieties to guard against loss, and, at every point, present an inducement or excite a sense of danger or insecurity.

Deeply considered, the wonder is, not that they have succeeded so greatly in procuring wealth from the community, but that, assisted by the supineness of their victims and the prevailing love of ease, they have not yet passed beyond the pale of damaging criticism and deserved and adequate exposure.

Whatever may be thought of the agencies, their own conduct betrays a consciousness of weakness. Their latest device to give something for nothing is apt and illustrative. They have caught at the conceit of a Health Intelligence Bureau, whereby insurance agencies and others may learn the condition of health of any person in a neighborhood for two dollars—one for the agency and one for the medical diagnoser. This small sum, we are to suppose, insures valuable medical information—as valuable in proportion as any furnished in regard to men's commercial standing. The reader can conceive the social and medical "rating" of a doctor whose restricted practice or estimate of the value of his own opinion induces him to examine, certify, and report a patient for one dollar, and can also approximate the caution of an insurance company which would accept a life risk on the recommendation of so cheap-priced and remote an Æsculapius. "All premiums, no responsibility" must be the motto and purpose of such a company, just as " all subscriptions and no accountability" is the true shibboleth of the agencies. The revenue derived from this experiment is not large, however, and we only allude to the matter to show the mean minuteness of rapacity which actuates the policy-makers of the institutions. By a natural sequence, projects known to their authors to be hollow and unsubstantial are constantly accreting accessories and helps to buoyancy. The "seventh son of a seventh son, born with a caul" is the natural progenitor of the boy who invents an insect-destroyer or becomes a corn-doctor, and supplements his precarious business by the sale of rat-paste. Credulity may have an end in one direction: and it is the part of conscious insolvency of merit to devise a change of base which may enable the old furniture to be applied to new uses.

Following out this idea, the gentlemen of the agencies may in the end drop on something useful. Why would not a matrimonial bureau, with its tin photos and weekly circular, graced with charades and rebuses, be an appropriate adjunct? Next to the need of being married is the need of being married well. How many aspiring widows and languishing young ladies would spend a dollar or two privately in the delusive hope of exact information in reference to the affairs of Mr. Scroggs, of the Swamp, or the expectations of Adolphus Boggs, of Madison avenue? Neither is the exchange of love-tokens in hair trinkets and cheap jewelry* an exhausted field for profit. Arrangements for private interviews would justify extra charges. The distribution of garden-seeds might also be adopted, at slight additional expense. Cures for the toothache, salves for wounds, recipes for cooking, phrenological charts, adapted to any head, might all be dispensed from the principal and branch offices, with the special advantage that the present clerical force would not find the employment beyond its capacity. As for fortune-telling and palmistry, that would entail the hiring of a madam; but could not her salary be readily produced by rating down one or two young merchants and calling their attention to the change?

We throw out these hints. They are suggested by the idea of the Health Bureau, or "Health Lift," as we prefer to term it. If the agencies have not determined to act on all of them already, they will be pleased, we are sure, at the appropriateness and timeliness of our suggestions.

---

* By the bye, as these pages go through the press we find our idea carried out by at least one agency. Dun, Barlow & Co. are now agents for the cheap French brass and leather jewelry of the period; and they are given as reference, in a late New-York *Herald*, on the efficiency of a moth exterminator.

CHAPTER V.

THE KEYS WHICH UNLOCK NOTHING—HOW BUSINESS CONFIDENCE IS REGULATED.

THE methods adopted by the agencies to decrease the chances of exposure of their ignorance and avarice are numerous enough to be classified and noticed separately, namely: those relating to the "key"; those adopted in the printing of their quarterly, half-yearly, or yearly reference-books; and those interposed by the deceptive form of contract made with subscribers. We shall devote a fitting space to each in turn.

As to the first class: the reader who will turn to the fly-leaf for the "key" of the three agencies will notice the exceeding *vagueness* of the scale of imputed capital and the *looseness* of the associate alphabetic or number designation, *in themselves considered.* For instance, the Dun, Barlow & Co. "L," meaning "$1000 and under" of capital, if correctly used, may convey an idea of some definiteness, but when you go backwards and reach "F," $10,000 to $25,000, *you have a margin of $15,000 associated with a pretended fact of $10,000!* Take "E," $25,000 to $50,000, you find a margin of doubt equal to the allegation of capital! In "D," $50,000 to $100,000, the mathematical relation of the capital is not changed; but it must be in "D's" case of greater importance to know whether an amount equal to the original $50,000 would be forthcoming if required. This is evidently not the opinion of the agency, as it proceeds at once to show in the very next letter, "C," which, it informs us, may be relied on anywhere it is found in the book as showing a capital of from $100,000 to $150,000? No! $175,000? No! $200,000? No! but from $100,000 to $250,000, or a margin of doubt *twice and a half times* greater than their pretence of certainty!

One would think this fluctuation of their testing standard ought to satisfy the agency and afford it room and verge enough, whatever thoughts it may evoke in the minds of the seeker for truth. Not so. It plumes its wings for a higher flight. " B " stands for $250,000 to $500,000 ! " A," $500,000 to a million, and A+ is equal to " A," that is $500,000, but, strange anomaly, it is also equal to $1,000,000 and as many millions over as you like ! At this point—A+—the accurate series of mathematical progression of the agency gives out. Precision can go no further. The millionaire and the $20,000,000 millionaire are " all one" to the agency; and the theretofore painstaking and deliberately precise calculator may be regarded as overcome by the algebraic term and its portentous meaning, "unlimited credit"! How strange it is that the deft processes of the mercantile agency ratings and those contrived to express the higher mathematical processes should yet illustrate the finiteness of human ingenuity. At one million the agency loses its power to calculate capital, or considers it immaterial whether a man have one or a dozen millions to fall back on. At a certain number in the trillions Babbage's brass and iron calculator ceases to record logarithms, and indulges in every kind of numerical freak as if under the dominion of a frenzy. But there is this difference. The brass and iron machine is *capable of giving certainty ;* is overcome, for a time only, by some law of numbers not yet discovered ; and *returns* to accuracy again as if animated with assured confidence in its own powers. The agency, on the other hand, glad to be rid of even this wild use of its crucial and metrical standards, at the first decent opportunity drops them, and never returns to their use. It is candid for the first time. It makes no pretence of applying them in the higher altitudes of commercial life—the very Alps where the storms sweep most destructively ; where the wild beasts, Speculation, Peculation, and Breach of Trust, choose their most inaccessible lairs, and from which pour down on society the very direst calamities and most permanent disasters !

To the rapt vision of the agency, one million and over means unlimited credit ; and yet, if we consider of mistakes in these higher altitudes of financial speculation, a single one affecting them would naturally lead to consequences more to be deplored than a thousand errors in the ordinary fields of enterprise.

But taking the limit of one million, set by the Agencies as the extreme within which they pretend to approximate the capital of commercial men, how dangerous and visionary and haphazard must be the collection of surmises on which the Agencies base even these widely divergent values! Have they no knowledge or *data* from which they could safely conclude the $100,000 merchant to be *only* worth $125,000 and *not* worth $250,000? If they have, why do they leave the matter of his means so horribly in doubt? If they have not, what security has the public that the Agency knows he controls even $100,000 capital, or knows he is possessed of any? On an *extreme* limit of a quarter of a million, they are uncertain as to two thirds of it. By what process of reasoning are we assured that, starting with the minimum limit of $100,000, they know any more positively whether it should have been $20,000 or $50,000 instead of the $100,000 selected? Is not the liberal latitude selected a plain proof of the known necessity of adopting it? Is it not reasonable to argue that, when they cannot presume to set up a fuller code of denominators, and graded to express responsibility in the all-important matter of capital more closely than from one hundred thousand to a quarter of a million, they are equally incapable of telling us whether the $10,000 minimum should not have been $5000, or the $50,000 maximum should not have been $20,000? Why, between these extremes there is, necessarily, in any given number of instances, a demonstrated preponderance of incertitude so great as to exclude the possibility of safe trading!

When we turn to the *Numerical* symbols of credit, we find "confusion worse confounded." By referring to the fly-leaf in which the "Keys" to credit are given, it will be seen that Dun, Barlow & Co. confine themselves to four designations, "Unlimited Credit," "High," "Good," "Fair," and that these are modified by seven numbers, A 1, 1, 1½, 2, 2½, 3, 3½. That is to say, "Fair 3" with "3½" added is less than "Fair"; "Good 2" with "2½" added is less than "Good"; "High 1" with "1½" added is less than "High"; and "A 1" is without limitation. If we consider that "High," "Good," and "Fair," with their numerical depreciators, can only represent *seven* states of credit, ranging from $1000 to $1,000,000, we see at once that the tests of credit are as lax and inexpressive of any fixed and ascertained condition as are the characterizations of capital. Seven symbols to express the credit of capitalists ranging from one thousand dollars

to one million or ten millions! Four numerals and three fractions
to designate the almost infinite variety of estimation in which the
possessors of credit really stand in the eyes of the trading world!
"$3\frac{1}{2}$"—less .than "Fair"—associated with, say, "F"—$10,000
to $25,000—must convey the same meaning as "$3\frac{1}{2}$" associated
with "E"—$25,000 to $50,000—or with "D"—$50,000 to $100,-
000—or with "C"—$100,000 to $250,000. It can mean, in itself or
its use, no less or more in the one case than in the others. The same
criticism holds good in regard to "2," "$2\frac{1}{2}$"—"Good" and less
than "Good"—and "1," "$1\frac{1}{2}$"—"High," less than "High"—which,
to mean anything, must mean less than "High" and not "Good"!
Was ever a more deceptive and self-confuting method adopted to
express, or aid in expressing, the grades of business confidence?
What condition of credit *can* that be which is less than "High"
and is not "Good"? which is less than "Good" and is not
"Fair"? which is less than "Fair" and not unworthy of credit?

But these self-confusing and self-convicting symbols are not
only absurd on their face: they are rendered supremely ridiculous
when it is considered that they pretend to be the product of processes of reasoning from such complex and involved *data* as the
personal habits of traders, or, as McKillop & Sprague Co. express
it, "the character and habits of each member of a firm; the
"*nature* of the business, hazardous or otherwise; business capa-
"city and promptness in payment; capital or worth in *propor-*
"*tion* to business done, and negotiability of acceptances." To
carry out the load of this exacting announcement, McKillop &
Sprague Co. call in the aid of a double line of symbols, and instead of the adjective of number "less," affected by Dun, Barlow
& Co., use the adverb "very," to give point to "High," "Good,"
"Fair," etc. But phrases do not change things, and we illustrate
this truth by asking what *can* be the state of a trader who *is* in
"very high," and *not* in "*undoubted*," credit, and who *is* in
"good," and *not* in "very good," credit; who *is* in "*very* good,"
and *not* in "high," credit; who *is* "fair for small lines," and *not*
"a Fair Business risk" in those lines? Is not a person in "good
credit" a fair business risk? Is not a person in "high credit" in
"very good" credit? Where does his title to the one begin and
to the other end? Can it be rationally pretended that a distinc-
tion so purely artificial and gossamer in import is founded on a

discovered balance of probability of credit arising from a calculation of the always variant habits of various members of a firm, their respective capacities, the constantly changing hazardousness of their business, and the no less constantly changing *proportion* of capital and worth compared with the business done? Of three members of a firm, one is abstemious, another drinks, a third plays poker at evening parties. Does the abstemious man neutralize the poker-player, or the drinking man neutralize the abstemious? From the conflict of characteristics, what is the final resultant— the true *caput mortuum* of the seers and alchemists of the Agencies?

Go a step further: McKillop & Sprague Co., and the other Agencies as well, although not on their title-pages, assure us, or desire us to be assured, that every "deficiency" in good habits of every member of a firm, every deficiency arising from various kinds of trading in the sense of increase of hazard, every modification or departure from effective business capacity, every change in the proportion of capital to trading done, is recognised and *allowed* for in applying these few designations to traders. The problem now becomes more intricate: "allowed for" as well!

A few letters and figures are declared equal to the work of conveying the wisest conclusion to be drawn, not alone from variations of habits, of capacity, of risk, of capital, not in a few cases, but in over 800,000 cases, although, as we have just shown, the same letters and figures are incapable of conveying any clear idea of one man's credit so as to distinguish it "less than high," and not "good"; less than "good," and not "fair"; "good," and not "very good," and not "high," credit. In the smallest town the wisest trader makes bad debts. In the same city and street the most alert speculator in others' credits gets taken in. Of one hundred individuals exercising their personal judgment at its best, all are daily more or less mistaken, and a large percentage greatly deceived, in business transactions and prognostications. And yet the Agencies have the effrontery, and their whole theory of right to exist is based on the presumption, to claim that their few vague phrases are a substitute for the aggregate business varieties of opinions and judgment of all the business men of the States and Canada, and are sufficient for the purpose of effectually advising the business community whether eight hundred thousand traders, merchants, and manufacturers are in credit, what kind of credit they are in from day to day, and to distinguish its shades and fluctuations with sufficient accuracy for wisely influencing and controlling dispositions of property!

We have seen the worthlessness of these Keys of capital and Keys to credit separately. Do they acquire a new virtue by being put alongside each other and attached to a name ?

Separately they are indefinite and unmeaning criteria. Putting them together only multiplies their indefiniteness and induces greater perplexity. What can be understood of a man with from $25,000 to $50,000 capital who is in " good," and not in " very good," credit ? Is he fit to be trusted to the extent of $5000 or $10,000, more or less, because of the credit rating indicating the one condition and not the other? or, indicating either, does the indication denote that his credit as to capital should be exhausted at a presumption of $20,000 and not at a presumption of $50,000 ? How can any sensible conclusion be drawn from the fact that a firm rated " C "—$100,000 to $250,000 capital—is rated at " very good," and not at " high," credit? Does the doubtful $150,- 000 of capital bear any secret relation or give any particular significance to the one credit rating and not to the other ? Is not the expressed possibility of a capital even twice as large as the presumed capital sufficient to convert " very good " into " high " credit, or *vice versa ?* If not, why not ? One would think that a man " very good " with $100,000 would be in " high " credit with $200,000, higher with $250,000. The Agencies know better. They can tell us *just when* a person having a capital of from $500,000 to $1,000,000 is in " very high " credit, and just when he is in " undoubted " credit, when with $100,000 to $250,000 he is just less than " high " and not " good." If this be not a claim of measuring water accurately with a sieve ; of producing certainty, or an approximation to it, by increasing the elements of uncertainty ; of regulating business confidences by enlarging the doubt-producing combinations whose fewness is the only possible basis for even prophecy, we do not know what to call it. The Bradstreet " Key," with its 93 letters and 80 figures, is better graded to represent presumed fact than either of the other two ; but it does not pretend to give capital, avoids estimates entirely, and is not applied with any regularity to even the states of circumstances indicated by the " Key" itself. Of course, the system proceeds on the same inexact information and misinformation, and the sliding scale becomes a toy, instead of an instrument, inevitably. The firm appreciates the paucity of terms and conditions of the other " Keys," recognizes their looseness and insufficiency, and tries to hide an equal barrenness under a deeper festoon of words.

We have referred to the " Keys " simply *as instruments* of relative calculation. Their actual use in the Reference Books of the Agencies deserves a separate chapter.

CHAPTER VI.

HOW THE "KEYS" ARE PLAYED AND RATINGS MADE UP—WHO SIT IN JUDGMENT AND DISPENSE AGENCY JUSTICE.

THE best and most experienced business man in the world, personally informed, so far as one man can ever be, of another man's affairs in his immediate vicinity, would be in some difficulty to fix a true capital and designate a safe credit rating.   Proceeding from the point that these ratings and " Keys" of ratings are necessarily false and inefficient as such, we come to the question, who affix them ?   The persons who do it are :

Firstly : Outside of sixty office centres, not persons of the neighborhood, but clerks to whom the letters and reports are sent from the neighborhood.

Secondly : In the cities, where the sixty offices are situated, reports concerning residents are first received by the managers, pigeon-holed until the convenient opportunity of copying has arrived, and then turned over to clerks, who affix the ratings.   The managers attend to the more useful work of increasing the subscription-lists.   The writer, with three others, was lately engaged for a period of six weeks affixing such ratings as he saw fit to the names of several thousand New-York merchants, the latest reports of whom (and on which the ratings were predicated) were in some instances eight years old, in the vast majority of cases four years old, and not a hundred less than one year old !   This habit, originating in choice and recklessness of the principal office, where the responsible managers and proprietors are supposed to give their judgment and experience to their work, is followed, by necessity, in smaller places, where none of the company resides ; and young men who never did business themselves, and boys who by reason of nonage could not do business, are the arbiters of the capital ratings and the affixers of the credit-marks of merchants longer in business than the lifetime of their inquisitors and judges.   It was this sublime absurdity—if the agencies were sincere in their claims—and this sublime indifference to results—if they were not so—which set the writer first inquiring what enabled *him* to extract truth as to the present condition of a merchant from an old report, or a new one, affording no sufficient elements for even a wild hypothesis. An intimate acquaintanceship, extending over twelve years, with the business :—commencing as an errand-boy, progressing to an assistant managership and cashiership of two leading branch offices—gave him facilities, with increase of age, to learn the grossness and hollowness of the pretences of the Agencies in this regard, and certainly enabled him to follow the system and apply the ratings as well as others of shorter experience in the business and his juniors in age. What wonder that, when he became conscious of his own incapacity to give any reason to himself why one man should be rated in poor credit and another in high credit; when he found himself doling out anathema from secret reports when the Reference Book ratings indicated large capital and high credit, or giving rosy pictures of men whom the Reference Book rated poorly or not at all ; when he saw the victim of the latest report coming in and paying his money to be unconsciously destroyed, he determined to inquire whether the whole system was not a crying fraud and injury to the business community. His opinions, he further found on examination, were the same as those of nearly all the other employees. They enjoyed the joke and took their salary. But none ever pretended to believe that the information sent out should determine the propriety of entering into a single bargain or executing a single sale! They simply profited by the system, and held their peace.

There were potent reasons for this conduct. The merchants affected were not *their* employers. The salaries paid were so meagre, averaging ten dollars per week, that only persons of pressing necessities and slight self-assertion were employed. The injury done to business hopes and reputation did not come immediately under their observation so as to excite sympathy, or, if it did, situations were hard to get, and labor was going a-begging for employment. The agency fed them, whoever else it hurt or betrayed. They did the work assigned to them, and cared nothing for the consequences.

Imagine a ten-dollar clerk poring over ten or twenty lines of

manuscript without a figure in it, and determining ratings of
capital and credit in the case of merchants doing a business of two
or five millions a year! Take an instance from the New-York
grocery trade. Tupper—Dun, Barlow & Co.'s reporter of this
line—is notorious for *seldom giving an estimate of means*. The
business in which he is employed engages the second largest capital—
barring the dry-goods trade—invested in the metropolis. The number of merchants and traders may be safely set down at 5000;
and yet, during seven years or nearly seven, Mr. Tupper has either
never secured information enough to communicate estimates,
or, to guard against the consequences of his ignorance, has seldom
dared to do so. Yet it is from the vague statements of this gentleman, couched in language which fits Talleyrand's ideal in its capacity to hide thought, that the boys of the Agency sit in judgment and award sentences which, within an hour after utterance,
may imperil a prosperous business or elevate a sinking firm into a
self-surprising credit.

In the city dry-goods trade Mr. Chase holds the like office that
Mr. Tupper sustains in the grocery line. Tupper's excessive
tendency to caution is not Chase's sole characteristic. He is a
sour, lymphatic old man, whose errors lie in the other extreme.
He jumps at conclusions without what we regard necessary information. The clerks have no difficulty in dealing with his statements. He decides summarily, and the reports indicate in what
spirit, where his curiosity has not been gratified, where his feelings
incline, or where he has been treated as an impertinent intermed-
dler by houses of known respectability. Indeed, Chase relieves the
clerks from superintending his estimates, just as he relieved Ed-
wards, his assistant, from presuming to have an opinion of a merchant's credit adverse to his. If Chase likes a dry-goods house, or
has had reason to like it, *that* house will get to the public and
trade through the agency in glowing colors. If any house *com-
petes* with Chase's favorite, *that* house will learn the result in the
next Reference Book, or earlier, if called for, in the secret reports
and in the best words of Chase. This peculiarity was generally
known and commented on in the office. Two effects of it are sufficient to illustrate its consequences. Vyse & Co., an old English
house, importing straw-goods, and rated by Chase in the Reference
Book equal to A. T. Stewart & Co., A + A 1, was a favorite with

this gentlemen so late as February, 1875, and his friendship or admiration for it caused the house to be reported to the Tenth National Bank in that month as in unquestionable credit after the house had failed! Of course the Tenth National Bank was only practising a joke on the Agency, for it knew of the failure when making the inquiry, and made the request in that spirit. How the Central National Bank of New-York, if it had confidence in the Agency, was misled by the same favorable report, obtained a few days previously, can be best told by Mr. William A. Wheelock, its president.

Take another case. Alsberg & Jordan, hosiery, etc., having, like the Tenth National Bank, little or no faith in the Agency information or in Chase, refused to make any statement of their affairs to him in January, 1875. They had been rated previously in "good credit." Forthwith they became "doubtful." The Dry Goods Bank made inquiries in anticipation of discounting their paper in the usual course. Chase's report stopped the chance of legitimate discount. The house still survives, and is in better credit than ever, if possible, from having weathered a test which a single man's repelled impertinence might have rendered fatal in the case of firms not so generally esteemed or of less mobile means. Still another instance. Shackman & Katski, cloths, etc., 229 Church street, New-York City, although solicited to become subscribers and pay $150 to the Agency, declined; they were rated down accordingly. Paine, Goodwin & Nowell, wholesale woollens, cloths, etc., advised Mr. Shackman to call at the Agency, subscribe, and "fix his rating," and they would sell to the firm, being willing to sell if Shackman & Katski could buy from others. Shackman stood on his right, did not go to the Agency, and is pursuing business on the joint capital of his own merit and the prevailing belief of the general incorrectness and pliability of the Agency's opinions.

The person in general charge of the New-York City department is Mr. Wiman, who began business about eighteen years ago by keeping a paper-stand and stationery store in Toronto, and by a series of judicious manœuvres succeeded in passing from a clerkship in the business at Toronto to a partnership interest and a residence in New-York, in the principal office. He is practically the controlling spirit of the institution. His fitness for presiding over the commercial credit of the old and young merchants of such an emporium as the Empire City can readily be determined. On the 9th of May, 1868, Erastus Wiman was compelled by process to depose before Hon. Charles Mondelet, judge of the Superior Court in Montreal, Canada East, that one Jay Lugsdin, who had been manager in that city from September, 1866, to March, 1868, " *was discharged because he borrowed* $800 *frow Andrew Mac-* "*farlan & Co., St. Paul street,* and neglected to advise the Lon- " don office with information about the firm until the information " had become valueless." The borrowing took place in February, 1867 ; the information was held back until 25th July, 1867, when the Macfarlans had effected all their foreign purchases. The Macfarlans became insolvent in the spring of 1868 ; and the removal of Lugsdin did not take place until the Insolvents had been brought into court. Dun, Barlow & Co., fearing the effect of such a transaction, sought to claim credit to their Agency for having " discharged " him ; but the falsity of this pretence was soon evidenced *by the appointment of Lugsdin to the manager- ship of the Philadelphia office,* and his subsequent promotion to San Francisco, the head-quarters for the Pacific Coast States, with the Portland (Oregon) Branch under his supervision—a posi- tion which he still holds. It was not the borrowing therefore, but *the being found out,* which stirred Dun, Barlow & Co.; it was not the keeping back of injurious information *relative to a subscriber,* and *withholding it from other subscribers entitled to it by having paid for it in advance,* which touched Dun, Barlow & Co.'s con- science most severely : all this could have been borne with; had been borne with one year, and would have been borne with longer if the facts had *not got into court,* and compelled Dun, Barlow & Co. to transfer Mr. Lugsdin's approved capacity to new fields. Nor is this surprising. Mr. Wiman himself had been a manager in Montreal, and had learned from personal experience the efficien- cy of his position to procure aid in difficulties from the mer- chants of that city. *In the very years* when Lugsdin was operat- ing with the Macfarlans, Wiman was borrowing from R. J. Dallas, manager of the Montreal branch of the Bank of Toronto (who subsequently absconded with $40,000), and from P. D. Browne, Exchange Broker, and getting the indorsements of David Morrice and others on notes discounted for his individual benefit by the

Bank and Browne! *This Browne was also indorser on the note given by Lugsdin in the Macfarlan transaction,* and evidently appreciated the necessity of affixing his name, on request, on the back of either Wiman's or Lugsdin's promises to pay, although both Lugsdin and Wiman were merely salaried persons, without property, capital, or business—besides reporting on the commercial standing of gentlemen who might refuse to afford them these convenient facilities of local credit. In the light of these facts, within the writer's personal knowledge, Wiman's exhibition of a testy sense of Merchantile Agency honor in the Superior Court was one of the coolest exhibitions of the season even in that climate, and gives pith and point to his further declaration, on coming to New-York, that he would never leave the broader and richer domain of Agency effort afforded by the Metropolis, without a clear million to his credit.

It is not for us to say whether he proposes to attain his object by worthy or unworthy means; but the reader may draw such conclusions as he shall see fit from the following data.

Edward Mathews, Nos. 4 and 6 Broad street, New-York City, is a real-estate owner worth, by the affidavits of half a dozen experts, $6,000,000 or more, and in receipt of $326,000 a year from it, clear income, over and above Taxes, Assessments, etc. Dun, Barlow & Co. rated this well-known capitalist as worth only from $500,000 to $1,000,000, with a credit rating such as is given to a man with from $25,000 to $50,000 capital! This rating appeared at a time when Mr. Mathews was about to negotiate a loan in England on property situated in Wall and Broad streets. The New-York City Department manager contrived to put himself in communication with Mr. Mathews by asking for a statement and sending a canvasser for a subscription. Mathews received the Gospel but dismissed the Missionary; that is, he called on Dun, Barlow & Co., made his statement, showed his proofs of value and liabilities under the oath of the best authorities in the city as to real estate, and told them that he would not subscribe; that the rating must be changed to represent the facts, or that his name must be wholly suppressed to avoid legal proceedings. No subscription or other inducement appearing, an unfavorable report was made and circulated. The name was suppressed *in the Reference Book* in view of the threat of legal proceedings, and the London *Times,* getting its misinformation from some American source, has lately been obliged to publicly retract its misstatements about Mr. Mathews, and to do justice to a man whom a subscription, or a judicious recognition of Dun, Barlow & Co.'s position, might have saved from all the annoyance and possible injury. *Dun, Barlow & Co., we know, received nothing but the statement from Mr. Mathews.* The uncharitable may say the fact accounts for the preservation, in the Agency and private circulation, of the unfavorable report up to the time of writing. At all events, Morrice and Browne, of Montreal, with a respective capital of $75,000 and $50,000, stand in higher credit, conceded by Dun, Barlow & Co., than Mr. Mathews, although McKillop & Sprague Co. rated Mr. Mathews " A 1, A 1, A 1 "—the highest capital rating and highest credit—and Bradstreet & Son at " A, A, A "—the most undoubted capital, business character, ability, and credit.

Query. If a capital of $50,000, with a liberal habit of indorsing paper, produce "High Credit," what would a capital of $6,000,000, *with the like habit,* produce?

Answer. "Unlimited Credit," at least.

The final moral remains to be drawn. Since the time mentioned, P. D. Browne has had his rating increased to an extraordinary amount within a short period. But all is not gold that glitters under the fructifying rays of friendship. Nathless the Agency, Browne incontinently failed in June, 1875, owing $60,000 and over, or an amount about equal to his last false increase of pretended capital and credit. These three gentlemen, Tupper, Chase, and Wiman, with a varying number of cheap assistants, are the reporters and raters of the Merchants, Bankers, Manufacturers, and Traders in and out of New-York for Dun, Barlow & Co. Of course the Agency must make a show of activity somewhere, and the chief city is the most profitable place for making it. Hence fine offices, a large array of old Books, a majority of illiterate clerks, and an increasing system of canvassing for subscriptions. Talk of the curse of the Locusts of Egypt or Kansas, of the infliction of the Sewing-Machine travellers and Lightning-Rod men : these Agency canvassers are to the business men of this country equally persistent and far more exacting. A new firm is engaged in taking down its shutters for the first time. *Enter* a canvasser. An old one is in the labor-pains of bringing forth a new Special. *Enter* a canvasser. A partner is retiring, and the rest of the firm are entitling their new Books and repainting the sign. *Enter* a canvasser. An unreported local house is inquired for at the Agency counter, in Broadway, or any of the Branches. While the inquirer is waiting for information the canvasser crosses a threshold in one of the down-town streets, and demands information and a subscription.

The amount ranges from $150 to $5000 yearly, as testified by Wiman in April, 1875, in the New-York Supreme Court, on trial of an action entitled "Robert G. Dun and others *vs.* J. Arthur Murphy"; but where $150 cannot be got, $50 placates or mollifies the itinerant. Even at the latter rate the profit is enormous and justifies all the effort expended by the Agency.

Outside of New-York, as the opportunities of getting Subscribers decrease, the efforts to get information decrease also. The Principal Office makes the subordinate ones self-supporting at least, or ceases to indulge in them. The Syracuse Office was started in this wise, in May, 1872. Two clerks got half their travelling expenses to that burgh. One resident Merchant, Duguid, of Duguid, Wells & Co., saddlery, etc., advanced the use of his rooms in place of a subscription, and got rated with unction. Another firm, Cooke, Carpenter, Coleman & Co., gave the furniture for the same consideration and with an abiding faith that their bread "would come back after many days." Less than $50 sufficed to impose on the people of that city an institution which now costs them annually $12,000, under the direction of a mere youth named Cargell, whose services as a Commercial Rhadamanthus of a large contiguous District are rated by the Agency at the weekly value of $15. It is but just to add that this compensation is fully commensurate. Cargell will admit he could not earn $10 a week marking boxes or in any other employment requiring special adaptability. It must be worth $5 more to calculate the average risks attending the investment and use of 500 or 600 millions of active capital within the radius of his District. Twelve dollars per week satisfy Marshall, in Erie, Pa. Nevill is content with the same stipend in Scranton, Pa. Pratt makes Cincinnati profitable on an infinitesimal portion of the revenue derived from the Porkopolites. Brock lives and flourishes like a Prince in Chicago, on a salary sufficient to justify his æsthetic tastes and open-handed expenditure in that fast-living and energetic community. In the staider City of Buffalo, John H. Smith has labored these six years past on a stinted compensation, and contrived, with a genius not unique in this business, to set aside savings variously estimated at $60,000 to $70,000. In St. John, N. B., Augustus P. Rolph performs the duty of Sweeper, Errand-boy, Reporter, and Manager all together for about $20 per week, and does not repine at the ways of Providence. Our friend Lugsdin disports by the Golden Horn on a light apparent capital; but who can say how many Macfarlans he may have met to lighten and brighten his Pacific exile?

But we are not restricted to generalization in judging of the average fitness of the managers and credit men of the institutions. The records of courts in the United States and Canada supply us with abundant proof of particular escapades; and even the instances of wrong-doing "hushed up" by the Agencies, in self-protection and as the better wisdom, are matters of common report. One of Dun, Barlow & Co.'s men, appointed through the influence of Erastus Wiman, absconded from Rochester in 1870 with about $4000, went to Canada, and was employed there by Bradstreet & Son. Another of Dun, Barlow & Co.'s defaulted in Mobile in 1873, was convicted, and imprisoned two years. A third, of the same Agency, embezzled at Evansville, Indiana, in March, 1875, and was not prosecuted, as we judge from a statement of an Evansville newspaper. In Pittsburg, a fourth depleted his friends $6000. A fifth absconded from Montreal, and subsequently entered the employment of McKillop & Sprague, at Chicago. A sixth is alleged to have depredated in Syracuse, in 1873. A seventh was arrested in Albany, charged by Henry Brock with fraud, etc., and was afterwards appointed to Scranton, Pa. An eighth—a city department reporter—has just been exposed in the courts as the keeper of a house of prostitution. A ninth, in Memphis, explained his deficiency in accounts by saying he lost his money in a Faro-bank and is now probably in charge of a less tempting neighborhood. A tenth is announced, under date of October 18th, 1875, in a circular issued in Houston, Texas, as having, within ten days, "practised divers frauds on some of the best citizens by obtaining money, etc.," on account of his Agency connection. The list might be increased *ad libitum ;* but we merely give these facts to show the carelessness as to character evinced by the Agencies in selecting their most trusted assistants. It is no wonder such aids turn out thieves or criminals, or are chosen from the criminal classes. No references are required; no preliminary examination into the antecedents of an applicant is had. If he will work for low salary, the Agencies give themselves little concern what else he may have done or may do. Indeed, one of the most amusing features of Agency life is their utter heedlessness of consequences in the case of credit men. The writer has often been amused at the return of credit men, after enforced absences in jail or on the Island, for reinstatement and back salary. He never knew one of them to be refused renewed service on such grounds. Whatever they did, they seemed to think they knew enough of Agency methods to brazen out their transgressions and enforce a re-employment. And so far as the writer's experience goes, they never calculated erroneously. If we only consider the scope for false, fabricated, or collusive reports given by and to the persons whose misdeeds we have just noted, what a terrible mass of misrepresentation must have got abroad at their hands! If we consider that the Agencies take no precaution against the recurrence of like offences, we may naturally infer that the *exposed* crime bears but an insignificant ratio to the hidden wrongs and offences daily committed by persons chosen, by such methods, for such work. And may we not reasonably ask the business classes: If the reputations of traders and the safety of sellers are both entrusted to carelessly or capriciously selected men, out of whose ranks the foregoing offenders have come, what is to be hoped for from the undetected remainder?

CHAPTER VII.

FURTHER ILLUSTRATIONS OF AGENCY IGNORANCE, CUPIDITY, AND AVARICE—DO THEY CONTRIBUTE TO MISLEAD CONFIDENCE?

This remarkable disparity between the known salaries of the employees of the Agency and their ostensible means and methods of living may have an innocent explanation. A man *may* be willing to carry on his shoulders, year after year, the responsibility of a Branch office in a leading city, and acting over a large adjoining District, on a fixed salary of from $10 to $20 or $30 a week. We know these men do so. But if they be not driven by stress of circumstances to take and hold such a position at such a price, they must be moved to the sacrifice by other motives than those supplied by their salaries. Are there no perquisites? If Wiman hopes to make a million dollars—he has already got $200,000—may not Smith aspire to one tenth thereof? If Wiman may have his stud and country villa and gorgeous retinue, why may not Brock look forward to the not far distant day when he may drive a four-in-hand instead of a team on Wabash avenue, nor excite the gall of the manager-makers? Whatever the true explanation, this argument results: the Agency selects cheap labor because it is cheap, and pays accordingly; and cheap labor is a dangerous inducement to poorly-paid men, whose position as raters and givers of commercial credit and standing is so grossly at variance with their stipulated income.

The McKillop & Sprague Co. and J. M. Bradstreet & Son Agencies claim to have as many Branch offices as Dun, Barlow & Co., and employ relatively illiterate men and cheap ones, in preference to any other, for like reasons. For all practical purposes of comparison, their methods of receiving gratuitous information and, outside of New-York City, relying wholly on volunteer and unpaid-for knowledge are the same as Dun, Barlow & Co.'s. In New-York City they have a certain number of credit men who either

solicit subscriptions or give names of probable subscribers to canvassers, with whom they divide the Commissions. These credit
Reporters pick up such rumors as they meet with in the streets ;
apply to particular houses in a given line for opinions of other
and rival houses in the same line ; inquire from strongly-rated, that
is, favorite, houses in the eyes of credit-givers, for estimates of the
financial condition of less favored ones, but make *no personal
critical examination* of the Records of the County Clerk's or Re-
gister's offices for the purpose of proving the true position of sole
Merchants and Traders or individual members of Firms or Companies. Apart from the street " say so," the statements of parties
in their own behalf when given, and the Real Estate *Record* of
current judgments, mortgages, liens, and foreclosures, these high-
ly-paid Agencies do nothing to earn the liberal contributions made
to them yearly by the business men of the country. Now the
Record does not give the business or addresses of persons against
whom judgments have been obtained, or who have mortgaged or
transferred their property, or who have created liens on it and had
them created in Law or Equity. The value of this daily re-
minder is determined, so far as the Agencies are concerned, by this
fact. The Smiths and Browns are numerous in any large city,
and hold their customary preponderance in the Empire State. If
judgment is got against Smith, some Smith is suspected of being
the right one ; his name is marked with a query ; but whether it
be the particular Smith of Broadway, or the same-named Smith of
Wall street, or another Smith in the Swamp, is "all Greek" to the
Agencies until a disturbance occur out of it. The inspection of
the Judgment is never attempted. What is worse follows.
No notice is taken of Satisfactions of Judgments, so that the
doomed and suspected Smith continues to be doomed and suspected until he either goes to the trouble of having a correction made, or goes to the grave in blessed ignorance of the cause
and origin of many unaccountable business experiences.

An incident which occurred in February, 1875, in Dun,
Barlow & Co.'s New-York office, will illustrate the common
danger in all other Agencies arising from the mistake of names.
The writer suspected, and called the Superintendent's attention to,
an unfavorable report applied to the house of Schuyler, Hartley
& Graham, Military Goods, etc., Maiden lane, New-York City.

It was meant for another firm, but had been sent to and recorded, with all its injurious import, in six or eight Branch offices. This error continued for more than a month, and was only corrected after several days of calling attention to it. It is of record in the Branch offices, owing to the negligence and carelessness of the Superintendent, and will remain so until this publication shall have compelled correction.

Another one occurs to us, as we write, where no correction has been made, and where one was prevented being made, to hide the ignorance of the Agency. Koehler & Kupfer are Distillers; Herman Koehler is a Brewer; I. M. Koehler is a Banker in New-York. The reports of each are mixed up with the others'. One was reported unfavorably, although all are men of assured capital. This report was tacked to the most conspicuous capitalist. The Dry Goods Bank got the bad report of the wealthiest man; and although the messenger could have been recalled or the correction made to the Bank, the Superintendent instructed the writer not to do either, choosing the Bank should be misled, and the citizen, it might be, ruined, rather than that the Agency should be found correcting its mistakes.

Still another. Robert Macdonald is a Wholesale Dealer in White Goods, etc., at 468 Broadway, New-York City, and a subscriber. Wiman does not allow the clerks to read Macdonald's report to subscribers, but refers inquirers to himself for those titbits which he dare not place on record or within Mac's reach.

What if Mac does drive a four-in-hand, or has married a *divorcée*, or failed in Belfast, or is disliked in Ireland, cannot this be written down, if true, in a manly way, and the consequences borne? Do Dun, Barlow & Co. fear to lose a subscription, or to incur a libel-suit, or to earn a thrashing from the man whose acquaintanceship is turned into a commodity? Of course whatever is offensive in this statement is necessarily untrue, and we repeat it merely for the purpose of contradicting it, in whole or in part, and with infinitely better authority for our contradiction than the Agency could ever have had for its first statement.

The Schuyler, Hartley & Graham and Koehler & Kupfer cases are not mere clerical blunders. They arise out of the *purposed neglect* of all the Agencies to print the *places of business* in connection with the names. In this course Bradstreet and McKillop & Sprague Co. imitate Dun, Barlow & Co. One would imagine that these *indicia* would facilitate references, and would, consequently, be adopted and used by the Agencies. There is a better reason why they should not be used. The number of a street would be an ineffaceable sign and proof of the *age or incompleteness* of the Agencies' pretended knowledge. When the inquirer found a firm located in Beaver street which he knew had moved two years ago to Barclay, or another put down in Wall street which had long since taken up its position in William or Nassau, what could he think of the freshness and value of the intelligence possessed by the Agencies? If so plain and apparent a circumstance is found overlooked or unknown, what warrant can he have that the associated syllabub of words is not guess-work of the veriest? Their plan is, therefore, to avoid every sign or token by which a tell-tale error might have ready demonstration, and to lessen the chances of discovery by reducing the available tests of comparative accuracy to the minimum.

We recur again to McKillop & Sprague Co. They are in the same box with the rest, as a few examples will show.

Hawkins & Hanken, Builders' Materials, Brooklyn, were rated by this Agency in July, 1873, " 3, 3½, 6 "—that is, capital, " $3000 to $4000 "; credit, " fair for small lines." In July, 1874, we find them rated " 1½, 2, 2 "—that is, capital, from " $100,000 to $200,000 "; credit, " very high and very good." How the firm managed to jump in one year from the extreme of $4000 to the extreme of $200,000 capital is best known to themselves, and is still a subject of serious consultation with the Stockholders of the New-York Plaster Works, who lost a round $5000 in a single transaction shortly after the appearance of the latter rating, and while Hawkins & Hanken were in the throes of monetary death!

Giroud Bros. & Co., Cuban Commission House, were rated in July, 1874, by McKillop & Sprague Co., at " 1, 1½, 1 "—that is, capital, from $300,000 to $500,000 ; credit, " very high and undoubted." Van Tuyl & Co., Bankers, being about to discount their paper, requested a special report. It confirmed the rating. Within a few weeks, and while the favorable report was still fresh in memory, Giroud Bros. & Co.'s first note, *for a small sum*, went to protest, and all the others followed suit, to the confusion of the National Park Bank and Van Tuyl & Co., the trusting subscribers to

McKillop & Sprague Co.'s unreliable information or unfortunate guesses. .

J. M. Bradstreet & Son will afford us the next illustration of procuring information on which their subscribers are expected to make safe bargains and sales. M. L. Oberdorfer & Co., Wholesale Liquors, Syracuse, were inquired about, in November, 1872, at the principal office, in New-York. Bradstreet had then no office in Syracuse, a city of 50,000 inhabitants and controlling one of the greatest staple products of the State—Salt. In the emergency they wrote—not telegraphed, for cheapness is everything—one William O'Conor, corner Fayette and South Salina Streets, the keeper of a small basement restaurant, who, although otherwise an excellent man, was as wholly unacquainted with the standing and credit of Oberdorfer & Co. as an Aborigine may be presumed ignorant of the Transit of Venus. O'Conor used to show the inquiry with commendable pride; joked his customers on the devious ways of commercial credit, and relied on the courtesy of some one to *write* an answer, which he could not do himself. To add to the value of the epistle, it ought to be said that neither O'Conor nor the writer ever heard of Oberdorfer until the arrival of Bradstreet's query !

One of the dangers of this method of repeating inquiries and trusting to random in the affair of an answer may be noticed in this connection. Bradstreet & Son were called on for a report of one Josiah Tasker in the same year. They sent by post two hundred and fifty miles for the material for an opinion—to Tasker's son-in-law ! The New-York creditor probably understands by this time the old gentleman's notions about his own standing. As to Bradstreet & Son, they will, of course, be obliged to the writer for posting them up in the Tasker family history, and hinting that a slight rebate of subscription ought to be allowed, in this case, to the inquiring firm.

Going back to Dun, Barlow & Co., we close this chapter with four pregnant examples of the consequences of their negligence or complicity, the reader can decide which or neither.

In Dun, Barlow & Co.'s Reference Book dated *January,* 1872, occurs the following :

" Oswego, N. Y.—W. H. Herrick, Sr., *Agt. for wife,* Commission, etc.," rated "K"—then the lowest rating, and meaning "*neither capital nor credit.*"

In the *next* issue of the Book, July, 1872, the same person was rated "C 2"—$100,000 to $250,000; credit, "High."

NOTHING HAD HAPPENED, MEANTIME, TO W. H. HERRICK, SR., EXCEPT THAT HE HAD PAID $100 SUBSCRIPTION, "PURELY ON GROUNDS OF PERSONAL FRIENDSHIP," AS HIS LETTER STATED!

In this month of July, 1872, McKillop & Sprague Co. left Herrick's rating *blank*, and Howlett, Lathrop & Co., of Oswego, N. Y., and others, subscribers to the Dun, Barlow & Co. Agency, bitterly complained of the effect of such a palpable perversion of ink and paper. They were Millers, and knew Herrick, Sr., well through grain speculation. Herrick knew the Agency, "went one better," and promptly failed for a sum which cannot be called less than respectable, and greatly enlarged by the friendly "C 2," on grounds of "personal friendship." His liabilities were $193,639.52, with very small assets, and the estate is now in Bankruptcy.

About the 29th April, 1875, the Toronto and Montreal subscribers of Dun, Barlow & Co. enjoyed a startling surprise—if we call that a surprise which the commonest acquaintance with Agencies should have taught them to expect. A fashionable young gentleman named Zevy, or rather going by that name, entered the City of Toronto suddenly, made his way to the Agency Office, and, after a short prelude of engaging conversation, told Mathews, a partner's cousin, in charge of the Branch, that he had just arrived from Germany, was about to open a Wine and Spice House in the City, and carried in his pocket a letter of credit on one of the local banks for $15,000 "to pay duties on the first consignments of stock of the parent German House" to its Toronto protégé. Mathews duly gave the customary attention to the statement, did not go to the trouble of verifying it by calling at the designated Bank, and wrote down Zevy & Co. as a new firm of undoubted capital and credit.

Whether from confidence in his arrangements with Mathews, or in utter contempt of the Agency's simulation of effective inquiry, Zevy did not deign to hurry himself in executing his swindle. He opened a Store; bought in Toronto, at his leisure; extended his speculations to Montreal, where the Agency report stood him in stead of capital; bought largely there; sold his purchases in the vicinity of Toronto without ever taking them from the Depot; and having amassed all the money he wanted, except what he had given to the Agency (if any), stuck up a card on his Toronto *magasin* that the death of his mother necessitated a return to Germany!

If any one wants to know what the Merchants of Montreal and Toronto think of Agencies in general and Dun, Barlow & Co.'s in particular, let them mention Zevy to J. Hope & Co., W. F. Lewis & Co., or any of the dozen other merchants swindled, and be convinced.

The present manager of the Montreal Branch is W. W. Johnson, who seems to have as ill luck in giving satisfaction to subscribers as either of his predecessors. A special friend of his, up to June, 1875, was his namesake Johnston, of the firm of Empey, Johnston & Co., Wholesale Dry Goods, St. Helen street, subscribers and rated " D 1½ "—that is, capital, " $50,000 to $100,000 "; credit, " High." In the last-mentioned month, notwithstanding the rating, the firm failed for $160,000, of which loss, largely distributed between the Bank of Montreal and Christian, Gault & Co., Bankers, Notre-Dame street, *over $70,000 may be fairly charged to have been rendered possible through the circumstances stated.* It appears that the Manager was not content with rating his friends favorably to the last: he "drummed them up" with Banks and Bankers. He represented to Mr. Angus, of the Bank of Montreal, that the firm were his particular friends; that he had access to their Books; and that they were unassailable in credit or capital. To Mr. Christian, of Christian, Gault & Co., he claimed the like personal knowledge. Both gentlemen believed him, and within a fortnight Empey, Johnston & Co. were insolvent, with $160,000 liabilities!

Some years ago Davis & Welsh failed in the same City, and Henry Davis & Co. rose on their ruin and commenced anew. They subscribed $75 to the Agency, and got a very favorable rating and private report, in consequence, from Manager Johnson. In June, 1875, they failed for between $700,000 and $800,000, and James Court, their Assignee, has offered *ten cents on the dollar on their liabilities to their victims.* In other words, there had been no capital of any account in the firm; but the private reports of the Agency had been used in their favor by some understanding, and a profitable bankruptcy became practicable. Like all the Managers, Johnson lives well, enjoys yachting and diversions, and would repel no one by either the dignity of his conversation nor the asceticism of his manners. For our own part, we are confident he did *not* lose a dollar by the suspension of either Empey, Johnston & Co. or Henry Davis & Co.

On the 4th day of May, 1868, Robert Macfarlan, deposing before Judge Mondelet, of the Superior Court of the Province of Quebec, answered as follows:

" I am aware that a number subscribe to the Agency; but the " information furnished is of such an unreliable nature that the " slightest dependence is not to be placed on it, as, from personal " experience, *we have made more bad debts through information* " *received from them as being correct, while we have afterwards* " *found it to be incorrect and not reliable,*"

Being further questioned:

" Do you mean to say that when a Merchant gives a correct " statement of his affairs to the Mercantile Agency, the latter " would give an incorrect or unreliable statement of the standing " of such Merchant ?"

He answered:

" ANY INSTITUTION WHICH ATTEMPTS TO LEVY BLACKMAIL AND " WILL MARK YOUR CREDIT ACCORDINGLY, I do not consider that " much reliance is to be placed on their statement, so that I think " they are not to be depended upon to give a correct statement, " even when they obtain correct information."

Further on in his examination the witness said:

" He " (Lugsdin, Manager for Dun, Barlow & Co.) " said that " the Agency was a powerful institution; that it could *raise* " *firms without any means* and cast down the best-established " institutions."

This Mr. Macfarlan is the gentleman who allowed an Agency Manager to borrow $800 from him; but he is under oath, and comes into court to explain how he became insolvent propitiously and soon after receiving large consignments from London on the repute of an Agency report. His relations with the Agency enabled him to speak with knowledge. If he evince no respect for their honesty, he is not inexperienced in its methods of exhibition; and if he think little of their usefulness to respectable traders, he certainly enables us to learn the highest claimed faculty of the institution—namely, "*that it could raise firms without any means.*"

Well, this is refreshing, whether we consider its candor or morality! "Raising firms without means"! Is it not decoying subscribers into crediting swindlers, and is not decoying subscribers into such credits playing the *role* of a confidence operator for a share of the "swag"? And yet this opportunity was the faculty which Manager Lugsdin thought to be most assuring and convincing when he wanted a loan or desired a subscription.

These facts, selected at random from thousands occurring all over the country, leave no room to doubt—

I. That the Agencies are a *danger*, as well as a *menace*, to the business community.

II. That they are often ignorant and profoundly reckless.

III. That they are moved to these extraordinary freaks by *considerations of some kind* sufficient to overcome the scruples and circumspection of an ordinary caution or a politic silence.

CHAPTER VIII.

THE CHANGES IN SUBSCRIPTIONS—WHAT CAUSES THEM ?—THE
AGENCIES AS WITNESSES AGAINST THEMSELVES—THE OLD AND
NEW AGREEMENTS AND SECRET CIRCULAR—ATTEMPTS TO
DUPE SUBSCRIBERS.

WHEN the agencies were first introduced they asked for confidence and patronage on the ground of promoting safe trading by
special knowledge, carefully acquired, by fitting persons. They
pretended to Merchants that they could supply the place of personal inquiry and secure accuracy, promptly, over a large extent of
territory with the same certainty as over a small one. They pitch-
ed their charges on this basis; and although the three agencies have
existed, in one form or another, a conjoint life of 90 years, they
have only been able to acquire from 25,000 to 30,000 yearly
subscribers in the United States and Canada. Even this, their
highest success as to numbers, is the result of a constantly shifting subscription—the number of subscribers who have paid and
withdrawn during the term, tired of the affair or indignant at its
uselessness or bad faith, being at least 200,000 ! That is to say
their existence has been preserved, not by the continued support
*of any respectable portion of the subscribers who have had experi-
ence of the merits of the Institutions,* but by the slowly-produced
results of canvassing in new quarters, rating new names, serving a
fraudulent end, or showing a rod to new enterprises. It may even
be doubted if, in the three Subscription Lists of Dun, Barlow &
Co., McKillop & Sprague Co., and J. M. Bradstreet & Son, one
hundred subscribers' names can be found who have kept their
subscriptions intact for a period of ten years consecutively, even
where the names, firms, and business continued identical !

This fact is a pregnant proof of what the subscribers think of
the system. Coaxed or bullied into it at the start ; using it as a
means of temporary credit for a passing purpose, we yet find

them dropping away from it at the first opportunity, and leaving the load of its exactions to be borne by more unsophisticated and less experienced recruits.

If we examine the lowering of the pretences in the agencies themselves, we will see a similar change going on year by year. In fact, nothing about them is so remarkable as the self-supplied proofs which they afford *of a desire to reduce their own claims to accuracy and responsibility as they grow older.* This is not the tendency of honest business. Whatever may happen to an old-established house, owing to vicissitudes of trade, it is always sure to claim an increase of facilities and a better experience in catering to the wants of customers, as time passes. On the other hand, the agencies, as they grow in age, lessen their pretensions; and after starting into life on the plea of promoting trade by giving reliable information about traders, they come out, after a long struggle for existence, and disclaim every thought of giving trustworthy or reliable intelligence !

The most flagrant example of this *reductio ad absurdum* process is to be found in contracts made by Dun, Barlow & Co. with their subscribers. *The facts and reasoning are equally applicable to McKillop & Sprague Co. and J. M. Bradstreet & Son,* but we select the first-named firm in preference, because they have more elaborately and lately supplied us with conclusive arguments out of their own mouths.

Here is a copy of the first, or old agreement, as it is known, made by the agency :

THE OLD AGREEMENT.

TERMS OF SUBSCRIPTION TO THE MERCANTILE AGENCY.

"In consideration of the agreement hereby entered into by Dun, Barlow & Co. to "furnish TO THE BEST OF THEIR ABILITY information of the Mercantile Standing and "Credit (in the communities wherein they respectively reside) of our customers among "the Manufacturers, Merchants, Traders, &c., throughout the United States and in the "Dominion of Canada concerning whom we have occasion to make inquiry *in order to* "*aid us in determining the propriety of giving credit,* we, the undersigned, do hereby "constitute and appoint said Dun, Barlow & Co. *our agents* to procure and furnish to "us the information aforesaid, in accordance with the following rules and stipulations, "and with which we agree to comply faithfully, to wit :

"1. All information furnished us by said Dun, Barlow & Co. shall be strictly confi-"dential, *and all extended reports are to be read at their office* to us or to such confiden-"tial clerk as may be authorized by us to receive the same subject to their regulations.

" And said Dun, Barlow & Co. shall prepare for our use, and place in our keeping, a
" printed copy of a Reference Book prepared by them containing ratings or markings
" of the credit of business men. *And all inquiries at their office,* as also all use we may
" make of said Reference Book, shall be exclusively confined to the legitimate business
" of our establishment.

" 2. The information, reports or ratings, and markings which we, our agents, or
" clerks may so obtain from Dun, Barlow & Co. *shall never in any way, by exhibit,*
" *copy, or otherwise, be communicated to the persons reported,* nor *to* any other person or
" persons whatever other than the members of our firm.

" 3. The said Dun, Barlow & Co. shall provide themselves with the names of Law-
" yers, throughout the United States and in the Dominion of Canada, carefully selected
" as to capability and reliability, of which we may avail ourselves from time to time as
" occasion for their professional services in our business may arise, or said Dun, Bar-
" low & Co. shall, if we prefer it, take charge of our collections themselves, on terms
" customary in that department of their business to regular subscribers.

" 4. We will pay, in advance, ... for one year's services of
" said Dun, Barlow & Co., together with the use of said Reference Book pursuant to
" the foregoing conditions, and at the end of .... months from the date hereof
" we will return the said Reference Book to said Dun, Barlow & Co.

....
" ...., ...day of ...., 18 ." .

It will be noticed that this agreement provides for the agency
becoming the agents of subscribers merely to furnish " to the best
of their ability information," etc., in order to aid the subscriber, or
principal, *in determining the propriety of giving credit,* BUT DOES
NOT RELIEVE THE AGENCY from the consequences of ignorance, error, or mistake, as such agents. Whatever else may be said about
it, it certainly held out, in fact and law, the idea of some responsibility for the information conveyed; and by just so much was an
earnest of a pretence, of some kind, for the compensation received.
Joined to a belief that the agency possessed facilities for examination superior to those of a private individual, and was in constant
and exclusive exercise of them, this strong presumption of being
responsible for the consequences of errors, mistakes, or ignorance
went far to deceive the public in the first instance. For a long
period, because of restricted circulation, or the few transactions
made *solely* on agency information, or the vagueness of the information conveyed, or the judicious settlement, by compromise,
higher ratings, or otherwise, of claims made against them, the
true intent and purpose of the agency, to be and remain irresponsible, was not suspected or brought into serious question.
The agency preferred the public should believe in accountability. The belief increased subscriptions. Subscriptions enough attained to assure the enterprise, the true intent of the agency

might be carried out and profitable evasion perpetuated. As time passéd, however, some subscribers here and there were foolish enough to rely wholly on statements furnished; the consequences were, of course, disastrous; the sufferers commenced reclamations on the agency, and the latter wheedled them into quiet as best it could, and turned to " seven or eight leading legal minds of the country" for the purpose of devising a " new agreement " which should leave them legally irresponsible to subscribers, without causing the subscribers to discover that they were being cozened out of rights already paid for. The following is the result of the labored consultation between the " leading legal minds of the country" :

THE NEW AGREEMENT.

TERMS OF SUBSCRIPTION TO THE MERCANTILE AGENCY.

" Memorandum of the agreement between Dun, Barlow & Co., proprietors of the " Mercantile Agency, on the one part, and the undersigned, subscribers to the said " agency, on the other part, namely :

" The said Proprietors are to communicate to us, on request, for our use in our busi- " ness, *as an aid to us in determining the propriety of giving credit*, such information " as they may possess concerning the mercantile standing and credit of Merchants, " Traders, Manufacturers, etc., throughout the United States and in the Dominion of " Canada. It is agreed that such information HAS MAINLY BEEN, AND SHALL MAINLY " BE, OBTAINED AND COMMUNICATED by servants, clerks, attorneys, and employees, " *appointed as our sub-agents in our behalf* by the said Dun, Barlow & Co. The said in- " formation to be communicated by the said Dun, Barlow & Co. in accordance with " the following rules and stipulations, with which we, subscribers to the agency as " aforesaid, agree to comply faithfully, to wit :—

" 1. All verbal, written, or printed information communicated to us, or to such confi- " dential clerk as may be authorized by us to receive the same, and all use of the Refer- " ence Book hereinafter named, and the Notification Sheet of corrections of said " Book, shall be strictly confidential and exclusively confined to the business of our " establishment, *and shall never be communicated to the persons reported*, nor to any other " person or persons whatever other than members of our firm.

" 2. The said Dun, Barlow & Co. SHALL NOT BE RESPONSIBLE FOR ANY LOSS CAUSED " BY THE NEGLECT OF ANY OF THE SAID SERVANTS, ATTORNEYS, CLERKS, AND EMPLOYEES " IN PROCURING, COLLECTING, AND COMMUNICATING THE SAID INFORMATION, AND THE " ACTUAL *truth or correctness of said information is in no manner guaranteed by the said Dun,* " *Barlow & Co.* The action of said agency being of necessity almost entirely confiden- " tial in all its departments and details, the said Dun, Barlow & Co. shall never, un- " der any circumstances, be required by the subscriber to disclose the name of any such " servant, clerk, attorney, or employee, or any fact whatever concerning him or her, or " concerning the means or sources by or from which any information so possessed or " communicated was obtained.

" 3. The said Dun, Barlow & Co. are hereby requested to place in our keeping, for " our exclusive use, a printed copy of a Reference-Book, containing ratings or markings

" of estimated capital and relative credit standing of such business men as aforesaid,
" prepared by them or servants, clerks, attorneys, and employees aforesaid, together
" with Notification Sheet of corrections. We further agree that, upon the delivery to
" us of any subsequent edition of the Reference Book, the one now placed in our hands
" shall be surrendered to them, and also that, upon the termination of our relation as
" subscribers, the copy then remaining in our hands shall be given up to the said Dun,
" Barlow & Co., it being clearly understood and agreed upon that the title to said Re-
" ference-Book is vested and remains in said Dun, Barlow & Co.

"4. We will pay, in advance, ... dollars for one year's services from the
" date hereof, of said Dun, Barlow & Co., together with the use of said Reference Book,
" pursuant to the foregoing conditions, and such other sum annually thereafter for the
" same as may be agreed upon between us verbally or otherwise, subject always to the
" conditions and obligations above mentioned.

" 5. Dun, Barlow & Co. are hereby permitted to *reserve to themselves the right to*
" *terminate this subscription at any time,* on the repayment of the amount for the unex-
" pired portion thereof.

....

" ...., ... day of ...., 18 ."

This new agreement, if only used with new subscribers, would
be simply an open confession that the agency had discovered, and
was ready to admit, in a roundabout way, its incompetency as a responsible adviser ; but used as a substitute with old subscribers, who
had paid their hundreds or thousands of dollars under the old contract, it was nothing less than a gross deceit, repugnant to the
minds of all honorable merchants, devised by the " seven or eight
leading legal minds of the country." Fortunately we need waste
no words in characterizing this conduct. The agency, by the following *secret circular,* dated March 9th, 1875, and forwarded to
branch offices, renders language other than its own superfluous :

" THE NEW AGREEMENT."

(PRIVATE.)

" To MANAGERS :
" The exigencies of business, and the adaptation of the Mercantile Agency thereto,
" have rendered necessary some alterations in the Terms of Subscription, in order to
" afford us effectual protection ; and, after very careful deliberation among ourselves,
" with the suggestions of seven or eight of the leading legal minds of the country, we
" have adopted the accompanying form, which, we think, affords us the protection
" sought, and which we desire shall hereafter be used, *to the exclusion of all others.* We
" further desire to have the present form *substituted* gradually (in making renewals,
" etc.,) for those already signed. *There may be some little trouble in doing this, in indi-*
" *vidual cases, but a little tact will overcome it.* All the old forms now in your possession
" must be destroyed at once, to prevent the possibility of their being used after this
" notice.

" In connection with this subject, we desire to draw your attention to a practice—

" now prevalent, more or less, everywhere—of asking, by telegraph or letter, whether
" parties named are good for specified sums or not. *It is an objectionable form of in-*
" *quiry, for no one can tell what amount any man is good for on an individual transaction*
" *without knowing all his other transactions at the same time. In giving information, never*
" *say a man or firm is good for any amount ; rather substitute for it a form of expression*
" *more guarded, by saying they are ' thought to be,' or ' supposed to be,' or ' our impression*
" *is they are so,'* etc., etc. We have a troublesome suit now in Montreal growing out of this
" objectionable practice, and although we have no great uneasiness about its final deci-
" sion, still, we feel satisfied, it would not have been commenced at all if the objec-
" tionable form of expression had not been used. We want to *discourage* suits quite
" as much as to *defend* them successfully.

" *It is very essential that the question of liability should be discussed as little as possible.*
" *We do not want public attention or the attention of our Subscribers drawn to it unnecessari-*
" *ly, and we therefore desire you to keep this communication as much as possible to yourselves.*
" The plea for the substitution of the new Terms of Subscription must be, that the
" original contract was framed many years ago, before the business had assumed any-
" thing like its present magnitude ; that it did not cover the Reference Book and Noti-
" fication Sheet ; that it required all reports to be read at the office ; *that the principle*
" *of privileged communications was not as well understood then as now,* and that the whole
" question of Agencies, owing to recent decisions in Court, had been so much chang-
" ed that, under the advice of eminent counsel, we had decided to make some neces-
" sary alterations, in order to have the relations between our subscribers and ourselves
" more clearly defined, etc., etc.

" We are truly yours,

(Signed) " DUN, BARLOW & CO.

" NEW-YORK, March 9, 1875."

This general order from the Agency to its clerks to enter on a
systematic course of deception with the principals of both, is a
rare and instructive lesson in Agency morality and methods.
Managers systematically taught to afford their Co-Agents " effectual protection" by lying to the man who employs both, must be
safe and fit persons from whom to expect conscientious ratings or
to withstand bribes ! Low-salaried clerks, far removed from the
protecting morality of the principal office in New-York, and
drilled with elaborate detail in tricks of sleight-of-hand substitution of one thing for another; enjoined to the use of tact and
the finest phrases of verbal dissimulation; exhorted to appreciate
the essential necessity, in this business, that the question of
liability should *not be drawn to the minds of subscribers ;* these
surely must be fit and proper guardians of business men's reputations and gaugers of commercial honor !

But the force of this circular lies in something else than its
inculcation of deceit, and dissimulation, and paltering words. It
concedes away the whole *raison d'être* of Agencies, their reason to
be, or to be regarded as, *bona-fide* establishments. If the Agencies

can *never* say " a man or firm *is good* for *any* amount ; " if " no " one can tell what amount any man *is* good for on an individual " transaction without knowing all his other transactions at the " same time ; " if the Agencies do not pretend to know these, or enough of them, to have an opinion ; if they can only say they " have an impression " of a man, or the man is " thought to be," or only " supposed to be," good, or in credit, what can the Agencies do to earn $8,000,000 a year ? They concede their incompetency by stipulating to evade responsibility. They admit their ignorance by providing for its expression in the most self-protecting words. They say, in effect, all we can say of them : they are willing and anxious to get the public's money, but what to return for it except facilities for fraud, by third parties, must remain a profound mystery to themselves and the public, " passing understanding."

CHAPTER IX.

DISPENSATIONS OF PROVIDENCE OR WHAT?—THE SECRET BLACK
LIST—WHAT IT IS, WITH ILLUSTRATIONS.

A REFERENCE to the Secret Reports and Black Lists, preserved,
read, and circulated on request but never published, is now in
order.

In Banking and negotiating Railroad Securities there are few
older or more stable houses than M. K. Jesup, Paton & Co., 52
William Street, New-York City. Their credit has never been
doubted. They are reported in the Reference Books as " in un-
" doubted credit." Call on Dun, Barlow & Co., and you will be
forthwith put on your guard. The person in charge of their New-
York City Department will tell you, with a knowing leer, " Jes-
" up has taken care of No. 1 all his life, and will continue to do so."
If this be not sufficient to startle you, he will add, " He is not
" considered by some very reliable, not strictly reliable, and only be-
" lieved safe for engagements when strictly defined." What effect
these sardonic utterances may have had on A. T. Stewart & Co.,
the Merchants' Bank of Canada, and the various others to whom
they have been retailed, we know not; but they are strange things
to say or write of a gentleman whom the Agency is obliged to admit is *worth over one million dollars and free of outstanding
debts!* We think it may be said, however, that A. T. Stewart
has bought no exchange through Jesup & Co. since this cowardly and unmerited imputation was imparted; and that Mr. Jesup
has continued to forward subscriptions to his secret assailants, without " caring so much for No. 1" as they would have people believe.
With the information now first imparted to Mr. Jesup, is it too
broad to advise that he increase his subscription and await results?

Among the long catalogue of merchants favorably reported in
the Reference Book and subjected in the Secret Reports to such

aspersions on their business ability, and such imputations on their integrity of character, as we have noticed, J. & W. Seligman & Co., the well-known German Banking House, whose estimated cash capital is $10,000,000, fills a conspicuous place. This great house has stood above criticism or suspicion since its organization. Panics have come and gone and left it unaffected. The especial favorites of Mercantile and Commercial Agencies have sunk around it by the hundred. Trial may be said never to have reached it, for its foundations were laid in the eternal verities of a practically inexhaustible capital operating on an unchangeably reliable German constituency. It could not be assailed or depreciated openly without stultification to the assailant; yet it is secretly represented as " not considered entirely reliable," and as a house " only believed safe for engagements when clearly defined, " *and which looks, above all things, well after its own interests.*" Not reliable! Where did any Agency find reason or authority for so sweeping a characterization? Only fit to be dealt with as a man would deal with a notorious rogue—on a " clearly defined " basis! Who has ever had such a thought of the Seligmans? The base fling is without the slightest pretence of truth, and must have been indulged in for some purpose discreditable to the utterer. How can it have an *honorable* explanation?

The contrasted case of Duncan, Sherman & Co. is more recent and as suggestive. William Butler Duncan, the Mæcenas of New-York Merchants, the exemplar of high business and personal honor—if the Agencies were to be trusted—was hopelessly involved when they complimented him as highest in credit and means; and it sounds odd to learn now, from the Courts and Orders of Arrest, that his father was a secret creditor all the time, holding the greater part of the son's real estate in unrecorded Deeds, placed on file for the first time two days before the failure. It turns out now that the firm was only worth a *third* of their indebtedness at the very hour when the Agencies were heralding their "money-making investments" and advertising them to all comers as in "unlimited credit," when many merchants, taking their information from more reliable sources, knew them to be embarrassed for years and in hourly danger of failure! In other words, the Agencies rated them worth " one million and over;" that is, over *all* liabilities; so that, in sober fact, they were about

three millions in error ! Besides, it is now stated that, instead of
having £30,000 to their credit in London, they really owed
£139,000 to the Union Bank of that city—a further error or fraud
of nearly $700,000! Of course they subscribed to the Agencies
and paid them liberally. How other subscribers were led into the
catastrophe is best known to the sufferers.

From these seriously-meant accusations of incapacity and want
of reliability against the very best men and firms in New-York,
and false and fulsome eulogies of the insolvent or fraudulent, the
transition of the illiterate ghouls of the Agency is easy and natural
to the drivel of scandal and stutterings of doubt against less remarkable but equally solvent persons and firms.

One gentleman, prominently identified with a leading Hotel,
and in excellent credit and standing judged by the Reference
Book, is announced in the Secret Reports to have "no, or only a
"doubtful, capital;" as a "frequent borrower of money, largely in
"debt to Mrs. James Fisk: from this source he has facilities for
"raising money; is of expensive and extravagant, as well as some
"disreputable, habits." We do not know what the commentator
meant by collocating "disreputable habits" with the source of the
means; but a more malignant and dangerous attack on the sacred-
ness of private reputation, male or female, is not often made.

In the successful Publisher of some of the best, purest, and
most enjoyable literature of the day, a man whose capital and
credit are certified in all the Agency Books, and whose social life
is certainly respectable judged by any standard, the same ghoul
has discovered a monster—"a man of notoriously bad character, a
"free-liver, a keeper of fast horses, and an associator with males
"and females of doubtful character." The gentleman so assailed
never had a fast horse, as matter of fact; but if he had, Belmont
has a dozen, Bonner more, and Vanderbilt enough to deserve the
stigma. The gentleman so assailed never associated with males
and females of doubtful character any more than every one is
compelled to do who passes through the world in any public position and is obliged, by his daily duties, to extend the courtesies of
life to those with whom he may come in contact. But there are
men who, in pursuit of some hobby, go out of their way to associate with persons of whose "character" there is no doubt whatever,
as that abused word is applied, and yet the Agency moralist is

exceedingly careful to overlook matter of common notoriety. We can point to at least one hundred names, highly complimented by them for " character," who travel away from their ostensible business, whenever an occasion offers, to frequent gambling-hells, to play " sport" on race-courses, and to lead a life of extravagance, excitement, and conspicuous sensuality. How these persons have escaped censure when better-conducted men have been singled out for attack and condemnation, the experts in human motives must imagine for themselves. Did they strike their colors and lighten their coffers on sighting a piratical craft? Did they purchase exemption from the penalties of the proscription by a timely ransom ? The mendacious details which enter into these infamous records are not worth further illustration. How some respectable and reputable business men are spoken of as " only fit for a public " institution where they could get their board and lodging for " nothing;" how family affairs of great age and no value are made to serve a present resentment ; how matrons' names are associated with fraudulent transactions of which they never heard, may be readily inferred from what has been written. It is sufficient for our present purpose to say : Over eight thousand four hundred Merchants and Firms in the City of New-York alone are rated well and favorably as to capital and credit in the Reference Books of the Agencies, and scandalously assailed, to every applicant, in their honor, character, and business integrity in these Private Reports. Throughout the United States and Canada over *ninety thousand* others are treated to the same public compliment and secret detraction. Is it possible to reconcile the printed report and spoken lie coming from the same origin ? If the slander be true, or believed to be true by the slanderers, why do they lie in print? If the printed statement be true, why do they asperse and falsify privately ?

The manner of these secret reports is as bad as the matter of them. The same hand can be traced in the same catch-phrases throughout. It is apparent to the initiated that ignorance and assumption have joined together to produce the worst possible kind of character-killing by the clumsiest possible kind of weapons. And yet is it not an additional indignity to be assailed in such sort by men whose own reputations have stood at zero, and whose first success in life was attained by obliging others, in self-defence, to

support them?   We may forget that the assailers of Seligman and
Jesup are the eulogists of all the most disastrous failures of the
last five years down to Vyse & Co., Duncan, Sherman & Co., Allen,
Stephens & Co., Henry Clews & Co., Howes & Macy, Jay Cooke
& Co., and innumerable others throughout the entire country;
but how *can* we become reconciled to having persons dispense
reputation to our great and reputable Merchants when one of them
waited ten years to announce to the writer that he performed a
wise and honest act by not absconding once with a sum of gold
entrusted to him by the Board of Trade of Toronto?   The ancient
Thersites was a low-minded and vulgar-faced ruffian.   He had
human characteristics and at least one qualification—excellence in
blackguardism.   But to be trampled in the dirt by a set of Satyrs
whose lower passions might be typified by a Goat's extremities,
and whose highest ornament is an Ass's ears—can human patience
be asked to stand such an extremity of ill-fortune?

CHAPTER X.

WHEELS WITHIN WHEELS—DOCTORS DIFFER—AND WHAT THEY SAY OF THEIR· PATIENTS.

IF the Agencies appreciate friends like Macfarlan, Browne, Morrice, Herrick, *et id omni genus*, the timorous merchant who visits them voluntarily to show his real means, or try to correct their misrepresentation, must not always expect justice or security as the complement of a subscription. *The rule is that subscriptions mollify just in proportion to the amount paid;* but the volunteer needs also to remember that all the owners of the concerns have not equal control of the private reports. If, for instance, you confess your business matters to Dun, of Dun, Barlow & Co., you may look for reprovals from the City Manager—for this person cannot suffer any one to think *he* does not hold the key to the innermost chambers of commercial credit. The importance of this hint is readily made manifest by the following facts:

R. W. Cameron, of R. W. Cameron & Co., shipping and commission, carried his heart on his sleeve to R. G. Dun, in January, 1872. He satisfied the senior, who knew him well, that his resources were adequate for all needs, and his right to credit, if he desired it, perfect. The manager of the New-York City department, however, was not consulted, and he accordingly acted on the constructive slight. Mr. Cameron has now for the first time the mortification of knowing that, although his capital was £60,000 ($240,000), the city-department manager could only find it convenient to place it at $60,000 to $70,000 while communicating with Charles Pratt & Co., Central National Bank, Bank of British North-America, Hanover National Bank, and others in and out of New-York City; and that, "although standing high among his "friends, he had conveyed the idea of unreliability to persons not "so intimately connected with him;" that is, like the manager, who probably never saw him in his life. He soon learned "he was, in "the main, an enigma, and of doubtful reliability, although cer- "tainly prompt, energetic, and capable." The mistake of calling on the wrong man in this case shrunk £60,000 into $60,000, and entailed on a merchant and firm of indubitable resources and the highest commercial standing, who should never have entered such a place, an ill-favored aroma still hanging, without any intentional fault of his, around all his enterprises. In the closing words of the manager, "If he should get into trouble to-morrow it would "not create a great deal of surprise, and the universal remark "would be, 'I told you so!'" This is what he gets from praying at the wrong shrine, and not recalling that a brass serpent was the idol to neutralize the poisons of the pilgrimage.

O. R. Dorman, president of the Metropolitan Collar Company, doing the largest business in the line in the world, made the same mistake as Cameron. Dun and he were acquaintances of twenty years. Dun thought him to be as *he* knew him to be. The city manager did not know him at all, but he saw through him in a flash—through him and his admitted half million capital—and gazetted him "as not the most reliable man in the world." He was not indeed "unsafe," but "your account with him ought to "be watched"—as if every man's account ought not to be watched, only his. These words of golden wisdom did the manager indite and cause to be communicated to A. T. Stewart & Co., Wheel-wright, Anderson & Co., Minot, Hooper & Co., and Kibbe, Chaf-fie, Shreve & Co. what time R. G. Dun, under the softening thoughts and pressing duties of a prospective day's recreation after the manner of Isaak Walton, committed his departing friend to the mercies of the guardian of the vestibule. Dun *may* have been hospitable for the hour; but why, when he left the shores of his ever-flowing Pactolus for Lake Simcoe, did he forget to whisper to Dorman, *Cave canem*—beware of the dog!

Even the paths of Law and Literature do not escape these per-turbations. A well-known legist, over whom the shadow of the *Tribune's* tall tower erstwhile cast its genial shade, has com-mitted (in Agency opinion) some dire offence against the stringent rules of morality and conduct favored by the Agency. He had had the fortune, or misfortune, to be retained and to plead for (say) a criminal and convict. He had had the further fortune, or misfortune, to be counsel (say) for an impeached judge. Both acts were in the due exercise of his profession ; were, indeed, duties in a professional sense ; but their due performance did not exalt him in Agency eyes; relegated him to doubtful company, and drew down on his unconscious head these potent *dicta* : "He "is not very popular with some of the leading members of the "bar ;" is only "in *some* quarters regarded responsible for legiti- "mate business wants; is *suspected* of having no property in his "own name; is dabbling in outside operations, and *cannot* be re- "commended to credit." It may be of slight importance to the learned gentleman what "some leading members of the bar," in opposition, think of him; less, how "some quarters" regard him ; none, what the Agency recommends or omits to recommend in his behalf ; for his credit is unimpeachable. But we should really like to know whether he lost the chance of a lawn-cutter, a plough, or a client in consequence of the inquiry of Vanderbilt Brothers, or the ignorance, malevolence, or political or personal prejudices of this Agency representative.

A well-known lawyer, residing near Rye, with an office in Liber- ty street, and estimated worth from $500,000 to $1,000,000, the owner of dozens of houses and the director of a bank, is another victim. He is denounced as a "sharp, shrewd man, who will get "the best of a bargain, and rather unscrupulous. Transactions "with him should also be clearly defined, and in ' black and "white.' " The iteration of the same phrases palls on the ear and indicates the poverty of language which may consort with sly malice and devious detraction. What Mr. C. did to merit these opinions, complimentary to his legal, at the expense of his moral, character, we know not; but we would wager a ducat that their utterer merely spoke from his own inner consciousness to Cleve- land and St. Louis inquirers, and wholly without a tittle of personal experience or other justification.

Passing from the legal fraternity, who are naturally measured by the Agency's standard of professional ability and integrity— itself indicated by their selection of one Whelp to superintend their collections and bark, in return, at the citizens of Staten Island —we come to the treatment of literary men and literary ventures. In this category of Agency effort, the jealous nature of ignorance and also the cautiousness of cowardice assert themselves. Where there is great risk of discovery, the Agencies either omit to rate newspapers as such, or rate them highly. This is a rule of the trade. But where the chance of discovery is lessened, and the publishers or editors come to be treated of in the private reports, they fare worse than others, in proportion. It seems as if the acrimony withheld for prudential reasons were poured out with greater unction because of the compelled restraint in regard to journalism proper.

Our first example under this head will be the treatment of a Dey street company of publishers. Their papers are declared to be valuable property, and rated very highly ; but between the months of February and November, 1874, a remarkable change must have come over the men engaged in the publications. In February they were " smart fellows "—a favorite term with the familiar bumpkins of the agencies—and, " on the whole, sat- "isfactory." In November the same gentlemen are persons " in whom little confidence is felt ;" who " will take care of their "own interests, *at all risks*," and who " are managing the "—————— much to the dissatisfaction of the proprietors," although " paying promptly and making money." It is not for us to re- concile these sudden contradictions of feeling and circumstances. But it is fair to ask how the same gentlemen, " satisfactory" in February and " making money" up to November, came, in No- vember, to be without public confidence and possessed of so little moral sense as to " take care of themselves, at all risks" ? And it is also fair to ask whether or not these gentlemen, and men like these, connected with the honorable profession of journalism, are pleased to find the boobies of the agencies presuming to say what is and what is not " good management" of one or more leading news- papers ? We do not know what effect the wise-saws of the Agency may have had on II. C. Hulbert & Co., F. G. Green & Co., J. F. Anderson, Jr., & Co., Bulkley, Dunton & Co., W. II. Parson & Co., and others. We do know that the assailed gentle- men could graphically resent the impertinence if they saw fit.

The publisher of another daily newspaper, and known to pos- sess a great deal of wealth, variously estimated from $500,000 to $1,000,000, a member of the Manhattan Club, and a Director of the Associated Press, is denounced in the severest terms as a

" slippery, unreliable man, unfitted for credit except on the basis of
" net cash." This is said of a person whose word of honor passes
current with all who know him for any amount of money; who
has never contested a claim unless he believed it fraudulent, and
who is rated in the Reference Book in " *very* good" credit!
We learn his libellers are anxious to retract their aspersions now
that their secret defamation is exposed ; but we should think as
little of the person who would be satisfied with such a requital for
so grievous a wrong as we do of his traducers.

The family circle is no safer from attack than the Bar or the
Press. Thus we learn of one H—— that " he takes too much
" wine, and is possessed of an *extravagant wife* and fast horses."
Of another " H——," that " he has recently been made no-
" torious by his love for the drama ; by being sued for divorce
" *by a notorious so-called vocalist of the Variety*, and by it being
" alleged that *this is the last of three marriages*, and that *his first*
" *wife is still living in Brooklyn*." The second " H." is conceded
to be in " excellent credit," but the opportunity of recording these
useless details in a record could not be missed. Of another gentleman it is told that " he is doing a large business and thought to
" be making money, *but is involved in a suit with the widow of*
" *a man he is said to have killed in a mêlée*." Of another, who
" is worth from $200,000 to $250,000," it is carefully related that
he is " amply safe and responsible for all contracts, but was at *one*
" *time* an inmate of the Binghamton Inebriate Asylum." Another will be surprised to learn that his daughters, living in his
house since their birth, " left him on account of a second marriage."

Indifferent to the reserve of home, the agencies are also indifferent to the sanctities of conscience, and betray the bigoted prepos-
sessions, of every temporary manager, in the record. Charles H.
Applegate, doing business in Dry Goods at 330 Broadway in 1874,
and associated as partner with a house reputed to be worth $200,000,
is made the scape-goat of a narrow religious prejudice. He is denounced as " an *ardent Methodist*, erratic, difficult to place, easily
" persuaded, sharp and tricky." As if " ardent Methodists" lost a
certain amount of business qualification in proportion to their ar-
dor of religious belief and their eagerness in practising it !

The editor of the " Quebec Saturday Budget," quoted in the
Montreal *Sun* of September 14th, 1875, is our authority for au-

other instance of offensive bigotry. Writing of the agencies under
a recent date, he says : " We well remember an occasion when, in
" reply to an inquiry concerning a certain house in Quebec, one
" of the agencies flashed back the reply by telegraph, ' *They are*
"Roman Catholics ; do not give them any credit.'" The descent
from bigotry to dirt is natural and inevitable. On the record of
one of the agencies in Albany, and New-York, is this entry in reference to Potsdam Junction, St. Lawrence County, New-York:
" Miss L. E. K——k. Is an orphan, twenty years old, *comely,*
" residing with the widow A——y, who is a woman of wealth
" and has no children of her own." And of another lady in New-
Jersey it is said " she has a neat millinery store, with a cozy room
" in the rear, and an inviting lounge."

Two others—partners—will find something more surprising
still in these ruffianly reports, namely : " that *each enjoyed the*
" companionship of the other wife's with her husband's consent."

We stop here. If the reader has any patience left after
perusing these examples of agency literature, we must ask him to
exercise it over a few questions which we submit to him in perfect sincerity.

I. Are men moved by the impulses displayed in the foregoing examples fit to be associated with on terms of equality,
or any terms, by self-respecting citizens ?

II. Are men who live by the sale of the false—where not
puerile ; scandalous, where not inane ; malicious where not in-
consequent—reports, hints, surmises, guesses, criticisms, and down-
right blackguardisms detailed in this chapter, fit to be recognized
as public benefactors ?

We select for our illustrations of the influence of personal
bias, etc., on Agency Reports these sample facts of a great
number germane to New-York City, because the principal office
cannot elude responsibility for them or pretend that it is not
affected by the spleen, narrow-mindedness, and ignorant pretensions to which we have referred. The effect of having the
same fellows who play these antics on citizens of assured
wealth and character in a position to gratify like feelings on
gentlemen of less means and equal integrity can be readily
conceived. Assuredly the knaves who receive men's money and
rate them well *openly* only to depreciate and degrade them *pri-*

vately are not likely to respect less wealth or greater sensibility to abuse, if a purpose may be served or a feeling gratified, in disregarding both.

It occurs to the writer that there ought to be a limit to public forbearance. The Courts, whose breath is publicity and whose prerogative is sovereign to correct and reprove things tending to the destruction of society, seal up from prying eyes the inevitable records of human frailty. Legislatures pass Statutes of Limitation to restrain and prevent discussions of personal character only calculated to foment strife and endanger social peace. Municipal governments set apart a time for removing the natural accumulations which might affect the health of localities by being brought in contact with the air at less propitious hours for human rest. The Agencies alone, bound up in their own selfish objects, and incapable, from their very constitution as depots of ignorance and rapacity, of respecting any tie however sacred, any reserve however urgent, any misfortune however retrieved, set no bounds to the accumulation of matter obnoxious in itself, and display their indifference to honor, and the comities of Society, by giving it a permanent hospitality and a perpetual circulation.

CHAPTER XI.

THE WEEKLY CHANGE SHEETS—THEIR INCOMPLETENESS—THEIR AGE.

BESIDE the yearly, half-yearly, and quarterly Reference Books, the three Agencies indulge their subscribers with "Notification Sheets." These are supposed to be a true exhibit of the changes happening within the period mentioned to over 800,000 persons. The average number of names on these Sheets is not over three hundred. Whatever the Branch Offices can pick up they report to the Principal Offices, and the Principal Offices print and distribute weekly or monthly, as their custom may be. The first objection to these Sheets is apparent. Among 800,000 persons the fluctuations of business, of a decisive kind, must number thousands weekly. Let any single Merchant in any town in this Country or in Canada recall the changes in business men's affairs within his own knowledge during a single week, and he will immediately discover how incomplete and inadequate the few hundred instances given in the Sheets must be to represent the changes by Death, Dissolutions of Firms, Insolvency, Judgments, Fire, and the thousand and one casualties incident to the business life of 45,000,000 of population. There is not a State in the Union, or a Province in the Dominion, which would not supply a larger roll; and single counties in the mercantile portions of either country, would, if adequately reported, require a much greater exhibit.

The second defect of these Sheets is that they are old when printed and older when received, as well as incomplete. The Post-office is the means of first communication with the Branch Offices; these offices transmit news also, by Post, once a week: the Principal Offices make up the Sheets from this slowly gathered matter, print it during two days, and, instead of mailing directly to subscribers, return the Sheets in packages to the Branch Offices for final distribution by mail.

In this manner the weekly list, when received, generally conveys information three weeks old.

Now, it is the common experience of business men that the period most dangerous to honest traders is always the period just previous to unexpected changes, or within a short time after they have happened, and in advance of their becoming notorious. If the Agencies meant to serve their subscribers in any way, the greatest expedition would be shown in this critical time. If they could not aid them by approximating correct ratings, they might, at least, make an effort to *promptly* announce such *open secrets* as Failures, Suspensions, Receiverships and Fires. They know better than to attempt it. However the defects and incompleteness of their arrangements may be to subscribers, they are fully appreciated by the Agencies. *Festina lente* is a meaningful motto to them. It is safer and better for them that the subscribers should wait and suffer, in their pockets and goods, than that the Agencies should be put to the additional cost and responsibility of telegraphing changes, etc., by means of the Associated Press, or report a financial death until it had stunk beyond providential resuscitation. This niggardliness and self-convicting caution distinguish all they do and determine all they decline and neglect to do. The use of the telegraph to and from their Branch Offices would cost from $20,000 to $30,000 yearly, perhaps more; but if it saved ten subscribers out of 30,000, during the whole time, from loss arising from want of information, it would be a partial, however inadequate, requital for the $8,000,000 extracted yearly from the business capital of the country. Even this slight chance of recompense is disregarded. The coercive features of the institution are relied on to make up for every shortcoming or omission.

The Agencies know they may snore if they choose, on the principle that *Apollo semper arcum tendit*, and a man capable of communicating contagious disease may thank no one for showing him a Hospital. A small-pox patient finds plenty of room and encounters little controversy in any community.

Let us, however, suppose the Change Sheet received in due course. Consignments have had plenty of time to reach the buyer's hands, or his Receivers, or his Assignees. *Pro rata* distribution, instead of recovery of the goods or payment in full, is the first consequence. The second is: entailed costs for Attorneys, and, in case of collection being made through the Agencies, *profit from the very loss which their negligence of subscribers' interests had already entailed or aggravated.*

If the Change Sheets arrive pending a negotiation instead of after an executed contract, the absence of a credit applicant's name is a deceiving assurance; while, on the other hand, if the name appear in connection with an honorable change or a suspension, nothing is said to show whether the change is for the better or the suspension likely to be short, protracted, or distinguished by circumstances justifying forbearance rather than pressure. It is of common occurrence to find Firms that had resumed within a week after suspension dropped out of the Change Sheets entirely, and thus excluded from the community of active traders to which many Merchants and Manufacturers look for desirable customers. But if the resumption be announced, it comes months after the time of happening; and the resuscitated firm has had a chance to secure new associations before the old ones could wisely take advantage of their longer acquaintance and former relations.

Of the Notification Sheets of McKillop & Sprague Co., J. M. Bradstreet & Son, and Dun, Barlow &. Co. the general charge holds good:—that they are made up from the same sources as the Reference Books; are slow to come, and useless or confusing when they do come. In a country of quick transportation, a device which gives contemplated or accomplished fraud even a week's start is necessarily valueless except as a test of patience; and after-the-fact knowledge becomes likewise a work of supererogation, in the instance of honorable business misfortune; for who ever heard of an honest man attempting to incur obligations when in a state of flagrant failure without apprising the credit-giver of his condition? They are, therefore, too tardy to prevent losses; too meagre not to deceive the trusting; and, although the most pretentious sign of activity and alertness of the Agencies, are of a piece with the decoy of the Prize Package and the trick of the Sawdust swindle.

As the yearly, half-yearly, and quarterly Reference Books are the standing capital and menace of the Agencies, they are made to do double duty—extort the yearly subscription principally, and extract a biennial tax of $10 besides from subscribers. One would think the yearly charge monstrous enough for the mass of trash supplied; but this supplementary piece of highwayism partakes more of the condign necessities of the footsore and barefaced "Secesh" who peeled his victim to the buff than the genteel Turpinism which should characterize already well-mounted and well-appointed footpads,—which the Agencies are *not*. 'Tis the old story over again. The business public did not resist beginnings. They might have singly and cheaply overcome the first assault. They have paid fifty or sixty millions for their remissness, and must now essay, with greater labor, to render unprofitable the very capital supplied by themselves, and used to harass the weak and levy tribute from the irresolute.

The half-yearly and quarterly volumes are merely the yearly matter with the Notification Sheet alterations. As subscribers receive the yearly volume for the subscription-price, and the little Sheets to modify a few of its many discovered inaccuracies, they have the very matter in their possession for which they are required to pay the additional $10. This is a very considerable item for Dun, Barlow & Co., and in a lesser, but also proportionably profitable, degree to McKillop & Sprague Co. and J. M. Bradstreet & Son.

The cost of these absolutely-needless books is merely the paper and printing, about $2.50 or $3.00 per volume. The difference is clear profit. But the dodge produces a further advantage. It makes the subscribers pay for the yearly Books: the profit of sales supplies enough to pay salaries, rents, and contingencies. The system of calling in the old volumes serves a treble purpose. It contributes to prevent Merchants from discovering the extent of obsolete or identical matter, by comparison; destroys the primary evidence of information which may have induced losses, or might furnish ground for libels, and enables the Agencies to recover all the paper and binding material of every edition to work up again into a next issue or sell to the paper manufacturer. A calculation will indicate the exquisite adaptation of means to ends in all this arrangement. It will show the absurdity of the popular impression that Jack cannot eat his cake and have it too. The Agencies prove the contrary. They can eat their cake a dozen times; be paid for the successive exertion; and only lose a few crumbs in the whole series of operations in the interests of Trade! The yearly subscriptions are, therefore, either wholly or nearly wholly, clear profit; so that, which ever way we turn, we find every appliance disadvantageous to the subscriber and of profit to the publishers.

As to the yearly volumes themselves, they can only contain, additional to the half-yearly or quarterly ones, as the case may be, the substance of the Change Sheets issued within the time of the publication of the last quarterly, and previous to the opening of the yearly, term. If no changes be reported, none, of course, are entered; if they are reported, they make a very inconsiderable addition to the last volume's; and, in all events, apart from these alterations, the old ratings of capital and credit are sold over again, year after year, with commendable persistence and constantly accumulating profits. The merchant who has not failed, and who has been quadrupling his means within three or four years, sees his old rating occupy the same place with the proverbial persistence of error. The merchant who has failed will, in ninety cases out of a hundred, either find himself paraded in all his pristine credit or overlooked, as is natural where only about *five per cent of the business population* of the United States and Canada is noticed in any manner. Administrators and Executors who have passed their accounts and been discharged, find their long-buried testator in active life and high credit. The members of long-since dissolved partnerships discover themselves still allied in effort and responsibility. Once in every two or three years a crusade for new subscribers is entered on, from the district offices, into the towns which appear to justify the effort, and these itinerancies have the effect of burying some of the notoriously dead, and bringing into agency life and meshes some new, traders; but as the solicited merchant who refuses to subscribe is sure to be remembered as a penalty to himself, an inducement to reformation, or a terror to others, the amount of consequential misrepresentation added is generally in startling excess of the correction made.

Between the necessity and policy of lying *in favor* of subscribers and the necessity and policy of lying *against* non-subscribers, Truth, it might be thought, is crucified with all the concomitants of gall and wormwood, while Barabbas is let loose, with loud acclaim, to rob and plunder.

If the agencies were even conceded to preserve, in a tempting employment, even the average morality of the day, why, it may be stated, should we expect them to properly perform a function more delicate than legislation; more remunerative by its abuse than lottery schemes; more involved and far-extending in purpose than any single enterprise of the time, excepting the United States Revenue Service; when we have just seen a national Legislature given over to the infernal gods by the rapacity of its most trusted members, and a carnival of greed for dishonest gain sweep into its vortex Cabinet Officers, Ministers Plenipotentiary, and thousands of the most revered characters in and out of places of official trust in the country? What right have we to imagine illiterate boys, working on a salary of $10 a week, more upright than Colfax, or managers, earning one thousand, and living at the rate of six, more self-denying than Tweed? We do not. But this is merely their apology for being as they are. It is no excuse or justification for their existence, as such.

The agencies are certainly *not* officered or controlled by men of exceptional mortification. Their staff is a promiscuous gathering that can have no other purpose in such a line of life than to make money quickly and retire. As with all enterprises attracting public odium, appeals to self-interest must preserve a constant excess of persuading force over deterrent or disgusting features. There must be compensation for shame suffered as well as labor done. The demeaning performance over, the petty assistant may be expected to count his petty knock-downs in rear of the establish- ment, while the higher priced and placed manager or confederate may be presumed to openly pass through the front door, to a luxurious retirement, with just such a portion of the goods of the concern as a feeling of perfect immunity from legal reprisal on the part of associates, or his own opportunities, may have defined for him. The reason is natural. Hangmen have always had, as of right, something for the executions, over and above the fees. The rope, or a part of it, is one. Other analogies will suggest themselves.

CHAPTER ' XII.

TAMPERING WITH THE LEGISLATURES OF CERTAIN STATES AND
THE PARLIAMENT OF THE DOMINION OF CANADA—MORE
SECRET CIRCULARS—FACTS AND METHODS.

CONSCIOUS wrong-doers fear the law. Are the Agencies an
exception? Ever since their introduction they have been haunted
by the fear of Legislative interference. As they progressed in
wealth and increased in age, fear gave way to attempts at precaution against it; and a large part of their energy and no insignificant
proportion of their profits are now devoted yearly to anticipating hostile movements set afoot by their victims, or suppressing
the honest efforts of enlightened and thoughtful law-makers to
abolish or restrain their abuses. Dun, Barlow & Co. make, no
mention in their Secret Circular, which follows, of the first inte-
resting episode had with the Canadian Parliament. They wholly
overlook their experience at the Dominion Capital in 1873. A
merchant of St. John, New-Brunswick, conceived himself grossly
aggrieved, and induced the local member to propose a General Act
of Parliament. A committee was appointed to take testimony.
Middlemiss, of McKillop & Sprague Co. (and then representing
that firm in Montreal), was summoned before it and examined. An
agent went in hot haste from New-York to appear for Dun, Barlow & Co. and give his notions. Feeling ran high—high enough
to induce the rival Agencies to confer together against the common
enemy. They conferred to advantage. The Agencies were
something poorer for a period; the Act was not urged; several
ambitious members were flush for a month or two; and the people
of the Dominion found themselves temporarily turned over to the
Agencies for further phlebotomy. The connection of McKillop
& Sprague Co.'s representative with the Canadian Crédit Mobilier
business, known as the " Canadian Land Swap," and the subsequent

judicious investments of Dun, Barlow & Co. at Harrisburg, render it unnecessary to assure the reader that both institutions used only *honorable* arguments, and persuaded one or more Canadian Legislative Committees solely by the innate force of *truth* and the example of uprightness.

The second instance of Legislative interference with the nefarious business was that originated by some excellent gentlemen in the Lower House of the Pennsylvania Legislature. The statesmen of that Commonwealth, brought up at the feet of Gamaliel, in all that pertains to popular rights, and fully appreciating the sacred rights of persons and character, early noticed the inroads of the new claims on the old-time reserves of business and society. They felt, too, that if privileges so general were asserted in the name of Right, they should be met at the threshold, and denied admittance in the name of the Commonwealth, without conditions calculated to insure safety to Merchants and traders in purse and character. This course was worthy of the Keystone State, and especially honorable to the legal profession, which has so long made its Councils a bulwark against individual wrongs and lax constitutional interpretation. The home of a Sharswood, a Black, or a Gurney was naturally the first in the Union to challenge the bold pretensions of the Agencies; and the ease with which the following Act passed an Assembly, largely composed of lawyers reared in the same school of jurisprudence, showed that there were not wanting many men who appreciated the danger and sought to avert it.

"AN ACT

" To punish commercial agents for false representations of the business condition "of certain persons

" WHEREAS There are persons travelling from time to time in different parts of the " Commonwealth claiming to be conducting or representing commercial agencies to " ascertain keep a record and publish the financial responsibility of business men in " different parts of the country

" AND WHEREAS Such persons from malicious or corrupt motives often wilfully and "*knowing* exaggerate and misrepresent the financial condition of persons engaged in "different kinds of business to the great injury of such persons and the general public
" Therefore

"SECTION 1 *Be it enacted by the Senate and House of Representatives of the Common-* " *wealth of Pennsylvania in General Assembly met and it is hereby enacted by the authority* "*of the same*

" That any person conducting the business of what is known as a commercial agency " established in this commonwealth or elsewhere for the purpose of ascertaining pub-

"lishing and keeping for public or private information a record of the financial re-
"sponsibility and business condition of bankers merchants traders builders manu-
"facturers or other persons engaged in any commercial business and any person
"claiming to be the representative of such commercial agency who shall knowingly
"heedlessly or wilfully exaggerate or misrepresent by writing printing or otherwise in
"book form or otherwise the credit financial responsibility or business condition of
"any banker merchant manufacturer tradesman builder or other person or persons en-
"gaged in any commercial business shall be guilty of a misdemeanor and upon con-
"viction thereof shall be sentenced to pay a fine of not less than two hundred and fifty
"dollars nor more than one thousand dollars one half of the fine imposed to be for the
"use of the informer A conviction for the foregoing offence shall not bar an action
"for damages by the person or persons injured."

No sooner had this Bill passed the Lower House than the
Agencies discovered it and took alarm. They counselled together
how to avoid the threatened restraints on unlicensed libel and irresponsible slander. One of their modes was the writing and private circulation, throughout the State, of the following confidential letter, copied from the original in the writer's possession, received from a merchant too honorable to act on it:

"THE MERCANTILE AGENCY.

"............, 1874.
"...................
"..............

"Dear Sir:
"On the next page you will please find an Act that has been introduced into the Le-
"gislature of Pennsylvania, and which, *with the very slightest consideration*, has actually
"passed the House of Representatives. There is a good prospect, however, of stopping
"its passage in the Senate, and we beg, therefore, to ask your good services to that end.
"If you can assist its opposition by letter, or otherwise, to the Representative of your
"District in the Senate, we beg that you will do so at once. As you will see, the Act is
"very loosely drawn, and contains a false declaration at the start, that information is
"' often ' wilfully erroneous, and moreover offers a bribe to unprincipled informers to
"annoy respectable persons for the hope of reward. The laws of the land are already
"adequate to protect the public, and the *penalties now in existence for slander and libel
"are heavier than even this Bill proposes.* It is therefore uncalled for. The merchants in
"the various cities are petitioning against the measure, and you will not be singular in
"your opposition to it if you will do us the favor to bring what influence you can to
"bear in the Senate. Inasmuch as action is likely to be taken very shortly after the 7th
"April, prompt measures are necessary. We should like to have a line from you
"whether you can help us in the matter or not.
"Respectfully yours,
"...................."

The FIRST falsehood in this shameful document is self-evident.
No bill *could* pass the House "with the very slightest consideration." It was referred to the Judiciary Committee. It had

received their *full consideration,* and we know that no law of this import could pass from that committee back to the House without having *received* the approval of the *best legal minds in the State.* The SECOND falsehood is meanly malignant. The wiseacres of the Agency affect to think the act "loosely drawn." To further this impression *they* print it *without* punctuation and *with* verbal in- accuracies, just as we have produced it. Every one knows, who can read it, that, even with these disadvantages, it is an exceedingly clear and well-expressed statute. The THIRD falsehood is worse than the other two in effrontery. The public are already better protected by the laws of slander and libel than the bill proposes! Why, as we have shown elsewhere in this work, the Agencies have always *claimed* immunity from the operation of these laws on the double ground that their communications were privileged between master and employee—principal (merchant) and agent (themselves) —and further, that their *interest* in the character of merchants and traders was a legal protection against either the claim for private damage or public prosecution! The FOURTH falsehood is "that merchants were petitioning against" the passage of the bill. There was not a word of truth in this statement. The circular was in- tended to induce them to do so, and in the hope that some might be got to sign against the bill, on the promises of *special* recogni- tion from the Agency. A few were caught by this bait, after a time; but their number and character were so insignificant that the names were never presented in the Senate, and the bill was de- feated by very different methods and ones more distinctly within the Agencies' immediate control. A member of one of the Agencies went on from New-York to Harrisburg, with means fur- nished by the Agencies, to *persuade* certain majorities of certain committees of the Pennsylvania Senate that the bill ought not to pass. It cost money to travel. It cost money to live in hotels. It was not without large additional expenditure, and much intrigue, that this agent was enabled to telegraph that all was right at last! The exact outlay will only be known in a court of justice; but it is safe to say the contingent or expense accounts of the Agencies show a marked rise in these spring months of 1874 to whoever may secure access to them.

The third interference with the Agencies occurred on the

banks of the Mississippi and Missouri. In December, 1874, King, the St. Louis office manager, learned that a bill was about to be introduced at Jefferson City creating greater responsibility, for false reports by Agencies, to the slandered and deceived, and defining their liability to parties injured by their *espionage*. These restrictions were barely just; but they would have destroyed the institution in the State within an hour after their passage. The fact was communicated to head-quarters in New-York, and the Agencies took alarm again. If this example were to spread, their career would be brought to a close. If it were generally known and canvassed even, there was danger that, although legislation might be prevented in Canada, Pennsylvania, and Missouri, some of the other States would legislate in the like wise spirit, and, by making the Agencies responsible for their malice and mistakes, practically prohibit them. In this emergency a consultation was had in New-York. As the result of the conference a telegram was agreed on and sent through the Western Union Telegraph Co. to King, instructing him to "spare neither money nor labor to kill the bill." King spared neither. The sum of *thirty thousand dollars*, at least, was expended among the Black Horse Cavalry of the St. Louis Delegation, and a few effective society men in the country districts; but we are bound to *state*, expended in a legal way: what we *believe* is another matter; and the proposed bill dropped out of sight after serving a few evenings as a scarecrow at the Capitol.

There is still, however, in that and other States, the germ of an active opposition which may lead to efficient legislation. Several energetic attorneys are badgering the Agencies in the courts; and we should not be surprised if the spring and winter of 1876 witnessed a new campaign led by honest men and supported by the leading presses of that and other high-spirited commonwealths.

Warned by this troublesome business in Canada, Pennsylvania, and Missouri, the Agencies conceived the idea of guarding against future surprise and, if possible, cheapening their legislative processes, both. In execution of this purpose the following circular, dated January 19th, 1875, was printed and sent to all branch-offices by the Mercantile Agency. It indicates the anxiety of the Agencies on this head:

" LEGISLATION.

" To Managers :

" We particularly wish to impress upon you the necessity of constantly perusing
" the official reports of your State Legislature, in order to discover if any bills or re-
" solutions are introduced affecting the Agency business. We had a *great deal of trouble*
" last winter from Legislation, especially in one or two cases, not having been advised
" sufficiently early to combat it as successfully as we could otherwise have done. The
" moment you discover anything affecting our business do not fail to notify us at once,
" and to send us copies of the documents. We presume the daily paper published at
" the State capital will contain all that is necessary, and a hasty glance at each day's
" proceeding will enable you to keep track of what we so much desire to know.

" Yours truly,

(signed) " DUN, BARLOW & CO.

" NEW-YORK, January 19, 1875."

The indorsement by the Manager of a Southern Branch on one of these circulars is curt and to the point. "Don't think the " Legislature, composed as it is of two thirds negroes, will ever " think of a ' Mercantile Agency,' much less pass laws affecting it. " *All they care for is the money !*"

The trouble which Dun, Barlow & Co. had in "two cases," during the winter of 1874, "to combat Legislation" must refer to their interference with the members of the Missouri Legislature through the exertions of their St. Louis manager, King, and the equally important manipulations of the Pennsylvania Legislature by their Secret Agents at Harrisburg and the various Senatorial Districts of that State. We must suppose all done within the Law. The confession of these two crimes against the public leaves many others of the same nature in the background, but we have preferred to use their own proofs and limit ourselves, for the time being, to the offences which they have admitted.

Can that be treated as a safe and legitimate business which adopts the methods indicated in the preceding circulars to elude legislative restraints? Ought the public countenance or sustain men who, by their own confession and these proofs, might be charged with following the practice of corrupting the fountains of Legislation?

Is there not a public danger, apart altogether from the question of private wrongs, in the growth of institutions which make a boast of anticipating reformatory measures by capturing the representative bodies, or enough of them to make the rest inefficient to carry out the popular will?

Our Representative Assemblies are bad enough already ; but it is full time to become alarmed for them when these Agency enterprises, " conceived in sin and brought forth in iniquity," are emboldened, by public apathy, to approach the very sanctuary of the law-making power, and lay their unclean hands on the ministrants at the Altar !

CHAPTER XIII.

SPREADING THE PLAGUE—THE FOREIGN OFFICES AND THEIR
USES—JONATHAN THE ONLY SUSPECT.

It is one of the wonders of the time how Mercantile or Commercial Agencies could establish themselves and prosper on this side
of the Atlantic, when public opinion would not suffer them to be
planted in many countries, or attain separate vitality in any, on the
other side of the Ocean.

In the British Islands they were not permitted to organize a
List or report Credits or Standings; and when, in 1872, they attempted, in view of the large California trade with Australia, to
plant themselves in Melbourne, the people of that Colony drove
them out ignominiously. Notwithstanding these effective exhibitions of feeling, a weak system of correspondence was inaugurated by McKillop & Sprague Co., J. M. Bradstreet & Son, and
Dun, Barlow & Co. in two or three European Cities; and those
firms were put on their "good behavior" to let all British and
European Citizens severely alone, and confine their attention to
Americans.

The Foreign Offices of the American Agencies are, therefore,
used, like the Home ones, to operate on American traders only.
They are not suffered to speak—would not be permitted to speak
—of the subjects and people in sight of their windows, in either
France, Germany, or the British Islands. Brother Jonathan is
their exclusive resource at home and abroad.

The fact is not flattering to national pride. Is the American
Citizen the sole Trader or Merchant who will permit himself to
be tried at home by these self-constituted tribunals of character;
followed beyond sea by their underlings; and harassed by their
impertinences and exactions, everywhere? Either the human race
requires this protection from his dishonesty, and he concedes the

necessity, or he is endowed with less self-assertion and independence, in affairs of Commerce, than John, Pat, Sawney or Pierre, and is content to have every one intermeddle with his affairs who may desire to make a trade of doing so.   However we essay to explain his forbearance, foreigners will fall back, at last, on his consciousness of special depravity, or his national bluntness of feeling.

Our National, State, Railroad, and Municipal loans are never effected through information of the Agency sort.   Special Agents go out; other Agents or Attorneys are sent here to inquire on the ground into the security of proposed investments; and the office of the Agencies is therefore reduced to that of prepared detectives in the lighter transactions between firms and individuals *cis* and *trans* Atlantic.   In these dealings, which ought to be on a plane of equality between the respective nationalities, the home American is always the inquired about, never the inquirer; and the purpose of the foreign offices can, therefore, only be to exercise in London or Paris the same profitable *surveillance* over our citizens which the Parent Agencies render so remunerative in this country.   As the American is the only man who submits to it in his native land, it is fitting, perhaps, when his business lies abroad, he should be made to pay toll again, or take the consequences.

Rightly or wrongly, no business man or firm having foreign relations can wholly afford to disregard the significance of the geographical position of these foreign branches.   An unfavorable rumor, however started—even if started to be silenced on proper inducement—obliges the inducement to be forthcoming.   Among his acquaintances, a man with average grit and sufficient capital may do business in a storm of detraction. Abroad, a whisper is ruinous; and he is inconsiderate of his interests who does not purchase silence or buy encomiums.

Our own impression is that these foreign branches are not growing in favor, and cannot become permanent, self-sustaining establishments.   *Their main revenue has always been collected on this side of the water from the class of persons who desire decoys to credit on the other side;* and they are so generally suspected now by British, French, and German Merchants, on account of recent occurrences, that their usefulness, even to the fraudulently disposed, must, before long, come to an end.   Their only duty will be purely scenic and spectacular.   In the show business every wagon and box adds to the effect of the cavalcade. In the Agency business every office is an advertisement. When, however, in the former calling, the audience discover that the beasts and performing animals bear an absurd proportion to the cages and conveyances, they invest in no more tickets for *that* circus. By parity, when the foreign man of trade will no longer be deceived, and the fraudulent trader here can procure no benefit, the foreign offices will be dispensed with as mere advertising luxuries, cheap indeed, but valueless for revenue in the New World or the Old. Jonathan will then cease to supply Europe with a standing proof of his want of confidence in himself. Besides, Bucket-shops are profitless when exposed to the authorities.

CHAPTER XIV.

DO THE AGENCIES CONTRIBUTE TO, OR LESSEN, PANICS IN TRADE ?

THE panic of 1837 is explained in various ways. Some say the Stock speculations of men like Nicholas Biddle, Jacob Barker, J. W. Bleecker, and Samuel J. Beebe—the king operators of ten years preceding the catastrophe—were the efficient cause. In support of this theory they contrast the great fluctuations in the favorite Stocks of the day, and give the following examples :

	Nov. 25, 1834.	Aug. 25, 1835.
Morris Railroad	70	200
Harlem Railroad	64	105
Dry-Dock Bank	118	145
Delaware and Hudson Canal	72	113

An advance so purely speculative indicated "corners" worthy of comparison with the worst of our time ; but mere Stock speculation could not have produced the wide-spread destruction of 1837.

Our own explanation takes a more commercial turn. Forty millions had been invested in the purchase of wild land in the fiscal year '35–6 ! The process of locking up private capital in unproductive land had been going on for years. The Railroad system, then just beginning to draw to itself, in the hope of future profit, private means and public credit both, had succeeded in absorbing forty millions more. Other schemes of internal improvement, Canals, Turnpikes, etc., had, to the extent of fifty millions for the former, and twenty-five millions for the latter, absorbed labor and resources "in drafts upon posterity," leaving Bonds and Scrips in the place of the (for all immediate purposes) destroyed values. Counting the Bank Bonds, there were at least $185,000,-000 of artificial representatives of removed or unproductive values in the country, and, coincidently, a great shrinkage in proportion to population of productive agricultural labor. A lax credit system extended from Europe to America and permeated every condition of life to an enormous extent. Men worked less and "indulged" more than ever before. The crisis came with the defective harvests of '36. When Flour was worth $22 per barrel in Chicago, twenty days of excessive rain destroyed the crops; and the West—so called—which, it was hoped, would come to the rescue, failed for a hundred millions, and brought the rest of the country tumbling down with her. In three years, according to Medbury, sixty Banks sank out of sight, dragging $132,000,000 into the vortex, and out of an aggregate indebtedness of $440,000,000 the Creditor Class could not realize over *one cent* on the dollar, the rest disappearing in collectors' fees, brokers' commissions, and the costs of Courts, Lawyers, and Juries. The sinking of active capital in wild lands; the neglect to cultivate arable lands in proportion to growth of population and trading needs; the withdrawal of the labor which should have gone to productive uses from them, and its diversion to heaping up dirt for future railroads, and sinking ditches for future canals, prepared the country for the catastrophe; and the elements, as if teaching the lesson that Nature should not always be relied on to compensate for any unwonted dependence on her, precipitated the disaster and made it universal.

Whatever explanation, however, be the true one, the Agency system had its birth shortly after the Panic of '37; and the periodical Trade panics since that time have occurred in presence of its continuous development, and as if in derisive commentary on its pretensions. If its claims were well founded, *trade* panics would have been reduced or impossible ever since 1850, when it claimed to embrace the greater part of the commercial class. As matter of fact, they have been constantly shortening the period of their recurrence and extending the area of their destructiveness. Of two things, one: either the Agencies have not served the purpose of their origin in giving correct estimates of business risks, or the trading body has disregarded their advice, and either credited when it should not, or injuriously refused to do business when it might credit safely and profitably. We do not argue *post hoc ergo propter hoc*, but we say that if we find commercial panics increase in number, volume, and intensity in the presence of a system which claims to afford protection against them by enabling business to be conducted on a rationally safe basis, we cannot escape denying the efficacy of the system or admitting that it is not followed. Either is true; and either leaves the system, we were about to say, a fraud on subscribers or a deception to the community.

Their difficulty does not end with this dilemma. If they do not convey a reliable basis for traffic, if they are not generally credited with doing so, why do they persist in urging unreliable ratings on the public and forcing a market which the customer's own conduct shows to be irksome and valueless? Are they Black-mailers—coercers of others' money, giving no equivalent, of right belonging to them? Certainly the persistent tender of a valueless commodity to our citizens, accompanied with the opportunity of rendering the commodity annoying and mischievous if not pur-chased, is a suspicious method of livelihood, especially when it is remembered that the standing, character, and worldly credit of others than themselves are the exclusive subjects of sale. If it be not Blackmailing, it is assuredly not commerce. There is such a thing as a purely sentimental traffic in Relics and Antiques. We should call it highway robbery, however, if the collector effected an exchange for gold at the muzzle of a pistol.

But the regular publication of Agency Reports is the introduc-tion into Trade channels of an affirmatively disturbing and injuri-ous element. Disregarded, in the main, at and near the residence of the Merchant whose credit is rated, well or ill, accurately by guess-work, or the reverse by design, the Printed Reports must have the effect, at a distance, of putting caution asleep and anæs-thetizing suspicion. Suppose twenty-five thousand Subscribers—Merchants, Manufacturers, Traders, and Bankers—in the principal commercial centres are rated to secure and preserve their subscrip-tions—that is, as they would wish to be—and an equal or greater number are rated so as to make them anxious to be rated better by subscribing: we have fifty or more thousand men, in the chief seats of commerce, magnified or diminished in capital and credit *for reasons wholly apart from Trade reasons* and at variance with the natural ebb and flow of commercial affairs. The actual condition of business is travestied, year in and year out, by an arti-

ficial one. A constantly active and aggressive interest is tampering with the weights and measures of credit and capital. If the
seller does not wholly believe in or act on them, he is not apt to
totally overlook them, and is more or less, although unconsciously,
likely to accept and be influenced by them in some degree. This
is the first disturbance of Trade. If we add to this that the capital ratings of the Reports represent, in the case of 800,000 names,
a variable excess over the minimum capital three and a half times
greater than the minimum of the Ratings, and vastly in excess of
the estimated census wealth of the whole country, we see, at once,
that the Agencies interject a second element of miscalculation, also
necessarily injurious and misleading. But when we know that the
Printed Ratings of Capital are constantly circulated by the three
Agencies to 30,000 Subscribers, while the Secret Reports, designed
to modify them, are never publicly sent out ; that the bane is sold
and scattered broadcast, and the antidote, real or pretended, is
locked up in the Agency archives to be shown to others than the
persons affected, only when specially applied for, we need no
further proof that in proportion to the growth of the Agencies
must be the growth of dangerous trading, and consequently of
Trade panics—the first-born of inconsiderate Adventure.

The panic of 1854 was precipitated by the loss of a California
steamer, which threw the house of Paige, Bacon & Co. into suspension, and so unsettled confidence in others that the single event
assumed the dimensions of a national calamity. If we consider the
usual risks taken by Traders, the narrow margin of true profit, and
the inevitable losses, we shall find no difficulty in believing that
the additional errors and losses brought about by Agency misinformation, in even one year, greatly exceed in volume the freight of any
dozen vessels that ever sailed the seas, or the capital of any dozen
trading firms in the United States. The growing dependence, too,
of one Trade interest on every other enlarges the area of influence
and danger, while, within the special Trade most directly concerned, a surprising suspension carries within itself the causes and
occasions of a series of others, each more alarming and calamitous
than the last. The suspension of one Bank or Trust Company
creates a run, more or less, on a dozen Banks. The unnecessary,
unexpected, and extra business losses caused by Agencies are, of

all others, the most apt to astonish and dismay merchants, and to create a partial or general panic in the line.

The preceding pages have barely touched the mass of losses caused, within the personal knowledge of the writer, in a few cities in a brief period by one Agency, and the list might be almost in. finitely extended if space permitted. We can only instance an aggravated additional example of the same kind, which has just found its way into Court.

About $10,000 or thereabouts, in paper, of a New-Orleans merchant was offered in Montreal in connection with an advantageous bargain to a merchant of the latter city named J. A. Converse. He applied to the Montreal office of Dun, Wiman & Co. for special information, stating the facts. The Agency, after some delay, gave him *special* assurance that the *drawee* was good for almost any amount. The bargain was effected under this advice, and the Montreal merchant placed the Notes in the Collection Bureau of the Agency for collection. The Collection Bureau, within a few days, and ignorant of the advice given by its Company, returned the Notes as valueless, and reported to the merchant that the New-Orleans trader had failed months before!

Here was not alone the gross neglect to inquire, and resulting ignorance, such as we have shown to be normal with the Agencies, but the exercise of a *special* effort to procure the truth resulting in a loss of $10,000 to Mr. Converse, whose damages may be recovered in the Courts, but whose serious loss must have produced in his line of trading many consequential losses, and perhaps failure to others having relations with him.

This occurrence—only one of many similar ones which our space does not permit us to detail—was no doubt the predisposing cause of the urgent haste with which the "New Agreement," referred to in a former chapter, was pressed on the attention of managers, and the old one surreptitiously withdrawn and cancelled. The Agency, accustomed heretofore to mere suits for Libel with incidents of Damage, was naturally alarmed at an action seeking to recover losses arising from false information; and it sought to interpose between itself and an inevitable Bankruptcy, for this cause, a double-dealing contract which protected it from the consequences of an almost universal ignorance. Under the last, or "New" Agreement, the Agency has secured a double purpose, that is, tied the hands of its subscribers and enabled itself to combine, if it should choose, with fraudulent traders with impunity.

What is to prevent the happening of such a fraud as Ross & Co. perpetrated on Wall street in 1866, if any member of any of the Agencies were induced, in view of the present want of responsibility under the new agreement, to enter into an arrangement for its repetition? Ross & Co. established themselves in the vicinity of Wall street at the time mentioned, and secured, by means which may be readily comprehended, Agency indorsement. With its assistance they collected $600,000 on deposit within a short period. Having a moderate ambition, this sum satisfied them, and they set about possessing it in their own right. Knowing that we had no Extradition Treaty with Brazil, they chartered a schooner for one of the ports of that country, set sail on a Saturday evening with the treasure, and paid $25,000 to the captain to land them in safety. Somewhere in the Gulf of Mexico the captain conceived a desire for a larger share of the plunder, and exacted one hundred thousand dollars. Ross & Co. paid it. The vessel and treasure landed; the indorsed Bankers have not since been heard of, and the deceived depositors passed quietly into the procession of Agency dupes.

If the Agencies had correctly rated Henry Clews & Co., Duncan, Sherman & Co., Jay Cooke & Co., Howes & Macy, and others, when they pretended to rate them at all, the last Panic, under which we are still laboring, would not have spread so far or struck so deep; but rating them as they did, in " Unlimited Credit" and with " Unlimited Capital," they spread a net for their patrons, and rendered disaster more disastrous by lulling inquiry.

At the best, Trade in the United States, ever since the close of the war, has been easily affected by comparatively small disturbances. Sixty thousand Books, issued half yearly and quarterly to thirty thousand merchants, and incorrectly rating 650,000 men out of 800,000, would seem to supply a sufficient explanation and to afford a reasonable solution for many untoward vicissitudes in the business of the United States and Canada. Panics have grown out of lesser influences; and it is our belief that the Agencies not only do not assist to give stability and security to Trade, but that they always and everywhere unsettle commercial relations just in proportion to the attention which they attract.

CHAPTER XV.

DO THE AGENCIES MAKE THE CORRECTIONS WHICH THEY CLAIM TO MAKE?—BETRAYING INQUIRERS TO EACH OTHER.

EVER since the writer announced his intention to introduce the public to the interior of the Agencies the latter have shown great alacrity in receiving corrections of their reports. Wanting other information, they are glad to take the merchant's estimate of himself, and, eager to be rid of the responsibility for grossly false or malicious statements already gathered or published, they promise amends and place the indignant merchant, *to all appearances*, just as much above his deserts as they had previously placed him below them.

They are as considerate and accommodating in all this as one of their own canvassers who, exhausting his eloquence in vain to get a statement and a subscription, recently informed a city merchant (a Mr. Wronkow) that he would be obliged by the loan of five dollars. But these appearances are misleading and designed to mislead. For one injured and misrepresented man who will call on them for a correction a dozen will neglect to do so, or remain ignorant of a reason for inquiring except as this book may suggest it. It is not yet understood by business men that the best public ratings in the Reference Books are often only cloaks behind which lurk the most damaging reports ; and that while ratings may remain constant, the private reports may be variable and contradictory, and *vice versa*. Persons satisfied with their ratings, and not learning their *status* on the Black Lists from us, will not think of calling ; whereas those who do call, with excerpts from the Black Lists, will be promised, and will apparently receive, an immediate correction on the Printed Reports, with many verbal placating apologies for libel. *But the old record will remain in the Books ; will be circulated from the Branch Offices ; and will be read with the complainants' " say so " every time the latter is requested, for years to come*—just as the secret reports of some of our most honored merchants contain, within twenty lines of writing, details of purely imaginary and scandalously malicious charges of fraud and crime alleged to have been committed thirty years ago! The new report is added, indeed, as the man's opinion of himself; the libels it was meant to correct remain too, to be read in every Branch Office in the United States, Canada, and Europe, and to go down and out with the modification, as the only "outside," and therefore controlling, estimate of the capital, credit, and character of the affected merchant. The Agencies escape punishment for wrongs done; the merchant goes about his business; but the first inquirer at the agency *will have* all that ever was written of him read on request, just as if no complaint had been made or amendment and reparation had been promised.

The erasure from the secret record of the offensive statements in the personal presence of the libelled, both in the principal and Branch offices, would alone destroy the offensive matter and correct the agencies' habit of perpetuating the wholly false and the half true indiscriminately. This has never been done—the agencies preferring to deceive the injured by an amiable exterior, a penitent expression, and an abundance of lies.

They think the present agitation only a storm after all; and they hope to quell it and reach quieter times by being " all things " to all men," and protesting they meant no harm while fatally stabbing reputations or imperilling the success of a lifetime.

To show the dovetailing of old slanders in new reports, and the system adopted of reading them out together, we select the instance of a well-known Builder in New-York City, condensed from the Black List of Dun, Barlow & Co. from June 1861 to 1874, giving also the names of persons and firms to whom this epitome was read at the periods hereunder, and the Branch offices to which the same was transmitted.

VOL. XI., PAGE 243, NEW-YORK CITY RECORD.

* * * * * * * * * * *

" June 3d, 1861.—Failed many years ago, and *settled at 25 cents on the dollar*. Was " some time out of business, but subsequently got a large contract on the S—— Insti-" tution, Washington. Of late years has been speculating and building in connection " with his brother-in-law, ——, who is well off and has supplied the means mostly. An-" tecedents are bad, and he is not reliable; parties who sold him previous to his failure " decline dealing with him except for cash down."

" October 17th, 1872.—Is still Director and Stockholder in the B—— National Bank;
" also in the New-York —— Insurance Company. Owns valuable farm at ——, Conn.,
" and several valuable pieces of real estate in this city. He says he is worth nearly a
" half million dollars, while more *conservative* men place him at from $100,000 to $200,-
" 000. Is sharp and shrewd, but inclined to be a little overreaching; consequently he
" is not popular. Parties dealing with him should have their contracts clearly defined."

6666—Syracuse Branch Office.	5564—C. F. Danbmann & Co.
4700—Albany Branch office.	4828—Equitable Life Assurance Society.
7061—Burr & Chichester.	653—Tappan & Carr.

" January 30th, 1874.—Owns considerable property, and is no doubt worth over
" $100,000. Some do not like his way of dealing, but still is regarded good where a
" fair understanding is had."

VOL. VIII., P. 558.

" October 22d, 1874.—*Failed in 1845, owing $64,000, and never settled.* Continued
" building on contracts, and has since accumulated real estate variously estimated
" worth $100,000 to $300,000. Is at present doing no active business. Is a Director
" and Stockholder in the B—— National Bank. Is regarded sharp, shrewd, and, his
" previous history shows, somewhat unscrupulous, although it is *thought* that for $2000
" to $3000 he would be a fair risk, and would doubtless settle if matters were clearly
" defined."

3798—Peoples' Bank.	5651—Harris, Richmond & Schaffer.
3028—E. Cole & Co.	5901—F. Krutina & Co.
3281—Dannatt & Brother.	

By Dun, Barlow & Co.'s *own* printed Report this well-known citizen, " who is not reliable," who " settled " and " did not settle," who is a " fair business risk for only $2000 or $3000 when clearly defined," is rated " D 2 "—$50,000 to $100,000—and good credit ! By McKillop & Sprague Co., A 1, 1, A a—$750,-000 to $1,000,000—highest, undoubted commercial credit ! By J. M. Bradstreet & Son, A A, B B—superior business character and ability, and in excellent credit!

Not alone is the contradiction of the report glaring and unaccountable, but the reader must not omit to notice that the subject-matter has passed from Vol. XI. back to Vol. VIII. of the Reports ; so that, even if the agency allowed the error to be amended and erased from the last volume, the derogatory matter would still remain on the earlier books, to be seen and used of all subscribers, on request.

Perhaps no class of persons are more persistently and continuously libelled than those engaged in competing with the collection bureaux of the Agencies, and we find hostile reports of these firms and associations running through the volumes in every direction. The Merchants' Law and Collection Association, Ulman & Remington, John H. Watson & Co., Cohn & Co., and others, are industriously assailed because they, each in their own way, lessen the product of the Agencies' collections; and it is to be hoped that men like Watson and associations like the Merchants' Law and Collection Association will not rest content with mere contradiction, but will show our merchants and traders the best method of having every thing offensive and false indubitably erased, as well as denied and excused. The advantage of such example would soon crowd the branch offices of the Agencies with clamorous subscribers and non-subscribers who have suffered for years, and these too-patient people would exact the same precaution against future wrongs to reputation and impediments to business.

Let it be understood that erasure is the *only* means of getting rid, for the time being, of erroneous and scandalous matter; that to be thorough it must be procured in the branch offices as well as in the principal offices; and that persons affected should not rest until they had assured themselves by personal inspection that the true Black List—the most destructive and injurious reports—had really been exhibited to them and destroyed. Many have complained and been put off. It rests with the readers of this work to secure effectual protection from at least the repetition of baseless rumors and groundless accusations.

The past wrong righted, however, what security can be devised for the future consistently with the existence of these Agencies? This is the true question. In the presence of almost innumerable libels and slanders emanating from certain of the persons employed by the Agencies during the past thirty-four years, they have not been brought face to face with more than fifty suits, owing to their methods of secrecy and prompt compromise of threatened difficulties. These same precautions and readiness to arrest legal exposure of their system will be taken hereafter. Suits brought will be compromised; suits threatened will be anticipated by friendly ratings; proposed legislation will be lobbied down with money; and, unless this exposure bear fruit in some concerted action against the institution, vast sums will be continued to be forced out of cowardly merchants, and private character will continue to

be at the mercy of every one who has a point to make against an
adversary or a business grief to gratify. Without private reports
the public ratings would be quickly discovered valueless, or
friendly and misleading; so that the preservation of these reports
is essential to the existence of the Agencies; must be persisted in
from necessity; and even if old libels are expunged, new ones must
be written and uttered. The only true cure is in the hands of
merchants themselves. Let them refuse to renew their subscriptions under such new agreement as Dun, Barlow & Co. tender,
and let the State Legislatures, under their influence, pass laws com-
pelling the Agencies, under the penalty of fine and imprisonment,
requiring every reference to a man's credit, business standing, or
private character to be open to the inspection of any citizen
who may consider himself interested. There is no hardship in
this proposition. Whatever the Agencies hold out as subject to
general sale ought to be subject to *general inspection.* If this re-
quirement would be onerous to the Agencies it would only be just
to the public, whose characters are the staple of the Agencies'
speculations and profits. If the Agencies should urge the needless
publicity of this plan, we answer, only those will examine who are
interested, as now; whereas, *not* as now, the party more interested
than all others, the reported, will have an opportunity of knowing
what is said about him, and to whom it is said. If it be true, the
Agencies will have saved their subscribers from loss, and should
stick to it as a portion of the venture, for which they are paid so
handsomely; if it is false, it may be corrected as soon as known,
and so save imperilled credit and assailed character from a slow,
secret, and assassin-like destruction.

But how can the Agencies pretend to lessen the publicity of
unfavorable matter ? Why, it occupies a great part of the time of
the Agencies *to give the names of subscribers who have secretly inquired about their neighbors, and these names are seldom refused!*
That is to say, the Agencies betray all parties in turn: inquirers to each other, and subscribers, for small and large yearly sums,
alike.

For instance, if Opdycke, Terry & Steele, or Evans, Peake &
Co., dry-goods, of New-York, wish to know if E. S. Jaffray & Co.,
H. B. Claflin & Co., A. T. Stewart & Co., or any other house in
their own or other lines of trade, have inquired about Clement,

Morton & Co., of Chicago, Jones, Warner & Co., of Philadelphia, or J. & L. Seasongood, of Baltimore, *they will learn the fact at once;* and the customers may readily be induced to change their place of trading by a representation of the *last* inquirer that the *others* had secretly inquired about them at the Agency, and had lost confidence in their credit! *We know* that subscribers receive this information not only from the clerks, but are formally betrayed, on system, and not as an isolated fact of the business. By this means many old and good customers are lost to merchants, the meanest and most knavish generally being successful in playing on the feelings of the solicitor for credit, and inducing him to withdraw from relations so derogatory to self-respect and business pride. If the Agencies do not regard the interest of merchants who apply to them in confidence, they cannot put on a show of consideration when the publicity of the trader's standing only is at stake. They give another illustration of "straining at a gnat and swallowing a camel." We know of dozens of subscribers to the Agencies who have lost in one year one hundred times the amount of their subscription by having their inquiries disclosed to competing merchants, who took advantage of the circumstance to acquire new customers. The best customers, in fact, were generally the efficient cause of cupidity; for who would desire a bad one? And when a good one could be got by so simple means, who would hesitate to adopt them?

CHAPTER XVI.

THE RELATIONS OF AGENCIES TO NON-SUBSCRIBERS AND "STREET"
RUMORS—COULD CREDITS BE GUARANTEED AND BUSINESS PRO-
FITS MADE TO DEPEND MORE EXCLUSIVELY ON THE AMOUNT
OF SALES?

WE have heretofore mainly addressed ourselves to Agency
subscribers, accustomed to see the Books, to read the Notification
Sheets, and to be brought into contact with the Solicitors, Offices,
or Collectors. Such a relation implies a certain amount of experience; and we have taken this experience for granted, and written
as if it relieved us from much of mere explanation and also a great
many illustrations. Every reader of this Book will have seen, in
his own limited circle, dozens of proofs of ignorance, mistake, or
malice; every one who has applied for a "private report" at the
offices has had an opportunity of securing a taste of the silly, rotten, or rancid stuff which they dole out as carefully and solemnly
as if it were honey from Hybla or the chrism of some tremendous
religious rite; and every one who has met the "Credit men," Canvassers, and Collectors need not be told, at any great length, of their
amenability to impression, properly made, their assiduity in urging threats under the disguise of applications, and their readiness
to receive, as honest supplement to salary, any loose change which
the merchant may desire to spare. For *subscribers* the usefulness
of this work is only in showing that their particular experience is
the result of a system which inevitably renders the same experience
common and consequential; and it would add nothing to its force
if we were to pile example upon example of the efficiency of a
five-dollar bill, the saving efficacy of a chest of tea, or the molli-
fying effect of one or more baskets of French wines, on these
Agency spies. If each reader were to add, to the sample proofs
supplied by us, his individual experience, a mass of incidents, corroborative of our statements, would be gathered sufficient to fill twenty
books as large as this; and it is manifestly useless for us to go on

further, page after page, in proving again and again what, with the evidence already in, and that possessed in every street, town, village, and hamlet in the land, cannot be questioned. We turn, therefore, to that vast body of Merchants and Traders who practically take little, if any, interest in the existence of the Agencies, or do not know of their existence *at all;* who buy and sell, give and get credit, on the reputation made or learned in the good old way of the good old time before Agencies existed; and who may see no danger in the System simply because they have never realized that it operates on them *without their knowledge.* Of this number more than 800,000 exist in the United States and Canada; for the 30,000 subscribers to the Agencies are really the only ones who make it a habit to learn how themselves are rated, how others are rated, or use the Reports to *indulge in efforts to control their own and others' ratings.*

Now, it is just among this great body of *non-*subscribers that the Agencies exert the most malign, because unknown, influences. The Subscribers get the Reference Books and learn what is *printed* about them—if not, what is on the secret records. The non-subscribers do not get the printed Reports; have no means of even suspecting what is said of them in the private records; and do business in perfect ignorance of the many ways of affecting their credit and dealings indulged in by the three Agencies and their Credit Raters and Detective Correspondents. A *non-*subscriber is refused credit, or is placed on a low margin of credit by a wholesaler. He sees only an exercise of individual caution in the circumstance. He is suddenly called on to pay up by a creditor from whom no such message is expected or apparently natural. He wonders at the novel urgency, and pays up indignantly, often at a sacrifice. He is in the habit of exchanging surplus lines of stock with another trader, and even this convenience is abruptly withdrawn. He wonders at the variableness of men, and still sets the occurrence down to accident or to an *uninfluenced* determination of his co-trader. The true explanation is to be found in the *unknown and uncalculated interference with his name by the Agencies;* and he either struggles with less profit or goes out of business under a cloud, without discovering the fact in time to avert the consequences.

There is a sort of wild justice in having subscribers hurt by

their own instrument ; but it is certainly inequitable for the men
who are either too respectful to enter into the league, or who
have learned to do business without reference to such an aid, to
be, as they really are, more hopelessly and unconsciously thwarted
and maligned than any other class of merchants. Whether they
seek credit or not, the Agencies *rate* them to induce subscription
or gratify a spite. Whether they conduct a cash trade or not, the
Agencies claim the right to *speculate* in public print and private
record about their affairs and character, and to circulate these speculations on the grounds that some one else's curiosity *may* be
gratified or their Book List swelled.

The Agencies have conceived the idea of making a separate
and profitable business for themselves out of other men's names
and reputations, and it is apparently immaterial to them whether
or not a third person should ever have occasion to desire information on the subject. The " world is their oyster," and non-subscribers must take their chance of being accurately or inaccurately
rated and criticised by every mendacious scoundrel who will render, gratuitously, his unworthy services. They have the capital of
a printing establishment; and other men's names must supply an
opportunity for its profitable use while ink and paper and printers can be had. If Agencies had any justification in playing with
the names of persons asking for credit, they have none for doing
so with traders who seek no credit. If they had any pretence of
justification in instituting inquiry on the basis of a real application
for confidence and trust, they have none for engaging in and pub-
lishing one where no present purpose of trade is to be subserved
—where none ever may rise to be subserved. If they were *infallible* it might be harmless to trust them with the privilege in either
event ; but, being fallible, why should the non-subscribing 800,000
merchants of the United States and Canada be compelled to undergo the risks attending their errors, for a purely hypothetical future interest ?

The wrong and impertinence do not end here. The non-sub-
scriber who is terrified by their assumption may think if he pay
one year's subscription all will be well. Not so ! " 'Tis the first
step that counts," but mainly because retreat out of the meshes
can only be accomplished at a risk which had better have been taken
at the start—namely, of incurring their displeasure. If a house is

satisfied with its rating, why should it refuse, not merely to pay at the same rate as the first year's subscription, but double the amount ? If it be not satisfied with its rating, then the greater reason exists why it should pay freely and generously any additional tax imposed on the succeeding subscription-day. Where a man of assured standing refuses plumply, at the first approach, to have anything to do with the system, he can only be rated low or ignored; and the system is generally glad to let him in on the cheapest rates of subscription, if he deign to apply. Where a trader voluntarily applies, or is easily persuaded to apply, either from an honest or fraudulent motive, he is made to pay a full price the first year, *and a constantly increasing one afterwards.* One hundred and fifty dollars entrance-fee in the larger cities may—often does—run up to $300 and $500 yearly after 2 or 3 years' association. The Agencies well know that every dollar given to them is an inducement to the trader to keep up the connection for this period at least; and that, between the consciousness of having thrown away so much money, the fear of being worse rated in the event of a discontinuance, and the hope of making profit out of the agency misrepresentation, many of those who enter the lists will struggle to meet the exaction for a few years. By and by, however, they see that concessions bring no relief : they must refuse to pay at all, or pay some time. After the expiration of the period mentioned they do refuse, and drop out of one agency only to find another at the door. The method taken to run up subscriptions is adroit and natural. A canvasser says to the merchant, "We rated "your business at so and so last year, and you paid only so much. "Your capital is larger this year, and your business increased. "You should be willing to pay a proportionate increase of subscrip- "tion." The merchant does not wish to admit either that his capital or business is less than during the past year ; he hopes to have it regarded more. He does not contradict the canvasser, therefore, but takes the hint and pays out his money, year after year, until its exceeding amount startles him and determines him to break with the monster, at whatever cost.

Some business men and firms are often induced to subscribe to the three Agencies in order to have their *own* ratings and reports in each institution agree with the other ; and where the credulous merchant, unfamiliar with Agency intrigue, finds uniformity in their separate estimates of the same trader, he attributes it to *honest precision* rather than *purchased accuracy*. This, however, is so costly an experiment that comparatively few indulge in it.

Any subscriber, paying yearly from $150 to $5000, who should volunteer a biassed opinion concerning a trader of whom he presumes to know, whether a rival in trade or otherwise, will find it readily accepted and permanently recorded as the prevailing belief, in preference to the opinion of a subscriber paying a less sum, or who does not pay the Agency at all. Herein is where subscribers with doubtful motives succeed in impressing on the Agencies, actively, their own impressions, real or pretended. A firm is found by its rival to be underselling the market or itself, having bought to greater advantage, at more propitious times, and in greater quantities. The rival need only say to the Agency that the shrewder firm is unloading its stock under market rates, and a suspicion of smuggling, or an intent to abscond or go out of business, is a natural conclusion. So, by these methods, the subscriber has his satisfaction of an enmity or a rivalry, the Agencies are paid handsomely, and the better merchants go to the wall in the long run.

But let us take the case of a merchant heavily interested in a debtor on the brink of bankruptcy. He wants to save whatever he can and reduce his losses by drawing others into the catastrophe. He has only to report to the Agencies his failing customer favorably. The insolvent increases his stock and enlarges his liabilities. In due time he tumbles into Bankruptcy; his assets show a diminution proportioned to the amount *paid meantime to the friendly creditor reporting.* There is nothing strange in this proceeding. Every *new* credit to an insolvent assists him to lessen his liabilities to his *old* creditor out of his *new stock ;* and a merchant, having a doubtful debtor on hand, would stand in his own light if he failed to speak well of him to all inquirers, *more particularly the Agencies.* The consequence is that insolvent men's names are made efficient, by Agency interference, to spread and assure greater disaster to the many, for the benefit of the one, or the few, in the secret.

While on this subject of the general circulation given to false information, designed by others for individual injury, we should not overlook the fact that the late Act of the New-York Legislature, enacted to punish the authors or circulators of false rumors intended to influence the " Street " or unsettle confidence, might be turned to good account on the Agencies, not *as* Agencies, but on the individual proprietors, on fit occasion.   If the law is worth anything it should be sufficient to support a prosecution in any one of the thousand flagrant instances afforded by Agency error ; and if it should not be sufficient as it stands, the insufficiency ought to be demonstrated, so that the next Legislature may apply a more stringent and efficient remedy by additional legislation.   The prosecution of a single individual " rumor-starter" would be a hunting of the wren when the atmosphere is alive with the bigger and baser birds of prey from Agency eyries.   We hear of two "stock" rumors, recently sent out with firm reports, which ought to be instantly ventilated in the Criminal Courts, and, we trust, will be.

The Agency system having been shown inefficient in its whole scope and purpose, as well as in its practical working, the question recurs, is there no way of increasing the certainties of merchants and traders in ordinary business transactions, of a sudden, and without putting these classes to the safest of all methods of inquiry—special individual examination ?

It occurs to the writer that a scheme of Commercial Assurance or Guarantee of Business Risks might be safely tried in the great cities.   It would require, when fitly developed, large capital, but, we think, not more at the start than could readily be got by calling out the latent resources of each city, and leaving every Company which might be formed a local field to operate in, independently.   By limiting each Company's operations to a convenient district of territory, it would be enabled to secure for its own use exclusively, and for the direction of its own investment *only*, the best attainable estimates of credit and capital of Business men, and would have the very highest inducement, self-interest, to judge accurately and invest cautiously.   A tariff of charges for contracts of Guarantee might be adopted ; undesirable risks would be refused ; the statements of seekers for credit could be reduced to writing and sworn to; if false, the Company would have cumulative civil or criminal remedies at its disposal; the wholesaler whose risks were accepted would secure a guarantee of prompt payment by the Company, for a reasonable sliding percentage, and, while the honest trader could find an increased facility for legitimate purchases, sellers might rely on the guarantee Company having the highest attainable certainty before it became surety. Given a certain capital and good management, it seems highly probable that an Institution of the kind mentioned in each city would, from comparatively small beginnings, soon supply a true gauge to credit, by *becoming a part of the credit process*, and profitable or ruinous to itself, according to its own accuracy of estimate.

Such a scheme possesses, in reality, several features which the Agencies claim, but do not possess. It assists in giving security to business dealings. It eliminates recklessness of statement; for a good risk brings profit, and a bad one loss, on the Guarantor,—the seller escaping in either event. *The information on which risks are taken is collected by the risk-taker, and preserved by him from outside parties as his permanent capital.* Whether accurate or inaccurate, it is harmless to the man who does not seek credit; and it is absolutely sacred in the instance of the man who is asking credit. Every honest and honorable end of business in commercial dealing is attained, and private character is even less discussed than it is now by the Agencies every discount day in our private Banks.

The common experience of business men leads them to expect in the safest credit trade a yearly loss of from five to ten per cent on their active capital. If they could be assured against this loss, or the possibility of a greater, Trading would become a Science and Panics impossible!

The problem to be solved is, therefore: Could capital see, in the experiment suggested, enough of profit to protect itself?

The same thing is done now, in a small way, by some of the better class of Commercial Travellers. Where a bad debt is made under their recommendation, the loss is deducted from their salaries and Commissions on good ones. So long as we find individuals ready to assume this responsibility, and able to make money by doing so, why should we not believe the like might be done by Guarantee Companies, in the leading Cities of the States and Canada? There is even a better illustration at hand. The Cotton and Tobacco firm of Fatman & Co., Broad street, New-York, with branches in various cities of this country and Europe, handle a business of over $20,000,000 a year on Guarantees from their Agents and Correspondents. They make immense sums yearly, and do not lose a dollar. The English houses of John Henry Schroder & Co., worth £12,000,000, and Freeling & Goshen, worth £3,000,000, and the Bremen House of D. H. Watgen & Co., worth $15,000,000, guarantee orders. Fatman & Co. buy for cash, and their Exchange is the first on the New-York market, being readily and eagerly taken by any of our Banks. If Schroder & Co. can guarantee orders enabling Fatman & Co. to pursue an absolutely safe business on a time margin of thirty days, why could not Guarantee Companies, selecting men of the best knowledge and talent for each trade to assist in their management, do the same? The salaries paid credit men in large Commercial Houses are enormous in the aggregate. These would be largely saved to the Mercantile community. The Guarantee Companies would afford greater facilities to their employees for the exhibition of the best judgment, and promotion for the best fidelity. In addition, the EIGHT MILLION yearly drain of the Agencies would be done away with, and merchants would find themselves guaranteed on every credit at an expense of only a small proportion of their present Profit and Loss Accounts. The effect on trade could not be otherwise than favorable. The trader who could not safely be guaranteed would be obliged to either confine himself to small purchases for cash, if no seller could be found speculative enough to take a credit risk, or go out of business. This would tend to weed trade of men who, from lack of financial responsibility, should not be in business, and would discourage intended fraud from a useless exertion. It would, we think, restore commerce to a healthy condition. The credit-seeker, if solvent, could have no motive in concealing his *true status* from the Company, knowing from its character that an honest disclosure by him could only inure to *his* benefit, and would not be perverted and circulated to his own detriment, as is now done by the Agencies, to promote the interests of a *rival* trader.

At present every merchant practically insures himself. The Agencies induce more losses than profits and eschew responsibility. They keep the word of promise to the ear and break it to the hope. You pay for their pretended information. When it turns

out erroneous, they show you that, by the very terms of your sub-
scription-contract with them, the men whom they employ or inquire from *are your own Agents,* and that Agencies are not responsible for their accuracy or inaccuracy! Now, if the mercantile
classes really insure themselves on all credits, so far as the Agencies
are concerned, and yet support the latter at great cost to themselves, it seems reasonable to expect that a scheme which would
remove the *modicum* of risk, and reduce the useless expenditure
at the same time, would be hailed as a public benefit. We make
these suggestions to anticipate the objection that, having demonstrated the inutility of the Agencies, we have no remedy to substitute which would partially or wholly relieve the trader from
special inquiry in regard to customers at a distance. The idea is
neither novel nor original with us. We find it entertained by
several large mercantile firms, and the same principle is practically illustrated by a firm in Cleveland, in a limited trade sphere, and
with perfect success. These gentlemen guarantee, for a small per
cent, all approved credits in a particular line, and have made
money by doing so. Why could not a series of companies do likewise in reference to all Trades? Another example is before us.
In New-York an association has just been formed, by some of the
most experienced capitalists, to guarantee contracts of Insurance,
etc., and there is reason to hope that at an early day the principle
will be extended to many other classes of contracts by the same
company. The plan is sketched to reflect the opinion of experienced business men rather than our own; and while we express the
possible arguments in favor of such a project, we do not commit
ourselves to it, for our experience of the Commercial Agency System has taught us the innumerable opportunities of misapplication
which even the best-devised arrangement might entail.

This discussion has brought us face to face with a circumstance
too often overlooked by merchants. How many business men
have fully considered the danger arising from the present method
of detailing to strangers and underlings of the several agencies, in
our large cities, the amount of negotiable securities on hand or the
quantity and kind of merchandise, of great value and small bulk,
in their stock? It is a well-authenticated fact that many burglar-
ies have occurred immediately after the delivery of these detailed
statements to agency reporters! A merchant wishing to confirm

his assertions of available assets, or requested to do so, gives the names of Stocks or the character of Bonds held by him, and, to remove all doubt, brings them out of his safe and shows them to the inquirer. Or he takes the searcher for knowledge over his premises and points out to him the most valuable kinds of stock, in bulk, or broken for custom. The dullest rascal could not fail to learn aids to crime, for himself or confederates, in these thoughtless disclosures. And certainly, when we learn that the police authorities of several large cities are discovered to have long been in league with the choice spirits of the various departments of Statutory Crime, we shall not be astonished to learn that more than one Bank, Insurance, and private robbery has been perpetrated to get hold of portable assets, stocks, bonds, and moneys, which the owner had carefully kept within his sole personal knowledge until the agency spy had also secured the important details of time, amount, character, and place. How few clerks are fully apprised, from day to day, of the state of their employer's capital, except in a small business too limited to afford chance of reserve ! Large concerns may have one or more confidential men, outside of the partners, who are fully informed ; but the general run of employees is kept in the dark, as a rule of discipline if not wholly as a matter of precaution. And yet the Business Classes have heretofore foolishly opened their business secrets to every poorly-paid Tom, Dick, and Harry who presented a Mercantile or Commercial Agency card and demanded to share in the confidences withheld from well-known and, in other respects, fully trusted servants. A Guarantee Company or Companies could entail no such danger as this on their patrons without suffering themselves. The agencies do not guard against it ; and if they could, have no interest in lessening the risk by employing only the best-known citizens, and at compensative salaries. Our advice to Merchants is : refuse details of stock or assets to inquirers until fully satisfied that the inquirer is not making an inventory which might reach and assist the principal cracksmen of the neighborhood.

CHAPTER XVII.

THE LEGAL DIFFICULTIES OF THE AGENCIES—HOW THEY STRIKE
THEIR COLORS OR ESCAPE FROM THE FIELD—STRAWS FROM
THE BAR.

An institution so offensive and aggressive as the agency system
very naturally ran athwart the reputations of honest business men
at a very early period in its career.   Started in 1842, as we have
stated, Church, its first traveller, contrived to libel (amongst
others) Taylor, Hale & Murdock, of Columbus, Miss., and when
the libel was discovered these gentlemen sued the libeller for
damages in the New-York Common Pleas.   Church defended on
the ground that he was employed by certain New-York merchants to " report" traders for them as their agent; that he reported plaintiffs to Wolfe and Gillespie, two of these merchants,
in a private and confidential letter; that he had never seen the
plaintiffs, bore them no malice, and merely repeated what he had
heard in reply to inquiry; and that the printing of his report was
done without his personal supervision, and solely by his employers.
He further claimed the communication was confidential.   For the
plaintiff it was contended that Church published the libel maliciously; that it was written to be published, if not " printed,"
and that it was not, and was not contained in, a privileged communication.   The case finally went to the Court of Appeals (4
Selden's Reports, p. 452), which decided by a unanimous bench
that the report was *not* privileged, but sent the case back for a
new trial on an exception to a ruling on the admissibility of evidence in the Court below.

    The decision in Taylor *et al. vs.* Church embodies all the
law learning on the subject of privileged communications up to
that time, and contains the test which renders all more recent
agency publications, if untrue (and, as some contend, even if true),
unprivileged and amenable to legal restraint and both compensa-

tory and exemplary damages. The printing for general circulation, and in a manner which might reach parties having, or intending to have, no business relations with the trader reported, was held to be against public policy, and to subject the reporter to such legal penalties as any jury might reasonably see fit to inflict. Since this decision, several cases have come before the Courts in other States; but in all of these the dedication, by printing and circulating the reports, to general use, of these estimates of traders' characters, qualifications, and standing, has been uniformly held to take them out of the class of privileged communications, and to leave the writers, compilers, and utterers subject to civil and *quasi*-criminal remedies on behalf of the persons affected by them.

The reason of this rule of law is very plain. While a merchant should be allowed to employ a clerk or agent to learn for his own use the standing of a dealer *proposing to have relations* with him, it would be unreasonable and impolitic to allow the same thing to be done on the mere hypothesis that *other* merchants at some future time *might* have like reason to desire information. Such a purely speculative interest in a future possibility could not be safely conceded to give a present immunity to such communications. The trader reported might never ask for credit. No one, in that event, could have any substantial reason for inquiry, still less could any one justify a purely anticipative and precautionary inquiry designed for general circulation. Where the necessity for privileged communication ceases, the permission ceases also. But even if one or a dozen merchants really desire information about a person proposing to enter into business relations with them, this fact gives no right to them, or any one in their behalf, to place the information in such a manner that it might reach a non-interested person. In other words, the interest must be a present and existing one to justify any communication designed to limit or curtail the chances of credit; and when this interest is satisfied, the qualified privilege lapses again, only to be revived by the occurrence of a new justification for it.

Judged by this standard, the whole Agency System, as now conducted by anticipatory inquiry and general publication, is practically at the mercy of the Courts and the public. It is protected in no manner by the subscription system—a device intended to create an agency character for it—for the subscriber has no present interest in any name in the book ; his ever having a future one is purely problematical; and it is certain he can never have any in eight or nine hundred thousand whose capital is guessed at and credit standing rated.

When the Court of Appeals determined that thirty-six sub-scribers did not justify the printing of seventy-five reports in 1846, it is very plain that thirty thousand could not authorize the use of several hundred thousand merchants' and traders' names, with "estimates" and "ratings" picked up and attached by the agencies, for sale and circulation to whoever might choose to purchase. It is quite probable, too, that the contract of subscription itself is a mere *nudum pactum*, and will be so held when the question shall have been squarely brought up. Fortunately for the agencies, their powers of coercion have been so great in other respects that they have had no reason to sue for subscriptions. They make no bad debts. But they cannot have this luck always. Some one will break with them ; and we shall then see whether or not they will have the courage to go into Court for redress. Our own opinion is quite decided that contracts contemplating a general system of commercial inquiry and the publication of its results, without the consent of the individuals reported, and wanting the element of a *subsisting* interest in the reported parties, as traders applying for credit, are void on the ground of public policy, and will be so declared. Whoever shall start the issue will prove a public benefactor. As we have shown in other places, " the System" has a holy horror of Courts of Law and Equity.

Its policy has therefore been, from the beginning, to keep out of Courts; to retain ownership in the Reference Books sent out and recall them, so that they could not furnish proof to injured parties ; and to supplement the dangerously-published books with a privately communicated plan of Secret Reports, where libellous matter may be gathered and doled out with greater impunity. In pursuance of this policy their clerks are instructed to read injurious details to " Principals only," or their confidential managers, meaning heads of trading houses and subscribers. Their contracts are drawn so as to make their clerks and informants servants of these " Principals," and they expressly require that the said Principals should *not* have any remedy against them for insufficient, defective, or mistaken information. The "New Agreement" of Dun, Barlow & Co. is a fruitful sample of this ever-active caution and desire for irresponsibility; and the conduct of all the agencies in settling, where compromise is possible, rather than litigating suits for damages, is a further proof of their judicious susceptibility to legal terrors.

For the purpose of securing the fullest information in relation to the recent or existing suits against the agencies in the Courts of the United States and Canada, we lately sent letters to the known plaintiffs or their attorneys. We have several responses in our possession, but we can only refer to a few of them. The suit of John A. Converse, of the Canada Cordage Factory and Plaster Mills, Montreal, recently instituted, has not yet come to trial, and Mr. Converse does not know how soon it may, but he is confident of a verdict. His claim is for damages arising from the purchase of mercantile paper of a New-Orleans merchant on the assurance of the agency, *after special inquiry*, that it was "per-" fectly good." He bought the paper, and placed it in the Collection Department of the same agency within a few days. Shortly afterwards the Collection Department informed him that it was worthless, and had been so at a time antecedent to the inquiry about the maker and the assurance of the agency that he was solvent and in good credit! So palpable an instance of agency effort is not likely to reach trial, and we should not be surprised to learn that, as it produced the immediate occasion for the "New Agree-" ment," it had been settled by the agency paying a round sum in damages and compromise to Mr. Converse.

In response to a letter of ours of the 28th of June, 1875, Hon. Francis Kernan, of Utica, writes that the action for libel commenced by his firm against Dun, Barlow & Co. "had been satisfactorily " adjusted without trial," and that there was " hence nothing in the " case to interest the public." Mr. Kernan concedes that the agency had made a "mistake" and circulated "an erroneous re-" port ;" hence we are at a loss to imagine how he comes to the conclusion that a "satisfactory settlement" leaves nothing to interest the public. Is it of no interest to the public to know that the agency *had* made a "mistake"? Is it of none that the agency *had* circulated wrong information? Is it a matter of indifference that the agency had been compelled to eat its words and pay $16,000 to his client? Why, what would the learned Senator have the public interested in, if not the standing danger to business character in agency "mistakes," in their opportunities of circulating "erroneous reports," and in their eagerness to settle privately sooner than go before a jury of their countrymen? For our own part, we know of few things of more actual interest to the business public than just such facts. They are certainly more important than the present intimate relations of Mr. Kernan's law partners with certain of the agencies in this city since the "satisfactory settlement" aforesaid.

From Missouri, where a Mr. Kinealey acted as attorney in an agency case some time ago, we have no direct information of the present condition of the controversy, but the silence is indicative of a settlement after the Utica fashion. From a State Senator and late member of the Constitutional Convention we learn that an active antagonism to the agency institution exists in that State, and we conclude from his letter that, however the agencies may "hush up" the injured by free payments, legislative action will be soon taken to render them responsible in a wider sense or keep them out of that Commonwealth.

An instructive instance of Agency methods, with Attorneys nearer home, occurs to us, and may be mentioned. A gentleman on Staten Island, some time ago, requested a well-known criminal lawyer and ex-Judge to sue an Agency in New-York. The legal gentleman was considerate enough to inform the prospective defendant, who forthwith took measures to get rid of the evidence against it to be found on its Records. No suit was commenced, and the legal gentleman is now the retained counsel of the prospective defendant, we are apprised, in any litigation which may be evoked by this publication!

A chapter on the legal relations of the Agencies would be incomplete without a reference to the late quarrel, by Chancery Suit, for $50,000 and Injunction, between themselves. Dun, Barlow & Co. claimed that Bradstreet & Son had "pirated" some of their matter in Canada. Bradstreet denied the charge, and countered by alleging the like of Dun in Pennsylvania and other States. On the trial it appeared that Dun, Barlow & Co. had *invented* a lot of towns and villages unknown to any Geography or Census, rated their imaginary merchants, and quietly waited for their competitor to appropriate the discovery. They even swore the latter did so; and the controversy is still smouldering in Court, neither being anxious to fan it into publicity.

The trick was conceived in the best manner, and showed a mutual appreciation of mutual weakness.

When the dead may be kept alive to swell a Reference Book, and City Directories laid under contribution without compensation, why, indeed, should not a few villages and towns be invented? The device was also the least harmful of any practised. Merchants who never existed could not well be misrepresented. Traders who had never been born or christened, could not easily be injured in credit or standing. And the Agency system, for the first time in its career, was sure to be safe and certain to be honest.

Of the recently commenced, or threatened, litigations against the institution it is not timely yet to write at any length. The terror awakened is indicative of the depths to which they must sink into Agency methods on the trials. One is for damages for charging a man with homicide committed in *self-defence by another!* A second is for charging bigamy! A third for accusations involving a female's chastity! A fourth is by a partnership for charging forgery on one of its members! A fifth—but these suffice to show that the Agencies are about to meet other questions than those simply relating to business solvency, and must defend their pretension to discuss and assail private character, under the guise of giving opinions concerning financial responsibility.

The eagerness of the Agencies to prevent legal reprisals was well illustrated to the writer, in an attempt to dissuade him from this publication, by a proposition to purchase his silence. The suggestion was met with contempt. When the resource failed, their next dodge was a published "Card," proposing to every one, *with whom the writer had communicated,* to correct mistakes on application. Redress for the past, however, was not promised. Nothing was said about showing to applicants the *private* reports upon which the public ratings were based, nor was it suggested that the names of informants would be given as a badge of good faith. This deceitful "Card" was merely a "stop-gap" to gain time, while an investigation was in progress, to learn the extent of the writer's acquaintance with "bottom facts." If a "Card" were to be issued *now,* the chances are altogether in favor of a more liberal array of terms for the dissatisfied, and a corresponding reduction in subscription-rates.

Perhaps the very meanest act on the part of the startled traffickers in the good name of so many of our first citizens, was the malignant manner in which they commenced dismissing or shifting clerks who might have secured special acquaintance with the Black Lists. The suspicion of being suspected was enough. The known opportunity to learn undesirable knowledge was sufficient to place under ban. A clearer confession of conscious weakness was never illustrated by a pretentious system, in the instance of its oldest and most devoted servants.

Besides this Carding, dismissing, and shifting process, another precautionary one was added. A secret circular—the trustiest weapon in the rusty catalogue of the system—was dispatched to Branch office managers, informing them that the writer had got great store of facts already, and might be in league with the clerks in the various Branches to get more. Extreme watchfulness was enjoined. Letters were withheld; post-marks scrutinized; any symptom of increased assiduity in labor was held of bad omen; and such a fluttering generally was never seen before since Coriolanus "fluttered the Volsci in Coriole." The unfortunate clerks were undecided whether to look sad or cheerful; to be active or remiss in duty; to speak or not to speak of the thunder in the Agency sky and the threatened blinding blaze of exposure. All these precautions came too late. The persons selected by the writer to unearth the hidden secrets of the Charnel House had closed their labors long before the System took exceptional precaution; and the writer intentionally gave the first alarm himself by informing injured subscribers and others, by letter, that they could learn what was said of them in the Reports, free of charge, on application to him at the Agency's counters! So the "Secret Circular" was just as valueless to avert exposure as the "Card" had been, and is now serving the only purpose it can ever subserve—namely, to show how eager the Agency Managers were to trample out the sparks which threatened their tinder-box institutions.

If this was the general conduct of one Agency, largely referred to in these pages, we can find no greater show of courage and self-confidence in the other two, in the presence of the threatened danger to their system. Bradstreet & Son were struck dumb, and dared not commit themselves to any statement designed to show either the comparative benefits or lesser defects of their establishment over others in the same line. They were willing to negotiate for the secret transfer of a competitor's good-will in the trade of a neighboring city, but they shrank from presenting to the public any claim on its confidence or respect. They appear to have suffered judgment to pass against them by default sooner than go on the stand or introduce a witness. The older and larger firm of McKillop & Sprague Co. met the emergency with a bolder front for a time, and, as we thought and hoped, proposed to show that, whatever might be said against its rivals' manner of doing business, it had no occasion, itself, to avoid controversy, not arising from the Agency System, as such. In this spirit it favored the writer, of its own motion, with a pamphlet, published by it when the System was less understood than now, and courteously solicited inquiries from him in reference to the firm's progress and painstaking. We acted on the suggestion in the same vein : and hoped, at last, to find some one who could show effective administration on even a wrong principle, or introduce some defence for the principle which had not occurred to us. Our disappointment was sincere when we found even this firm declined to commit itself, on the pretence that facts could have no force coming from them. As if the mere making of such statement to us, in the expectation of a critical analysis, were not a straightforward and manly thing, certain to be favorably thought of by the public! This determination, however, coming after a proffer, indicates that the Commercial Agency preferred trusting to luck to showing its hand; and was just as unwilling to have the facts of its management submitted, over its own signature, to examination and comment, as the younger and less generally recognized firm of J. M. Bradstreet & Son. It matters very little, however, to any one who shall read this work, and particularly the chapter containing the Comparative Tables of McKillop & Sprague Co. and Dun, Barlow & Co., whether the former firm employs more " help" than the latter, or spends more subscriptions, in arriving at the self-confuting statistics with which we have knocked both their heads together and demonstrated their worse than inutility. It is of no consequence, whatever, whether the one or the other firm employs the greater number of hands and the more experienced managers; our issue is with the System, out of which both extract their wealth ; and so long as the System cannot be defended, it is not worth while to enter into a calculation for the purpose of determining which of the two is the greater trifler with private rights or public patience.

Between eluding the light of controversy and creeping or crawling out of litigations on its belly, the Agency Business may be said to lead a reptile life of secret warfare for its own ends, but of cowardly retreat and elusion when fairly challenged. It can bite and sting the unconscious and unsuspecting; but it is wily enough to risk nothing when its opponents are prepared. If we may judge from the past history of Agencies, they will pursue the same course which has stood them in good stead of courage or merit. They will seek to avoid responsibility for injuries done, by a swift show of deceitful meekness and simulated regret at their occurrence; they will compromise, where they can, at the last moment, rather than try actions brought against them for libel ; they will lure to their side the Attorneys of the opponents, at every opportunity; they will watch the Journals of State Legislatures to anticipate legislation inimical to their pretensions ; where it is attempted, they will call in the "Lobby"; they will do anything and everything, except enter, voluntarily, on a public discussion or a legal investigation.

CHAPTER XVIII.

THE AGENCIES' ESTIMATES COMPARED AND APPLIED TO INDI-
VIDUALS IN VARIOUS CITIES—THE RIDICULOUS FIGURE CUT
BY THE "WISDOM-SELLERS."

WE come now, by an easy and natural transition, from allega-
tions relating to the capacity and fitness of the Agencies to advise
in business risks, to the proof of their unfitness, which is found in
their own works and under their own signatures. If we have,
heretofore, reasoned wrongly or assailed maliciously, we are
about to be confuted; for who in the wrong can afford to be
judged by the evidence of his adversary? But if we have merely
told the truth, and fairly weighed our subject *pro* and *con.*, the
Agencies themselves will supply us with incontrovertible testimony.

Of the three Agencies Bradstreets', alone, gives no capital ratings, so that it escapes, for the time being, from the common pil-
lory of comparison into which we press the other two. But its
competitors' "figures" must cast a deep shadow of suspicion over
its own "words," and satisfy any reflecting person that greater
wariness is no indication of equal or superior knowledge, but may
be a sign and symbol of either more conscious ignorance or more
alert self-conviction.

Take up, reader, the July (1875) Reports or Reference Books
of the McKillop & Sprague Co. and Dun, Barlow & Co. They
are the latest published by these firms at the hour of writing.
They should be the most perfect. They are sold for high prices.
They ought to be worth something. They are ponderous and im-
posing in exterior looks and interior matter; so that they ought
to serve, or be able to serve, some useful purpose in the Agency
economy. They pretend to more practical wisdom than the
Tables of Moses or the Ten Commandments; for those merely
give moral axioms, and these claim to give lessons of successful
business life to a people ten times as numerous as the Jews at their

best, and engaged in transactions involving ten times more wealth than the treasures of Judea or Egypt. They are the ripe result and full fruition (it is said) of the efforts of a standing army of correspondents numbered by the 50,000; an auxiliary corps of municipal sappers and miners counting well up in the hundreds; headed and directed by the inherited and attained generalship and discretion of a staff of superb appointments and magnificent incomes, and they ought to be—well, worth more than waste paper. Alas! the anti-climax. These ponderous tomes, out of whose feculent growth several fortunes have been made—out of whose hoped-for continuance several more fortunes are expected to be made—are self-convicting impostures. These mammoth accumulations of names and figures are discovered to be neither more nor less than utensils for withdrawing money from business men's pockets under the disguise of improving their understandings and facilitating their intercourse.

Open the two Books at the State of "Maryland," take the title "Baltimore," and for greater convenience, while picking at hazard from the roll of names for our examples, select them alphabetically and set them down tabularly. Having chosen the names for contrast, note the ratings, and put down their equivalents, by the respective keys, in numerals. As both Agencies give the extremes of capital ratings, let us take their lowest and their highest, each as to itself, and next as to each other, and contemplate the result. It is certainly startling; and if the Agencies can profitably exist in an intelligent community after the exposure, the fault will not lie at our door.

BALTIMORE, MARYLAND.

NAME.	Business.	Dun, Barlow & Co.'s estimate of capital.	McKillop & Sprague Co.'s estimate of capital.	Margin of combined ignorance of both Agencies.
Abrahams, J. J., & Son	Ship-builders	$100,000	$750,000	$650,000
Armstrong, James, & Co	Soap	50,000	300,000	250,000
Baltimore Bridge Co	....	50,000	500,000	450,000
Baltimore Steam-Packet Co.	....	1,000,000	100,000	900,000
Barnum & Co	City Hotel	50,000	300,000	250,000
Bevan & Sons	Marble	25,000	200,000	175,000
Cahn, Belt & Co	Liquors	250,000	20,000	230,000
Eaton Bros. & Co	Dry Goods	50,000	300,000	250,000
Ellicott, William M., & Sons	General Commission	250,000	20,000	230,000
Fisher, James J	Capitalist	1,000,000	200,000	800,000
Goldsborough & Johnston	Commission	250,000	30,000	220,000
Hicks, George C., & Co	Fire-bricks	100,000	4,000	96,000
Howell, William, & Son	Shipping, etc.	1,000,000	200,000	800,000
				$5,301,000

Is it necessary to waste words with a "system" which produces, for pay, and in the name of thrifty commerce and judicious trading, work like this? The mere figures must convince the general public; how much more absurd and stultifying they may appear to the gentlemen and firms above named can only be truly known to themselves. But perhaps this example in Baltimore is anomalous. Not so! Turn to

BOSTON, MASSACHUSETTS.

NAME.	Business.	E. Russell & Co.'s estimate of capital.	McKillop & Sprague Co.'s estimate of capital.	Margin of combined ignorance of both Agencies.
Bacon, Jerome A	Paper	$100,000	$500,000	$400,000
Baldwin & Heald	Provisions	250,000	30,000	230,000
Barnard, George M., & Co.	Commission	100,000	500,000	400,000
Belknap, Lyman & Co.	Produce	250,000	50,000	200,000
Bigelow, J. R., & Co.	Paper-hanging	1,000,000	300,000	700,000
Blake & Alden	Furniture	250,000	1,000,000 and over	750,000 and over
Boston Button Co.	Book-binders	250,000	4,000	246,000
Bradley, Ira, & Co.	Importers, etc.	50,000	300,000	250,000
Bray & Hayes	Publishers	250,000	80,000	220,000
Brewer & Tileston	Saloon	1,000,000	75,000	925,000
Brigham, Robert B.	Matches	250,000	20,000	230,000
Byam, Carlton & Co.		100,000	750,000	650,000
				$5,201,000 and over

Neither Agency, it will be noticed, observes any *uniformity* of mistake in comparison with the other. If it did, some vicious rule—but still a rule—would be found at the bottom as the cause of the uniformity. But there is evidently no rhyme or reason in the case. At one time, Dun, Barlow & Co. is the latitudinarian in estimates; at another, McKillop & Sprague Co. rises into the seventh heaven. The disparity lies in the purely guess-work character of the information sought to be conveyed, and, relatively, in the want of all useful or approximate information.

BUFFALO, NEW-YORK.

NAME.	Business.	Dun, Barlow & Co.'s estimate of capital.	McKillop & Sprague Co.'s estimate of capital.	Margin of combined ignorance of both Agencies.
Alberger, John L., & Co.	Pork-packers	$250,000	$30,000	$220,000
Beardsley & Belden	Malsters	25,000	200,000	175,000
Bissell, A. A., & Co.	Commission and Fwdg.	25,000	200,000	175,000
Buffalo Dental Manufacturing Co.	....	25,000	200,000	175,000
Crocker, L. L.	Malster and Cattle-dealer	50,000	300,000	250,000
Dawley, Job S.	Sewing-machines	25,000	200,000	175,000
Dodge, H, & C.	Planing-mill, etc.	10,000	200,000	190,000
Enos, George T., & Co.	Millers	100,000	500,000	400,000
Felthousen & Russell	Stoves, etc.	250,000	30,000	220,000
Fish, Armstrong & Co.	Insurance Agents	10,000	75,000	65,000
Fisher Bros. & Co.	Malsters	250,000	30,000	220,000
Haines & Co.	Lumber	250,000	50,000	200,000
				$2,465,000

If these terrible disparities are found in the case of leading houses of leading trade interests in leading cities, where the Agencies have their largest offices, and canvassers and credit-men at the highest-paid compensation, what must be the greater wildness of Agency prophecy in reference to less-known traders, in smaller centres of traffic, where there are only branch offices, or no offices, and where the transmitting media are mere youths on beggarly weekly salaries, and volunteer correspondents, whose *own* antecedents and business standing are purely matter of surmise, or not even surmised?

CHARLESTON, SOUTH-CAROLINA.

NAME.	Business.	Dun, Barlow & Co.'s estimate of capital.	McKillop & Sprague Co.'s estimate of capital.	Margin of combined Ignorance of both Agencies.
Bardin, Parker & Co.	Cotton, etc.	$250,000	$20,000	$230,000
Boyd, Bernard	Liquors, etc.	25,000	3,000	22,000
Brandt, H. F.	Confectioner	500	6,000	5,500
Brown, Edmonds T.	Hats	100,000	10,000	90,000
Charleston Mining and Manufacturing Co.	Shipping Agent	1,000,000	100,000	900,000
Courtney, W. A.	....	5,000	50,000	45,000
Enterprise Railroad Co.	....	250,000	50,000	200,000
Gage, A., & Co.	Ice	100,000	20,000	80,000
Hastie, William S., & Son	Bankers, etc.	100,000	10,000	90,000
Holmes, Calder & Co.	Paints	100,000	20,000	80,000
Lowndes, C. T., & Co.	Bankers	100,000	20,000	80,000
Lowndes & Grimball	Auctioneers	1,000	20,000	19,000
Marine and River Phosphate Mining and Manufac'g Co. of S. Charleston	....	100,000	750,000	650,000
Planters and Mechanics' Bank	....	250,000	50,000	200,000
Ryan, W. K.	Cotton Factor	250,000	30,000	220,000
Sulphuric Acid and Super-Phosphate Co.	....	500,000	50,000	450,000
Tecklenburgh, John	Grocer	5,000	200,000	195,000
				$3.556,500

But the fluctuations of rating have a deeper meaning than we have yet assigned. Where the capital figures are low, relatively, the credit rating, which involves the question of integrity, punctuality in fulfilling obligations, etc., is lost sight of or drops to zero, and the safest trader and most honorable finds his admitted capital, within which he operates well and wisely, a deprecatory circumstance never permitting a recognition of good standing. In other words, the demonstration proves that business character may rise with capital but cannot be preserved in connection with small or sufficient capital, simply because it is small in amount, though it may be sufficient for the trader.

CHICAGO, ILLINOIS.

NAME.	Business.	Dun, Barlow & Co.'s estimate of capital.	McKillop & Sprague Co.'s estimate of capital.	Margin of combined ignorance of both Agencies.
Adams, B., & Co	Grain	$250,000	$30,000	$220,000
Austin, H. W., & Co	Pumps	1,000,000	200,000	800,000
Botsford, H., & Co	Packers	500,000	75,000	425,000
Brachvogel, Charles	Picture-Frames	10,000	100,000	90,000
Buehler, John	Banker, etc.	250,000	20,000	230,000
Burley & Tyrrell	Crockery	100,000	500,000	400,000
Clacius, C. E., & Co	Drugs	250,000	30,000	220,000
Clowry, Jeremiah	Grocer	100,000	10,000	90,000
Cole, Newell & Mosher	Real Estate	250,000	20,000	230,000
Collins & Co	Brokers	500	10,000	9,500
Cook & McLain	Dyers	250,000	30,000	220,000
				$3,134,500

The next consideration suggested by these tables is: What determined the choice of *sources* of information leading to such discrepancies, conceding even that the estimates are correctly based on the information given? Which company went—if either ever went—to the best? How did they choose—in the line of competitors in the trade or business, or from parties not in the same line of trade or business? Why did they, or on what principle of policy did they, respectively, come to any distinct choice of one set of figures instead of any, or all, others? A variation of over $3,000,000 capital in connection with only eleven Chicago names is greater than the mean possible capital, high or low, of the same names. The sources must have been muddy which belch out such drumlie stuff.

CINCINNATI, OHIO.

NAME.	Business	Dun; Barlow & Co.'s estimate of capital.	McKillop & Sprague Co.'s estimate of capital.	Margin of combined ignorance of both Agencies.
Andrews, Bates & Co.	Wholesale Grocers	$50,000	$300,000	$250,000
Andrews & Conklin	Liquors	50,000	300,000	250,000
Britt, Patrick	Boots and Shoes	250,000	50,000	200,000
Bruce, B., & Co.	Carriages	100,000	750,000	650,000
Cincinnati Ice Co.	......	500,000	100,000	400,000
Cochnower, John	Coal	250,000	1,000,000 and over	750,000 and over
Cunningham, Curtiss & Co.	Pork	25,000	200,000	175,000
Daniels, Nichols & Co.	Tailors	250,000	20,000	230,000
Driver, H. L., & Co.	Japanned Ware	500,000	100,000	400,000
Eagle White-Lead Co.	......	100,000	500,000	400,000
Eckert, Michael	Tanner	100,000	500,000	400,000
Evans, Lippincott & Cunningham	Pork	1,000,000 and over	300,000	700,000 and over
Evans & Kinney	Pork-Packers	1,000,000	200,000	800,000
				$5,605,000

In this city we see the two Agencies differ one million and a half in reference to two houses engaged in the pork and pork-packing business. The highest estimate of the capital of both firms is $2,000,000. We have an incertitude, consequently, of monstrous dimensions in regard to two dealers in one of the most clearly defined and staple investments. In these cases McKillop & Sprague Co. are the moderate estimators. But we must not give them credit, hastily, on this head. In the instance of the coal-dealer, Cochnower, they excel Dun, Barlow & Co. at least $750,000, and exceed them, in five other cases, as much more. There is no thread of Ariadne to lead either out of this labyrinth.

CLEVELAND, OHIO.

NAME.	Business.	Dun, Barlow & Co.'s estimate of capital.	McKillop & Sprague Co.'s estimate of capital.	Margin of combined ignorance of both Agencies.
Babcock, Hurd & Co.	Grocers	$100,000	$750,000	$650,000
Baker, George A.	Lightning-Rods	50,000	500,000	450,000
Childs, O. A., & Co.	Boots and Shoes	100,000	500,000	400,000
Cleveland Spring Co.	Manufacturers (Springs)	250,000	50,000	200,000
Clough Stone Co	....	250,000	50,000	200,000
Commercial Oil Co	....	500,000	100,000	400,000
Fulton Foundry Co.	....	100,000	750,000	650,000
Gaensslen Brothers	Leather, etc.	100,000	500,000	400,000
Heisel, N., & Son.	Wholesale Confectioners	250,000	80,000	230,000
Hoffman, Isaac, & Son.	Hides, etc.	10,000	100,000	90,000
King, Z., & Son.	Manufacturers (Bridges)	100,000	750,000	650,000
				$4,320,000

Is there anything in the business atmosphere of the place to account for such results? Here are eleven names—the same number chosen as example in Chicago. The margin of doubt, over and above that shown in the latter city, is one million two hundred thousand nearly. And yet, one would think, two Cleveland branch offices ought to be able to approximate closer in the smaller city instead of becoming more variable and discrepant. The *size* of a place is thus seen to bear no relation to the accuracy or inaccuracy of the reports of its trading classes. So the reduction of area or of names affords no material for imputing the increased probability of an approach to uniformity of opinion.

DETROIT, MICHIGAN.

NAME.	Business.	Dun, Barlow & Co.'s estimate of capital.	McKillop & Sprague Co.'s estimate of capital.	Margin of combined ignorance of both Agencies.
Beecher, Luther...............	"Biddle House"	$100,000	$1,000,000 and over	$900,000 and over
Darmstaetter, William.........	Brewer	250,000	50,000	200,000
Detroit Emery-Wheel Co.......	....	2,000	20,000	18,000
Detroit, Lansing and L. Michigan R.R.	....	1,000,000	......	1,000,000
Ducharne, Fletcher & Co........	Hardware	250,000	1,000,000	750,000
Ford, J. N., & Co.............	Steam-Forge	250,000	50,000	200,000
Greusel, John, & Sons.........	Drain-Pipes, etc.	250,000	50,000	200,000
Gunn, C. K...................	Dry-Goods	100,000	20,000	80,000
Holmes & Webster.............	Plumbers	100,000	20,000	80,000
Hubbard & King..............	Lumber	250,000	50,000	200,000
Kling P., & Co..............	Brewers	50,000	300,000	250,000
				$3,878,000 and over

In this city we take merely one case for comment. Dun, Barlow & Co. rate the D., L. & L. Michigan R.R. at $1,000,000. McKillop & Sprague Co. cannot say it is worth a dollar. They have heard of the company, or they would not put down its name. Of what use is the name without an estimate? Any Directory of Detroit would supply that much without injury or responsibility. Were they in doubt after investigation? Then why do they not indicate their doubt instead of simply want of information? Again, if a railroad which D., B. & Co. find to be worth $1,000,000 cannot convince McK. & S. Co. that it is worth anything, how did the railroad satisfy D, B. & Co.? Secondly, what chance is there for clearness about dealers with less authentic evidences, officially or otherwise?

NASHVILLE, TENNESSEE.

NAME.	Business.	Dun, Barlow & Co.'s estimate of capital.	McKillop & Sprague Co.'s estimate of capital.	Margin of combined ignorance of both Agencies.
Adams, Thorne & Co.	Dry-Goods, etc.	$100,000	$500,000	$400,000
Akers, George F.	Tobacco	50,000	6,000	44,000
Arrington, Farrar & Weakley	Real Estate	10,000	100,000	90,000
Burns & Co.	Saddlery	25,000	750,000	725,000
Cooley, S.	Grocer	50,000	1,000	49,000
Dale, J. P., & Co.	Machinery	1,000	50,000	49,000
Deschamps, George	Saloon	500	10,000	9,500
Ellis, J.	Clothing	25,000	1,000	24,000
Gauthier, Charles H.	Paints	50,000	6,000	44,000
Hanmer & Co.	Livery and Commission	100,000	10,000	90,000
Hicks, Houston & Co.	China	250,000	50,000	200,000
Hunt, William G. or S.	Carriages	2,000	200,000	198,000
				$1,922,500

We have now before us a city of the smallest population yet reached in our examination of these absurd reports, and one largely affected by its relations to the Civil War. An approach to uniformity of estimate might reasonably be looked for in its case, if made even by two distinct inquirers who should open a Nashville Directory and send letters of inquiry to the first names which presented themselves. And yet to these professed specialists William G. Hunt is worth either $2000 or $200,000, and Burns & Co. are good for either $25,000 or $750,000! Hunt and Burns may be worth, considered together, $27,000 or $950,000, and the person who wishes to trade with either is considerately left either figure to choose from at his leisure.

NEW-ORLEANS, LOUISIANA.

NAME.	Business.	Dun, Barlow & Co.'s estimate of capital.	McKillop & Sprague Co.'s estimate of capital.	Margin of combined ignorance of both Agencies.
Abbott, Robert..........	Cotton-Press	$500,000	$100,000	$400,000
Alcus, Scherck & Antey.....	Cotton Factors	100,000	500,000	400,000
Bayly, G. M., & Pond....	Wholesale Grocers	500,000	100,000	400,000
Belden, F........	Hats	500,000	100,000	400,000
Block & Brittin	Wholesale Grocers, etc.	250,000	50,000	200,000
Briggs, Payne & Co......	Wholesale Grocers	250,000	30,000	220,000
Brousseau, A......	Carpets	250,000	50,000	200,000
Brulatour, P. E.....	Liquors	250,000	50,000	200,000
Buddecke, C. T., & Co.....	Commission	100,000	10,000	90,000
Burbridge, J. W., & Co.....	Commission	1,000,000	200,000	800,000
Camors, J. B., & Co....	Flour	250,000	50,000	200,000
Chaffe, John, Bro. & Son...	Commission	1,000,000	200,000	800,000
Chopin, Oscar......	Commission	100,000	10,000	90,000
Clason & Co.......	Commission	500,000	50,000	450,000
				$4,850,000

It must not be forgotten that, in picking out these names, we neither exhaust the alphabet nor go over the leading enterprises of the merchants. We merely take a few names under the first few letters of the alphabet, and disregard the innumerable discrepancies of from 20 to $50,000 even in connection with these. If we should depart from this course in our further comparisons, we shall do so solely to prove to the reader that there is no occult significance in any letter, as such, making in our favor and against the Agencies.

NEW-YORK CITY.

NAME.	Business.	Dun, Barlow & Co.'s estimate of capital.	McKillop & Sprague Co.'s estimate of capital.	Margin of combined ignorance of both Agencies.
Abecasis, J. S.	India-Rubber Belts	$25,000	$300,000	$275,000
Allen, J. T., & Co.	Furniture	50,000	300,000	250,000
American Clock Co.	....	10,000	500,000	490,000
American Metalline Co.	....	50,000	1,000,000 and over	950,000 and over
American Sardine Co.	....	25,000	750,000	725,000
Atwood, Thomas S.	White-Lead	25,000	500,000	475,000
Babcock, David, & Co.	Naval Supplies	50,000	750,000	700,000
Bacon & Hyde	Copper	100,000	1,000,000 and over	900,000 and over
Barling & Davis	Commission	500,000	75,000	425,000
New-York & Ohio Coal Co.	....	25,000	750,000	725,000
New-York Rectifying Co.	....	50,000	500,000	450,000
Nichols, William B.	Real Estate	50,000	1,000,000 and over	950,000 and over
Nichol, Cowlishaw & Co.	Upholstery Goods	100,000	750,000	650,000
Noel, Saurel & Marniffe.	French Plate-Glass	1,000,000 and over	300,000	700,000 and over
				$8,665,000 and over

Out of (say) 40,000 New-York merchants we pick fourteen names, and find a disparity of nearly $9,000,-000! In this city all the Agencies have their principal offices, their largest number of canvassers and credit-men, their imposing array of books, clerks, etc. From this city, pre-eminently, is drawn yearly a great part of their royal revenues. Facilities for acquiring accurate or proximately accurate estimates of capital are ne-cessarily abundant in the Court Records, in the Register's Office, in the Banks, in the Real-estate publications. Surrounded by these opportunities, the Agencies must have shut their eyes and stuffed their ears, or allowed themselves to be deceived or persuaded, before achieving so eminent success in blundering.

PHILADELPHIA, PENNSYLVANIA.

NAME.	Business.	Dun, Barlow & Co.'s estimate of capital.	McKillop & Sprague Co.'s estimate of capital.	Margin of combined ignorance of both Agencies.
Alexander Bros.	Leather-Belting	$100,000	$10,000	$90,000
Andrews, A. J., & Son	Grain and Storage	250,000	20,000	230,000
Ashmead, Henry B.	Printer	250,000	30,000	220,000
Atlantic Refining Co.	......	500,000	50,000	450,000
Audendried, W. G., & Co.	Coal, Iron, etc.	1,000,000 and over	100,000	900,000 and over
Bailey & Co.	Jewelers	100,000	750,000	650,000
Baker, Arnold & Co.	Gas Fixtures	1,000,000	200,000	800,000
Baugh & Sons	Fertilizers	100,000	500,000	400,000
Beckhaus, Joseph	Coaches	250,000	50,000	200,000
Bement, William B., & Son	Tools	1,000,000	200,000	800,000
Berwind, White & Co.	Coal	500,000	100,000	400,000
Billington, James H., & Co.	Factory Findings	250,000	10,000	240,000
Bloomingdale, Rhine & Co.	Clothing	50,000	300,000	250,000
Borie, C. & H.	Bill Brokers	1,000,000 and over	500,000	500,000 and over
Bower, John & Co.	Hams, Lard, etc.	100,000	750,000	650,000
Boyer, I. S. & Co.	Coal	5,000	300,000	295,000
Bradlee & Co.	Chain Manufacturers	25,000	200,000	175,000
Broad-Top Improvement Co.	......	1,000,000	30,000	970,000
Buist, Robert, Jr.	Seeds	25,000	300,000	275,000
				$8,495,500 and over

(Continued.)

PHILADELPHIA, PENNSYLVANIA.—(Continued.)

NAME.	Business.	Dun, Barlow & Co.'s estimate of capital.	McKillop & Sprague Co.'s estimate of capital.	Margin of combined Ignorance of both Agencies.
				$8,495,500(br't forw'd)
Bunting & McDonnell	Liquors	$1,000,000	$200,000	800,000
Burns & McMenamey	Coal	10,000	100,000	90,000
Button, Conyers & Co	Manufacturers	250,000	1,000,000 and over	750,000 and over
Callaghan & Brothers	Cottons	100,000	750,000	650,000
Carrow, John	Silver-Plater	250,000	30,000	220,000
				$11,005,500 and over

Twenty-four names (in three letters) produce over eleven millions of disparity between the two Agencies in Philadelphia, a city only four hours' ride from New-York. Out of 165 names, in twelve cities, the margin of doubt already counts up over $60,000,000. The conundrum is: Where would the discrepancies stop if, instead of comparing the ratings of one hundred and sixty-five traders, in the twelve cities, we had pursued a comparison between the one hundred and fifty thousand persons engaged in business in those centres? A parallel puzzle also occurs to us, and we submit it to the agency experts: What certitude could the Agencies have had about the correctness, or approximation to correctness, of the very lowest ratings? Any basis of knowledge whatever cannot rationally be imputed to them; for any elements of proof would have led to less flagrantly absurd conclusions. Is not the true explanation this: That the Agency giving the low estimates is waiting for patronage, and the Agency giving high estimates is working to repay subscription?

PITTSBURG, PENNSYLVANIA.

NAME.	Business.	Dun, Barlow & Co.'s estimate of capital.	McKillop & Sprague Co.'s estimate of capital.	Margin of combined ignorance of both Agencies.
Adams & Co.	Glass	$250,000	$20,000	$230,000
Armstrong, C. H., & Son	Coal	50,000	500,000	450,000
Bailey, Farrell & Co.	Lead Pipes, etc.	100,000	750,000	650,000
Bakewell, Pears & Co.	Glass	1,000,000	200,000	800,000
Bigley, N. J.	Coal	100,000	750,000	650,000
Bovard, Rose & Co.	Carpets	100,000	500,000	400,000
Coffin, G. W.	Lumber	100,000	20,000	80,000
Crossan, J. McDonald	Hotel	250,000	50,000	200,000
Davis, Chambers & Co.	White-Lead	1,000,000	300,000	700,000
Dilworth, Porter & Co.	Spikes	250,000	1,000,000 and over	750,000 and over
Fort Pitt Coal Co.	....	250,000	30,000	220,000
French, Aaron & Co.	Railroad Springs	250,000	30,000	220,000
German Fire Insurance Co.	....	50,000	300,000	250,000
German Savings Bank	....	500,000	100,000	400,000
				$6,000,000 and over

In this table the glass-dealers are favorites with Dun, Barlow & Co., and the coal-dealers favorites with McKillop & Sprague Co.; but when the Agencies cannot guess closer than in the last two items about a Bank and an Insurance company, whose standing and capital are matters of verified record in the State Department at Harrisburg, it is quite impossible to ascribe to them any energy in looking for data. Even if we overlooked their see-saw vaticination where many channels would need to be searched, it is surely unpardonable to discover from this table how negligent they must be in looking at the most patent evidence.

PORTLAND, MAINE.

NAME.	Business.	Dun, Barlow & Co.'s estimate of capital.	McKillop & Sprague Co.'s estimate of capital.	Margin of combined Ignorance of both Agencies.
Alden, W. L.	Commissioner, etc.	$25,000	$200,000	$175,000
Bailey & Noyes.	Books	250,000	50,000	200,000
Bond, J. H., & Co.	Plumbers	10,000	500	9,500
Cahoon Manufacturing Co.	Lamps	250,000	20,000	230,000
International Steamship Co.	......	100,000	500,000	400,000
Jose, Charles E., & Co.	Crockery	250,000	50,000	200,000
Locke, Twitchell & Co.	Dry-Goods	500,000	100,000	400,000
McGlinchy, James.	Brewer	500,000	100,000	400,000
McLaughlin, C., & Co.	Grocers	250,000	50,000	200,000
Portland Kerosene Oil Co.	......	100,000	500,000	400,000
				$2,614,500

It would be entertaining, if our space were not so valuable, to insert here a few extracts from Agencies' circulars claiming superiority over each other. Were we to believe each sapient self-lauder, *it* is the only correct, reliable, and thorough one, and its competitors are charlatans and impostors. Put face to face, as we place them, the reader can readily agree with what each one says, and come to a conclusion common to all.

PROVIDENCE, RHODE ISLAND.

NAME.	Business.	Dun, Barlow & Co.'s estimate of capital.	McKillop & Sprague Co.'s estimate of capital.	Margin of combined ignorance of both Agencies.
Abbott Rim Co.	Prints, Cloths	$50,000	$1,000,000 and over	$950,000 and over
Adams Bros.	Flour and Grain	250,000	50,000	200,000
Aldrich, H. L.	Cotton	100,000	750,000	650,000
Alexander, Andrews & Co.	Grocers	250,000	50,000	200,000
American Corset-Shield Manuf'g Co.	....	250,000	50,000	200,000
American Steamboat Co.	....	250,000	1,000,000 and over	750,000
Angell & Lansing	Lumber	250,000	50,000	200,000
Anthony, A., & Co.	Tanners, etc.	500,000	100,000	400,000
Arkwright Manufacturing Co.	Sheetings	100,000	1,000,000 and over	900,000 and over
Ashland Co.	Cotton	50,000	1,000,000 and over	950,000 and over
Austin, John, & Co.	Gold-Refiners	250,000	8,000	247,000
Babcock, George W.	Watchmaker	100,000	6,000	94,000
Beckwith, A. N.	Cotton	250,000	1,000,000 and over	750,000 and over
Blodgett, L. M.	Cotton Brokers	250,000	20,000	230,000
Borden & Bowen	Cotton	250,000	1,000,000 and over	750,000 and over
Bridge Mill Manufacturing Co.	Cotton	250,000	1,000,000 and over	750,000 and over
Brown, J. A., & Co.	Jewelers	250,000	3,000	247,000
				$8,468,500 and over

From this list, it is evident McKillop & Sprague Co. are the favorites with Agency subscribers in Providence. The Spragues, indeed, are all-powerful in Rhode Island, and blood—as the adage runs—is thicker than water. On the other hand, Dun, Barlow & Co. are plainly in a huff with the Providence men, but not averse, we should think, to conciliation.

RICHMOND, VIRGINIA.

NAME.	Business.	Dun, Barlow & Co.'s estimate of capital.	McKillop & Sprague Co.'s estimate of capital.	Margin of combined ignorance of both Agencies.
Allison & Addison............	Agricultural Implements	$100,000	$20,000	$80,000
Archer, Goodwin & Co........	Founders	100,000	20,000	80,000
Booker, John................	Commission	5,000	50,000	45,000
Christian & Gunn............	Commission (Tobacco)	100,000	6,000	94,000
Davenport & Morris..........	Commission	1,000,000	200,000	800,000
Grant, L. J., & Co..........	Tobacco	5,000	750,000	745,000
Hannewickle, F. W., & Co....	Tobacco	500,000	100,000	400,000
Hill & Skinker..............	Wholesale Grocers, etc.	500,000	30,000	470,000
Lyne & Bro.................	R. E. and Auctioneers	250,000	30,000	220,000
Nowlan & Co................	Jewelers	100,000	10,000	90,000
Patterson, R. A., & Co......	Tobacco	1,000,000	10,000	990,000
Piedmont & Arlington Life Ins. Co....	....	1,000,000 and over	50,000	950,000 and over
				$4,064,000 and over

In this schedule, two items will naturally arrest special notice—the discrepancy between $5000 and $750,000, alleged capital limit of L. J. Grant & Co., and $1,000,000 and $10,000, applied to Patterson & Co. These are competing tobacco firms, and each has its partisan at the Agency bellows. The result is seen in the figures. Is it possible to explain the contrariety of view on the theory of *innocent error* ?

SACRAMENTO, CALIFORNIA.

NAME.	Business.	Dun, Barlow & Co.'s estimate of capital.	McKillop & Sprague Co.'s estimate of capital.	Margin of combined ignorance of both Agencies.
Adams, McNeil & Co	Wholesale Grocers	$100,000	$500,000	$400,000
Booth & Co	Grocers	500,000	100,000	400,000
Capital Savings Bank...	....	250,000	1,000,000	750,000
Cohen, Benjamin	Carpets, etc.	10,000	300,000	290,000
Cooper, John F.....	Music, etc.	1,000	20,000	19,000
Deolin, Robert.....	Grocer	2,000	20,000	18,000
Doherty, D........	Grocer	500	20,000	19,500
Guth, George.....	Grocer	500	10,000	9,500
Locke & Lewenson.....	Carpets, etc.	250,000	50,000	200,000
Stoll, J. T......	Harness	25,000	3,000	22,000
Stone, R., & Co.....	Harness	250,000	1,000,000 and over	750,000 and over
				$2,877,000 and over

Messrs. Guth and Doherty possess between them $1000 or $30,000, and we can take our choice of estimates. If $1000, we should think they could readily lose their capital in a day ; if $30,000, a longer period might be required to absorb it. But the moral in the case is this: *low* ranges of capital give us no greater tendency to approximation of estimate than high ones ; and, one by one, the only conceivable excuses of the Agencies are shown to be merest moonshine.

SAN FRANCISCO, CALIFORNIA.

NAME.	Business.	Dun, Barlow & Co.'s estimate of capital.	McKillop & Sprague Co.'s estimate of capital.	Margin of combined ignorance of both Agencies.
Baum, J. & Co.	Clothing	$500,000	$100,000	$400,000
Brown Bros. & Co.	Agents for Oregon City Woollen Mills	500,000	100,000	400,000
Crane & Brigham	Drugs, etc.	1,000,000	100,000	900,000
Crocker, H. S., & Co.	Printers, etc.	50,000	500,000	450,000
Falkenstein & Co.	Tobacco, etc.	50,000	300,000	250,000
Fechheimer, Goodkind & Co.	Clothing	1,000,000	100,000	900,000
Giant Powder Co.	....	25,000	1,000,000 and over	975,000 and over
Goodall, Nelson & Perkins' S.S. Co.	Commission, etc.	100,000	500,000	400,000
Grace, J. W. & Co.	Shipping & Commission	50,000	500,000	450,000
Hastings, C. C., & Co.	Clothing	1,000,000	100,000	900,000
Hawley, Marcus C., & Co.	Hardware	500,000	100,000	400,000
Hecht Bros. & Co.	Boots and Shoes	1,000,000	200,000	800,000
Heller, M., & Bros.	Dry Goods	1,000,000	200,000	800,000
Hooper & Co., William B.	Shipping, etc.	1,000,000	200,000	800,000
Hooper, E. P. & J. A.	Lumber	50,000	300,000	250,000
Hotaling, A. P., & Co.	Liquors	250,000	1,000,000 and over	750,000 and over
Jones, S. L., & Co.	Auction and Commission	500,000	75,000	425,000
Knowland & Doe.	Lumber	50,000	500,000	450,000
				$10,700,000 and over

ST. LOUIS, MISSOURI.

NAME.	Business.	Dun, Barlow & Co.'s estimate of capital.	McKillop & Sprague Co.'s estimate of capital.	Margin of combined ignorance of both Agencies.
American Wine Co	......	$1,000,000	$200,000	$800,000
Blackman, James, & Co	Hides, etc.	100,000	750,000	650,000
Bouton, Smith & Wandell	Imp'ters Carriage Goods, etc.	100,000	500,000	400,000
Catlin, D	Tobacco	250,000	750,000	500,000
Eisenstadt, M. & Co	Jewelry	250,000	50,000	200,000
Espenchied & Benning	Awnings, etc.	500,000	20,000	480,000
Garneau, Hillard & Co	Steam Bakery	500,000	100,000	400,000
Jacoby, F., & Co	Liquors	500,000	100,000	400,000
Keokuk Northern Line Packet Co. of St. Louis	......	1,000,000	200,000	800,000
Kingsland, Ferguson & Co	Foundry	100,000	750,000	650,000
Lemp, William J	Brewery	100,000	750,000	650,000
Maramec Iron and Mining Co ..	......	100,000	500,000	400,000
				$6,330,000

In this and the preceding city, we pick out the first chance names which open to us on the Reference Books, down to the letter M. Thirty names give us a variation of $17,000,000! Up to this point 258 names produce $101,852,000 of demonstrated doubt in regard to capital possessed by them. If we had chosen to load our work with five hundred, we could have reached a mass of erroneously imputed capital equal to the whole available currency of the United States!

ST. JOHN, NEW-BRUNSWICK.

NAME.	Business.	Dun, Wiman & Co.'s estimate of capital.	McKillop & Sprague Co.'s estimate of capital.	Margin of combined ignorance of both Agencies.
Davidson, William...........	Mills	$50,000	$500,000	$450,000
De Veber, L. H., & Sons......	General Merchants	500,000	75,000	425,000
Dunn, James L...............	Iron and Shipping	250,000	50,000	200,000
Kennedy, E. T., & Co........	Steam Heating, etc.	10,000	500,000	490,000
				$1,565,000

We must stop this tiring process somewhere, and this is as good and convenient a place as any. A few hundred names out of 800,000 produce over *one hundred and three millions of variety of estimate.* What good can be subscrved by going on and demonstrating an aggregate inaccuracy or doubt, superior in amount to all the active capital in the universe? And these be the oracles ye bow down to, business men of the United States and Canada! These be the guides to the unwary, lights to the blind, and voices for the deaf and unheeding traders and capitalists of fifty millions of the human family! The serpent was worshipped on the Nile; but serpents are wise in their order. Who ever before heard of a community which erected large edifices to commemorate Ignorance, or paid eight millions of money yearly to perpetuate the dynasty of the Incapables?

CHAPTER XIX.

IMPORTANT LEGAL DECISION—THE McLEAN CASE IN TORONTO—
THE AGENCY PRINCIPLE OF NON-ACCOUNTABILITY DENIED
BY A CANADIAN JURY—A VERDICT FOR THE PLAINTIFF IN A
TEST CASE.

THE Toronto *Globe* and Toronto *Mail* of December 8th and
9th, 1875, contain a full report of the trial of an action brought
by one Andrew McLean against Dun, Wiman & Co.'s Agency
for damages sustained in consequence of relying on information
given to him by their clerks and servants. The gist of the action
goes, of course, to the very marrow of the controversy in which
we are engaged; and the thoroughness of the contention in the
Canadian court, the strong array of counsel employed, the direct-
ness of the testimony on the question of negligence, and the final
result in favor of the plaintiff at the hands of the jury, render an
extended notice of the case eminently proper in these pages. In
fact, we have purposely delayed this publication so as to spread
this corroborative proof of our arguments of principle and policy
before our readers, believing that nothing could be more acceptable
or convincing than a legal determination of a plainly test case
coming after our own proofs, and showing their legal, as well as
practical, bearings.

Mr. Bethune opened the case for plaintiff. He said the facts
were as follow:

Mr. McLean was a dealer in leather, and in June last E. M.
Wilson, who at that time was doing business in the shoe trade on
King street, called at plaintiff's to purchase goods. Mr. McLean
was not at home, but on his return he had sent to the agency of
Dun, Wiman & Co. to get a report of Wilson's standing and
character and business. The information was to the effect that
Wilson claimed to be worth $7000; that he had $5000 or $6000
in his business; that he was doing a fair business, and that his
credit was fair. The inquirer as to this information resorted to it

about April, it seemed, or perhaps an earlier date. The action was fixed on the alleged duty of the defendants to use ordinary diligence in obtaining information according to their contract, and in regard to the standing of business men, and diligently and faithfully to report to their subscribers the result of such inquiries. Mr. McLean had been in the habit for years before of paying his subscription, and the plaintiff claimed that he had a right to the damages he asked as a compensation for the loss he had sustained owing to the incorrect information they had given to him. The defendants, Mr. Bethune said, came into court, and were prepared to deny everything—that they were not a mercantile agency, and that they had not signed the agreement. The plaintiff had a right to compensation here just as much as if he had engaged a private detective, who had acted in negligence of his orders; or against a physician who had been negligent or ignorant of his engagement.

Mr. J. H. Cameron argued that the plaintiff had no ground for his action, quoting authorities, the principal of which were the Statute of Frauds, and the clause relating to such actions in Lord Tenterden's Act, and the Act 9, George IV.; Swan *vs.* Phillips, 8; Adolphus *vs.* Ellis, 4, 5, 7. But in this action, Mr. Cameron said, they would have to confine themselves to the grounds permitted in the 4th Sec. of the Statute of Frauds, or Sec. 6 in the Act relating to promises and agreements, and in which the mischief intended to be guarded against was sufficiently pointed out. The plaintiff's case, as they had heard it, could not be sustained, as there had been no written contract, and he would ask for a nonsuit.

Mr. Bethune said the only case he would offer was a recent English decision, Lloyd *vs.* Pernywas, an action against the *Weekly Bankrupt Gazette* for not supplying information in agreement with a published prospectus. The jury had found that a contract had been made, and gave the plaintiff damages. He thought the cases to which Mr. Cameron had referred were entirely outside the argument here. He would ask his Lordship to let the case go to the jury, although he would have preferred the matter to come up by demurrer.

Mr. J. H. Cameron replied that the case cited by Mr. Bethune did not sustain the argument or form a sufficient ground for action.

His Lordship decided that the case did not come within the Statute of Frauds, and the question of whether it came within the scope of Lord Tenterden's Act was one of greater difficulty, but his impression was that it did not apply either. His Lordship decided that the case should go to the jury, with leave to Mr. Cameron to move generally.

After proving by other witnesses the demand for information, its receipt, its context stating that " Wilson was worth $7000, and in good local credit," the sale and delivery of goods under this information, and the loss, Mr. Bethune called D. McLean, who testified:

"I am in the leather business here; I have been in business about twelve years; I had a partner, Mr. Daly, about ten years ago, and I think we became connected with the Agency *about the same time;* I had a book called a subscriber's book." (A book was produced and identified as one he had had. A smaller book was produced, also a subscribers' book, which he had had when the action commenced. These books contained the names and ratings spoken of by Mr. Bethune.)

Witness.—We rely on these books, and have them at hand for use; I paid $75 a year; I gave instructions to obtain information from the Agency, and a day or two after I saw Wilson; I sold him goods to the amount of $524.17, on the usual terms; I applied for no other information except that I got from the defendants; it was so explicit and so strong I had no doubt about it; I got information early in July that Wilson had cleared out; I sent my bookkeeper to find out the particulars, and found there was nothing left; I never questioned the truth of the information I got from the defendants; I know Mr. Wiman personally.•

By Mr. M. C. Cameron.—I knew the elder Wilson, who was carrying on business before in the same stand as his son afterwards; I knew as a fact that Wilson, the son, carried on business in the same place as his father had done before; I have been connected for about ten years with the defendants, and have made a great many inquiries in that time.

Erastus Wiman.—I am one of the defendants; I live in New-York; we do our business here by deputy; our deputy here is W. C. Mathews; there are twelve or thirteen in the office; I was not here in June; I have been told that one of our clerks gave the information to Mr. McLean. We give the information we have; we do not pretend to give the information down to the day we give it; we generally get information twice a year, *and do not consider it necessary to do so oftener;* we make up the reports in the spring and fall; the April report was gotten probably for our London (England) office for the subscribers there.

By Mr. J. H. Cameron.—They had the book with the rating of March in this year, and the information they got was probably a month later.

John Gillies.—I knew Mr. Wilson, who ran away July last: I was in his employ about two or three weeks in June, but not when he went away; I was going messages; he had not much stock; he had a great many boxes, but they were empty; he was always talking about getting stock, but he did not get any; I do not think he was doing a prosperous trade, as I did not see much doing.

By Mr. M. C. Cameron.—A stranger going into the shop would not see much hanging around; there was a great number of small boxes, but they were empty, and the boxes *had only one or two pairs in them.*

William Thompson, a boy of 14.—I was in the employ of Mr. Wilson; I was there up to the evening before he went away: I took some goods of his down to the auction-room—to Henderson & McFarlane's; I could not tell how often I took goods down there; I took them in a wheelbarrow; I took some in the daytime and some in the morning; they were in boxes; a good many people came in but they did not buy much, *for he had not much to sell.*

By Mr. M. C. Cameron.—I do not know how much goods he had in January when I went there; *I knew the boxes were empty,* for I used to put them upon the shelves.

John McFarlane.—I am one of the firm of Henderson & McFarlane, auctioneers; we made a sale of boots and shoes on account of E. M. Wilson; they were advertised as bankrupt stock: they were sold by the dozen pairs, and he gave me the cost price on the margin of my sale-book.

Mr. M. C. Cameron asked what this evidence amounted to.

Mr. Bethune said they expected to show such a notorious state of matters, that other people knew, if the defendants did not.

what was the low state of credit. I propose to show that from
March he had sold probably up to $1000 worth of goods at auc-
tion. We will want to go further, and show that it was well
known that Wilson was in embarrassed circumstances.

Philip Jacobi.—Was a dealer in shoe-findings and leather;
knew Wilson, and had some talk last winter about his credit; it
was said to be very bad; the talk was ever since he (E. M. Wilson) was in business; I would not have trusted him; I did trust
him for about $55, and he gave a check, but before I could get it
cashed he was gone; I am a subscriber to the Dun-Wiman
agency; I never made any inquiry there; I knew enough myself;
it was currently reported that he had been travelling in the States
with a troupe of negro minstrels. (On cross-examination the witness said it was not a good experience for business to have been
going with a minstrel troupe.)

Walter Beardmore, wholesale dealer on Front street.—Wilson
had asked for a credit at our house, and had ordered a quantity of
goods which I refused to deliver; I had an idea that he would not
succeed in business; his father had spoken to us about his son and
regretted that he was so unsteady, but hoped now he was going to
turn over a new leaf; I had spoken to several parties during the
spring, and there was an impression that Wilson was not in good
credit.

Joseph Priestman.—I am manager of Bradstreet's agency in
this city; I ascertained E. M. Wilson's credit through the ordinary channels.

Mr. Cameron objected to this evidence of obtaining information. It might have been gotten by some person who was evilly
disposed towards Mr. Wilson.

Witness, proceeding.—It was one of our city reporters who
got the information.

Mr. Cameron.—The sources may be all wrong. Mr. Priestman
tells us he has no personal knowledge of the matter.

Witness.—We do not interchange with the other agencies in
the city; our clerks are forbidden to have any communication with
Dun, Wiman & Co.'s office.

Charles Blair.—I am employed by Mr. Blachford; I was also
in the service of the elder Mr. Wilson for about twenty-five years,
and in the employment of the young man after he got the busi-

ness; he had very irregular habits, not strictly sober nor particular in his company ; *I did hear last winter some people say they would not trust him ; business men said so ;* he was not an honorable man.

William Rodgers.—Was in the employ of Mr. Hay last summer ; Mr. Hay was Wilson's landlord ; I went into the store after he ran away and found a lot of empty boxes; there might have been $15 or $20 worth of stock left.

Mr. Bethune said he now proposed to call Mr. McFarlane to show that Wilson had been in the habit of selling parcels of goods below cost. He had a double proposition to demonstrate—the fact that Wilson was insolvent, and then that the defendants might have known this fact.

His Lordship said there could be no difficulty about proving the insolvency.

Mr. Cobley, recalled.—There was nothing said of the date up to which the information was given; if there had been I would have made a note of it in my report.

Mr. Donald, recalled, said the agent told him they never gave dates; there was nothing said as to the date up to which they gave the information.

Mr. Bethune.—Does the Agency issue a change-list?

Witness.—They give us a change-list twice a week; they will not give a messenger a date, but they put the date of the statement on the papers they supply; *if they send a report a week after it is asked,* for example, they will send the date up to which they know about the person, but if I was getting the information they would not tell me up to what time they had made it up.

Mr. Bethune said this was the plaintiff's case.

Mr. M. C. Cameron said the plaintiff has failed to prove that the defendant had made breach of contract, as they had given the information up to 29th April, and had not given it as information up to June 10th. Then the information was given up to the time when it was stated, and it did not therefore appear that there had been any breach.

Mr. Bethune replied that the contract could not mean to be merely the information they had, *but they agreed to give with reasonable correctness at a given time or a particular time, and not any time, as it might be five or six years.* The information must be of some use, and to be of this character it must be therefore of such dates that it could be relied on.

Mr. Bethune asked to be allowed to amend the declaration to sustain the averment that the report of the 29th April was incorrect, and upon the merits. Mr. Bethune said the report following was misleading. This report was:

"E. M. Wilson, Toronto, June, 1875, has stock about $1000, formerly of Wilson & Co., dissolved. He is son of D. Wilson, who sold out to E. M. Wilson and E. A. Philip. Wilson owns no real estate; has some $5000 or $6000 in the business; he claims to be worth $7000; character and habits are good; is doing a fair trade; buys mostly American goods; credit good locally."

There was evidence to show that as far back as January the young man's habits were not good, and that his business was not at any time in a good condition.

Mr. M. C. Cameron said no evidence had been offered ot prove that E. M. Wilson was not all that was stated in April when the report was made.

His Lordship decided that there was sufficient to go to the jury on the question of Wilson's standing even on the 29th of April.

THE DEFENCE.

W. T. Pridham testified that he was in the employ of Dun, Wiman & Co. as city reporter; remembered getting a report from Ernest Wilson; called at Mr. Wilson's store, and saw a person whom he believed to be Mr. Wilson; inquired from others as to the verification of Mr. Wilson; speak in confidence to all parties doing business with us; believed that Mr. Wilson was speaking the truth, but did not until he verified it.

By Mr. Bethune.—Have been for the past five years engaged in the Mercantile Agency Company; was an occasional reporter with Murray, Middlemiss & Co., Montreal; had no previous acquaintance with Mr. Wilson; knew the firm was about dissolving, and went to get particulars; came to the conclusion that he was not worth more than from $3000 to $4000; he claimed to be worth $4000 in property; *did not ask him his indebtedness;* he may have had some cash besides, for all I know; *did not ask them to show their books;* consulted some of the boot and shoe manufacturers of the city ; *do not remember whom I consulted ;* Mr. Hewson was reporting for the company besides myself ; *have no knowledge of the shoe trade ; know nothing about Wilson's habits.*

Edwin Paul, examined, said—I am employed in Dun, Wiman & Co.'s ; have been in their employ for eight years ; had been city reporter in Toronto in 1865 ; remember getting report of Mr. Wilson in that year ; called on Mr. Wilson, who said business was very good ; had no reason to doubt him ; made further inquiries among the wholesale shoe trade, *" he presumed ";* was making reports of other houses at the time ; heard nothing against his credit.

By Mr. Bethune.—Was not the regular reporter at the time ; performed the duties of city reporter for three months ; had a good general knowledge of the trades of the city ; told me he had a stock of $10,000 worth, but could not say ; remember hearing of Wilson running away ; *cannot recall the name of the person who gave me the information ;* had no reason to be suspicious of Wilson.

Thomas Houston, examined, stated that he was a city reporter of the firm of Dun, Wiman & Co. ; made the proper inquiries ; the business was increasing slowly, but from other sources ; the stock looked full in the shop ; it was the leading trade in town.

By Mr. Bethune.—David Wilson was not a partner at the time of my visit ; the firm claimed to be worth over $7000 ; think he claimed himself to be worth $7000 ; put him down at between $5000 and $6000, *allowing for contingencies ; don't remember whether I made a report or not of the circumstance of Wilson running away.*

Henry Moffatt.—I am a reporter for John McKillop & Co. ; a similar company to that of the defendants' ; I made a report of E. M. Wilson on the 7th April, 1875 ; the result of my inquiry was favorable ; I saw E. M. Wilson personally ; I looked through the stock and saw the insurance papers he held, and he gave me a statement of the trade he was doing, the insurance, and the rental he was paying. I reported him worth from $4000 to $5000, and his stock worth $7000 ; I made inquiries from others ; he appeared to be doing a good business, and his stock was well assorted.

By Mr. Bethune.—I have not a copy of the report I made; I spoke to Mr. Jacobi about Wilson in September, 1874; it was the firm then; I reported the firm worth from $7000 to $10,000; on the April report I thought he (Wilson) had a stock of over $6000; he told me he had; *I could not swear that I asked what his debts were,* but I reported him worth $4000 to $5000.

This was the case.

His Lordship remarked that he would hold the action to be one of breach of contract, and he said the contract would be that part of the general conditions that referred to the obligation of the defendants to supply information to the subscribers. His Lordship asked them how they were to estimate the damages under this assumption.

Mr. Bethune said they would ask just as much as they had lost by the sale to Wilson. He thought they should recover the whole loss or merely nominal damages.

Mr. J. H. Cameron said he was prepared to show that the utmost the plaintiff could recover were nominal damages. In the case of Kinghorn *vs.* Montreal Telegraph Co., 18 U. C. Q. B., he presented a case where his contention was sustained, and that more than nominal damages could not be assessed; Stephenson *vs.* Montreal Telegraph Co., 16 U. C. Q. B., was a similar case, and in which the decision was that the plaintiff could not recover unless there was fraud in the delay by the Company's official delivering the message. . Mr. Cameron said also there was no breach of the contract. He asked again if the plaintiff had any case to go to the jury.

His Lordship answered that he thought it would be most proper to allow the case to go to the jury. There would be the single issue of the breach of contract, but he was not at all sure whether Mr. McLean had acted with reasonable care. He said it would be better to place the matter in a specific manner before the jury by asking their answers to the two questions:

1. Did the defendants, who are persons engaged in the Mercantile Agency business, furnish to the best of their ability information to the plaintiff of the standing and credit of Ernest M. Wilson?

2. Did the plaintiff act as an ordinarily prudent man in not making any further inquiries in view of the fact that Wilson re-

sided and carried on business in his immediate neighborhood, and was well known in the city, and that the goods were not furnished for a fortnight after the application ?

Mr. J. H. Cameron addressed the jury, remarking that they would have nothing to do with figures, as that, by arrangement between counsel, had been withdrawn from the question. But they would have to decide upon a matter that was of as great consequence to the mercantile agencies as to the public. And although these agencies had been in existence for about forty years, there was not a case reported in the courts that could be called an example, except the one cited by Mr. Bethune, which was the English case he mentioned. Mr. Cameron said this case was not a contract of guarantee. The question, Did the defendants give information to the best of their ability? was what they would have to consider. After a recapitulation of the evidence and a statement of the case, Mr. Cameron laid down the proposition that if the Company gave all the information they possessed at the time, they had done their duty ; and he said the Company had done this. Further, Mr. Cameron said it could not be expected that these agencies should be held to such a strict account as was sought to be imposed on them in this case, and that all that could be expected of them was a fair report of the individual at the moment when they were asked.

Mr. Bethune, addressing the jury, observed that many people thought these agencies were not advantageous to trade, and it was a question on which the mercantile public were divided whether they should be tolerated at all.

The law would not look at the question of consideration, based upon the amount paid by the plaintiff; illustrated by the example of an accident insurance policy, where a mere trifle would yield a large sum back in case of accident. That they have not been sued before is no argument not to deal fairly with the question. That, if they escape scot-free now, will be an argument and an inducement for, perhaps, greater carelessness than heretofore, and greater risk to the subscribers. All the plaintiff asked the defendants to perform was to give a fair report. It was easy to see the power and facility the company possessed. It was in the power of this company to puff any man, to rate him highly, and place him above suspicion ; and it was in their power also to blast any man's prospects and reputation. In this case the first report they made of Wilson was not correct, if almost he had been the most honest man in the community, after all the opportunities they had of making inquiries. It was said that Mr. McLean might have made inquiries himself, but it was not to be supposed that Mr. McLean would have been satisfied that he could know, or get to know, in any way, as much about Wilson's business by any inquiries he could make as the Agency, with all their means of promoting inquiries, could do. Mr. Bethune proceeded to show the amount of stock that Wilson had received and owned at any time, and all the stock he had been possessed of, and to prove that he could not have had the quantity of stock that was credited to him by the Agency. The operations of the reporters of the Agency were criticised as not being of the sort that entitled them to confidence. There were no particular inquiries, and no verification of the answers given by any one person by answers of another. Mr. Bethune asked the jury to infer that the reporters had forgotten all about the matter, and that really no inquiries had been made at all. The entries in the Agency book, too, were not assuring as far as they could be ascertained, either for their order or for their correctness. It appeared, indeed, that the Agency had not made their inquiries at the very places where they might have learned most, and where common-sense would have pointed as the best sources of information. Wilson's stock and property in April could not exceed a value of $4000. It was shown that he had a balance at the bank indeed, but the amount at the bank was made by the sales made at auction. The company said they did not know that he was selling off the stock at a sacrifice in an auction-room; but a number of private persons, merchants in the city, knew all about this. It was the blame of the servants of the company; but it should not be asked that Mr. McLean should suffer for these servants' mistakes. And when, two weeks after he got a certification of the character and standing of this man Wilson, Mr. McLean gave him a credit, a few days only before he ran away, it was surely not too much to expect that the defendants should compensate him for the loss he had sustained by their negligence. Then, if the defendants repudiated their contract in this case, a certain result would be that the public would lose confidence in them, and require to make a safer contract with them, and require greater certainty in the information they pretend to give. For it was clear that the representations made upon Wilson's character and business were not true. He would repeat that the value of these institutions was the degree of care given to the information they professed to afford to their subscribers. He closed by asking a verdict for the plaintiff on both the questions that were submitted to them. The whole system of mercantile agency was to day on its trial, and their verdict would go far to enforce a closer inspection by the reporters and officials in these offices. If they allowed this to go it would be a step towards making these agencies mere offices for blackmailing the commercial community.

His Lordship said the case involved a number of questions of difficulty, but they had been instructed in those that were to be decided by them. He pointed out what the duties of the defendants were which they had undertaken to execute. And it was only just to mention, too, that Wilson had not been dealing much with any of the wholesale merchants here. He made these remarks as to the standing of Wilson and the facility the defendants had of making an accurate report of Wilson's business. This report, His Lordship did not hesitate to say, as his opinion, was not correct; and he thought there were still avenues of information by which a more correct report might have been obtained by the defendants, and, if a knowledge of the sales at auction had been in possession of the company, they would certainly have been at fault if they had not reported that knowledge to Mr. McLean. His Lordship read passages of the evidence to strengthen the idea that there had been a remissness in the company in obtaining information of the commercial value of E. M. Wilson, and in not noticing that he possessed no aptitude for business. The evidence of the employees was not satisfactory; they could not tell how they got their information exactly, with the exception of one who said he had communicated with Mr. Jacobi. And if they took their information from Wilson's communication alone, they were not doing all their duty. McKillop's reporter gave evidence, it had to be remembered, similar to that of the defendants, but the jury would consider whether he had made sufficient inquiries as well, before they would determine on its value. His Lordship then glanced at the question of whether the plaintiff had acted with ordinary prudence in accepting the information and acting on it without making any inquiries on his own part.

The jury then retired.

The jury returned, after a short absence, with a verdict for the plaintiff, being an answer to the first question in the negative, and to the second question in the affirmative. His Lordship re-corded a verdict for the amount claimed.

The local opinion on this verdict is also of great importance. We append two editorials from the *Globe* and *Mail* respectively under date December 9th, 1875.

MCLEAN VS. DUN, WIMAN & CO.

The verdict rendered in this case yesterday by a petty jury in the Toronto Assize Court *appears to strike a very serious blow at the existence of the commercial associations known as* MERCANTILE AGENCIES. Mr. McLean, a highly respectable and extensive dealer in leather, in this city, was applied to in April last by Mr. E. M. Wilson, then a shoe-dealer in King street, to supply him (Wilson) with a quantity of leather. Mr. McLean was a subscriber to the Mer-cantile Agency of Dun, Wiman & Co., and entitled to obtain from them from time to time reports as to the solvency of parties pur-chasing from them on credit, for the consideration of seventy-five dollars *per annum*. Mr. McLean accordingly applied to Dun, Wiman & Co. for a report as to the standing of Mr. Wilson; and, having received a favorable reply, sold $500 worth of leather, or thereby, to that person. In July following Wilson absconded, and Mr. McLean lost his money. Mr. McLean thereupon com-menced suit against Dun, Wiman & Co. for the amount of his loss, not alleging for a moment any want of good faith on the part of the agency, or that different information from that given was in possession of the Agency or its employees, but simply on the ground that its report was erroneous, and that the Agency had not used due diligence in obtaining information. The jury sus-tained Mr. McLean in this pretension, and gave a verdict against Dun, Wiman & Co. for the full amount of his loss, $500.

In the examination of witnesses it was brought out that some parties were aware, previous to Wilson's absconding, that he was not worthy of credit; and that if Dun, Wiman & Co. had gone to certain parties for information, they would have learned much more about him than they told to Mr. McLean.

*　　*　　*　　*　　*　　*　　*　　*

[*The Mail*—Toronto.]

LIABILITY OF MERCANTILE AGENCIES.

The case of McLean *vs.* Dun, Wiman & Co., which has occupied the attention of the Assize Court for the last two days, was concluded yesterday: a verdict being returned for the plaintiff for the amount of damages claimed, subject to certain considerations reserved for the full Court. Two questions were left to the jury, as will be seen in our report of the case, and both were answered in favor of the plaintiff. The jury in point of fact have determined that Dun, Wiman & Co. did not use due diligence when they gave a favorable report of Wilson's standing, and that Mr. McLean was perfectly justified in relying solely on the Company's statement. The mercantile community will be glad to hear that even thus far the case is in favor of their rights. They are dragooned into subscribing to these agencies, and the least they can expect is that the information received is so accurate that it may be safely acted on. The Court above will have to decide whether the plaintiff can really recover more than nominal damages, and even if the so-called Mercantile Agency should succeed in escaping the heavier penalty, it and kindred institutions will have been taught a useful lesson. The popularity of these agencies is on the wane, and merchants are beginning to quote the long list of failures which have occurred in direct contradiction of agencies' reports and hieroglyphics. There is something un-British and repugnant to most right-thinking men in a system of espionage that has · become a huge Mercantile Inquisition, by no means infallible, and, it now appears, not always very careful of the way in which it conducts its inquiries. As a matter of fact, the cases are few in which private inquiry will not discover all a merchant wants to know of a purchaser seeking credit. New customers are bought at too high a price whose standing has to be certified by an Agency. The system of credit may thereby be infinitely extended; but old firms will tell you· a much safer business was done before this new-fangled system came

into operation. Without impugning the *bona fides* of this particular Agency, we are of opinion that collectively quite as much
harm as good has resulted to those merchants who have been
satisfied to take a customer's "rating" as conclusive evidence of
his worth. Of some other associations formed for the purpose
of enlightening the trading public it is not too much to say that
they are merely snares and delusions got up for the profit of
their promoters.

The great significance of this case justifies us in calling special
attention to two or three points not dwelt on at any length by
counsel. McLean was a subscriber for ten years, at the yearly
cost of $75. He had, therefore, paid $750 to the Agencies
when he lost his bill against Wilson, in addition. This is not a
consolatory or exceptional experience.

The McKillop & Sprague Co. is caught in the legal trap as
well as Dun, Wiman & Co. *Neither* knew the true condition of
Wilson *when it reported him;* their clerks did not even ask him
how much he owed; they failed to examine his books or look into
his empty boxes, and a jury, in finding Dun, Wiman & Co. guilty
of gross negligence, has really passed on evidence sufficient, if unexplained, to mulct the rival Agency if the contract had been
with it. The "institutions," as they like to term themselves, may
not allow their clerks to associate with each other or exchange
opinions: but it is quite apparent that the young gentlemen of
both establishments are very much alike in industry and business
acumen.

Whatever way we look at this McLean case, its effect cannot be
exaggerated. The System, instead of compromising it at the start
according to custom, relied on achieving a success on account of
the two special features—McLean's propinquity to the buyer and
the buyer's fraudulent absconding. The former fact, it was hoped,
would raise the presumption of contributive negligence in
McLean; the latter, as the result of *mala fides* rather than financial insolvency alone, was relied on to relieve against mere contract
damages. Had the Agency any doubt whatever of victory it
would willingly have paid up; so that the result may be taken as
a success over them in their own selected field, and against large
and unusual legal odds.

CHAPTER XX.

THE BEST MEANS OF REDUCING THE DANGER FROM THE IN-
QUISITION—CORRESPONDENTS BEHIND A MASK—WHAT MER-
CHANTS THINK OF THE NEED OF CHANGE—FREE TALKERS
ABOUT OTHERS SURE TO BE BROUGHT TO TASK.

WE come to the question, How shall the opposition to the
Agency system find full, effective, and fitting expression?

Half the force of the agitation against an evil—we had almost
said all—is found in the fact that its movers have not alone arguments to convince, but also measures of correction to advance.
The practical value of any and every opposition to the Agency
system must submit to this test; and if, while the wrongs committed by the system are conceded, no method be proposed to remove them, or, wanting method, there be no independent means
adopted for their repression, it will matter little, in the end,
whether the whole scheme of traffic in men's reputations for personal benefit shall have been approved or reprobated by the public.
In this connection, as in most others, faith without works avails
not; and he is the best reformer who, having demonstrated the
necessity of reform, goes on and illustrates the most direct means
of its accomplishment.

Our FIRST proposition is a plain one. No honest man can
support the system believing it to be noxious and dangerous.
Our SECOND one is a natural corollary to the other. No sincere
man can, having the same belief, omit to become actively antagonistic to it. What, then, should a sincere and honest opponent of
the system do to illustrate his faith and bring forth fruit?

In the first place, such a man should cease using the system at
the earliest possible moment, or   least (if we must adapt our
sense of duty to the average of business moralities) at the close of
his present subscription. Even if he avoid selling on its estimates,
he owes it to himself, as a conscientious man, to withdraw his support from an institution on which his own opinion has already

passed judgment. If he continue paying for pretended information on which he cannot or does not rely, he is merely lending his
name and means to the perpetuation of an exacting and unscrupulous combination against the purses and reputations of other men,
and thereby making himself a party to whatever of wrong or injustice may be done to them.   He may be satisfied, for peace's sake
or a hoped-for benefit, to stand a yearly loss of subscription ; but
does he not owe something to the class to which he belongs, and
should he not be ready to resent, reprove, and repress any and
every flagrant assault on honorable trading so far, at least, as his
own contributive example may go?   We lay it down as a true rule
of commercial honor, that *no one should countenance in another
acts which he would not perform himself.*

Besides refusing to bear the yearly tax of subscription and
Reference Book buying, our merchants should studiously avoid
aiding the parasitic appliances of Collection Bureaux added to
the system, and acting as feeders to it.   Even if the classification
of a trader's doubtful debts for purposes of collection and turning
over to the Agencies had no depreciatory effect on the trader's
own standing as a careful credit-giver, he must see, in a moment,
that the Agencies' attorneys are not apt to be efficient, in any litigated cases, against the generally more competent lawyers who
will be found retained by the defence.   Is it to be believed that
the Agencies' creature will exert all his energies against an Agency
supporter, or that the Agencies would encourage him to press collections for a small percentage when the withdrawal of subscriptions may reasonably be expected to induce a much greater loss
than any possible profit so obtained?   But even if his utmost
ability were seriously exerted, what security can a creditor have
for prompt returns from a person capable of the personal mean-
ness of giving up his time to double service as an *unpaid* spy and
a *poorly-paid* lawyer?   If he exacted a salary from the Agencies,
even that fact would indicate a certain amount of moral stamina,
and a certain respect for his professional calling ; but, being either
too weak to impose terms, or too eager, from want, to secure even
a pittance of agreed compensation, he is certainly more amenable
to temptation than his more independent and self-asserting
brethren.

A THIRD means of decreasing the evil effects of the Agencies is the very simple one of not applying to them for information. We have shown that, according to their own statements, they cannot really tell whether or not any single trader is good for any single transaction. *Of what service, then, can any statement of his affairs prove which does not go to the extent of justifying a single bargain?* Indeed, must it not be more calculated to *lull* useful inquiry than to *suggest* caution? If a trader exercise ordinary prudence he can form a fresh opinion himself based on the most recent available information; but if he trust ever so little to Agency reports, he is sure to judge from evidence incoherent in itself, in almost every instance, of dubious age, and of dubious origin. Of what value, in the majority of cases, is an opinion six months old? Why should any man part with his goods on the strength of it, when the Agencies confess their own want of confidence in it by stipulating against any liability for imparting it? But over and above all these considerations, have we not shown that the system is the natural parent of constantly-aggravating errors and misreports?

A FOURTH means of lessening the ill effects of the Agencies would be persistent refusal to supply them with unpaid-for information. Why should not a merchant impart whatever he may find necessary or useful *directly to the person or persons from whom he seeks credit?* Already this is done in the vast majority of cases; and the credit-giver is accustomed to write down the statement or to carry it in his mind. He can have it verified or confuted by telegraph or letter within a short time—within as short or shorter time than the Agencies. They must inquire specially, at his special expense, if he insist on the latest attainable rumors. *They must deal with a volunteer unpaid correspondent who insists on keeping behind a mask.* The merchant, on the other hand, can inquire from other merchants of known standing, whose answers would be infinitely preferable, and whose statements, if knowingly erroneous and not coupled with reservations, might even be followed by legal recourse, on fit occasion. Besides insuring known channels of information, this practice, if generally adopted, would also leave the whole non-credit seeking mass of traders free from even the possibility of being injured in character or standing within their self-limited lines and methods of trade. The credit-seeker would not be, could not be, aware of the course of inquiry beforehand, and therefore could not anticipate it. He might rely on a good report from his neighborhood if he had earned a good reputation. If he had not earned it, or the matter were in doubt, he could personally convince the credit-giver of any injustice done him, and indicate the direction from which injurious remarks might have, or might be expected to have, come. In every event, he would have the double satisfaction of knowing that his business affairs were only laid bare to a person rightfully interested in them, and that he merely had one or more known merchants to satisfy instead of the same number supplemented by the loose guesses of a secret series of anonymous correspondents, juvenile clerks, needy credit-raters, or vague-writing managers.

A FIFTH means of correcting the growing wrong of the Agency system would be the prompt request, monthly, of every person whose name appears in the Books *to see the secret report on which it is based.* If the Agencies refuse to show it, *in the original record, book, and page,* to the applicant, he may rely that it is libellous, and should secure counsel who could either cause the name to be suppressed or require the record to be produced, or both. If the Agencies allow the record to be examined on application, the person affected should then choose whether they shall continue to trade in *his* reputation or desist. The result, in either hypothesis, must cripple the system. Of what service to any one except the person rated satisfactorily could the system be, in the one case? In the other, merchants could have no inducement for paying for a system of inquisition which, in its net product, realized the sole perfection of a mutual-admiration coterie.

A SIXTH means, and, to our mind, the fittest of all mentioned, is resort to the law to repress their libels and recover damages, as well, for breaches of contract to supply information correctly under their old or existing subscription contracts. By what right are ten men in the United States and Canada enabled to set themselves up as irresponsible censors of their fellow-citizens' characters and business standing? Simple agreements at large with third parties on the subject are certainly no protection so long as the really interested party's tastes are not consulted. Even if the principle of agency were allowed as a shield, in a single case, where actual trading had been contemplated in good faith, it would be manifestly against public policy to permit universal reporting and irresponsible criticism simply because, *at some time*, one or more thousands of one and a quarter millions of men *might* seek credit from one of thirty thousand other men, subscribers to and employers, so called, of the Agencies. But this is not the whole of the objection. Of the million and over rated and criticised by the Agencies not one half have ever had, or have ever sought to have, a single transaction with the thirty thousand subscribers! How can a theory of constructive agency be stretched so as to cover these innumerable and wholly indefensible interferences with private character and commercial standing? Then, as to the fitness of exacting damages from professional news-givers, what can be fairer than to insist that men who live by the business should lose by it, also, when found destroying their fellow-citizens, for private gain, in character and substance?

Lest the reader should consider these suggestions, however just in themselves, the result of bias in the writer, and any effort to carry them out singular and exceptional, and to be avoided for that reason, we proceed to supplement them by the personal testimony, conveyed to the writer within a single fortnight, of a few of many leading citizens. It will be seen that our advice is already adopted by great numbers of merchants, and that whoever would imitate them need have no fear of being without good company. L. H. P., a leading liquor merchant, says his experience is " that, with the use of an agency, and the expenditure of a bottle " of wine with its spy, he can break the credit and reputation of " his neighbor. He knows of no other purpose it can serve, and " wishes it suppressed."

The President of the —— Savings Bank says : " I have borne " the double relation of subscriber and correspondent. While " acting in the former capacity, I always took care to compliment " my own friends and keep my own credit in the meridian. As " a partner in a firm without more than $30,000 capital I found " no difficulty in getting the agencies to rate the house at $400,- " 000 (!) up to the moment of its failure. I think them a colossal " humbug, and carefully avoid them in the sense of giving a dol- " lar to them."

The President of the —— and ——'s Bank says: " I would not " throw away wine on any of them. A glass of lager is enough to " reach the credit men and raters."

An iron merchant on —— street says : "I never subscribed "to any but McKillop's, and I found they always omitted to rate "me when my subscription was discontinued. I finally got so " indignant I forcibly ejected one of the canvassers from my " office, and kicked his hat after him."

A shipping-house in South street regards them as " blackmail- " ers, to whom he would neither give a statement nor subscription, " and forbade their canvassers to come on our premises. Our "ratings have suffered, and are false, but we are too well known " to care."

A member of another shipping house writes : " A canvasser in- " sinuated that an attack on our credit would be made if we did " not subscribe. His threat is fulfilled. But I regret its vague- "ness prevents legal proceedings, although, to himself, the mean- " ing and malice are quite clear."

Another gentleman, well known as a leading political economist, sends a long letter declaring in the most positive terms that " the " system is a curse, and ought to be abated by legislation."

A hair importer of another city says : " I discovered I was li- " belled through the effort of a rival trader, who used the agency " against me. He pretended to be friendly, but was on the inside. " I now know how to get even, and will surely try."

The President of the N. T. Co. states : " If merchants are "attacked it serves them right for supporting such an institution. " Let them blame themselves, and turn a new leaf."

A gentleman, only second to Henry C. Carey in deep study of the economics of trade, etc., says : " They are dollar and cent con- " cerns, started and continued for a livelihood under a public pre- " tence. I hope to see them placed on the defensive in the press, " in the courts, and in the State legislatures. For my part, I am " quite certain the District Attorneys in some States could take "them in hand criminally."

Mr. H., of H. & A., Wall street, says : " We subscribed at one "time, but, finding the reports vague, incorrect, and useless, dis- " continued. Since then the agencies have thought less of us, " and in their reports say ' the father of one of our firm,' who died " twenty years ago, ' is still interested,' and place us with our " $400,000 capital below where they did when we had not a quar- " ter of it."

A large Broad-street Liquor Merchant regards it the "essence "of recklessness to pay any attention to the reports. It is a quick "way, a perfect short-cut, to Bankruptcy."

A leading Clothier says : "Our traveller lately found an agen- "cy correspondent in league with a trader to purchase all he could "on a favorable report and share the profits. I trust your agita- "tion will give us an organization or common system of action "against them."

These few samples, selected at random from a mass of city correspondence, with two exceptions received within fourteen days, barely give an idea of the extent and depth of feeling already eager to be directed against the obnoxious system. If we were to insert a tenth part of the general denunciation, by letter or word of mouth, of which we have been· made the receiver or hearer within the same period, our book would not contain pages enough to print it in detail. But even these examples will suffice to show the hesitating trader that *his* views are also those of many, many other active and reputable merchants in every city and town in the country, and that he can rely on efficient countenance and support, from this time henceforward, in every justifiable aggressive movement which he may contemplate against the agency system, its aiders and abettors.

While this proof of an' aroused public opinion must be assur- ing to long-patient and long-suffering traders, it carries a very dif- ferent lesson to those who have heretofore freely expressed opin- ions of their neighbors to agency detectives. Such persons must .hear, in these rumblings of an approaching controversy, the pre- sage of disclosures very painful and surprising. Victims will soon be demanding the names of their traducers. Courts will compel discovery. The natural anxiety of informants to avoid disclos- ure ought to be a warning to others that every statement made to the agencies may entail disagreeable consequences and should be sedulously avoided hereafter. A habit of strict refusal to say any- thing about neighbors, under any circumstance, to the minions of the Inquisition, is our last recommendation in this connection. Its wisdom is apparent. The neglect of it, whether from thought-, lessness or misapprehension of the scope and purpose of the system, is certain to bring trouble and annoyance, in the near future, to hundreds who thought they could stab in the dark and never be

detected. What honorable merchant would like to find himself
cheek by jowl with the army of purposeful or purposeless informers ?   Which one, with his own proper business to look after, is
prepared to act as a sleuth-hound, at the whip and beck of every
agency adventurer who may propose to retail, for hire and profit,
neighbors' opinions of each other ?   The occupation is certainly
not very dignified or gracious, at any time.   After the publication
of this book, we think we may say it will also be very apt to become both troublesome and disreputable.

Each of the means above suggested is good, in its way, in the
effort to reduce the harmfulness of the agencies. A few of
them, faithfully persisted in, will give back to injured business
men a large part of the fortunes made out of their characters. The
use, by any respectable number of men, of all the means indicated,
will speedily put an end to the system, and release American commerce from the filthy beak and strident talons of the agency vul-
ture.

CHAPTER XXI.

THE ENORMITY OF THE BLACK LISTS—THE NUMBER OF PERSONS AND AMOUNTS OF INVESTED CAPITAL PLACED UNDER BAN —MUDDLED CREDITS AND PARALYZED TRADE.

Having demonstrated in a preceding chapter, by indubitable proofs extracted from Agency Reference Books, the absurd position occupied by the System, judged with its own standard, it only remains for us to direct attention to the private reports, or *Black Lists*, from which, while favorable ratings appear in the Reference Books, opprobrious matters find constant circulation.

We have seen that small capital ratings are never associated with good credit ratings, even for small amounts; that is, the Agencies do not consider business character or private character, as such, sufficient to determine the right to credit proportionate to recognized capital, or worth recognition. But, on the other hand, large capital, although rated in the Reference Books generally in conjunction with "good" or "high" credit, preserves no fixed relation to business or private character even *in* the Reference Books, and, *outside* of them, in the private reports, is often associated with the most damaging statements. The ordinary reader, consequently, can discover no method of detecting whether or not the private reports of himself are carried into the Reference Book ratings for either low or high capital, and is led, if rated satisfactorily, to believe that his character has *not* been attacked, or, if rated unsatisfactorily, that the worst appears instead of being reserved for private sale and distribution.

On the other hand, the expert in Agency literature written or printed, even if he never read a line of the private reports, can lay his finger in the Reference Books on every name smirched by masked correspondents or secret spies and recorded for permanent blackening. Wherever the least discrimination is shown in the application of the movable *criteria* or symbols to the capital *criteria* or symbols, it is caused by suppressed information or pretended information of a damaging kind; but, as we have said, the absence of such discrimination is no guarantee whatever that matter tending to justify it is *not* on the record. The Agencies are indisposed, except for selfish reasons, to publish low ranges of credit in connection with large capital, and therefore avoid doing so as much as possible; for their subscribers are expected to come from such persons, in the main; but if we deduct *thirty thousand* (present subscribers') names from the lists of the three Agencies, and allow as many more to represent the very highest ranges of capital from which *future* subscribers are to come, we shall still have about *seven hundred thousand* persons *subject* to private detraction or false rating, and outside the purview of a selfish policy of suppression or favoritism. When we are able to say that a *tenth* of the trading population of New-York is on the Black Lists of a single Agency, it will not appear exaggeration when we add that the total number of Merchants and Traders in the United States and Canada *actually* derogatorily written about, to, or in, the three Agencies sum up NINETY THOUSAND, at least!

As we have seen, in a former chapter, how the capital ratings of TWO HUNDRED AND SIXTY-TWO Merchants are made to differ ONE HUNDRED AND THREE MILLIONS OF DOLLARS, it is not difficult to conceive a similar discordance, many times multiplied, between the Agencies, in reference to estimates and reports of *personal character*. Under the most favorable conditions, one man's *real*, as distinguished from his *supposititious*, merit is, necessarily, a puzzle seldom solved and never demonstrable. When we add to the ordinary inherent trouble of determination the accessory drawbacks of distance, anonymity, unfiltered prejudice, or undetected partisanship, the impediments to accuracy become infinite, and even the uninformed are prepared to believe that the contradictions of capital ratings are slight in comparison with the raging incoherencies of the comparative Black Lists on the subject of *character*.

The reader must have noticed, and can recall, several instances in former chapters where a single Agency is found rating Merchants in good credit whose character as business men is assailed with acrimony in the private reports. When persons in good credit by Agency admission are so attacked, it is nothing wonderful to find that persons *not* in good credit by Agency authority suffer to a monstrous extent in the secret archives. Common experience shows that cowardly detraction is seldom lessened by increased immunity from punishment.

The BLACK LISTS, therefore, are the designation we employ to characterize the vast mass of names blackened by slander or charred by envy. An iceberg is known to be two thirds under water. The Black Lists are sunk out of sight with their accumulated weight of multiplied impurities.

The Appendix which follows contains the initials of about TEN THOUSAND Merchants' and Traders' names, with city, State, and business added. It represents selections from the Reports of the three Agencies under late dates, and is the result of several months' almost constant labor. In our second and future editions we propose to enlarge the List until we shall have given, for his *and its personal satisfaction and identification only*, the name and business of every assailed Trader and Corporation in the United States and Canada.

In making up this terrible array of inculpatory matter our purpose was to enable our readers, *individually*, to learn, without *others* doing so, whether or not the Agencies had taken liberties with *their* names. We therefore confine ourselves to initials; and where even this slight clue might, in small places or very peculiar Trades, lead to identification, we have omitted selection. The Lists, taken in connection with the Comparative Tables in Chapter XVIII., supply incontrovertible proof of every allegation made in these pages, and leave our readers in possession of a fund of information not merely novel and convincing, but never before attainable, nor apt to be amplified or extended, except by the author. Its publication will induce and compel such changes in the Agency System that the future inquirer will be wholly at a loss to secure materials, and few, or none, will be found willing to devote the same amount of labor or time to their compilation. Luckily the author's opportunities for enlarging his proofs and exposing the Agencies can only cease with the System; for while they continue to publish he can continue to confute, and will assuredly do so. In some form, it may even become necessary and desirable to business men that a weekly record of Agency mistakes, omissions, calumnies, etc., should be made up and circulated, and the recep-

tion of this volume will show whether there exists a desire for a
cheaper, more convenient, and periodical form of current corrections, accessible to business men, side by side with the costly and
cumbersome Agency System infamies.

Our immediate duty, however, is with the Black Lists and
such portions of them as are appended. How *can* any rational
being wonder at the condition of trade when told that this vast
army of maligned Merchants and Traders is simply the advance-
guard of a host of other Merchants and Traders who may finally
number SIX HUNDRED THOUSAND! Even in the cities selected for
illustration we only cull a few names out of the general mass.
The vast multitude is not notably lessened. In all its mighty pro-
portions of numbers, wealth, accumulated hopes and aspirations, it
awaits the next roll-call. Why, if a foreigner were to hear from
these Agencies that the proportion of reputable and trustworthy
Merchants and Traders in the United States was less than *ten per
cent*, could we blame him for believing that our social fabric was
incorrigibly rotten? And yet the passivists will say it makes no
matter how much the Agencies belie or misreport so long as only
a few dozen persons, in the case of each trader, are let into the
secret! They forget that the falsehoods or libels themselves are
not reduced in intensity by the method of repetition, and that the
aggregate result to the business character of the country is pre-
cisely the same as if hundreds were made the confidants of the
Agencies in each instance. All who have reason to ask are
answered; *and those ask whose opinion, when formed, assists to
assure success or failure in trade to the person inquired about.*
What else is wanted to leave the Trade of the country and
commercial confidence both prostrate so far as Agencies can prostrate them?

Even if we leave out of account the wrong committed on private
feelings, or the danger to individual prospects, here are thousands of
millions of business capital confessedly in the hands of cheats or
swindlers! Is it nothing to throw a cloud round the utilization of
this wealth? to place its owners in a sort of moral quarantine destructive to energy and only reached by the desperate? Our experience with Agency capital estimates was certainly bad enough, but
in all that ministers to evil, and evil only, these character-killings
of the Black Lists are inconceivably the most infamous and most

deadly to legitimate commerce. If they enable our readers to exact relief and redress, our labor in compiling them will have been amply rewarded.

To renew our line of argument:

I. We set out to prove that the Agency "System" was a sham and a swindle of the first magnitude in its MANAGEMENT. *We have produced its own records to abundantly support this claim.*

II. We proposed to show that it was really no *System*, having neither coherent principle nor coherent illustration in its length or breadth! *The chapter on the "Keys" and the chapter illustrating the discordance of the Agencies as to third parties and each other, are conclusive on these questions.*

III. We commenced writing with the design of fairly discussing the right of such an anomalous "Institution" to exist in an intelligent community at all, or without special legislation directed against its abuse. *Who can say we have come to a negative conclusion without careful study or from an insufficient array of facts?*

IV. We designed to suggest to the business classes remedial measures against the System. What the suggestion in regard to Guarantee Companies does not provide for is amply compensated by the maxim sedulously inculcated throughout these pages, *Cease to support it; try legal conclusions with it, if wronged!*

It only remains for us to anticipate the methods in which the System will essay to meet our arguments:

I. *Its first effort will be to stop the circulation of this work.* To defeat this purpose we rely on the justice of Courts, the goodwill of the independent press, and the assistance of the long-suffering and grossly-betrayed business public.

II. *Its second device will be to assail the author.* If *he* have anything in his humble life to specially regret more seriously than his association with the System, he has yet to learn it.

III. *The third and last effort will be either to combat his reasoning or join issue on his facts.* This is the least likely of all, but the one which the writer naturally desires. Should the System, however, find *one* defender, we shall challenge him,

Firstly, To point to a single line in the work which is *not* a rational deduction from facts stated in it.

Secondly, To CONTRADICT, BY PROOF, A SINGLE ALLEGATION OF FACT IN THE WHOLE BOOK !

If we have written with warmth betimes, we have been unconscious of the spirit of either malice or uncharitableness. If, on looking over our pages, we see much that might be bettered, *we see nothing which we have not original proof to sustain and illustrate.* Our fears are caused by a sense of our incapacity to do justice to the subject; we have none about either the amount of preparation or the material at our disposal.

But whether the Agencies enter on a labored defence or not, they are sure to rely somewhat on the use of their cheap talent for private circulars. These will reach subscribers—will be practically exclusive and difficult for the *outside public* or the *author* to obtain—and may be made more efficient in retaining patronage than all other instrumentalities combined. They possess all the advantages of partisan statements without entailing the penalty of open confutation like a newspaper article or a pamphlet issued for general reading. We must rely on some one of our readers for any specimen of this kind of missile which may be stealthily put into his hand. The open defence, if any, we can find for ourselves.

One additional device occurs to us. The Agencies are certain to revamp and republish an *old collection* of Commendatory Letters written by a few subscribers, years ago, in return for overrating. These letters are simply poor imitations of the ones found in any Cherry Pectoral almanac or in any Stomach Bitters pronunciamento. When not manufactured outright, they are simply eulogies compiled by knaves for misleading fools.

Recommendations dated *subsequent to the reading* of this publication would not deserve the same characterization—for we are bound to believe the writers must proceed on some knowledge of their topic; but we predict that they will be so few that the apocalyptic duty of eating them would be within the capacity of an ordinary digestion.

CHAPTER XXII.

LAST WORDS.

So far of the past. What is the best method of crippling this dangerous and destructive system in the future?

Most of the suggestions already made are limited in application to subscribers. Those about to be made may be acted on by the whole trading community, and, on our theory, should be carried out promptly and persistently until relief from the Agency incubus shall have been attained.

One of the most effective of weapons will be the accumulation at some centre, for prompt distribution, of proofs of Agency errors, whether arising from ignorance or malice. It will readily occur to a merchant who has, at any time, been deceived by Agency reports, that the value of his information depends wholly on giving it publicity, and, so far as may be, in connection with like information from other merchants. Its point, too, will greatly depend on its circulation in the neighborhood where it originated, and might have quick confirmation in the personal experience of other traders. Given a common depository, nothing will be more easy than to direct these proofs, in the most efficient way, at the system, and so preserve a constant fire along the whole line of Agency occupation. The writer will be glad to constitute himself this common repository.

Even superior in importance to this gathering of proofs is the necessity that they should be irrefragable and incontestable. The opponents of the System must not imitate its looseness of statement, or looseness of reasoning. What is not capable of judicial demonstration to a common intent should not be used. Whatever contains an element of inference should be strictly scrutinized if not wholly disregarded. Where personal feelings might essay to get a hearing, they should be watched, weighed, and eliminated.

In illustration of the great care which should be exercised in accepting statements, even at one remove, we cannot do better than mention our own cautiousness in the same connection. Since the appearance of our Prospectus we have been pestered with innumerable offers of testimony against the Agencies from their Managers, Ex-Managers, and Clerks, but we have not taken a single illustration from their experience, fearing that, as our time did not permit us to go to the various places referred to and verify the tendered evidence, we might fall into even unintentional error and give expression to individual griefs and selfish purposes. When, for instance, one De Lestre, an Agency employee, wrote from Utica that "he knew of several instances of *undermining* the merchants of that city," and would be glad to place the information at our service; or when one Francey, in like employment, informed us, among other things, that the Erie *Dispatch* had shown certain favor to the institution, and several others tendered us lists of correspondents and damaging details for a consideration, we threw their propositions in the waste-basket. We could not give any weight to statements incapable of ready proof, and disregarded them at once. Each merchant must exercise a similar watchfulness in taking nothing for granted, and only vouch for alleged facts near at hand and capable of instant verification if disputed.

If subscribers have strong motives to assist in furnishing evidences of Agency mistakes and mismanagement, *non*-subscribers have infinitely more reasons for doing so. Non-subscribers are the subjects of Agency dissection for the pretended benefit of subscribers. Their character and standing are the System's stock-in-trade. Their financial assistance, through yearly subscriptions, is one of the constantly-pursued objects of Agency effort. If they would escape the alternative of propitiating Dagon by gifts, or of being in hourly fear of his malignity, let them strike hands with every man who has already set his face against the monster, and who proposes to destroy him. The ruined may retrieve themselves in time; but it behooves *selected* victims, as well, to do everything in their power to escape either the penalties of a worshipper or the pains of a sacrifice.

We have now finished our initiatory work in these subterranean crypts, and are about to emerge again into the open air. 'Tis a pleasing riddance—the escape, even for a short time, from the rank vapors of these lower regions, reeking with fœtid exhalations of assailed or decaying characters. But some one must have gone down into their depths to explore and expose their secrets, and we are confident that, however poorly we have performed our duty, the world of business will be the better for it.

Much that we could have added must wait for another occasion. We could not wisely have given more sample facts, for we rather wish to gain the attention of the public to a great outrage, and enlist it in a campaign for its extirpation, than to exhaust resources which, to be most effective, must be held in a prudent reserve and only applied to revive a flagging interest or reinforce a waning controversy. Like any other agitation, the one initiated by the writer against the Commercial Agency System in America should *grow* with discussion, and should be supplied, in its progress, with new weapons and missiles suited to the varying phases of the contest. He is not a careful soldier who brings all his troops into action at the opening of the engagement. The knowledge of a powerful reserve force is also as encouraging to friends as dispiriting to the enemy. We have this reserve, and intend to use it where and when it may reasonably be hoped to do most good to paralyzed trade and sadly-beset traders.

As for the Agency system itself, this work places it on trial in the United States and Canada. We call upon it to plead, and go to the country on the issue framed. Here is our evidence in part. Where is theirs to contradict or refute it?

The question is not, " What is the writer's motive?" although we can argue on motives, if necessary; but, " Can his facts be refuted?" Not, " Does he hope to be benefited by assailing the institution?" but, " Is the institution, in its principle or as conducted, fit to exist in a free community?" We say it is not, call on its defenders to come forth, and, with an assured faith in the outcome, leave the result to the final opinion of an intelligent press and an educated public.

The Detective and Informer belong to the paths of illicit trade or the skulking-places of accomplished crime. They should have no countenance in the marts of legitimate commerce or among the men whose pre-eminent achievements have placed us in the position of one of the Great Powers of the World.

If we *must* have Inquiry, let it be open, straightforward, re-

sponsible, intelligent, interested inquiry, affording facilities to both
Creditor and Debtor, Buyer and Seller, amenable to both, and regu-
lated by Law; an Inquiry befitting the manliness of the American
character, and recognizing its fitness to be judged by the highest
standards of business probity and commercial honor.

THE

SECRET

BLACK LISTS

OF THE

"SYSTEM."

PART I.

EMBRACING THE PRINCIPAL COMMERCIAL AND
MANUFACTURING CENTRES IN THE

United States and Canada.

NEW-YORK CITY.

A——I................Pawnbroker.
A——P.............Ret. Clothing.
A——G. W..................Stocks.
A——J. L..........Cotton Brokers.
A——J. E.........R. R. Contractor.
A——& C——.................Hotel.
A——& H——.........Com'n Flour.
A——J. S......India-Rubber Broker.
A——J.................Beer Saloon.
A——N..............'...Painter.
A——S. & Son..............Tailors.
A——A..Ret. Hats and Men's Furn'g.
A——P...........Boots and Shoes.
A——& C——...Com'n Tob. and Cig.
A——B. N......Sewing M. Findings.
A——C........... ......Mnfr. Boxes.
A——G. B....Whol. Wines and Liq.
A——J. H...............Stoves, etc.
A——I......................Watches.
A——G. & Son.......Wheelwrights.
A——J........................Tailor.
A——W. A. & Co..............Teas.
A——B. F..Com'n Prod. and Confec.
A——S. M...........Glass Stainer.
A——W. C..............Bottles, etc.
A——W. E...................Prov.
A——W. H., Jr.........Pickles, etc.
A——G—— & Co.........Chemicals.
A——H. M. & Co..........Liquors.
A——McH—— & Co...Stock Brokers.
A——R. W. & Co.......Lumber, etc.
A——& A——......Jobbers and Ret.
                                    Cloths.
A——& Co.................Jewelry.
A——M. M....Ret. Fancy Goods, etc.
A——M.............Com'n Trim'gs.
A——M.............Jobber Jewelry.
A——W....................Tailor.
A——A...................Flour.
A——I—— W——.......Founders.
A——F..........Artificial Flowers.
A——S—— & Co........Flour Mills.
A——J....................Saloon.
A——& D——........Leaf Tobacco.
A——H. F..................Coal.

A——J. G. H..............Liquors.
A——& F——.................Gro.
A——& B——.......Com'n Flour and
                                    Storage.
A——& F——.......Sugar Refiners.
A——W. C.........R. E. Broker.
A——F—— P—— Co..............
A——W. E. & Co......Spring Beds.
A——W. H.................Builder.
A——L............Boots and Shoes.
A——M.........Ret. Millinery.
A——& Co....................Drugs.
A——C. G. & Co....Mnfg. Jewellers.
A——B—— & Co.....Refrigerators.
A——C. C.............Stock Broker.
A——Mrs. F...Hoopskirts and Fancy
                                    Goods.
A——G. C.................Watches.
A——H.......Ret. Boots and Shoes.
A——J. H................Drugs.
A——D. Sons.........Jobbers Rope.
A——H. B. & Co.......Printers' Ink.
A——J. T. & Co..........Furniture.
A——L—— and P—— Co..........
A——& Co.................Tobacco.
A——& S.........Lumber, etc.
A——G. B. & Co.....Stock Brokers.
A——E. S..........Wine and Fruit.
A——Bros..............Ins. Agents.
A——R...........Felt Horse Cloths.
A——& J——......Jobbers Hosiery.
A——C....Optician and Mathematical
                                    Insts.
A——Bros..........Hops and Malt.
A——& Co............Upholsterers.
A——& K——...........Ret. D. G.
A——& H——............:.Rectifiers.
A——J. C...................Tailor.
A——G. B., Jr., Agent.....Ret. Hats.
American B—— T—— Co...........
American B—— B—— Co...........
American C—— Co.................
American D—— D—— Co.
American E—— C—— Co.
American F—— Co.

American F—— D—— Co.
American G—— W—— C—— and
   S—— Co.
American G—— Co.
American M—— and B—— Co.
American P—— C—— Co.
American P—— I—— T—— Co.
American P—— F—— Co.
American P—— L——. Co
American P—— P—— P—— Co.
American P—— Co.
American S—— S—— B—— H——
   M—— Co.
American S—— E—— Co.
American S—— Co...........Plating.
American W—— P—— Co.
American Z—— Co.
A—— R.................R. E. Agent.
A—— & T——...Druggists' Sundries.
A—— J. H.............Cabinetmaker.
A—— A.............Press Rooms.
A—— J. C.................Jeweller.
A—— J....................Drugs.
A—— S............Whol. Hats, etc.
A—— W................Crockery.
A—— & Co................Shipping.
A—— C................Machinery.
A—— C. E..........Ret. Millinery.
A—— & S——.......Whol. Millinery.
A—— G. N...................Drugs.
A—— E. C..........Turkish Baths.
A—— W. B., Agent.........Liquors.
A—— A—— R—— Co...Felt Roofing.
A—— J................Ret. D. G.
A—— & Co.......Sashes and Blinds.
A—— & G——.......Jobbers Jewelry.
A—— A.....Ladies' Undergarments.
A—— S. H..Peddler Millinery Goods.
A—— L. L. F.........Tob. and Cig.
A—— R.............Tobacco Broker.
A—— A........Shipping and Com'n
A—— C. S.,.........Whol. Liquors.
A—— W. A.....Ret. Hats and Caps.
A—— J. L.................Teas, etc.
A—— W. T...........Fruit Dealer.
A—— P—— Co.......Mnfrs. Pianos.
A—— T—— & Co..Shipping and Com.
A—— A. J..................Stables.
A—— J. G............Liq. and Res't.
A—— J. E...Coffees, Teas, and Spices.
A—— T. W...................Stoves.
A—— E. V. & Co...........Printers.
A—— & B——...Saddles and Harness.
A—— L...................Clothing.
A—— J. & W——....Mnfrs. Hats and
   Caps.
A—— J. E...................Feed.
A—— Mfg. Co.........Gas Fixtures.
A—— & W——.....Essential Oils and
   Drugs.
A—— J. & L......Ret. Men's Furn'g.

A—— & A——.Mnfrs. and Com. Mers.
A—— S. J..Mnfr. Ladies' Underwear.
A—— H............Glass and Frames.
A—— N..............Paper collars.
A—— F—— Co.........Mnfrs. Felt.
A—— S.........Mnfr. Ladies' Suits.
A—— G. A.................Shirts.
A—— M..............Mnfr. Caps.
A—— & B——...,.......Plumbers.
A—— P.......Ret. Fancy Goods.
A—— & A——..Mnfrs. Ladies' Suits.
A—— & R——..Mnfrs. Lace and Hair
   Goods.
A—— W. T..................Fruit.
A—— & M——.............Hotel.
A—— A. D.............Undertaker.
A—— J.............Ret. Millinery.
A—— W. B................Liquors.
A—— & T——.............Hardware.
A—— & B——.............Stationery.
A—— T. H................Liquors.
A—— T. & Co ....Com'n Prod.
A—— E. M..........R. E. Broker.
A—— T. S.......Mnfr. White Lead.
A—— C. B. & Co....Mnfrs. Ribbons.
A—— J......German Fruit and Prod.
A—— J..........Whol. Clothing.
A—— J....................Gro.
A—— W. F....Auction Fancy Goods.
A—— P—— Co.
A—— H—— and G—— Co.
A—— S—— V—— P—— Mnfg. Co.
A—— J........Metropolitan Bakery.
A—— G. W...........Lithographer.
A—— T—— ....Coppersmith.
A—— & Co.........Paper Fashions.
A—— J....................Printer.
A—— A......Mnfr. Boots and Shoes.
B—— C. B., Jr...............Tailor.
B—— J. A.............Plated Ware.
B—— E. & Son........Leaf Tobacco.
B—— Bros.......Ret. Clothing.
B—— S—— & Co.....Imps. Window
   Glass.
B—— S......Mnfr. Balmoral Skirts.
B—— Bros.........Jobbers Cloth.
B—— M. M. & Co............ Furs.
B—— E. F...........Jobber Cloth.
B—— Bros.............Gasburners.
B—— & K——...............Pianos.
B—— J...........Peddler D. G.
B—— M............. Ret. Hats.
B—— & M——.........Note Brokers.
B—— M. B...........,.R. E. Agent.
B—— H... ....Shipping and Com'n.
B—— G. F..........Mnfg. Jeweller.
B—— & B——.........Silverplaters.
B—— & C——...............Marble.
B—— H. E........Mnfr. Cane Fibre.
B—— H ....Spring Beds.
B—— H. & Son........R. E. Brokers.

B—— & C——..Fish, Prov. and Prod.	B—— & Sons............ Founders.
B—— & Co.............Coal Brokers.	B—— F. J..............Dyewoods.
B—— E. J...........Liquor Broker.	B—— P—— & H——.....Dyeing, etc.
B—— C...........Butter and Cheese.	B—— J. H..............Diamonds.
B—— A. F.................Lumber.	B—— & B——...........Mnfrs. Shoes.
B—— J. H............House Furn'g.	B—— J................Paper, etc.
B—— Bros. & Co............Express.	B—— J. W...............Liquors.
B—— R. J.............Syrups, etc.	B—— Bros...........Flour and Feed.
B—— P—— Co.	B—— M....................Cigars.
B—— G. H.................Hosiery.	B—— C....................Com'n.
B—— Bros............Mnfrs. Shirts.	B—— H. K........Jobber and Com'n.
B—— G. & J....Imps. German Linen.	B—— & S——..........Jobbers Tea.
B—— C. C...........Mnfr. Shirts.	B—— & S——......Mnfrs. Jewelry.
B——V......Mnfr. Ostrich Feathers.	B—— G. Z.................Bottles.
B—— R. & Co.....Prod. and Com'n.	B—— E.................Saddlery.
B—— & G——.....Ladies' Undergarments.	B—— W. H................Tailor.
	B—— C. B........Repairer Jewelry.
B—— Bros.....Shipping and Com'n. Prov., etc.	B—— J. B........Butter, Cheese, etc.
B—— J................Ret. Clothing.	B—— J. E....Domestic Gloves.
B—— J. S......Mnfr. Hats and Caps.	B—— M....................Stoves.
B—— F. J..............Restaurant.	B—— I. & F——......Leaf Tobacco.
B—— H. F.....House Furn'g Goods.	B—— W...........Ret. Shoes.
B—— Bros ....Clothing.	B—— A—— & Co....Mnfrs. Clothing.
B—— T—— & B—— Co.......Trusses	B—— W. A.........Com'n Tobacco.
B—— P................Contractor.	B—— A...........Artificial Flowers.
B—— S...............Ret. Clothing.	B—— E., Est. of.......House Furn'g.
B—— J.............Metal Roofer.	B—— J..............Ret. D. G.
B—— W. J...........Wigs and Hair.	B—— P.....................D. G.
B—— Bros..............Lumber, etc.	B—— M—— Co.........Ag'l Implts.
B—— J. F............Com'n Prod.	B—— J. A.................Clocks.
B—— L.............Mnfr. Clothing.	B—— T. & Son.............Printers.
B—— M....................Gro.	B—— T. H. & Co.....Fishing Tackle.
B—— O. H............Mnfr. Skirts.	B—— S—— & Co...Mnfrs. Straw Gds.
B—— S. W...............Banker.	B—— & Co.............Patent Meds.
B—— C. N. & Co............Bankers.	B—— & Co............Jobbers Tea.
B—— J. T. & Sons....Wood and Coal.	B—— C. M...........Wool Broker.
B—— C.........Mnfr. Cigar-Boxes.	B—— F. W.................Teas.
B—— J. O.............Paint Broker.	B—— A................Broker D. G.
B—— P....................Printer.	B—— E................Furniture.
B—— Bros.......Ret. Men's Furn'g.	B—— Bros....Mnfrs. Boots and Shoes.
B—— L. W. & Son......Canned Soup.	B—— & F——...............Gro.
B—— & B——.....D. G. Brokers and Com'n Mers.	B—— A.................Teas.
	B—— & Co....Shipping and Com'n.
B—— & J——..............Fruits.	B—— M. & Co.....Manfrs. Shirts and Drawers.
B—— I.................Pawnbroker.	
B—— J..Foreign and Domestic Fruit.	B—— & K——..........Willowware.
B—— J........Ret. Boots and Shoes.	B—— H. H.................Banker.
B—— S.& M——..........Leaf Tob.	B—— W. C...........Grain Broker.
B—— & K——...........Furniture.	B—— E. W. & Co.........Furniture.
B—— & Son.........Foreign Fruits.	B—— J. C. & Sons........Chandlers.
B—— A. J.................Liquors.	B—— S—— C—— T—— Co.
B—— G. W....Watches, Chains, etc.	B—— S—— E—— Co.
B—— C....................Baker.	B—— G. D..........Liquor Broker.
B—— & Co.....Shipping and Com'n.	B—— B..........Pipes and Tobacco.
B—— C.............Manfr. Clothing.	B—— M.........Ret. Fancy Goods.
B—— T....................Hotel.	B—— M.................Auctioneer.
B—— J....................Tailor.	B—— S....................Painter.
B—— C. & Co..........Bookbinders.	B—— L. P. & Co......Stock Brokers.
B—— J..................Butcher.	B—— E. R..........Agent Furniture.
B—— S. R....................Gro.	B—— W. D..........Mnfr. Bonnets.
	B—— N. B.................Painter.

B—— I. & Son	Imps. Toys, etc.
B—— D. N.	R. R. Ties.
B—— J. W. & Sons	Prov.
B—— W. H. & Co	Mnfrs. Laces and Embroideries.
B——H. M. & Son	Coopers.
B—— A. W. & Co	Bond Dealers.
B—— & J——	Homœopathic Meds.
B—— S. B.	Cotton Broker.
B—— E. L.	Shipping and Com'n.
B—— & G——	Jobbers Fancy Goods.
B—— A.	Paper Collars and Cuffs.
B—— J.	Artificial Flowers.
B—— C.	Liquors.
B—— J.	Plumber.
B—— W. L.	Drugs.
B—— W.	Gro.
B—— M.	Hardware.
B—— A.	Oysters.
B—— E. W.	Braids.
B—— J. L.	Pianofortes.
B—— C.	Leather and Findings.
B—— O.	Tobacco.
B—— A. & Son	R. E. Brokers.
B—— A. H. & Co	S. M. Needles.
B—— & G——	Com'n Paper.
B—— L. & T. H.	R. E. Brokers.
B—— & Bro	Gro.
B—— W. N.	Hardware.
B—— P. F.	Liquors.
B—— J. W.	Painter.
B—— J.	Liquors.
B——S. & Co.	Com'n Prod.
B—— A.	Whol. Gro.
B—— M.	Trusses.
B—— A. & J.	Mnfrs. Curled Hair.
B—— & H——	Brushes.
B—— J.	Ret. Fancy Goods.
B—— W. H.	Rules.
B—— & P——	Stained Glass.
B—— G. H.	—— Nickel Works.
B—— L. F.	Brassworker.
B—— W. S.	Mnfr. Hair Goods.
B—— A. C.	Tailor.
B—— J. W.	Tailor, etc.
B——I. Jr. & Co	Com'n Cotton, etc.
B—— J. A. & Co	Plumbers.
B—— J. & Co.	Carpenters.
B—— & B——	Ret. Clothing.
B—— & Co.	Gen'l Com'n.
B—— & K——	Mnfrs. Plastique Goods.
B—— W. H.	R. E. Broker.
B—— R. T.	Hair.
B—— W.	Ret. Hats, Clothing, etc.
B—— W.	Builder, etc.
B—— G. H.	Stocks.
B—— L.	Ret. Boots and Shoes.
B—— J. & Co	Human Hair.
B—— J.	Men's Furn'g.
B—— J. E.	Patternmaker.
B—— C. F.	Restaurant.
B—— C. W.	Paper.
B—— C. P.	Linen Collars.
B—— M.	Meat.
B—— Bros.	Jewellers.
B—— C. A. & S. H.	Undertakers.
B—— L. & Sons.	Prod.
B—— F. A.	Leaf Tobacco.
B—— I.	Jobber Shirts.
B—— J. P.	Shoe Findings and Fittings.
B—— L.	Fancy Goods.
B—— & W——	Fish.
B—— D.	Mdse. Broker.
B—— I.	Leather and Findings.
B—— H.	Ret. Boots and Shoes.
B—— C. H. & Co.	Brokers and Dealers Syrups, etc.
B—— B.	Ret. Boots and Shoes.
B—— B.	Sailmaker.
B—— G.	Corks.
B—— S. T.	Liquors.
B—— W.	Paints.
B—— Z. R.	Printer.
B—— A. V.	Artists' Materials.
B—— M. J.	Ladies' and Children's Underwear.
B—— D. & A.	Leaf Tobacco.
B—— B.	Flour.
B—— J. McJ. & Co.	Tobacco Inspectors.
B—— A.	Tea Broker.
B—— J. H.	Wool.
B—— Bros.	Carriages.
B—— G—— & Co	Shipping and Com'n.
B—— J.	Hardware.
B—— G.	Gilder, etc.
B—— R.	Books.
B—— G. N.	Umbrellas, etc.
B—— S.	Stoves.
B—— L.	Pianos.
B—— & L——	Bonnet Frames.
B—— E.	Mnfr. Cigars.
B—— M.	Confec.
B—— L. & Co.	Tob. and Cig.
B—— H.	Liquors.
B—— J.	Ret. Boots and Shoes.
B—— G.	Liquors.
B—— J.	Carpets.
B—— A.	Ret. Fancy Goods.
B—— A. & Co.	Mnfrs. Jewelry.
B—— B. J.	Kid Gloves.
B—— B.	Com'n Foreign D. Goods.
B—— H.	Butcher.
B—— Mrs. M.	Ret. Fancy G.
B—— I.	Ret. Fancy Goods.
B—— A. & Co.	Men's Furn'g.
B—— & M——	Mnfrs. Fringes, etc.
B—— I—— & R——	Pencils, etc.
B—— C.	Tailor.

B—— F............,.........Restaurant.
B—— S.......Ret. Shoes and Trunks.
B—— J. F. & Co....Pawnbrokers and
Diamond Dealers.
B—— & U——.........Stock Brokers.
B—— C. W......Shipping and Com'n.
B—— P. D........Mnfr. Pocketbooks.
B—— C.....................Tailor.
B—— R............Repacker Fruit.
B—— & H——...........Trimmings.
B—— P....................Trimmings.
B—— W. J. & Co......Imps. Linens,
White Goods, etc.
B—— L......................Gro.
B—— B—— & Co......R. E. Brokers.
B—— G. & Co..........Auctioneers.
B—— J. H. & Bro.............Hotel.
B—— & C——............Ret. D. G.
B—— E. & Co.........Com'n Cotton.
B—— & Co.........Financial Agents.
B—— & Bro....Tinware and Roofers.
B—— R.....................Tailor.
B—— J.....................Pianos.
B—— J....................Hardware.
B—— L—— & Co.....Imps. Toys, etc.
B—— W. H.....Baking Powder, etc.
B—— M—— Co......Soda Apparatus.
B—— H.............Ship Chandler.
B—— Bros. & Co...............Bags.
B—— I.....................Tobacco.
B—— H. E...................Hotel.
B—— & W——..............Organs.
B—— C & Co................Stoves.
B—— F. & Co.....Imps. Upholstery.
B—— S. Son........Printers' Rollers.
B—— A........... ....Com'n Liquors.
B—— I...............Ret. Millinery.
B—— J. C......Ret. Boots and Shoes.
B—— P. J....................Cigars.
B—— J. & Co....Shipping and Com'n.
B—— H.....................Tinsmith.
B—— G. & Co................Books.
B—— C.....Com'n Broom Corn, etc.
B—— O. P....................Wines.
B—— & Co........R. E. Auctioneers.
B—— & W——......Whol. Liquors.
B—— A. J....................Baker.
B—— W..................Sailmaker.
B—— J. W..............Perfumery.
B—— & S——.................Gro.
B—— J.............Horseshoeing.
B—— M.....................Shirts.
B—— C. Jr.......Ret. Fancy Goods.
B—— C. S.....House Furn'g Goods.
B—— & C——.................Oils.
B—— S. Son & Co..German Prod., etc.
B—— G.....................Toys.
B—— H.......Jobber Men's Furn'g.
B—— I.....................Cigars.
B—— S. H. & Co....Jobbers White G.
B—— W. T.................Varnish.

B—— F. W..........Felt Cushions.
B—— W....:........Carriage Trim'gs.
B—— C. F..................Printer.
B—— I. & Bro....Ret. Fancy Goods.
B—— & B——......Imps. and Jobbers
Fancy Goods.
B—— & R——...........D. G., etc.
B—— K—— & Co.....Mnfrs. Shirts.
B—— & Co..........Feed and Grain.
B—— & S——.........Ret. Clothing.
B—— S.................Ret. Shoes.
B—— & O——...............Pianos.
B—— Bros........Ret. F'cy and D. G.
B—— R. S...............Com'n Prod.
B—— A. J....................D. G.
B—— E. M......Ret. Wines and Liq.
B—— J. N...................Liquors.
B—— L................Jobber D. G.
B—— Bros.........Jobbers Hosiery.
B—— B....................Liquors.
B—— I.............Wines and Liq.
B—— L...........Tailors' Trim'gs.
B—— S. & Bro.......Stoves and Tins.
B—— & C——.........Leaf Tobacco.
B—— E., Jr...........Mnfr. Paints.
B—— J. A..............Ret. Laces.
B—— W..........Mnfr. Trunks, etc.
B—— H..................... ...Coal.
B—— H. M.........Whol. Straw G.
B—— L...............Straw Goods.
B—— Bros...............Medicines.
B—— F.......................Gro.
B—— G. M.................Watches.
B—— A.....................Stoves.
B—— Mrs. J..................Coal.
B—— & T——....Homœopathic Books
and Med.
B—— A. W..........Cabinet-maker.
B—— C. L.....Note, Stock, and Gold
Broker.
B—— S. M............Stock Broker.
B—— & G——........Stationery, etc.
B—— J. L........Ret. Men's Furn'g.
B—— T..............Ret. D. G.
B—— & S——.............Furniture.
B—— H.......................Gro.
B—— & B........Mineral Waters.
B—— E. D.........Livery Stable.
B—— C... ....Cabinetmkr.
B—— J.........Toys, Whips, etc.
B—— W. F......Paper Warehouse.
B—— D.....Imp. Italian and French
Prod.
B—— T...........Engraver, etc.
B—— & P——.......Mnfrs. Cigars.
B—— F. Jr. & Bro.......Pianofortes.
B—— J. & Co........Stock Brokers.
B—— S. W. & Co.....Stock Brokers.
B—— H. H..................Banker.
B—— & D——.............Presses.
B—— R.....................Painter.

B—— S................Boilermkr.	B—— & N——... ....Carpenters.
B—— & C——...Crockery, Chinaware, etc.	B—— J. G...............Furniture.
	B—— F............Stationery, etc.
B—— L.......Jobber Hats and Caps.	B—— O..............Foreign Fruit.
B—— & S——...............Tailors.	B—— C................Builder.
B—— M.........Ret. Fancy Goods.	B—— A...............Bookseller.
B—— & C——....Printers and Stat'rs.	B—— Coal Co.
B—— H..............Restaurant.	B—— J....................Liquors.
B—— P..........Canned Fruits.	B—— P.............. ....Liquors.
B—— F...............Tailor.	B—— L—— Co....Lithographers and Printers.
B—— T. E...........S. Am. Com'n.	
B—— L.................Tailor.	B—— Son & Co..Shipping and Com'n.
B—— F. E...Com'n Rivets, Bolts, etc.	B—— F. L.................Butcher.
B—— G...............Liquors.	B—— J. & Co..........Manfrs. Desks.
B—— L...................Gro.	B—— J. A............Com'n Prod.
B—— & F——........Cabinetmkrs.	B—— G. R. & Son........Hardware.
B—— M—— & Co.......Com'n Prod.	B—— J. B. & Co............Carriages.
B—— & Z——.......Cotton Brokers.	B—— N. S.........Com'n Paper.
B—— A. & Co.......Com'n Flour and Grain.	B—— R. B. & Co.......Paper Stock.
	B—— N. H...........Ship Broker.
B—— E. C.............Com'n Furs.	B—— C. I..........Jobber Millinery.
B—— J.................Liquors.	B—— & M——...............Prod.
B—— & S——....Auction and Com'n.	B—— J. P........German Silverware.
B—— P.......Ret. Fancy Goods.	B—— V. W.................Drugs.
B—— W.H...........Ret. Clothing.	B—— W. Jr. & Co......Mnfrs. B. & S.
B—— J. M......Com'n Fancy Goods.	B—— J. W...............Builder.
B——W. J. & Co...Drug and Chemical Brokers.	B—— D. B..........Com'n Liquors.
	B—— Van V—— & Co..Stock Brokers.
B—— W ....Patternmkr.	B—— H.................Liquors.
B—— J. J. & Bro......Iron Railings.	B—— G. H..................Coal.
B—— D............Crockery.	B—— M...............Tobacco.
B—— G........ Mnfr. Skirts.	B—— Bros.............Furs, etc.
B—— & S——.........Wheelwrights.	B—— F...Exchange and Ticket Office.
B—— J. W.........Grain, Feed, etc.	B—— S............Mnfr. Trimmings.
B—— R...............H. Tea Co.	B—— & Co............Scroll Mill.
B—— & G——.........Jobbers Flour.	B—— L.........Ret. Hats, etc.
B—— W. J.................Iron.	B—— H...........Glass Moulds.
B—— F. ...Mnfr. Children's Carriages.	B—— H. D. & J. U........Shipping.
B—— T. W............Tip Printing.	B—— C. C......Ret. Boots and Shoes.
B—— E. A......Com'n Fancy Goods.	B—— L. & Son.........Ret. B. & S.
B—— Bros...............Ret. D. G.	B—— & W.............Zincworkers.
B—— J. A.............Sail Duck.	B—— A. E.........Exchange Broker.
B—— E...............House Furn'g.	B—— C. A.........Eureka Solvent.
B—— J. S..............Engravings.	B—— De W. C...........Coffee-Pots.
B—— S. L.................Builder.	B—— E.................Machinist.
B—— P—— & Co.........Carriages.	B—— E. S............Com'n Grain.
B—— A. P........Ret. Men's Furn'g.	B—— J. B..W. I. Shipping and Com'n.
B—— & T——.......Fruit Brokers.	B—— J...........Brewers' Supplies.
B—— & O——...........Whol. Gro.	B—— J................Clothing.
B—— C............Kindling-Wood.	B—— J.............Ret. Hats.
B—— J.............Ret. Hats.	B—— J. H......Hats, Caps, Furs, etc.
B—— & Son............Dentists.	B—— L.................Drugs.
B—— N. S.............Jewelry.	B—— M.............Tailor, etc.
B—— P...........Liquor Broker.	B—— M...........Mnfr. Shirts.
B—— C. E....Backgammon and Chess Boards.	B—— M. B.........Job Printer.
	B—— M. P.....Jobber Fancy Goods.
B—— De P—— & Co....Com'n Wines and Liq.	B—— R.................Laces.
	B—— R. J............Mnfr. Cacks.
B—— B...............Hotel.	B—— T. E...............Contractor.
B—— F. & Co..............Dyestuffs.	B—— W. A. Jr..Leather and Findings.
B—— H...........Ret. Fancy Goods.	B—— A. & F............Machinists.

B—— Bros.............Ret. Clothing.
B—— E. E. & Co..........Envelopes.
B—— J. & Son...Bankers and Agents.
B—— S. & Co...........Hide Brokers.
B—— W. Sons..Lighters and Towing.
B—— W. Son & Co.....Com'n Wools.
B—— & Co........Heating Apparatus.
B—— & Co............Stock Brokers.
B—— G. F..................Saloon.
B—— J. F. & G. H. B——....Musical Instruments.
B—— P—— M—— W—— S—— Co.
B—— J. L. & Bro........Bankers and Brokers.
B—— H. L. & Co...........Woolens.
B—— W. M...............Printer.
B—— C—— & Co.......Com'n Prod.
B—— & Co.......Shipping and Com'n, Flour and Grain.
B—— Mrs. D......Ret. Fancy Goods.
B—— J.............. ....Ret. D. G.
B—— A.............Whol. Clothing.
B—— R. M..............Crockery.
B—— & K——.....Mnfrs. Cloth Caps.
B—— & M——........Cabinetmkrs.
B—— C....................Liquors.
B—— P..................Tailor.
B—— T...........Card Engraver.
B—— G. & Co.....Mnfrs. Cloth Caps.
B—— J.............Ret. Clothing.
B—— C. L............Storage, etc.
B—— J.............Upholsterer.
B—— H................Jeweller.
B—— M. L.Ret. Hats, Caps, Furs, etc.
B—— & Co...............Paper.
B—— C.................Costumes.
B—— J...............Mer. Tailor.
B—— W—— & L—— Co.
B—— J. A. & Co.......Stock Brokers.
B—— & F——............Builders.
B—— L.............Ret. Clothing.
B—— A. W.............Lumber.
B—— W. H...............Liquors.
B—— M—— Co.
B—— F.................Gro.
B—— E. S ....Stationery.
B—— M. Y. & Co.............Gro.
B—— & R——.........Imps. Laces.
B—— C. C..............Roofer.
B—— J........Ret. Boots and Shoes.
B—— F. A. & Co......Hardware, etc.
B—— H—— & L——..Sugar Refiners.
B—— L..........Ret. B. and S.
B—— E. G. & Co....Flour and Grain.
B—— E...............Ret. Meat.
B—— W. L.......Ret. Hats, Caps, Furs, etc.
B—— J.................Deskmkr.
B—— & McC——....Com'n Grain and Flour.
B—— J.................Carpenter.

B—— Mme. E. E.........Millinery.
B—— F. M. & Co.....Carriage Upholstery.
B—— G. W. & F. A....Furniture and Express.
B—— A. S........Ret. Men's Furn'g.
B—— R...................Oysters.
B—— T...................Liquors.
B—— R. & W............Jewellers.
B—— G. L...........Ret. Clothing.
B—— H................Carriages.
B—— D....................Lamps.
B—— T.................Old Iron.
B—— & P——.....Sewing Machines.
B—— P...............Raw Silks.
B—— R....................Gro.
B—— G. A................Paints.
B—— R. T. &Co.....Patent Metallic White Wire.
B—— J. J................Leather.
B—— & J——, Agents for R—— Bros.
B—— E. & Co...............Timber.
B—— J. A...............Jeweller.
B—— A. T............Com'n Paper.
B—— E............Imp. Crockery.
B—— M. J.............Liquors.
B—— W. R., Estate of.......Stoves.
B—— & Co.................Drugs.
B—— & H——...Builders' Hardware.
B—— & J——...............Paper.
B—— C..............Soap, etc.
B—— G. W.....Livery Stables.
B—— J. C................Coal.
B—— P....................Coal.
B—— R..........Woodenware, etc.
B—— & L——...Mnfrs. Straw Goods.
B—— C.........Shoe Findings.
B—— C. A................Drugs.
B—— J. C...............Engraver.
B—— A. K. & P——..Mnfrs.' Agents, etc.
B—— Mrs. C......Ret. Men's Furn'g.
B—— E. W...............Painter.
B—— F. J.................Liquors.
B—— J. J.............Ret. Clothing.
B—— M.................Tailor.
B—— W. P......Mineral Waters.
B—— Bros. & Co............Bitters.
B—— M..............Builder, etc.
C—— J. B.................Stables.
C—— A..................D. G.
C—— E. C..............Pictures.
C—— T.............Ret. D. G.
C—— L. F. & Co........Mnfrs. Gold Chains, etc.
C—— D. G...........R. E. Broker.
C—— A. M. & Co......Stock Brokers.
C—— & B——............Feathers.
C—— W—— & Co............Coal.
C—— V—— & Co........Pianofortes.
C—— D—— Co.

186 THE COMMERCIAL AGENCIES.

C—— H. C.............Plumber.
C—— A. F. & Co......Iron Founders.
C—— A. F. & H. C..Wood Pavements.
C—— C....................Liquors.
C—— J.................Ret. Hats.
C—— C........Jobber Straw Goods.
C—— G. A.................Butcher.
C—— H.................Ironworker.
C—— C—— Co.
C—— P—— & Co...........Linens.
C—— P...............Mnfr. Hats.
C—— J. T. & Co..Mnfrs. Trimmings.
C—— & B——.......Cotton Goods.
C—— A. J...........Iron Founder.
C—— J..................Liquors.
C—— S....................Drugs.
C—— E. & Son.........Com'n Prod.
C—— S. L................. Gro.
C—— & S——....Builders' Materials.
C—— A. T.................Books.
C—— M............Ret. Clothing.
C—— L.............Imp. Wines.
C—— H............Wines and Liq.
C—— D...China, Glass and Crockery.
C—— H. T...........Stock Broker.
C—— S.Millstones and Bolting Cloth.
C—— & Y——........Ship Brokers.
C—— T. J...............Distiller.
C—— & S——.................Gro.
C—— W. S..............Banker.
C—— S. & Co......California Wines.
C—— F........Com'n Woollens.
C—— J...........Looking-Glasses.
C—— D....................Iron.
C—— E. D..........Grain Broker.
C—— H., Agent............Baskets.
C—— F. H. & Co........Patent Sash
                        Fastenings.
C—— & H——.......Coal and Feed.
C—— & R——.................Prod.
C—— A.............Iron Pipe, etc.
C—— J.............Carpet Weaver.
C—— W.........Hides and Tallow.
C—— & R——...Com'n Foreign D. G.
C—— T..................Liquors.
C—— A. H............Jobber D. G.
C—— A. L....Stat'y and Fancy G.
C—— J. H. & Co..............Oils.
C—— J. F. & Son...........Tailors.
C—— T..................Liquors.
C—— L..............Pickles, etc.
C—— W. H............Gen'l Com'n.
C—— W. A..........Auctioneer.
C—— E. R........ .....Ret. D. G.
C—— & Co...........Imps. Teas.
C—— & Co...........Silverplaters.
C—— F....................Tailor.
C—— J.............Electrotyper.
C—— J. H..............Liquors,
C—— R. C............Auctioneer.
C—— J...Imp. Toys and Fancy Goods.

C—— C.........Peddlers' Supplies.
C—— Mrs. H. J...Ladies' Underwear.
C—— J........Pawnbrokers' Goods.
C—— W. J...........Fruit Broker.
C—— H. & Co.........Whol. Gro.
C—— J..................Builder.
C—— J........Pawnbrokers' Goods.
C—— A. V. & Co.....Stock Brokers.
C—— S. A. & Co..Com'n Smallwares.
C—— J. & Co......Imps. and Dealers
                            Teas.
C—— R. B.........R. R. Contractor.
C—— C................Reflectors.
C—— M........Shipping and Com'n.
C—— J. F...............Liquors.
C—— P............Ret. Liquors.
C—— E., B—— & Co...Shipping and
              Com'n Wines and Prod.
C—— J. M. & Co........Shipping and
                      Com'n Prod.
C—— & D——.........Mnfrs. Shirts.
C—— & B——....Agents French and
                      Italian Prod.
C—— P—— Co.
C—— S—— Co................Slates.
C—— & D——..........Pickles, etc.
C—— O. M......Sewing Machine At-
                      tachments.
C—— B. S...............Com'n Prod.
C—— & Co.Shipping and Com'n Prod.
C—— & C——.......Whol. Liquors.
C—— H. & G.——....R. R. Supplies.
C—— S—— M—— Co.
C—— & Co.........R. R. Contractors.
C—— M—— Co........Mnfrs. Frames.
C—— A. & W. & Bro....Lumber, etc.
C—— W............Stoves and Tin.
C—— & T——....Stat'y and Printers.
C—— R. P.........Bolting Cloths.
C—— M. W..............Furniture.
C—— T. B............Ship Broker.
C—— F. B. & Co.....Mnfrs. Jewelry.
C—— W. L. & Co.........Machinery.
C—— & P——.............Printers.
C—— A............Artificial Flowers.
C—— F. C.................Liquors.
C—— F—— E—— Co.
C—— Bros.......Chairs and Cradles.
C—— J. & Co.........Com'n Tobacco.
C—— & Co.........Com'n Whiskey.
C—— J. W. & K. & Co........Whol.
                      Fancy Goods.
C—— M. I..............Ret. D. G.
C—— E. T. & Co........Wholesale &
                      Retail Teas.
C—— D.........Mason and Builder.
C—— J. S...........Real Estate, etc.
C—— J...................Stages.
C—— W..............Hardware.
C—— & C——..........Whol. Hats.
C—— J. J. & Son...........Bankers.

C—— A. & Co........Whol. B. and S.	C—— D. L..Imp. Gloves and Fancy G.
C—— D. T.............Crockery, etc.	C—— L. H..................Painter.
C—— A. S.....Ret. Boots and Shoes.	C—— S........Ret. Boots and Shoes.
C—— G. M.......Machinery Agent.	C—— S...............Ret. Clothing.
C—— H. B..............Ret. D. G.	C—— S................Ret. D. G.
C—— S. E............Pearl Buttons.	C—— W.............Ret. Clothing.
C—— W. & Co.......Stock Brokers.	C—— J. & Son.....Peddlers' Supplies.
C—— D.....................Florist.	C—— A. & T....... Jobbers Flowers.
C—— D.....................Painter.	C—— I. P.....Hats, Caps, Furs, etc.
C—— H.....................Liquors.	C—— J. R.................Tinware.
C—— J. B......................Teas.	C—— R. F. & Co......Type-Founders.
C—— J. M.............Wagonmaker.	C—— & C—.............Veneers.
C—— T. H......Ret. Boots and Shoes.	C—— & V—............Marble.
C—— A. & Co.................Grain.	C—— J. B. & Co.....Gold and Stock
C—— D. W. & J. D..........Twines.	Brokers.
C—— D—— & Co...........Bankers.	C—— & S—.................Coal.
C—— J. A. & Son...........Tailors.	C—— J. W...........Wines and Liq.
C—— L. S. & Co.......Jobber Fancy	C—— F. A.............Trees, etc.
Goods.	C—— & S.............Printers.
C—— W. S. & Co.........Live Stock.	C—— G. G..........Ship Chandler.
C—— & H—.....Coffee and Spices.	C—— S— & O—....R. R. Cont'rs.
C—— & T—..........Horse Nails.	C—— G— S— Co.
C—— A. N.....Shipping and Com'n.	C—— I— Co.
C—— & C—.Mnfrs. Lace Goods, etc.	C—— Mrs. R........Ret. Fancy G.
C—— & B—......Imps. Laces, etc.	C—— W. A..........Piano H'ware.
C—— A.....Ship and Freight Broker.	C—— C. B. & Co...............Coal.
C—— & K—.........Wines, etc.	C—— S. M........Whol. Gro.
C—— J.....Cotton and Cotton Waste.	C—— E. A. & Co............Brokers.
C—— M..................Liquors.	C—— C....................Baker.
C—— T...................Bluestone.	C—— C.........Wines, Cigars, etc.
C—— & S—.................Paper.	C—— C.........Iron and Steel.
C—— & W—.....Mdse. Brokers.	C—— C. W.................Butcher.
C—— A.................Wines, etc.	C—— C— Co.
C—— O. B.............Dollar Store.	C—— D........Flour Broker.
C—— H....................Liquors.	C—— J...........Looking-Glasses.
C—— F— P— Co.......Plating.	C—— & Q—......Patent Fire-Proof
C—— M.....................Coal.	Roofers.
C—— & S—..................Coal.	C—— A..............Carpenter.
C—— E. H...........Whol. Liquors.	C—— F...................Liquors.
C—— J. W..........Paperhangings.	C—— & Co.....Ret. Fancy Goods.
C—— A. H..................Paper.	C—— I. B................Cigars.
C—— O. B.................Liquors.	C—— J. T..................Mason.
C—— J. W..................Builder.	C—— J. A. & Son....Kindling-Wood
C—— E. P............Job Printer.	and Children's Carriages.
C—— T. J. & Son.............Hotel.	C—— L. V. & Co.....Iron Founders.
C—— A. M.............Prod., etc.	C—— C— Co. of Maryland.
C—— & V—...........Com. Prod.	C—— & Co.........Lumber Storage.
C—— B. L...........Mnfr. Neckties.	C—— F...............Ironworker.
C—— J.............Ret. Clothing.	C—— N................Umbrellas.
C—— J.............Jobber Clothing.	C—— R— & Co.....Sugar Refiners.
C—— L. M..........Toys, Stat'y, and	C—— & B—........Whol. Liquors.
Fancy G.	C—— & C—.................Stone.
C—— M...................Millinery.	C—— E. P.................Shades.
C—— S. A...........Whol. Clothing.	C—— E. P. & Co............Brooms.
C—— S...........Jobber Cloths.	C—— J. & Co...................Hotel.
C—— B. & Co...Jobbers Clothing and	C—— & A—........Botanic Meds.
Fancy Goods.	C—— O....................Music.
C—— Bros...........Whol. Jewelry.	C—— O. H. & Co...............Gro.
C—— I. & S—..Ret. Hats and Caps.	C—— H. P.............Mer. Tailor.
C—— A.................Tobacco.	C—— W. B. & Co..Brokers Hemp and
C—— Mrs. C.........Jobber Ribbons.	Jute.

C—— & W——............Builders.
C—— J. & F............Mahogany.
C—— J.........Ret. Boots and Shoes.
C—— H. W.............Prod.
C—— F. & J. & Co........Red Cedar.
C—— D.............Hats and Caps.
C—— S. & Bro.............A. Fur Co.
C—— J.............Restaurant.
C—— J. F.............Wireworker.
C—— & Co..........Cotton Brokers.
C—— Bros...........Ret. D. G., etc.
C—— U...... ....Furnaces.
C—— Co......Mnfrs. Insect Powder.
C—— M. & Co................Oils.
C—— R. & Co..........Job Printers.
C—— & Co.....Shipping and Com'n.
C—— & S——............Liquors.
C—— M. & Co.......Cotton Dealers.
C—— & Co............Liquors.
C—— F. W. & Co....Hops and Essential Oils.
C—— A—— & Co...........Storage.
C—— C...................Stone.
C—— J. S.............Ret. B. and S.
C—— B. F......House Furn'g Goods.
C—— & H——.......Whol. Clothing.
C—— J. O......Imp. Lace Collars, etc.
C—— G. A.........:.Mnfr. Ink, etc.
C—— F. H..E. I. Shipping and Com'n.
C—— B. M. & Co.........Furniture.
C—— D................Towing.
C—— & B——..............Oils.
C—— H. H. & Son.....Plumber's Materials.
C—— B.........Ret. Fancy Goods.
C—— Bros......Shipping and Com'n.
C—— & Co.....Com'n Foreign Pickles and Sauces.
C—— & Co............Stock Brokers.
C—— E. M.....Jobber Leaf Tobacco.
C—— C—— Co.
C—— G. H.............Naval Stores.
C—— J. S.............Com'n Lumber.
C—— G. M..............Gro.
C—— A. M.............Auctioneer.
C—— D.............Ret. D. G.
C—— W. A...........R. E. Broker.
C—— H. H. & Co......Mdse. Brokers.
C—— & K——.........Mnfrs. Hats.
C—— H............Grain Broker.
C—— & B——.............Painters.
C—— T. J.............Lumber.
C—— H.............Hardware.
C—— J. F.........Prov. Broker.
C—— W. B. & Co......Advg. Agents.
C—— J. S...........Imp. Cigars, etc.
C—— J. M.....Architect and Builder.
C—— W. H. & Bro...Com'n Hardware.
C—— J............Mason and Builder.
C—— L. N...............Builder.
C—— & R——.............Painters.

C—— J...............Contractor.
C—— & Bro............Mnfrs. Mats.
C—— J. & Co...........Oil Brokers.
C—— & A—— M—— Co....Ammonia.
C—— F...............Liquors.
C—— T....Smoker and Packer Prov.
C—— & W——......Plaster Moulds.
C—— A...............Millinery.
C—— J. W............Carpets, etc.
C—— B—— & Co.......Com'n Prod.
C—— J.........Mnfr. Wire Goods.
C—— R. & J..........Contractors.
C—— & Co.......Mnfrs. Lace Goods.
C—— H. A. & Co....Imps. and Com'n Liquors, etc.
C—— M................Carriages.
C—— J...............Furniture.
C—— J.................Iron.
C—— & S——.....California Wines.
C—— & B——.............Printers.
C—— J...............Liquors.
C—— H. E........Com'n Fancy Goods.
C—— & S——...............Coal.
D—— A. W.....Children's Carriages.
D—— L....Imp. Wines and Brandies.
D—— E. G.............Ret. Clothing.
D—— S. S.............Ret. Clothing.
D—— M—— Co.............Silks.
D—— W. H.............Paints, etc.
D—— W................Coal.
D—— J............Mnfr. Head Nets.
D—— R...............Liquors.
D—— D................Rags.
D—— J...............Builder.
D—— J................Coal.
D—— M. & Co............Coal.
D—— C..........Ret. Men's Furn'g.
D'A—— J. N............Com'n Fruit.
D—— F. B. & Co........Forwarders.
D—— I. & W....Mnfrs. Cloaks, etc.
D—— H. T. & Co......Hide Brokers.
D—— J. & Son.....Ret. Fancy Goods.
D—— & W——.............Drugs.
D—— Bros.............Awnings.
D—— J. & Son..........Bookbinders.
D—— C. F............Stock Broker.
D—— J. G.............Pickles.
D—— & Co..Woolen Mnfrs. Supplies.
D—— J.............Grain Broker.
D—— & N——.....Mnfrs. Clothing.
D—— J...............Ret. Shoes.
D—— J..............Ret. D. G.
D—— W. M..............Coal.
D—— A. Sons............Prod.
D—— Bros...Pipes and Leaf Tobacco.
D—— H. J.............Clocks.
D—— J. L............:.Ret. D. G.
D—— T—— & Co...........Express.
D—— H. J.......Shipping and Com'n.
D—— J.........Ret. Clothing.
D—— J. S.............Silk Broker.

D—— J.....................Lumber.	D—— C. H.............Stock Broker.
D—— J. B..................Builder.	D—— A. W............Drug Broker.
D—— J. S.............Imp. Liquors.	D—— J. H..............Hair Goods.
D—— J. F............Paintings, etc.	D—— W.............Leaf Tobacco.
D—— S....................Watches.	D—— R. & H..........Cabinetmkrs.
D—— S.................Bells, etc.	D—— J............Fancy Goods.
D—— W. H.........Silk Broker.	D—— S. & Co...........Real Estate.
D—— W...............Ret. Liquors.	D—— L. G................Tailor.
D—— A. G. & Co.......Fancy Goods.	D—— J..Com'n Brooms, Brushes, etc.
D—— F—— & Co..Jobbers Millinery.	D—— C................Contractor.
D—— A. Sons.................Prod.	D—— J....................Drugs.
D—— T. R..................Printer.	D—— H. & Co......Clothing and Liq.
D—— E. & Son............Coaches.	D—— C....................Baker.
D—— F—— & Co.....Mufrs. Locks.	D—— J. & Co.............Printers.
D—— H—— & S——.........Drugs.	D—— & M——.........Drug Brokers.
D—— & B——....Petroleum Brokers.	D—— J....................Harness.
D—— & M——........Com'n Prod.	D—— M....Secondhand Clothing.
D—— F. W......Syrups and Sugars.	D—— B. S.........Diamond Broker.
D—— J. M..........Whol. Jewelry.	D—— & R——.....Artificial Flowers.
D—— W.................Ret. D. G.	D—— C................Confec.
D—— F. P..........Prod. Dealer.	D—— & M——.......Sugar Refiners.
D—— C. A. & Co.............Confec.	D—— E................Hardware.
D—— B. H..............Furniture.	D—— & B——......Mnfrs. Silk Hats.
D—— E. & Co............Imps. Laces.	D—— A. S..............Bluestone.
D—— G. H.................Com'n.	D—— & T——..........Hardware.
D—— A. B.............Blindmkr.	D—— C..................Liquors.
D—— W. H......Tea Broker.	D—— J. H. & Co. Com'n Domestic D. G.
D—— Bros............Pianofortes.	D—— H. E.............Knit Goods.
D—— L. & Co..Mnfrs. Billiard Tables.	D—— G....Stoves and House Furn'g.
D—— & Bro.............Pianos.	D—— J....................Painter.
D—— & S——........Com'n Meats.	D—— & T——........Chronometers.
De —— S....Shipping and Com'n.	D—— S........Jobber Millinery, etc.
De —— G. & Co...Mnfrs. Drugs, etc.	D—— & S——.....Mnfrs. Cigars.
D—— J. C. F........Military Goods.	D—— H. & Co............Pie Bakers.
D—— P—— B—— Co.	D—— J..............Wheelwright.
D—— G....................Builder.	D—— P............Shoe Uppers.
D—— F.........California Wines.	D—— G. S................Mason.
D—— A. B.......Com'n Fancy Goods.	D—— M. J...........Ice Cream, etc.
D—— W..................Furniture.	D—— H. R. & Co. Shipping and Com'n.
D—— A................Stationery.	D—— & M............Books.
D—— & B——....Mnfrs. Hair Goods.	D—— E. S. & Co. Printers and Stat'rs.
D—— J. A. & Co...Imitation Jewelry.	D—— A. & Co..............Liquors.
D—— & Co............Mnfrs. Soap.	D—— F. J...............Liquors.
D—— C. S..............Note Broker.	D—— H.................Hardware.
D—— L......Shipping and Com'n.	D—— A.........Pianoforte Materials.
D—— D.............Pawnbroker.	D—— N...................Tailor.
D—— Mrs. M....Milliner and Dress-	D—— S—— M—— Co.
mkr.	D—— H. W............Stock Broker.
D—— J. O.................Jeweller.	D—— F. R................Butter.
D—— A. T. & Co.........Carriages.	D—— & H——...........Jewellers
D—— & Co.........Shoe Findings.	D—— Bros.........Lithographers.
D—— E. L....'.........Fashions.	D—— W. & Co...Shipping and Com'n
D—— M. E............Jewelry.	Flour and Grain.
D—— W. J..............Publisher.	D—— J. Jr. & Co.........Cigars.
D—— A................Ret. D. G.	D—— & H——.Locksmiths and Mnfrs.
D—— A. & Co..........Imps. Books.	Trunks.
D—— G...........Horse-Shoe Co.	D—— J..............Bagmkr.
D—— M—— & Co......Gen'l Com'n.	D—— E. J..........Cotton Broker.
D—— M—— & Co.....Upholsterers.	D—— L—— & Co.........Bankers.
D—— L.............Wine Broker.	D—— J.................Coal.
D—— Bros............Cabinetmkrs.	D—— J...................Prod

D—— D. H............Frames.	D—— A. & Son............Lumber.
D—— & Bro...Mnfrs. Yeast Powders.	D—— & G——............Hay, etc.
D—— H. B........Gen'l Com'n Mer.	D—— W. M. & Co..........Cutlery.
D—— H............Cuban Com'n.	D—— J., Estate of....Printer and Sta-
D—— C. D.............Liquors.	tioner.
D—— & H——........Com'n Prod.	D—— T. N..........Packing Boxes.
D—— Miss A.....Ret. Fancy Goods.	D—— Bros.................Teas.
D—— J. A..Ret. Hats, Caps, Furs, etc.	D—— & C——..........Real Estate.
D—— J................Glasscutter.	E—— M—— W—— Co.
D—— W. & Son.............Coal.	E——E............Liquors.
D—— & B——.......Iron Founders.	E—— J................Corsets.
D—— W. & Co.........Com'n Fruit.	E—— M—— Co..........Crockery.
D—— A. Jr.................Cigars.	E—— Z—— Co.
D—— P..............Butter, etc.	E—— G. & Co........Cabinetmakers.
D—— P...........Mnfr. Shoes, etc.	E—— L............Hotel and Liq.
D—— & St. J——....Drug Brokers.	E—— L—— Co.
D—— Miss M.........Ret. Millinery.	E—— K—— & Co........Bankers and
D—— H. R. & Co...Buying and Ship-	Brokers.
ping Agents.	E—— & W——............Brewers.
D—— J...............Stoneyard.	E—— P. C........Ret. Fancy Goods.
D—— E. M..Com'n Foreign and Do-	E—— & Co.....Shipping and Com'n.
mestic Rubber Goods.	E—— N..............Ret. D. G.
D—— J. N..........Com'n Tobacco.	E—— Bros............Perfumery.
D—— Mrs. P. G...........Ret. Hats.	E—— R—— & Co.......Paper Boxes.
D—— E. T..............Ret. D. G.	E—— & R——..............Coal.
D—— & R——....Undertakers' Goods.	E—— J.................Stoves.
D—— F................Tassels.	E—— M. C..............Patent Meds.
D—— B. J.............Cabooses.	E—— W. A..............Lighters.
D—— H. L.................Gro.	E—— A.............Plumber.
D—— B. & Co.....California Wines.	E—— J. M., Jr..........Ret. D. G.
D—— J. G. & Co..Mnfrs. Cream Tartar.	E—— C—— & Co.........Whol. Liq.
D—— E..........Teas, Coffees, etc.	E—— M. & Son............Teas.
D—— F—— & A——.....Fancy Gro.	E—— J. D.........Mnfrs.' Agent.
D—— J. T.............Jewelry.	E—— J..........Freight Broker.
D—— E.............Ret. Millinery.	E—— A. R.......Ret. Fancy Goods.
D—— M. J........Fancy Goods.	E—— Mrs. M..........Fancy Goods.
D—— B. A.....Jobber Fancy Goods.	E—— I. D..............Chemist.
D—— J................Liquors.	E—— & R——.......Mdse. Brokers.
D—— J...S. Am. Shipping and Com'n.	E—— & T——.......Ladies' Cloaks.
D—— U. H. & Co.....Canned Fruits.	E—— J............Ret. Liquors.
D—— J. E..........Mineral Waters.	E—— D. E.............Oysters.
D—— J.............Mnfr. Suits.	E—— W. & Co........Leaf Tobacco.
D—— T...............Builder.	E—— C—— D—— P—— Co.
D—— Mrs. O.............D. G.	E—— J. C. R. & Co.........Glue.
D—— P. C..............Baker.	F—— P.........Com'n Trimmings.
D—— & O'S——........Com'n D. G.	E—— G..............Brewer.
D—— & H——...........Roofers.	E—— I..Imp. Toys and Fancy Goods.
D—— & C——...Architects and Build-	E—— H. & Co..........Shirts.
ers.	E—— S—— & Co.....Jobbers Fancy
D—— J. F.......Ret. Men's Furn'g.	Goods.
D—— J. & Co..........Mnfrs. Boxes.	E—— B..............Ret. D. G.
D—— S................Tailor.	E—— H.....Gilder and Silver Plater.
D—— & R——............Liquors.	E—— & W——.........Upholstery.
D—— D. S.............Speculator.	E—— Bros..............Drugs, etc.
D—— & Co..Ret. Hats, Caps, Furs, etc.	E—— E...............Rectifier.
D—— A.................Hay.	E—— G—— L—— Co.
D—— L. & H——..........Ranges.	E—— & Co..............Jewellers.
D—— A..............Com'n Cotton.	E—— R. H.............Jeweller.
D—— C................Com'n.	E—— R. & Co............Shirts.
D—— J...Cuban Shipping and Com'n.	E—— W. M. & Co.....Variety Store.
D—— E.................Tin Toys.	E—— A.........Ret. Hats and Caps.

E—— & G	Roofers.
E—— L	Mnfr. Dress Trim'gs.
E—— W	Teas.
E—— J. H. & Co	Cotton Brokers.
E—— G	Clothing.
E—— J. & Co	Oil Refiners.
E—— T. P. & Co	Loans and Bonds.
E—— W. & Son	Prov.
E—— J. N	Glassware.
E—— J. & J. W	Oysters.
E—— J. W. & Co	Shipping and Com'n.
E—— G. B. & Co	Pumps.
E—— L. L	Com'n Silks, etc.
E—— M	Ret. Fancy Goods.
E—— E	Ret. D. G.
E—— E	Prov.
E—— B. & Co	Beef.
E—— J	Imp. French Clocks.
E—— J	Shipping and Com'n.
E—— B	Tailors' Trim'gs.
E—— B. & Co	Mnfrs. Shirts.
E—— & M—— P—— Co.	
E—— M	Jewelry.
E—— R. S	Clothing.
E—— M	Sausagemkr.
E—— & K——Jobbers Trimmings, etc.	
E—— J	Liquors.
E—— E. W.,	Contractor.
E—— J	Shoe Findings.
E—— L—— & Co	Bankers.
E—— H. M. & Co	Mnfrs. Boys' Clothing.
E—— H	Tailor.
E—— G—— & C—— Co.	
E—— P—— Co	Canned Goods.
E—— & G——	Mnfrs. Cloaks, etc.
E—— F. A. L	Mining.
E—— H	Ret. Fancy D. G.
E—— O	Men's Furn'g.
E—— R	Restaurant.
E—— L	Fancy Goods.
E—— L	Mnfr. Metal Cornices.
E—— A	Teas, etc.
E—— Bros	Silks and Ribbons.
E—— F. J	Paper Boxes.
E—— J. W. & Co	Printers' Materials.
E—— Bros	Fancy and Military Goods.
E—— A. E	Mnfr. Neckties.
E—— M	Extension Tables.
E—— G	Upholsterer.
E—— S—— Co	Counter Scales.
E—— A	Com'n Prod.
E—— J. B	Gro.
E—— W. M	Carpet Stretcher, etc.
E—— B—— & Co	Shipping and Com'n.
E—— T. & G	Cotton Shipping and Com'n.
E—— W. & Co	Shipping and Com'n Prod.
E—— & Co	Ret. Clothing.
E—— & G——	Blankbooks.
E—— J	Engraver.
E—— H. W	Drug Broker.
E—— J	Ret. Liquors.
E—— S. H. & C	Hotel.
E—— Bros	Stationers.
E—— F	Doors, etc.
E—— J	Gro.
E—— J. H	Whol. Gro.
E—— & T——	Stock Brokers.
E—— C—— Co	R. R. Chairs.
E—— M—— Co	Coffee Urns.
E—— H	Com'n Teas and Coffee.
F—— Bros	Shipping and Com'n Cotton.
F—— E	Dentist.
F—— J. C	Paperhangings.
F—— J	Wood Engraver.
F—— & B——	Yarns.
F—— & J——	Stamping and Fancy Goods.
F—— J	Furniture.
F—— J. G	Liquors.
F—— D. & Co	Fwdg. Agents.
F—— A	Real Estate.
F—— S	Mnfr. Cigars.
F—— G. & Bro	Mnfrs. Cigars.
F—— M. & Co	Tobacco.
F—— J	Gro. and D. G.
F—— G. W	R. E. Agent.
F—— S	Tailor.
F—— I	Watches, etc.
F—— Miss A	Millinery, etc.
F—— C. J	Stable.
F—— R. G	Liquors.
F—— C	Cabinetmkr.
F—— B—— & Co	Note Brokers.
F—— H. F	Liquors.
F—— J	Liquors.
F—— J	Liquors.
F—— P	Liquors.
F—— & Son	Books.
F—— M	Custom-house Broker.
F—— M. J. & Co	Wines.
F—— T	Furdresser.
F—— Bros	Saddlers' Hardware.
F—— & T——	Auction Boots and Shoes.
F—— J	Plumber.
F—— T	Paperhangings.
F—— M	Liquors.
F—— & D——	Marble.
F—— J. H. & Son	Liquors.
F—— I	Whol. Clothing.
F—— & R——	Mnfrs. Woollen Shirts.
F—— M	Restaurant.
F—— W—— Co	Stationery.
F—— & Co	Com'n Prod.

F—— H. D.................Liquors.
F—— & C——..........B—— House.
F—— H. & Co....Auction and Com'n.
F——L. & K——............Collars.
F—— G. L. & Co........Ret. Notions.
F—— J. N...Broker Flour, Seeds, etc.
F—— J. B....Com'n Flour and Grain.
F—— I....................Cattle Hair.
F—— & S——........Com'n Hardware.
F—— W. & Sons........Undertakers'
                              Goods.
F—— & Co............Cuban Com'n.
F—— S. M.......Cuban Shipping and
                              Com'n.
F—— E....................Hull.
F—— Mme. J.........Ret. Millinery.
F—— & S——............Liquors.
F——J. J..............Flour and Feed.
F—— E. & Co...................Salt.
F—— E. & Son...........Ret. B. & S.
F—— C. B...............Ship Agent.
F—— C.....................Drugs.
F—— & K——.....Havana Tobacco.
F—— B....................Drugs.
F—— H. & Co................Rags.
F—— J.....................Builder.
F—— S.................Ret. D. G.
F—— L. & Son............Chemists.
F—— A...........Imp. White Beer.
F—— L. & E. H... Ret. Fancy Goods.
F—— F................Fancy Goods.
F—— J. H................Glassware.
F—— C. Sons........Mnfrs. Gloves.
F—— & J.——........Stock Brokers.
F—— A.....Upholsterers' Goods.
F—— W. S..............Note Broker.
F—— G—— & Co.......Tobacco and
                              Cotton.
F—— A.................Ret. D. G.
F—— J. J........Rubber Car Springs.
F—— R. H............ ...Furniture.
F—— F................Wines, etc.
F—— A.............Imp. Liquors.
F—— C. E....................Teas.
F—— E.......Ret. Boots and Shoes.
F—— L. & Co.....Artificial Flowers.
F—— & L——....Peddlers' Supplies.
F—— W. B...............Liquors.
F—— J. F..................Plumber.
F—— M.............Men's Furn'g.
F—— G. M.....Shipping and Com'n.
F—— B—— Co.........Roofing, etc.
F—— M..............Rhine Wines.
F——   M——   B——   and   S——
M——   A——.
F—— C....................Liquors.
F—— W. H. A....Petroleum Broker.
F—— J. & Co.Mouldings and Frames.
F—— & R——....Curtain Ornaments.
F—— W. L................Hotel.
F—— T. B. & Co...........Guns, etc.

F—— E., Agent.......   .Jewelry.
F—— M.........Mnfr. Silk Trim'gs.
F—— C. J. & Co.............Liquors.
F—— J. W...Ornamental Iron Work.
F—— N.............Fancy D. G.
F—— Dr. S. S..........Patent Meds.
F—— E. A. & Son.............Feed.
F—— & B——...........Com'n Prod.
F—— J....Ret. Hats, Caps, Furs, etc.
F—— J................Horseshoer.
F—— & H——...Mnfrs. Watch Cases.
F—— & Co.......Pasting Machines.
F—— & H——.......Com'n Southern
                              Prod.
F—— D. J.................Crockery.
F—— C. H......Rubber Goods, etc.
F—— & B——.........Furniture, etc.
F—— A. F.................Crockery.
F—— H..................Ret. Hats.
F—— S.......Men's Furn'g Goods.
F—— A........Books and Stat'y.
F—— S. D.................Ret. Hats.
F—— W....................Gro.
F—— A. & D. & Co.....Imps. Fancy
                              Goods.
F—— C.................Painter.
F—— J. W.............Cooperage.
F—— Bros......Imps. Kid Gloves and
                              Laces.
F—— B.................Liquors.
F—— M.................Liquors.
F—— S—— M—— Co.
F—— J.........Ret. Boots and Shoes.
F—— P. F...................Gro.
F—— M..............Dressmaker.
F—— E.....................Cotton.
F—— W. S..............Bedding.
F—— W. S. & Bro..........Bedding.
F—— J.............Mnfr. Gold Pens.
F—— M. W....Ret. Boots and Shoes.
F—— P.................Restaurant.
F—— C.....Guns, Pistols, Caps, etc.
F—— M............Com'n Prod.
F—— F..................Builder.
F—— A. G.................Drugs.
F—— R. H............Broker, etc.
F—— D..............Com'n Hats.
F—— J. J.......Ret. Men's Furn'g.
F—— P.........Jewelry, etc.
F—— F. & Co.........Jobbers Hats.
F—— R. B. & Co......Cotton Brokers.
F—— C. B. & Son..........Leather.
F—— J. & Sons........Paper Stock.
F—— G. F............. Spool Cotton.
F—— Mrs. J..............Ret. D. G.
F—— C. F. & Co.........Com'n Prod.
F—— & H——.......Jobbers F'cy G.
F—— J. Sons......Com'n W. I. Prod.
F—— F—— Co.
F—— A. E..................Builder.
F—— J. A. & Co.......Wool Brokers.

F—— G. W.	Drugs.
F—— C. R. & Bro.	Imps. Rice.
F—— H.	Mnfr. Shoes.
F—— I.	Mnfr. Cloth Hats and Caps.
F—— C. Son & Co.	Mnfrs. Hats, Caps, etc.
F—— G. W. & Co.	Com'n Carpets.
F—— & F——.	Cotton and Prov. Brokers.
F—— & W——.	Iron Founders.
F—— J. R. & Co.	Imps. Woollens.
F—— D. G.	Bookseller.
F—— A—— & Co.	Cotton.
F—— H.	Ret. Shoes.
F—— J.	Ret. Clothing.
F—— J.	Whol. Clo.
F—— L. J.	Gold Broker.
F—— L. & Son.	Jobber Shirts.
F—— M. M.	Mnfr. White Goods.
F—— S.	D. G., etc.
F—— S.	Ret. Boots and Shoes.
F—— S.	Leaf Tobacco.
F—— B—— & Co.	Whol. Liquors.
F—— L. Il. & Co.	Printers and Pub'rs.
F—— & K——.	Mnfrs. and Jobbers Shirts.
F—— & K——.	Liquors.
F—— M.	Cigars.
F—— L.	Ret. Men's Furn'g.
F—— & W——.	Jobbers White Goods.
F—— L, Jr.	Tailor.
F—— B.	Mnfr. Lace Goods.
F—— C—— Co. of W——, Pa.	
F—— R. & Co.	Mnfrs. Clock Cases.
F—— J.	Oyster Saloon.
F—— Bros.	Shipping and Com'n.
F—— & Co.	Watchmkrs.' Tools.
F—— J. W.	Military Goods.
F—— F.	Billiard Tables.
F—— T. A	Furn.
F—— Mrs.	Whol. Ladies' Goods.
F—— J.	Mnfr. Shirt Bosoms.
F—— M.	D. G. Broker.
F—— B—— & Co.	Whol. Clo.
F—— L. N. & Co.	Cotton Brokers.
F—— F.	Whol. Jewelry.
F—— E. F. Mnfg. Co.	Sewing-Machine Cases.
F—— G. P. & Co.	Gen'l Com'n, etc.
F—— S. & Son.	Publishers.
F—— F.	Gro.
F—— N.	Ret. Boots and Shoes.
F—— J. A.	Ret. Clothing.
F—— M. H.	Tobacco.
F—— T. Son.	Enamelled Cloth.
F—— Bros. & Co.	Mnfrs. Cigars.
F—— C.	Liquors.
F—— L.	Tailor.
F—— I.	Tobacco.
F—— S.	Clothing.
F—— H.	Tailor.

F—— O. O.	Com'n Liquors.
F—— S.	Whol. Jewelry.
F—— & O——.	Leaf Tobacco.
F—— & W——.	Mnfrs. Felt Skirts.
F—— & L——.	Cutlery.
F—— S.	Mnfr. Ladies' Garments.
F—— E. & G. & Co.	Tobacco.
F—— B.	Ret. Boots and Shoes.
F—— I.	Imp. Jewelry.
F—— & McH——.	Jobbers Notions.
F—— R—— & S——.	Leaf Tobacco.
F—— R.	Shipping and Com'n Italian Prod.
F—— Bros.	Stoves.
F—— C. & Sons.	Stamping.
F—— M.	Ret. Boots and Shoes.
F—— T.	Drugs.
F—— W. T.	Mnfr. Pocketbooks, etc.
F—— H.	Livery Stables.
F—— K—— & Co.	Whol. Liquors.
F—— S.	Ret. D. G.
F—— J. & Son.	Turner and Canes.
F—— & W——.	Sewing Machines.
F—— C. M.	Imp. Toys.
F—— & T——.	Mustard Mills.
F—— H. C.	Ret. Men's Furn'g.
G—— J.	Ret. Fancy Goods.
G—— C. L.	Paper Boxes.
G—— I. B.	Ship Broker.
G—— E. & Co.	Coal.
G—— M.	Morocco.
G—— T.	Ret. Boots and Shoes.
G—— B. & A.	Mnfrs. Ladies' Undergarments.
G——F—— M—— Co.	Electric Machines.
G—— H.	Crockery, etc.
G—— J. J.	Liquors.
G—— M.	Ret. D. G.
G—— S. M.	Whol. Clothing.
G—— Bros.	Ret. D. G.
G—— B.	Gro.
G—— W., Estate of.	Iron.
G—— Mrs. W.	Hotel.
G—— T.	Ret. D. G.
G—— J.	Imp. Watches and Jewelry.
G—— J.	Hotel.
G—— M.	Contractor.
G—— F—— & S——.	Military Goods.
G—— Mrs. E.	Milliner.
G—— Mrs. C. A.	Corsets.
G—— W. H. & C.	Carpenters.
G—— I.	Ret. Fancy Goods.
G—— C.	Stoves, etc.
G—— E.	Broker.
G—— G.	Imp. Photo. Materials.
G—— H.	Furs.
G—— E.	Mer. Tailor.
G—— J. W.	Stock Speculator.
G——C. E. & Co.	Mnfrs. Perfumery.
G—— N. G.	Hardware, etc.

G—— F. & J.........Dutch Cheese.
G—— Bros.....California Wines and Brandies
G—— J. G.............Liquors.
G—— A—— W—— Co.
G—— T—— & C——...........Iron.
G—— J............Imp. Trimmings.
G—— T. F......R. E. and Ins. Agent.
G—— F. C............Furniture.
G—— & G——...........Glassware.
G—— J...................Jeweller.
G—— J............Lithographer.
G—— W. Jr............Saddlery.
G—— W. H. & Co......Com'n Prod.
G—— J. L........Ret. Fancy Goods.
G—— & B—— M—— Co.
G—— & Co................Plaster.
G—— J. & Co........Whol. Liquors.
G—— B.............Hardware.
G—— D............Paperhangings.
G—— M. T............Pickles, etc.
G—— D............Mnfr. Spectacles.
G—— W.W..Whol. Boots and Shoes.
G—— J...................Carpenter.
G—— & P——....Bonnet Bleachers.
G—— J. A. Jr............Umbrellas.
G—— C—— E—— & S—— House.
G—— J. B.................Wine.
G—— J............Jobber Cloths.
G—— W. H. & Co.....Stock Brokers.
G—— G. A. & Co...Com'n Wines, etc.
G—— Co....................Soap.
G—— M. & J............Imps. Linen.
G—— J. & Sons. Jobbers Fancy Goods.
G—— A..................Ret. Shoes.
G—— & Son....Ret. Boots and Shoes.
G—— R. W..Steam-Engines, Boilers, etc.
G—— McL—— & Co..Linen Handkerchiefs.
G—— J. C. & Co...Jobbers F'cy Goods.
G—— R.............Mnfr. Shoes.
G—— & T——.......Cotton Brokers.
G—— A. E.......Broker H'ware, etc.
G—— E. A.......Wines and Liq.
G—— & B——.............Corks.
G—— & Co........Mnfrs. Silk Hats.
G—— G. W............Liquors.
G—— S. & Co...........Whol. Furs.
G—— H—— Co. Furnaces and Heaters.
G—— P................Optician.
G—— & G——............Liquors.
G—— A.........Mnfr. Flowers.
G—— & R——.........Photographs.
G—— H. N. J.....Mnfr. Shirt Fronts.
G—— Bros..............Cloaks, etc.
G—— T. A.............Stationer.
G—— R.............Crockery.
G—— S. & Co............Tobacco.
G—— J.............Hats and Caps.
G—— M............Fancy Goods.

G—— S.................Cigars.
G—— H. & Co............Clothing.
G—— S. & Co......Mnfrs. Neckties.
G—— & B——.........Mnfrs. Ladies' Trimmed Hats.
G—— P. Bro..........Pawnbroker.
G—— & Bro........Whol. Clothing.
G—— H............Cotton Broker.
G—— A. & Co.....Mnfrs. and Imps. Swiss Embroideries.
G—— & A——....Imps. Fruit, Wines, etc.
G—— M. J....Mnfr. Feather Dusters.
G—— & E——...Shipping and Com'n Flour, Grain, etc.
G—— W.........Ret. Fancy Goods.
G—— Bros...........Whol. Liquors.
G—— B......Mnfr. Collars and Cuffs.
G—— H...........Jobber Cloths.
G—— J.........Ret. Boots and Shoes.
G—— M...............Butcher.
G—— F.......Ret. Boots and Shoes.
G—— C. T. & Sons...Cracker Bakers.
G—— J. & Co..............Paper.
G—— I—— R—— H—— P—— Co.
G—— A. D........Com'n and Agent.
G—— & S——............Ret. D. G.
G—— S—— & Co.......Mnfrs. Hats.
G—— S. D...............Findings.
G—— J...............Com'n Cement.
G—— S. A. & Co.............Drugs.
G—— & Co............Iron Foundry.
G—— J............Artificial Flowers.
G—— L. G..............Pub'r Books.
G—— F. T..............Perfumer.
G—— J. S...............Tobacco.
G—— F........Jobber White Goods.
G—— C................Saddler.
G—— J. F..........Ret. Shoes.
G—— T......................Gro.
G—— T.........Painters' Supplies.
G—— J. & Son......Mnfrs. Bindings.
G—— A—— P—— Co.
G—— C..................Liquors.
G—— H—— C—— W——.
G—— H.............Restaurant.
G—— D. H.............Sulphur.
G—— M.............Flour Dealer.
G—— R......................Gro.
G—— & P——.............Plumbers.
G—— H—— & Co....Mnfrs. Jewelry.
G—— G..................Builder.
G—— G. B..........Com'n Flour.
G—— I. H.................Tailor.
G—— J. C.............Hardware.
G—— S. W..............Printer.
G—— A. & Co.........Com'n Prod.
G—— Bros..........Cotton Brokers.
G—— J. A. & Co...R. R. Contractors.
G—— P—— I—— M—— Co.
G—— S. H.................Hats.

G—— D................Furs.
G—— N—— & Co.....Stock Brokers.
G—— & R——.....Ret. Fancy Goods.
G—— R...............Ret. Clothing.
G—— G. G.............Carpenter.
G—— J........Ret. Boots and Shoes.
G—— C ....Silk Dyer.
G—— H...................Tailor.
G—— F. J.............Cabinetmkr.
G—— H. A.........Fruits and Gro.
G—— J. L & Co................Gro.
G—— M. F................Liquors.
G—— R......Ladies' Undergarments.
G—— & W——..Safety Boiler Works.
G—— & F—............Builders.
G—— S. M.....Mnfr. Gold Pens, etc.
G—— C. E. & Co....Imps. E. I. Goods.
G—— F. D. & Co...........Painters.
G—— G..................Millinery.
G—— J...................Brewer.
G—— M...................Brewer.
G—— & McL——...Com'n Prod.
G—— A......Mnfr. Woollen Shirts.
G—— M.....Mnfr. Fancy Furs, etc.
G—— W & Co.....Cabinet Materials.
G—— & Co......Sewing-Machine At-
                         tachments.
G—— F. & Co........Ivory Turners.
G—— E................Lighters.
G—— J. P.................Scales.
G—— R. & Bro.....Jobbers Hosiery.
G—— J. E. & Co...........Flags, etc.
G—— & K...............Hardware.
G—— J. H..............Telegraph.
G—— S......................D. G.
G—— G. G. & Co.......Patent Meds.
G—— K. J.............Carriages.
G—— & Son............Ironworkers.
G—— & F——..............Stoves.
G—— J..............Fancy Goods.
G—— P.........Mnfr. Lace Goods.
G—— Mrs. M. L. & Co......Printing
                          Presses.
G—— P. & Co........Com'n Cotton.
G—— J. F. J..........Iron Foundry.
G—— M. G.............Stoves.
G—— Bros................Drugs.
G—— C. G. & Co.............Furs.
G—— & S——........Jobbers Cloth.
G—— G. B.........Suspenders.
G—— & Co.......R. R. Ties, etc.
G—— F. W........Carriage Painter.
G—— E..................Builder.
G—— & C——...Picture Frames, etc.
G—— J...............Lager Beer.
G—— Mrs. J.............Milliner.
G—— J................Clothing.
G—— C. B...........Com'n Cotton.
G—— S. A............Imp. Gloves.
G—— & Co................Builders.
G—— E................Tin Cans.

G—— G...............Carriages.
H—— A.....................Coal.
H—— & Co.............Bankers.
H—— N................Builder.
H—— D. Sons..........Imps. Silk.
H—— & B——.Imps. German Wines.
H—— I., F—— & Co....Whol. D. G.
H—— J. W......Manfr. Fireworks.
H—— C. L.............Hardware.
H—— H. C.............Crockery.
H—— W...............Crockery.
H—— H. & T.............Hotel.
H—— & B——.......Gold and Specie
                        Brokers.
H—— F....................Tailor.
H—— & Co..................Oils.
H—— J. G................Confec.
H—— I. H........Mnfr. Cigars.
H—— L...................Tailor.
H—— J. & Son........Ret. Clothing.
H—— & B——......Imps. Cameo.
H—— V..........Oil Paintings.
H—— & K——...........Stone.
H—— T.................Corsets.
H—— H. M.............Jewelry.
H—— C. & Co.......Com'n Flour.
H—— G. L. & L..Bankers and Brokers.
H—— Bros...........Pianofortes.
H—— S..............Fruits.
H—— & O——...........Furniture.
H—— F.............Glass Signs.
H—— H. W..........Com'n Chairs.
H—— J. M...Shoe-Pegs, Lastings and
                          Gorings.
H—— B. E. & Co...Printed Wrapping
                          Paper.
H—— C. B...........R. E. Agent.
H—— Mrs. E......Ret. Fancy Goods.
H—— H. P.............Butcher.
H—— J. H....Agent and Com'n.
H—— R. W.............Ret. Hats.
H—— S.............Ret. Clothing.
H—— T.............Mnfr. Head Nets.
H—— C. H. & Co...Steam Pumps, etc.
H—— C. & J................Gro.
H—— & F——......Balloon Hanging
                          Baskets.
H—— F. E......Mnfr. Neckties.
H—— S. E............Stationer.
H—— L...............Feathers.
H—— G. G..............Stoves.
H—— A. T...............Hotel.
H—— W........Millinery, Hats, etc.
H—— J...................Marble.
H—— T. B...........Com'n Prod.
H—— M..................Hotel.
H—— P—— B—— & C—— Co. Mnfrs.
                   Rubber Watchcases.
H—— M—— Co...........Tinware.
H—— J. C............Carriages.
H—— J. H...................Gro.

H—— I.....................Chromos.
H—— E.....................Coal.
H—— & F——..........Framemkrs.
H—— H.............Ret. Clothing.
H—— J. Jr................ Trunks.
H—— J.....................Stationer.
H—— W. H........Mnfr. Brooms.
H—— J. G. & Co.......Jobbers Teas.
H—— P—— & Co......Mnfrs. Shoes.
H—— S. Sons.............Printers.
H—— & C——...............Cotton.
H—— & T——...........Ret. D. G.
H—— L. & Co......Watch Materials.
H—— B.............Ret. Hats.
H—— H.................Leather.
H—— A.....................Gro.
H—— J. W.............Steamboats.
H—— T...................Liquors.
H—— M—— & Co..Com'n Chemicals.
H—— T...................Liquors.
H—— C. H..........Wool and Hops.
H—— & Co.....Sugar and Molasses.
H—— & D——................Prod.
H—— J...Moulding and Planing Mill.
H—— G. D................Tailor.
H—— A.............Embroideries.
H—— T. L........Ret. Men's Furn'g.
H—— H.............Pianofortes.
H—— M. J. & Co..Com'n Whiskey, etc.
H—— P. & Co......Oars, Sculls, etc.
H—— S.............Whol. Clothing.
H—— & Co.............Tailors.
H—— W.................Builder.
H—— G. P.................Hotel.
H—— I...........Secondhand Furn.
H—— E. R...............Coal.
H—— F................. Liquors.
H—— C—— L—— Co.
H—— & B——.............Safes.
H—— C. W...............Music.
H—— F. G.............Clothing.
H—— J..................Painter.
H—— J..................Clothing.
H—— L...... Hats, Caps, Furs, etc.
H—— M........Peddlers' Supplies.
H—— M.........Ret. Hats and Caps.
H—— P...........Ret. Clothing.
H—— S. M.............Embroideries.
H—— A. W. & Co.......Tobacconists.
H—— F—— Co...........Showcards.
H—— & Co.........Jobbers Clothing.
H—— & H——........Woollen Rags.
H—— & H——......Whol. Clothing.
H—— A. C.............Bookbinder.
H—— G.................Brewery.
H—— H.............Mnfr. Jewelry.
H—— & H——.............Tobacco.
H—— G. K...............Lumber.
H—— C.............Lithographer.
H—— H.............Mnfr. Shirts.
H—— H. I............Planing Mill.

H—— I. Jr.................Clothing.
H—— J.............Imp. Corsets.
H—— P...................Tobacco.
H—— W...................Liquors.
H—— L. M—— Co......Silverplated Ware.
H—— & Bro............Com'n Prod.
H—— & H——.....Mnfrs. Neckties.
H—— Bros.....White Goods, Shawls, etc.
H—— L......................Hotel
H—— W...................Cigars.
H—— & Co.............Imps. Colors.
H—— J.....................Paints.
H—— J.....................Painter.
H—— E.....................Drugs.
H—— C. E. & Co........Imps. Hair.
H—— H. & Co.........Mnfrs. Tassels.
H—— J. & Co...........Ret. Clothing.
H—— W. A.....Jobber Fancy Goods.
H—— & V——...................Meat.
H—— & Co............Mnfrs. Bags.
H—— & B——.......Stock Brokers.
H—— U................ .Tailor.
H—— J. L.........Books and Stat'y.
H—— W...................Liquors.
H—— C. C...........Fancy Goods.
H—— A. L. & Co.....Stoves and Tin-ware.
H—— L—— Co.
H—— & Sons.............Tailors.
H—— & K——.......Mnfrs. Dress Trimmings.
H—— J. P. & Son...............Prod.
H—— & F——.........Imps. Drugs.
H—— C. & Co.........Pocketbooks.
H—— M. G...........Cotton Broker.
H—— N...................Liquors.
H—— B...................Plumber.
H—— & E——.......Sugar Refiners.
H—— G. G. & Co........Bankers and Brokers.
H—— J. N.........Com'n Lumber.
H—— J. H. & Son..........Lumber.
H—— & C——........Ret. Clothing.
H—— W. Jr...............Builder.
H—— W.............Com'n Flour.
H—— C.............Packer, etc
H—— H. S.......Corsets and Skirts.
H—— A...............Banker, etc.
H—— J..............Lithographer.
H—— W...................Linens.
H—— A. & Co.....Soap, Candles, etc.
H—— H.........Ship Chandlery.
H—— E. L.......R. E. Broker.
H—— P...................Tailor.
H—— T. E.......Ink and Mucilage.
H—— Bros........Patent Skylights.
H—— J. E. & Co......Com'n Paper.
H—— & F——.........Printers.
H—— C..........Boots and Shoes.

H—— Bros. & Co	Sponges.
H—— C. & H	Stables.
H—— & Co	Com'n Bedding Moss.
H—— J	Ret. Hats, Caps, Furs, etc.
H—— J. H	Com'n Prod.
H—— R	Mnfr. Cloaks, etc.
H—— C. H. & Co	Com'n.
H—— T. S	Distillers.
H—— & S——	Mnfrs. Jewelry and Emblems.
H—— & Co	Paperhangings.
H—— C. P	Iron Railings.
H—— & M——	Refrigerators.
H—— J	Gro.
H—— J	Marble.
H—— C. & Co	Ret. D. G.
H—— M	Ret. D. G.
H—— I	Jobber Linen.
H—— A. H	Stock Broker.
H—— E. A. & Co	House Furn'g.
H—— W. & Co	Stock Brokers.
H—— R	Coal.
H—— & Co	Woodenware.
H—— G	Ret. Drugs.
H—— H. B	Grain Broker.
H—— J. H	Grain Broker.
H—— J	Jobber Hosiery.
H—— S. A	Ret. D. G.
H—— A. & Co	Mnfrs. Tinware
H—— & M——	Ret. D. G.
H—— P. J	Skirt Materials.
H—— R. Jr	Coal Broker.
H—— C. B. & Son	Syrups and Molasses.
H—— F. L	Furnaces.
H—— G	Real Estate.
H—— C	Builder.
H—— F	Kid Gloves.
H—— J. S	Hardware.
H—— D. & W	Jobbers Cloths.
H—— S	Ret. D. G.
H—— & Son	Coal.
H—— E	Liquors.
H—— J	Ret. Clothing.
H—— G	Com'n Cotton.
H—— & C——	E. I. Shipping and Com'n.
H—— & Z	Imps. and Com'n D. G.
H—— F. S. & Co	Note Brokers.
H—— J	Diamond Setter.
H—— S	Fancy Goods.
H—— Mrs. C	Men's Furn'g.
H—— E. D	Ret. Boots and Shoes.
H—— Br s, & Co	Jobbers Hosiery.
H—— M	Laces and Embroideries.
H—— G	Confectionery.
H—— J	Cabooses.
H—— S	Sailmaker.
H—— H	Leather.
H—— J	Plumber.
H—— J. J. & Son	Paper.

H—— M—— & B——	Jobbers Hats.
H—— & M——	Hardware, etc.
H—— M	Metals.
H—— N. E	Com'n Prod.
H—— W	Imps. Drugs and Colors.
H—— W. F	Drugs.
H—— & P——	Ship Brokers.
H—— C	Liquors.
H—— H. Jr	Leather and Findings.
H—— & Co	Mnfrs. Jewelry.
H—— E	Ret. Boots and Shoes.
H—— G. F	Butter.
H—— & N——	Mnfrs. Quilts.
H—— J. L. & Co	Prov.
H—— E. E	Liquors.
H—— J. C	Drugs.
H—— J. J	Ret. Boots and Shoes.
H—— & Van R——	Com'n Tobacco and Cigars.
H—— I	Mnfr. Children's Clothing. etc.
H—— S	Auctioneer.
H—— & G——	Butter and Cheese.
H—— D—— & Co	S. Am. Prod.
H—— R—— & Co	Shipping and Com'n.
H—— S. W	Leather.
H—— A. Sons	Printers and Pub'rs.
H—— G	Butcher.
H—— H	Furniture.
H—— M	Clothing.
H—— M. S	Woollen Rags.
H—— N	Clothing.
H—— F	Roofer.
H—— A. C., Agt	Diamond Broker.
H—— F. & Co	Cotton Shipping and Com'n.
H—— M	Manf. Lace Goods.
H—— M. & Co	Imps. Kid Gloves.
H—— Bros	Furs.
H—— L. & W	Watches and Jewelry.
H—— D. S	Furniture.
H—— N	Metals.
H—— A. & Co	Whol. Jewelry.
H—— J. & Co	Shipping and Com'n.
H—— & H——	Whol. D. G.
H—— & M——	Publishers.
H—— C	Imp. Cigar Ribbons.
H—— H. L	Tailor.
H—— J. L	Tailor.
H—— I	Ret. Boots and Shoes.
H—— L	Ret. Clothing.
H—— Bros	Whol. Liquors.
H—— J. R	Mdse. Broker.
H—— M—— Co	Stencil Dies and Plates.
H—— W. C. & J. M	Agents Sewing Machines.
H—— E. S	Brass Founder.
H—— A	Whol. Carpets.
H—— G. W	Jeweller.

H—— H.	Saloon.
H—— C. & Co	Com'n Gro.
H—— M—— & Co	Ret. D. G.
H—— W. & Co	D. G.
H—— S. C.	Machinery.
H—— W. A.	Paperhangings and Clothing.
H—— F.	Imp. Teas.
H—— R. H.	Imp. Embroideries.
H—— H. G.	Liquors.
H—— D.	Coal.
H—— M.	Mnfr. Trimmings.
H—— Mrs. T.	Ret. B. and S.
H—— C. & Co.	Whol. Liquors.
H—— H. & Co.	Imps. Dress Trim'gs.
H—— B.	Cloths, etc.
H——L. & Co	Tobacco.
H—— & N——	Ship Chandlers.
H—— L.	Chemicals.
H—— A.	Patent Rights.
H—— B. W.	Music Pub'r, etc.
H—— C. B.	Restaurant.
H—— F.	Ret. Cigars.
H—— & T——	Imps. Millinery.
H—— G. D.	Drugs.
H—— J. T.	Com'n Flour, etc.
H—— R. S.	Paperhangings.
H—— & W——	Hatters.
H—— & C——	Mnfrs. Straw Hats.
H—— & S——	Mnfrs. Hats and Straw Goods.
H—— A. D.	Nickelplating.
H——D. & Co.	Rubber Goods.
H—— W.	Lager Beer.
H—— W. C.	Leaf Tobacco.
H—— C. C. M.	Human Hair.
H—— P.	Restaurant.
H—— C.	Real Estate.
H—— J. M.	Musical Insts.
H—— M. & Co.	Bedding.
H—— J. E.	Shipjoiner.
H—— W. & Co.	Iron.
H—— H. & Co.	Com'n F. Gro.
H—— C.	Hall.
H—— C. F. L.	Ret. Drugs.
H—— & F——	Mnfrs. Fancy Boxes and Baskets.
H—— H.	Liquors.
H—— T. G.	Painter.
H—— G.	Furniture, etc.
H—— E. J. & Co.	Mnfrs. Files and Saws.
H—— & S——	Shipwrights.
H—— J. F.	Hotel.
H—— T.	Mnfr. Glass Oilers.
H—— H.	Cigars.
H—— L.	Cigars.
H—— C. & Co.	Scroll Sawing.
H—— E.	Restaurant and Beer.
H—— & Co.	Lager Beer, etc.
H—— & D——	Mirrors.
H—— B.	Operator.
H—— & B——	Flour and Feed.
H—— & C——	Flour and Feed.
H—— J.	Stevedore and Liq.
H—— M. & Son	Whol. Gro.
H—— W. B. & Co.	Photo. Materials.
H—— & Co.	Feed.
H—— & I.	Metals.
H—— L. & Co.	Whol. Liquors.
H—— H. N.	Coal.
H—— H.	Cancelling Stamps.
H—— H. & Co.	Book Pub'rs.
H—— L. V.	Imp. Gloves.
H—— & D——	Tobacco.
H—— H. O. & Co.	Wines.
H—— M.	Whol. Fancy Goods.
H—— & M——	Jewelry, etc.
H—— Mrs. A.	Ret. F'cy Goods.
H—— J. M.	R. E. Broker.
H—— & Co.	Canned Fish.
H—— J. D.	Gro., etc.
H—— & D—— M—— Co.	Locks.
H—— & F——	Cabinetmkrs.
H—— C. & Co.	Mnfr. Caps.
H—— B—— & Co.	Men's Furn'g.
H—— J. H.	Jeweller.
H—— T. C.	Whol. Millinery Goods.
H—— T. B. & Son	Hay and Grain.
H—— A.	Imp. Watches.
H—— D. & Co.	Metal Brokers.
H—— & F——	Builders.
H—— C. N. & Co.	Com'n Prod.
H—— K—— & S——	Boots and Shoes.
H—— W. K. & Co.	Com'n Prod.
H—— C. H.	Painter.
H—— N. F.	Com'n Hops, etc.
H—— J. & Co.	Com'n Flour and Grain.
H—— M—— Co.	Machines.
H—— C. B.	Printer.
H—— M. H.	Iron Railings.
H—— W. R.	Photographer.
H—— & Co.	Silverplated Ware.
H—— & Co.	Bankers.
H—— F. & H.	Com'n Cotton.
H—— J.	Twines.
H—— J. O.	R. E. Broker.
H—— L. T.	Stock Broker.
H—— R.	Mnfr. Camphorine.
H—— S. W. & J. I.	Prod., etc.
H—— S.W. & Co.	Hatters' Trimmings.
H—— C. O.	Coal.
H—— J. E.	Hardware.
H—— S—— & Co.	Paper.
H—— W. F.	Hardware.
H—— G.	Hotel.
H—— A.	Drugs.
H—— H—— C—— & B—— Co.
H—— I. N. & Co.	Advg. Agents.
H—— R—— G—— Co.
H—— & B——	Shipping and Com'n.

H—— T. W. B.........Stock Broker.
H—— M—— Co.....Patent Window
  Fastenings.
H—— D...................Tailor.
H—— H. I.............Hide Broker.
H—— S. E.................Clothing.
H—— & B——.......Flour and Feed.
H—— & H——.....Jobbers Millinery.
H—— A. W. & T............Tailors.
H—— S—— H—— M—— Co.
H—— R ....Jeweller.
H—— H..................Liquors.
H—— J. Jr.............Com'n Paper.
H—— M. J....•....Sewing Machines.
H—— D. B. & Co..........Com'n Hats.
H—— P—— C—— W——.
H—— & M——................Teas.
H—— C. T..................Meds.
H—— W. H...............Com'n.
H—— P—— L—— Co.
H—— & C——.........Electrotypers.
H—— F. W. & Bro..Com'n Chemicals.
H—— H. G.....Brushes and Brooms.
H—— P. V..................Hotel.
H—— & G——.......Mnfrs. Trim'gs.
H—— D. W............Woodenware.
H—— E. W. & Son........Furniture.
H—— S. A.............Ret. Shirts.
H—— Bros................Jewelry.
H—— & Co...............Varnish.
H—— B. Jr......Window Shades.
H—— J......Whol. and Ret. Liquors.
H—— S. & Son........Jobbers D. G.
H—— J. & Co....Milliners and Dress-
  mkrs.
I—— B—— M—— Co....Roofing, etc.
I—— F....................Rags.
I—— M—— & Co.......Vault Lights.
I—— S...............Drug Broker.
I—— W—— & Co.........Furniture.
I—— L. & Co..................Prod.
I—— J............. ......Ret. D. G.
I—— P—— Co.
I—— M. & Son........Cabinetmkrs.
I—— & C——.....Jobbers Silks, Rib-
  bons, etc.
I—— H.............Mnfr. Syrups.
I—— A. & Co.............Sponges.
I—— D. J....................Ice.
I—— P—— L—— Co....Lamps, etc.
J—— H...............Mnfg. Chemist.
J—— J.............Jobber Cloths.
J—— R.....................Cigars.
J—— S. C....Mnfr. Silverware Cases.
J—— W................Com'n Prod.
J—— W. W................Twines.
J—— C. W. & Co....Mnfrs. Fringes.
J—— W. & Co.........Imps. Cutlery.
J—— M..................Glassware.
J—— F...... Sugars and Molasses.
J—— E........Broker Naval Stores.

J—— G. M.....Imp. Precious Stones.
J—— Mrs. H.....Tailors' Trimmings.
J—— L..............Ret. Clothing.
J—— L....................Jewelry.
J—— L. J............Jobber Liquors.
J—— S...................Clothing.
J—— & R........Whol. Clothing.
J—— O. H............Whol. Drugs.
J—— T..........Mnfr. Dress Caps.
J—— F. P. & Co.......Stock Brokers.
J—— R—— C—— Co.
J—— P. & Bro ......Jobbers Jewelry.
J—— R..................Contractor.
J—— D. & J.............Architects.
J—— G..............Mnfr. Shirts.
J—— & C——..Tea, Coffee and Spices.
J—— & J..............Imps. Hair.
J—— S. H............Spring Beds.
J—— E. Jr.......Patent Suspenders.
J—— L. D. F.......Fishing Tackle.
J—— & B——... ....Builders.
J—— & Co...............Clothing.
J—— & A..................Hotel.
J—— J. C. & Co.......Com'n Coal.
J—— J. & Sons....Mnfrs. White Lead
  and Linseed Oil.
J—— J. P. & Co.........Book Pub'rs.
J—— C.........Gen'l. Mdse. Broker.
J—— H. W..........R. E. Operator.
J—— N...........School Furniture.
J—— B. & Sons.......Sugar Refiners.
J—— R—— L—— Co.
J—— S. & Co..............Lighters.
J—— V—— Co.....Mnfrs. Valves.
J—— W. M. & R. H.........Lumber.
J—— & M——..........Bookbinders.
J—— A.................Auctioneer.
J—— G. R................Toys, etc.
J—— J. P..........Oils and Glue.
J—— J. J. & Co...Jobbers Hats, Caps,
  and Furs.
J—— F. & Co....Imps. and Mnfrs. Al-
  bums and Fancy Goods.
J—— C.............House Furn'g.
J—— J................Prov. Broker.
J—— S....................Wines.
J—— S...................Painter.
J—— W. H....................Gro.
J—— B. & Co........Grain Brokers.
J—— D. S. & A. G...Com'n Flour and
  Feed.
J—— E. & Co.......Com'n Lumber.
J—— & S——.Bond and Loan Brokers.
J—— & O——....Shipping and Com'n
  Prod.
J—— Bros......Printers and Stat'rs.
J—— M. J. & Co......Tea and Coffee.
J—— L........Mnfr. Lace Goods, etc.
J—— G. A..................Jewelry.
J—— C..............Stationery, etc.
J—— W. A...... ....Builder.

J—— & E——.................Hotel.	K—— T. D.............Advg. Agent.
J—— P.............Com'n Prod.	K—— O—— & Co...........Tobacco.
J—— H............Com'n For. D. G.	K—— D. D..............Spice Mills.
J—— H. & Co........Imitation Hair.	K—— D................Carpets.
J—— J. S. & Co..............Prod.	K—— J.................Liquors.
J—— H.................Liquors.	K—— W...............Rectifier.
J—— D. J.............Com'n Prod.	K—— & Co.............Furniture.
J—— W.............Crockery.	K—— & E——........ Paper Stock.
K—— E.......Ret. Millinery.	K—— & M——............Lumber.
K—— S. W...........Mnfr. Cloaks.	K—— F. C. & Co....Men's Furn'g.
K—— F. J... Meerschaum Pipes, etc.	K—— & H............Stationery.
K—— G...........Worsted Goods.	K—— J. F.........R. E. Broker.
K—— L.................Stoves.	K—— G. W...............Oils.
K—— J. & Bro....Mnfrs. Pocketbooks.	K—— & H—— Stationery and Printing.
K—— J..................Calfskins.	K—— D. T.................Builder.
K—— M....................Cigars.	K—— W. H............Undertaker.
K—— J. & Co.........Mnfrs. Pipes.	K—— H. C. & Co.............Com'n.
K—— P...................Wines.	K—— & Co.............Ret. D. G.
K—— M..............Imp. Cutlery.	K—— & M....Children's Carriages.
K—— J. J.............Trimmings.	K—— F. A.....Theatrical Hosiery.
K—— E.......Jobber Dress Trim'gs.	K—— C. B.....Sashes, Doors, and
K—— I..................Peddler.	Blinds.
K—— S. L. & Son.......Restaurant.	K—— J............Mnfr. Morocco.
K—— J. K...................Furs.	K—— F. O..........Com'n Oils.
K—— E.............Diamonds, etc.	K—— A. W. & Co....Silk and Fancy
K—— J. & Co.............Clothing.	D. G.
K—— A. & Bro.......Mnfrs. Cigars.	K—— & P——......Mnfrs. B. and S.
K—— J.........Gro. and Baker.	K—— A........Jobber Clothing
K—— L...........Mnfr. B. and S.	K—— & B——.......Stock Brokers.
K—— & Co.........Mnfrs. Boilers.	K—— Bros............Com'n Mers.
K—— Mrs. M.............Ret. D. G.	K—— & C———....Prov. and Fish.
K—— & Co.........Shoe Bows.	K—— T. & T——......Auctioneers.
K—— C................Butcher.	K—— & J——........Silverware.
K—— J...........Whol. Clothing.	K—— H. T. & Son......Patent Meds.
K—— S. & Co.........Com'n Cotton.	K—— C. T. P..........Furniture.
K—— & Co.............Clothing.	K—— E................Confec.
K—— & J——....Imps. Pictures, etc.	K—— H. H.................Banker.
K—— & Co........Imps. Pictures.	K—— B.......Mnfr. Ladies' Wear.
K—— P..................Liquors.	K—— J.......Broker Naval Stores.
K—— & D——.......Billiard Saloon.	K—— M. A...........Mnfr. Corsets.
K—— J..........Imps. F'cy G.	K—— W.................Liquors.
K—— & M——........Mnfrs. Cloaks.	K—— A. & Co.........Gen'l Com'n.
K—— & Co.....Shipping and Com'n.	K—— C—— M—— Co........Syrups.
K—— & Co...........Patent Meds.	K—— F—— & Co....R. R. Supplies.
K—— J. & Son...............Flour.	K—— J. & Co................Prov.
K—— & Co.....t. Mnfrs. Letter Files.	K—— W. & Co......Imps. and Mnfrs.
K—— A. T..............Liquors.	Corks.
K—— D. B., Jr.......Ins. Broker, etc.	K—— & Co............R. E. Brokers.
K—— S. C. & Co. Lumber and Veneers.	K—— & M——................Sauce.
K—— J...............Furniture.	K—— W. P.............Furniture.
K—— D. & Co.............Liquors.	K—— N. & Son.........Pickles, etc.
K—— J. M. Manufacturing Co.	K—— R—— & Co.....Com'n Lumber.
K—— R................Jewelry.	K—— C. N...........Cotton Broker.
K—— M. & Son.............Liquors.	K—— F. S............Mnfr. Cigars.
K—— & W......Whol. Clothing.	K—— J. P................Hay.
K—— B. & Co............Chemists.	K—— G. T. & Co............Liquors.
K—— S—— & Co....Mnfrs. Jewelry.	K—— W.........Ret. Fancy Goods.
K—— C ....Mer. Tailor.	K—— & L——........Lithographers.
K—— E. G....................Oils.	K—— E. R...............Sailmkr.
K—— C. G........Leather Weigher.	K—— J. C..................Tailor.
K—— J. Q.............Patent Meds.	K—— J. H..........Card Engraver.

K—— Bros. & Co......... Gen'l Mdse. Brokers.
K—— W..................... Fwd'r.
K—— A..................... Builder.
K—— H..................... Shirts.
K—— S. P............... Mattresses.
K—— V. & Co...... Imps. and Com'n Drugs.
K—— F. W........... Cotton Broker.
K—— F................. Rhine Wines.
K—— A..................... Lamps.
K—— C. E.................... Gro.
K—— J. F................... Gro.
K—— S. H................ Builder.
K—— H. & Son............ Bricks.
K—— J. G. Mnfg. Co.... Mufrs. Steam Gauges.
K—— & Co........... Prov. Brokers.
K—— T. B. & Co........... Crockery.
K—— A. Jr....... Lard and Lard Oil Broker.
K—— G. T..... Agent and Imp. D. G.
K—— T. M............. Liq. Broker.
K—— W................. Ins. Broker.
K—— W. H..... Shipping and Com'n.
K—— J. J............. Iron Foundry.
K—— & M—............ Carriages.
K—— E. M........... Stock Broker.
K—— G. & Sons.. Imps. Musical Insts.
K——J................... ....Liquors.
K—— S ns & Co.......... Stationers.
K—— S...... ... ...Mnfr. Flowers.
K—— H. & Co.......... Piano Legs.
K—— C................. Cabinetmkr.
K—— J. F................... Pies.
K—— C................. D. G. Broker.
K—— M............. Jobber Gloves.
K—— L. C. & Co...... Advg. Agents and Printing.
K—— & J—............ Fruits, etc.
K—— & S—........... Whol. Gro.
K—— H................ Ret. Gro.
K—— P— & Co.... Pipes and Cig.
K—— L..... Cotton Bats and Twines.
K—— & H—.......... Showcases.
K—— & S—........ Fruit Brokers.
K—— Bros.................. Drugs.
K—— K................. Safes, etc.
K—— A....... Leather and Findings.
K—— J.......... Mnfr. Door Knobs.
K—— Bros.................. Slate.
K——G. G—— Bronze Powder Works.
K—— K—— & S..... Jobbers Cloths.
K—— L—— & Co........... Bankers.
K—— & S—........... Carriages.
K—— A. & Co.... Mnfrs. Lace Goods.
K—— & F—..... Jobbers Hosiery.
K—— M............. Oils and D. G.
L—— J., Estate of............. Carpets.
L—— A. W.... Broker R. R. Supplies.
L—— G. W.. Mnfr. Soda-Water Cups.

L—— & Co..... Sewing-Machine Attachments.
L—— L................. Bookbinder.
L—— J. J................. Liquors.
L—— W................. Butcher.
L—— M. C.... Jobber Men's Furn'g.
L—— T. J....... Upholstery Goods.
L—— P. W. & Co..... Mnfrs. Ladies' Belts, etc.
L—— S—— & Co..... Mnfrs. Tables.
L—— H............... Furniture.
L—— B—— & Co........ Bankers.
L—— G—— R—— & T—— Co
L—— P......... Whol. Shirts, etc.
L—— F—— & C—.. Mnfrs. Cutlery.
L—— A. & Co....... Mnfrs. Neckties.
L—— R. E................... Furs.
L—— S... ......Imp. Watches and Jewelry.
L—— K.... Jobber Dress Trimmings.
L—— M—— Co....... Rubber Goods.
L—— H............... Stock Broker.
L—— & B—....... Stock Brokers.
L—— J............. Liq. and Billiards.
L—— & N—......... Mnfrs. Hats.
L—— & B—....... Imps. Sponges.
L—— F. K....... Teas and Coffees.
L—— C—— S—— M—— Co.
L—— J. & Co..... Flour, Grain, and Gen'l Com'n.
L—— & S—......... Cabinetmkrs.
L—— S—— & Co.... Com'n Shipping.
L—— M............... Cattle Drover.
L—— N............... Leather, etc.
L—— & Bro........ Bankers, etc.
L—— G.. Ship and Steamboat Owner.
L—— M................... Prod.
L—— Bros........... Prod. Dealers.
L—— J. W................... Baker.
L—— J................... Jeweller.
L—— W. S......... Jobber Flour.
L—— A. C. & Co........... Liquors.
L—— Bros. & Co...... Bankers and Brokers.
L—— C—— Co............. Cement.
L—— & Co................. Storage.
L—— & N—.. Wines, Liq. and Teas.
L—— J. & Co......... Mnfrs. Bags.
L—— R. M............. Com'n Grain.
L—— J................. Stationer.
L—— S. B........... Metal Broker.
L—— L. T................... Prod.
L—— J. & Co......... D. G. Brokers.
L—— & P—...... Petroleum Cans.
L—— Bros.............. Stationers.
L—— I.............. Ret. D. G.
L—— S. M............. Ret. D. G.
L—— & F—.... Tobacco and Pipes.
L—— Bros.................. Tobacco.
L—— & D—........ Whol. Liquors.
L—— B—— & L—— Co.

L—— C. F. & Co.........Pickles, etc.
L—— J. F. & Co.....Mnfrs. Brooms.
L—— & B——.........Fancy Goods.
L—— J. S....Mnfr. and Jobber Draw-
                ers, Shirts, etc.
L—— M., Jr........Galvanized Iron.
L—— E................Hair Goods.
L—— E. & L DeF——..Gen'l Com'n.
L—— Bros.................Books.
L—— A. Sons...........Whol. Gro.
L—— A. W. & F. W.....Com'n Prod.
L—— J. & Co......Pocketbooks, etc.
L—— C. B.............Flour Broker.
L—— S. W...........Com'n Flour.
L—— P. & Son........Ret. Clothing.
L—— C. H.............Com'n Piod.
L—— L. & G. S................Hotel.
L—— M. L....Fancy Goods and Pins.
L—— F.....................Liquors.
L—— F. & H...............Liquors.
L—— M—— & Co.....Leaf Tobacco.
L—— P. & Co................Wines.
L—— J. & E.........D. G. Folders.
L—— C. & S. E..............Hotel.
L—— DeW. C. & Co......Pub'rs and
                    Booksellers.
L—— T. F. & A——.....Com'n Prod.
L—— L. H., Bro. & Co.......Clothing.
L—— & E——......Lubricating Oils.
L—— F. W. & Co....Imps. Piano and
                Table Covers.
L—— P.................Hog Broker.
L—— F. & Co............Trimmings.
L—— T. F. & Co...........Printers.
L—— & F——........R. E. Brokers.
L—— A. & Co.........Jobbers D. G.
L—— O—— Co.
L—— J. H......Precious Stones and
                        Silks.
L—— F. H. & Co........Printers' Ink.
L—— S—— & Co.....Whol. Liquors.
L—— A...................Jeweller.
L—— Mrs. J.............Stoves, etc.
L—— L...........Mnfr. Shirts, etc.
L—— S.............Hats and Caps.
L—— A. D.........Mnfr. Clothing.
L—— B.......Ret. Fancy Goods.
L—— J. E.......Mnfr. Ladies' Suits.
L—— M............Wines and Liq.
L—— O. S......Com'n Fancy Goods.
L—— S.................Imp. Laces.
L—— S........Ret. Boots and Shoes.
L—— A. & J.......Mnfrs. Clothing.
L—— Bros ....Mnfrs. Cigars.
L—— J. & M......Whol. Clothing.
L—— J. & Co.................Lye.
L—— & B——.........Stock Brokers.
L—— & K——.......Mnfrs. Shoes.
L—— & Bro.........Fancy Goods.
L—— A. & Bros.....Mnfrs. Clothing.
L—— Mrs. R....Mnfr. Ladies' Suits.

L—— T. M.......Ret. Men's Furn'g.
L—— Bros..............Law Books.
L—— E. & Co.........Mnfrs.' Agents.
L—— W. R. & Co.........Rectifiers.
L—— & B——......Prov. and Tallow
                    Brokers.
L—— S............Imp. Kid Gloves.
L—— R..........Ret. Men's Furn'g.
L—— M—— Co....Machinery.
L—— J...................Vinegar.
L—— & E——..........Pianofortes.
L—— & I——........Mnfrs. Hats.
L—— J.................Boxmkr.
L—— A. W...........Gro. and Liq.
L—— J.................Liquors.
L—— & Sons...........Pianofortes.
L—— Bros.................Liquors.
L—— & Co.....Imps. Laces, White
            Goods, Embroideries, etc.
L—— A....................Cigars.
L—— S............Whol Millinery.
L—— R. J. & A. W...Type Founders.
L—— C. A..............Tea Broker.
L—— J. A...........Hair Jewelry.
L—— A. B.....Hop and Malt Broker.
L—— W. O................Tailor.
L—— & G.......Bronze Powder.
L—— S...............Mnfr. Frames.
L—— B—— & Co......Mnfrs. Boys'
                        Clothing.
L—— L. & Son......Whol. Clothing.
L—— M............Auction Goods.
L—— & S——....Watches and Watch
                    Materials.
L—— H....................Metals.
L—— A..........Ret. Fancy Goods.
L—— S. & B......Jobbers Millinery.
L—— E. C..........R. R. Operator.
L—— E. B.........R. R. Operator.
L—— L...........Whol. Clothing.
L—— F. N..........Mnfr. Brooms.
L—— J. H.........Mineral Water.
L—— H. & Co.......Knitting Cotton
                and Cotton Yarn.
L—— & M——............Stationers.
L—— & Co..............Bankers.
L—— & H——............Bankers.
L—— & G——.........Cigar Moulds.
L—— B—— Co......Mnfrs. Buttons.
L—— G..................Tailor.
L—— M. W....Broker Naval Stores.
L—— & Co......Wines, Teas and To-
                        bacco.
L—— & H——......Looking-Glasses.
L—— & Z——....Specie Brokers, etc.
L—— & K——.......Mnfrs. Jewelry.
L—— C.................Trimmings.
L—— & M——...Mnfrs. Ladies' Belts
L—— R................Furniture.
L—— & Co...............Guano.
L—— D. H........Com'n Cotton, etc.

L—— J.........Ret. Boots and Shoes.
l,—— H—— A——..........Harness.
L—— I. M.............Gloves, etc.
L—— & Co.............Kid Gloves.
l,—— K. H.,Steam-Engine and Cut-off.
L—— Bros. & Co...Imps. Tobacco and
Cigars.
L—— W. A. & T——....Mnfrs. Neck-
ties.
L—— J. H................Liquors.
L—— C. H. G. & Co....Mnfrs. Valises.
l,—— S................Furniture.
L—— S. & Co........Whol. Clothing.
l,—— & G——....Fringes and Tassels.
L—— S. C...............Hats, etc.
l,—— H. P.............Prov. Broker.
L—— J ....Com'n Grain, etc.
L—— D. H. & Co........Gas Stoves.
L—— I.........Broker Crockery, etc.
l,—— I................Flowers.
L—— L........Jobber Millinery, etc.
L—— S................Neckties.
l,—— & G——...........Wallpaper.
L—— C............Com'n Prod.
l,—— E ....Mnfr. Lace Goods.
l,—— J. L................Teas.
l,—— M—— Co............Mining.
L—— W—— & Co.........Foundry.
L—— G—— P—— & P—— C——
M—— Co.
L—— C. & Co...S. Am. Shipping and
Com'n.
l,—— H.................Printer.
l,—— & S——............Wagons.
l,—— E. S.....Railway and Carriage
Cloth.
L—— A..............Real Estate.
L—— & S——..Jobbers Jewelry, etc.
L—— M............Watches, etc.
L—— J............Com'n Silks.
l,—— H........Ret. Boots and Shoes.
L—— & S——.......Piano Materials.
l,—— & G——.......R. R. Supplies.
L—— T. C. & Co...........Brewers.
l, —— E................Florist.
L—— J..............Furniture.
l,—— J.................Lumber.
l,—— T.................Liquors.
L—— T. P ....Liquors.
l,—— C. & Co........Mdse. Brokers.
L—— J. T. & S——.........Neckties.
L—— R. V. & Co....Imps. Laces, etc.
L—— & G ——..............Pianos.
l,—— E..............Patent Jacks.
l,—— H............Com'n Liquors.
l,—— L...........Sewing-Machines.
l,—— T.............Jewelry.
l,—— J. M............Com'n Paper.
L—— J. & Co........Mnfrs.' Agents.
l,—— & A——....Mnfrs. Jewelry Set-
tings.

L—— & B——.........Ship Chandlers.
McB—— S. V.............Hats, etc.
McB—— J. D. & Co.....Imps. Laces.
McC—— B.................Tailor.
McC—— & C——.....Jobbers Fancy
Goods.
McC—— J.........Tobacco and Cigars.
McC—— J...............Tobacco.
McC—— W.........Tobacco Broker.
McC—— N. & Bro.......Leather and
Findings.
McC—— P...............Ret. D. G.
McC—— & Co................Drugs.
McC—— Bros............Hardware.
McC—— J. & Co...........Lumber.
McC—— J. G...Mnfr. Women's and
Children's Lace Caps.
McC—— & Co....Galvanized and Re-
fined Sheet Iron.
McC—— J. M........Gen'l Com'n.
McC—— J..........Malt, Hops, etc.
McC—— W.............Builder.
McC—— J..............Builder.
McC—— J. E.............Builder.
McC—— R., Agent....Ship Chandler.
McC—— S. G........Drug Broker.
McC—— H....Mnfr. Shirt Bosoms and
Women's Skirts.
McC—— J. J..............Lumber.
McC—— J. W.......Prov. Broker.
McC—— L—— Co.
McD—— & R——......Ret. B. and S.
McD—— G.............Com'n Prod.
McD—— J.............Restaurant.
McD—— R. G...Contractors' Supplies.
McD—— L—— & Co.........Fruits.
McE—— T..............Imp. Seeds.
McE——T. B.........Ret. Clothing.
McE—— H—— & Co....Mosquito Net-
ting, etc.
McG—— & W——.......Com'n Prod.
McG—— E........Wines, Liqs., etc.
McG—— G. W..Paper Fasteners, etc.
McG—— Miss L........Fancy Goods.
McG—— J. D........Mdse. Broker.
McG—— T. & Co........Oil Works.
McG—— H............Plumber.
McG—— J.........Lard and Grease.
McG—— R..........Writing Fluids.
McH—— J. V...............Shoes.
McH—— P.............Ret. D. G.
McI—— & B——.....Wines and Liq.
McI—— T.................Marble.
McK—— C. W.......Com'n Timber.
McK—— & F...............Drugs.
McK—— & W...Shipping and Com'n.
McK—— W.............Machinist.
McK—— H.............Liquors.
McK—— J.....Ret. Boots and Shoes.
McL—— E.......Shades and Paper-
hangings.

McL—— J.............. .....Hotel.
McL—— & Co....Gas Fixtures, China,
                             etc.
McM—— D—— & Co....Shipping and
                             Com'n.
McM—— Mrs. J....Ret. Fancy Goods.
McM—— R.....Bonnet-Frame Wire.
McM—— & D——....Ship Chandlers.
McN—— F.....Whol. H. and C., etc.
McQ—— & M——..........Liquors.
McR—— A...............Stoneyard.
McW—— W—— & Co.....Printers.
M—— & V——......Looking Glasses.
M—— & Co............Com'n Cotton.
M—— & W——..........Com'n Prod.
M—— F. S............Prod. Broker.
M—— Bros...............Furniture.
M—— W. & Co..Shipping and Com'n.
M—— W. A......Com'n Twines, etc.
M—— J. O'N...Dealer Auction Goods.
M—— P. A.....Shipping and Com'n.
M—— C—— Co...............Colors.
M—— W. & Co.................Prod.
M—— J.........Ret. Fancy Goods.
M—— J. T.............Scrap Iron.
M—— C. W. B—— Co........Mnfrs.
                             Brushes.
M—— & L——....Coffee and Mustard
                             Mills.
M—— P.................Varnisher.
M—— M......Mnfr. and Whol. Furs.
M—— H...............Whol. Gro.
M—— J.................Liquors.
M—— & M——........Whol. Gro.
M—— M................Bluestone.
M—— & Q——..Shipping and Com'n.
M—— J. S......Mnfr. Ladies' Suits.
M—— M.....:.......Mdse. Broker.
M—— & M——......Imps. and Com'n
                             Sauces.
M—— & Co................Storage.
M—— B—— M—— Co...Paper Bags.
M—— L......................Feed.
M—— T........ .Com'n Italian Prod.
M—— Mme. C...Ladies' Underwear.
M—— H........ ....Hair Goods.
M—— J..............Advg. Agent.
M—— L. L..........Southern Com'n.
M—— Mrs. F.......Ret. F'cy Goods.
M—— S.......Imp. Druggists' Ware.
M—— D. D......Com'n Flour, Grain
                             and Feed.
M—— M—— & C—— Co.
M—— P—— Co.
M—— P—— Co.
M—— S—— M—— Co.
M—— S—— M—— Co. of Nevada.
M—— S—— Co.
M—— & Bro............Kid Gloves.
M—— W......Mnfr. Harness Loops.
M—— H. & Co..Bankers and Brokers.

M—— & M——..........Hardware.
M—— A. W.................Slate.
M—— M...................Leather.
M—— A.............Ret. Clothing.
M—— J.............Jobber Hosiery.
M—— J. W...................D. G.
M—— M......Ret. Boots and Shoes.
M—— J. & Co.....Imps. Bronze, etc.
M—— J. C........Com'n Silk Goods.
M—— S.................Trusses.
M—— J. A. & Co......Stock Brokers.
M—— & Co............Printers.
M—— & R——.............Stationers.
M—— J. P...............Fruit, etc.
M—— H—— C—— Co.
M—— M—— & Co....Wines and Liq.
M—— M—— C—— W——.
M—— H.................Liquors.
M—— M.................Uphol-terer.
M—— E. H.......Toilet Soaps.
M—— W. D...................Coal.
M—— G........Mnfr. Straw Goods.
M—— S—— Co...............Safes.
M—— J...........Ret. Fancy Goods.
M—— M..........Boots and Shoes.
M—— Bros.. .....Imps. Kid Gloves.
M—— & Co...........Stock Brokers.
M—— A...........Publisher.
M—— R—— E—— Co.
M—— & E——......Whol. Liquors.
M—— J. S...............Contractor.
M—— F. O. & W—— S—— R—— Co.
M—— J. W.........Leather Broker.
M—— L..........Whol. Furs.
M—— & D——.............Marble.
M—— & P——..........Prod.
M—— A.............Hatters' Goods.
M—— J.....Ladies' and Men's Furn'g.
M—— R...............Organs, etc.
M—— & U——..........Prod.
M—— M.....:.......Whol. Jewelry.
M—— & VanR——.Mining Engineers.
M—— J. M. & Co.....Havana Leaf
                             Tobacco.
M—— A...............Brewer.
M—— & B—— H—— E—— Co.
M—— M. E.......Engravings, etc.
M—— E. L..............Patents.
M—— C. & D——..Com'n Barrels, etc.
M—— L. J.. ......Com'n Liquors.
M—— & C——.........Stationers.
M—— & I.——.........Imps. Linens.
M—— A...........Ret. Fancy Goods.
M—— Bros............Japan Trade.
M—— C.......Cotton Shipping and
                             Com'n.
M—— G. W.............Tool Works.
M—— J......................Gro.
M—— C. L...Whol. Boots and Shoes.
M—— J.........Ret. Men's Furn'g.
M—— C. S.............Pickles, etc.

M—— S................Gro.
M—— J. D. & Co...........Liquors.
M—— C. H............ .....Tobacco.
M—— J. J...........Crockery.
M—— J. R. & Co....Com'n and Imps.
　　　　　Cigars and Sugars.
M—— & Co.................Tailors.
M—— J.................Stoves.
M—— C. F.........Mnfr. Stationery.
M—— M. & Co......Window Shades.
M—— S. M.........Mnfg. Silks, etc.
M—— M..............Fancy Goods.
M—— N................Jeweller.
M—— N................Ret. Hats.
M—— W................Gro.
M—— F. & B................Gro.
M—— & M——...............Saw Mill.
M—— I...........Men's Furn'g.
M—— M. & H.........Liq. and Oils.
M—— & L................Cigars.
M—— M. H...............Clothing.
M—— T.... ....Liquors.
M—— T..........Ship Broker.
M—— & Co................Jewelry.
M—— J. F. & Co...........Prov.
M—— & H——.............Toys.
M—— A. H............Mdse. Broker.
M—— J. B......Ret. Boots and Shoes.
M—— T. J....Tea, Coffee and Spices.
M—— T................Furniture.
M—— W. C....Tinware and Roofing.
M—— C. R. & J. W.........Tailors.
M—— C. S. & Co..Sashes and Blinds.
M—— J. & Co..............Liquors.
M—— J. H. & Son......Gen'l Com'n.
M—— M. R. & Co........Com'n Prod.
M—— & Co.................Drugs.
M—— & Co.................Painters.
M—— W. E. & Son..........Music.
M—— Bros......Agents Thread, etc.
M—— Miss A.....Ret. Millinery, etc.
M—— S. A...........Stock Broker.
M—— T. B.......Fishing Tackle, etc.
M—— S. H. & Son..Purchasing Agts.
M—— C. J. & Co..........Ret. Hats.
M—— B. R........Tobacco and Cig.
M—— J. H.............Drug Broker.
M—— C. S................Drugs.
M—— M. S........Ret. Fancy Goods.
M—— & H——........Stock Brokers.
M—— G. M............Prov. Broker.
M—— A. C................Tailor.
M—— M..............R. E. Broker.
M—— & K——................Hotel.
M—— F. B....South American Com'n.
M—— W. C..Stoves and House Furn'g.
M—— D. & Co...........Wines, etc.
M—— F...............Mnfr. Combs.
M—— Mrs. A................Liquors.
M—— P. & F............Liquors.
M—— N. F............Com'n Furs.

M—— C...............Sign Painter.
M—— & D——.............Builders.
M—— C. P................Tailor.
M—— B. F.............Silver Chaser.
M—— E......Diamonds and F'cy G.
M—— J.............Fancy Goods.
M—— J.......Ret. Boots and Shoes.
M—— G. W. & Co ....Rubber Paints.
M—— Mrs. A......Ret. Fancy Goods.
M—— J.................Marble.
M—— T. F.............Lapidary.
M—— H. N............Com'n Prod.
M—— D. P. & Co......Stock Brokers.
M—— E. E. Sons.....Shipping and
　　　　　Com'n.
M—— H—— & Co...Financial Agents
　　　　　and Brokers.
M—— L. & Son...........Founders.
M—— B—— & Co....Bond Brokers,
　　　　　etc.
M—— H. E. & Co..Com'n E. I. Goods.
M—— S............Whol. Clothing.
M—— E............Stock Operator.
M—— C—— & Co.....Wines and Liq.
M—— G. F........Printers' Ink.
M—— H. G..............Prod.
M—— Mrs. A........Crockery, etc.
M—— I—— B—— & C—— R—— Co.
M—— H................Ins. Broker.
M—— J.............Patent Meds.
M—— & B——.........Ret. Clothing.
M—— & M——.........Spectacles.
M—— M..........Mnfr. Hair Goods.
M—— N...............Cigars.
M—— J. W..............Flour.
M—— Mrs. E. P......House Furn'g.
M—— & K——.............Gilders.
M—— J. E........Ret. Fancy Goods.
M—— J................Tailor.
M—— J................Hotel.
M—— J. G............Ret. D. G.
M—— & C——........Whol. Men's
　　　　　Furn'g.
M—— Bros......Drugs and Essential
　　　　　Oils.
M—— & G——...............Gro.
M—— N. L. & Co........Publishers.
M—— & Bro.........Jobbers D. G.
M—— & Co....Gro. and Com'n South-
　　　　　ern Prod.
M—— A.......Mustard, Spices, etc.
M—— P. & Son....Carriage Painters.
M—— W. H. & Co..Extension Tables.
M—— B. Jr. & Co...........Bankers.
M—— M................Liquors.
M—— P................Chemicals.
M—— R. Jr.....Shipping and Com'n.
M—— D. & Co....Mnfrs. and Jobbers
　　　　　Lace Goods.
M——F—— & Co.Shipping and Com'n.
M—— J. & Co.............Lumber.

M—— & Co...........Stock Brokers.
M—— & Co............Com'n Prod.
M—— F........Ret. Boots and Shoes.
M—— H.................Printer.
M—— H............Jobber Cloths.
M—— S............Women's Caps.
M—— S. F.....Ret. Fancy and D. G.
M—— M—— Co....Smoothing Irons.
M—— & G——............Pickles.
M—— & U——.....Com'n Flour and
                    Feed.
M—— & P——.........Laces, etc.
N—— M.............Lager Beer.
N—— M.......House Furn'g Goods.
N—— A.............Photographer.
N—— G.................Liquors.
N—— & L——....Mnfrs. Suspenders.
N—— R. H.Ret. Hats,Caps, Furs, etc.
N—— S—— Co.
N—— & G——.............Jewelry.
N—— R. W.................Broker.
N—— E. & Son.....Jobbers Clothing.
N—— & P——......Mnfrs. Imitation
                    Hair.
N—— C—— Co.
N—— T—— Co.
N—— W—— L—— & Z—— Co.
N—— W—— M—— Co.
N—— A....................Stoves.
N—— S. & Co......Imps. Wines and
                    Liq.
N—— A.....................Metals.
N—— L.............Whol. Clothing.
N—— K—— & G——....Fireworks,
                    etc.
N—— Mrs. R..........Gen'l Com'n.
N—— F. A.................Brewer.
N—— D.................Cabinetmkr.
N—— & H——.....Mnfrs. Neckties.
N—— J—— Z—— Co.
N—— H......Mnfr. Boots and Shoes.
N—— A.........Jobber Straw Goods.
N—— C. E. & Co.......Men's Furn'g.
N—— G. & Bro......Ret. F'cy Goods.
N—— J. & Sons.......Jobbers Fancy
                    Goods.
New-York A—— Co.
New-York A—— C—— P—— & P——
Co.
New-York A—— Co.
New-York C—— S—— Co.
New-York C—— Co.
New-York C—— P—— Co.
New-York C—— & S—— Co.
New-York C—— W——.
New-York E—— & P——Co.
New-York F—— S—— Co.
New-York G—— & H—— Co.
New-York G—— S—— Co.
New-York & H—— P—— Co.
New-York H—— E—— Co.

New-York L—— P—— Co.
New-York M—— Co.
New-York & N—— S—— S—— Co.
New-York & O—— C—— Co.
New-York O—— Co.
New-York P—— C—— Co.
New-York P—— M——.
New-York P—— W——.
New-York R—— Co.
New-York S—— M—— Co.
New-York S—— W——.
New-York S—— S—— Co.
New-York & S—— C—— & I—— Co.
New-York S—— M—— Co.
New-York T—— & D—— Co.
New-York T—— & E—— Co.
New-York V—— Co.
New-York W—— & S—— Co.
New-York W—— P—— Co.
New-York W—— & P—— Co.
N—— E. S.................Saddlery.
N—— L.............Stock Broker.
N—— Bros.......Imps. Fancy Goods.
N—— G....................Coal.
N—— I. U.........Ret. Shoes.
N—— J....................Coal.
N—— D—— & Co.........China, etc.
N—— A. H. & Co......Stock Brokers
             and Auctioneers.
N—— A.................Mer. Tailor.
N—— & K——.........Passage and
            Ticket Agents.
N—— O. R.......Mnfr. Fancy Goods.
N—— S. A.................Lumber.
N—— M.................Contractor.
N—— & G——.............Lumber.
N—— Bros.................Watches.
N—— H.W.................Jewelry.
N—— E. S. & Co......Jobbers Cloths.
N—— A—— N—— R—— P—— Co.
N—— R—— I—— Co.
N—— C. M. & Co.........Furniture.
N—— M. C.& Co...............Coal.
N—— P.................Contractor.
N—— & D—— M—— Co....Saddlery
           H'ware.
N—— T.................Furniture.
O'B—— J. R.........Paints and Oils.
O'B—— J.............Ret. Liquors.
O'B—— R...............Liquors.
O'C—— P. J. & Co..........Dry Dock
           Owners.
O'C—— & Son............Ret. D. G.
O'C—— F......Mnfr. Imitation Hair.
O'D—— J.............Iron Foundry.
O'D—— D.............Silk Broker.
O'H—— J. & Bro......Ret. Boots and
           Shoes.
O'K—— T.................Stationery.
O'M—— Bros..Ret. Boots and Shoes.
O'N—— B.................Liquors.

O'N—— P. H..................Coffins.
O'N—— & Co........Marble Mantels.
O'N—— A. & Co.............Liquors.
O'R—— C...................Builder.
O—— F. C.....................Coal.
O—— & K——....Washing Machines.
O—— P......Mnfr. Cloaks and Suits.
O—— Mrs. S........Ret. F'cy Goods.
O—— & W——.......Mnfrs. Shirts.
O—— S...............Ret. Clothing.
O—— F. & Son.........Cabinetmkrs.
O—— A. S. & E........Livery Stables.
O—— & Co.....Shipping and Com'n.
O—— & C——.......Moulding Mill.
O—— R..................Wines, etc.
O—— I. J..............Printer, etc.
O—— J. C...........Jobber Notions.
O—— C.............Paperhangings.
O—— & Co...................Bitters.
O—— & Co...............Teas, etc.
O—— J. W. & Son.....House Furn'g.
O—— & C——...............Guns.
O—— G. & Co...............Bankers.
O—— S—— V—— Co.
O—— S.............Sausage Casings.
O—— M—— & S——....Sausage Casing Mnfg.
O—— P.........Jobber Hosiery, etc.
O—— M—— Co....Patented Articles.
O—— E...................Harness.
O—— G.................Mnfr. Caps.
O—— J. U. & Co.............Bankers.
O—— W.....................Tailor.
O—— W. C.....Hemp, Bagging and Twine.
O—— J..... ....Wines.
O—— F. A. & Co...................Oil.
O—— H. D..........Mattresses, etc.
O—— & W——...........Laces, etc.
O—— L................Fancy Goods.
O—— D. E..................Carpets.
O—— O. C. & Co.........Stationers.
P—— K—— & F——......Roofing Materials and Varnish.
P—— M. J. & Co.......Music Boxes.
P—— N—— & Co....Leather Brokers.
P—— J. R.............Wireworker.
P—— A................Mnfr. Suits.
P—— A—— B—— W—— Co.
P—— Bros.....Jobbers Cotton Goods.
P—— & Co...................Confec.
P—— M....................Tobacco.
P—— R. R....................Prod.
P—— Bros.. ....Drugs.
P—— J. A......Lithographic Presses.
P—— N. O. & Co...............Oils.
P—— W. S...........Woodenware.
P—— G.................Fireworks.
P—— M. H...................Oils.
P—— W. J..................Chemist.
P—— J. & Co..........Gen'l Com'n.

P—— & C——........Mnfrs. Cigars.
P—— J.....................Chairs.
P—— P. J...................Drugs.
P—— Bros.........Stock Brokers.
P—— B—— R—— Co.
P—— C—— S—— R—— & W—— Co.
P—— R—— T—— L—— Co.
P—— S—— A—— S—— Co.
P—— R. & Co...Shipping and Com'n.
P—— L. & Bro........Photo. Goods.
P—— C. G................Operator.
P—— G T...............Bookbinder.
P—— H. A............Stock Broker.
P—— F. & Co....Druggists' Sundries, etc.
P—— K—— & Co.....Foundry.
P—— F. C. & Co......Billiard Saloon.
P—— I—— M—— Co.
P—— W. & Co..........Com'n Flour.
P—— G. W.......Jobber Dry Goods.
P—— L. M. & Co..........Tea Dealers.
P—— P. L...........Ship Chandler.
P—— M. M................Carriages.
P—— & B—— M——..Children's Carriages.
P—— C. H.................Banker.
P—— & M——..Mnfrs. Silk Ribbons.
P—— C...........Artificial Flowers.
P—— & P——..........Com'n Furs.
P—— Bros. & Co......Shipping and Com'n.
P—— & O——...Shipping and Com'n.
P—— & S——........R. R. Securities.
P—— J. A.............Gen'l Com'n.
P—— J. L..............Music Pub'r.
P—— S. D.............Wheelwright.
P—— Bros...........Imps. Cutlery.
P—— C. & E. J......Com'n Lumber.
P—— & Co...............Publishers.
P—— & O——....Wheelwrights, etc.
P—— J. T...................Tailor.
P—— L. A....Liq. and Canned Fruits.
P—— W. K...........Ret. D. G.
P—— T...................Wines.
P—— J. & Co..........Paper Boxes.
P—— E..........Ret. Men's Furn'g.
P—— G. E......Mnfr. Billiard Tables.
P—— & E——.......Jobbers Fancy Goods.
P—— & G——.............Jewelry.
P—— & S——.........Mnfrs. Clo.
P—— J....................Tailor.
P—— A—— & Co........ Publishers.
P—— J. B. & Son.....Shipping and Com'n.
P—— M—— Co.....Camera Obscuras.
P—— & Co......Gen'l Mdse. Brokers.
P—— F...........Insect Powders.
P—— E. S. & Co...............Feed.
P—— E—— Co.
P—— & D——.....Steam Governors.

P—— A............Liquors.	P—— W. B..................Drugs.
P—— Bros. & Co...........Hops, etc.	P—— T. L......Mnfr. Piano H'ware.
P—— R. L............Fruit Broker.	P—— S—— & Co......Mnfrs. Ladies'
P—— J. B.................Fwdg.	Suits, etc.
P—— B. Son..............Optician.	P—— M—— Co.
P—— H. H....Bookseller and Stat'y.	Q—— F................Publisher.
P—— & Co.........Gold and Specie.	Q—— Mrs. G.........Hair Goods.
P—— F. H. & Co.........Publishers.	Q—— H.................Mahogany.
P—— I...........Ret. Fancy Goods.	Q—— J...........Boots and Shoes.
P—— G............Machinery Agent.	Q—— H—— & Co.......Cut and En-
P—— & Co..................Spices.	graved Glass.
P—— M. A............Stock Broker.	Q—— E. A...................Coal.
P—— H. R. & J. L .. ....Furniture.	Q—— O. C..................Safes.
P—— H.............Ret. Clothing.	R—— J. H....................Fish.
P—— H. & Co..................Lye.	R—— & Bro.........Ship Brokers.
P—— J. & Bro.............Confec.	R—— S—— & Co....Mnfrs. Hats and
P—— & L——...Mnfrs. Ladies' Caps,	Caps.
etc.	R—— O—— Co.
P—— & Co..................Store.	R—— P—— Co.
P—— E. D............Com'n Prod.	R—— & K——........ ....Manures.
P—— E—— Co.	R—— M...........W. I. Com'n.
P—— & B——...........Founders.	R—— P—— I—— Co.
P—— W. E...........Mnfg. Agent.	R—— J. R. & Co....Blasting Powder.
P—— B—— A—— Co.	R—— & T——.........Bookbinders.
P—— Bros...........Cabinetmkrs.	R—— O. A.............Printer.
P—— E ....Ret. Millinery.	R—— S...............Confec.
P—— J..............Hardware.	R—— S. R.............Hardware
P—— & S—— M—— Co.......Furn.	R—— I. C. B............Crockery.
P—— Bros...Sewing Machine Attach-	R—— W.....................Gro.
ments.	R—— & S——. ....Ins. Brokers.
P—— & M——........R. E. Agents.	R—— M. L...:.....Mnfr. Umbrellas.
P—— D...............Chairs.	R—— G. H................Baker.
P—— P. F................Tailor.	R—— & Son.............Jewellers.
P—— M—— & S——........Printers.	R—— & Bro........Woollen Rags.
P—— M. & Bro... .....Whol. Shirts.	R—— W. M. M—— Co...Burial Cases.
P—— S. L.......Imp. Feathers and	R—— G. W...Ginger Beer and Cider.
Flowers.	R—— J. A..................Banker.
P—— J. P.................Printer.	R—— C. H..:.......... ....Hotel.
P—— R. M..........Ret. Shoes.	R—— J. Jr........Cider, Brandy, etc.
P—— Bros.................Cloaks.	R—— W. J...............Printer.
P—— J. H...................Gro.	R—— W. H...............Liquors.
P—— & Sons........Wines and Liq.	R—— G. H.............Envelopes.
P—— W. I....Com'n Flour and Grain.	R—— S—— G—— Co.
P—— Dr. C. T.........Patent Meds.	R—— & Co.............Books, etc.
P—— D... ....Drugs.	R—— & S——............Tobacco.
P—— J. D........Ret. Clothing, etc.	R—— J. E......House Furn'g Goods.
P—— J..................Books.	R—— C. E...............Jeweller.
P—— J. & Son..........Japanners.	R—— G. R.........Ret. Millinery.
P—— D. H.............Printer.	R—— H. C. Jr.........Platedware.
P—— J. L..............Ret. Hats.	R—— J. A..............Machinery.
P—— J. D. & Co......Stock Brokers.	R—— J. J................Printer.
P—— & T——........Mnfrs. Plated	R—— P..........Prod. Dealer.
Jewelry.	R—— I. T..............Stables.
P—— M—— P—— Co.	R—— A. M.......Men's Furn'g.
P—— R........ ....Ret. Men's Furn'g.	R—— J. T Jr.............Billiards.
P—— & P——........R. R. Supplies.	R—— S — & Co....Confec. Supplies.
P—— J. B....Jobber Toys and Fancy	R—— F. A....Imp. Drugs, Paints, etc.
Goods.	R—— J. J. & Son...Mnfrs. Furniture.
P—— A—— & M——........Mnfrs.	R—— & S........ ......Varnishes.
Ladies' Suits.	R—— F..........Photo. Materials.
P—— C. J..............R. R. Iron.	R—— C. B.................Feed.

O'N—— P. H.................Coffins.
O'N—— & Co........Marble Mantels.
O'N—— A. & Co.............Liquors.
O'R—— C....................Builder.
O—— F. C.....................Coal.
O—— & K——....Washing Machines.
O—— P......Mnfr. Cloaks and Suits.
O—— Mrs. S........Ret. F'cy Goods.
O—— & W——.......Mnfrs. Shirts.
O—— S.............Ret. Clothing.
O—— F. & Son.........Cabinetmkrs.
O—— A. S. & E......Livery Stables.
O—— & Co.....Shipping and Com'n.
O—— & C——.......Moulding Mill.
O—— R.............Wines, etc.
O—— I. J...............Printer, etc.
O—— J. C............Jobber Notions.
O—— C.............Paperhangings.
O—— & Co..................Bitters.
O—— & Co.................Teas, etc.
O—— J. W. & Son....House Furn'g.
O—— & C——..............Guns.
O—— G. & Co..............Bankers.
O—— S—— V—— Co.
O—— S.............Sausage Casings.
O—— M—— & S——....Sausage Casing Mnfg.
O—— P.........Jobber Hosiery, etc.
O—— M—— Co....Patented Articles.
O—— E....................Harness.
O—— G................Mnfr. Caps.
O—— J. U. & Co.............Bankers.
O—— W.....................Tailor.
O—— W. C.....Hemp, Bagging and Twine.
O—— J.....................Wines.
O—— F. A. & Co................Oil.
O—— H. D..........Mattresses, etc.
O—— & W——............Laces, etc.
O—— L................Fancy Goods.
O—— D. E................Carpets.
O—— O. C. & Co.........Stationers.
P—— K—— & F——....Roofing Materials and Varnish.
P—— M. J. & Co.......Music Boxes.
P—— N—— & Co....Leather Brokers.
P—— J. R............Wireworker.
P—— A.............Mnfr. Suits.
P—— A—— B—— W—— Co.
P—— Bros.....Jobbers Cotton Goods.
P—— & Co..................Confec.
P—— M..................Tobacco.
P—— R. R....................Prod.
P—— Bros....................Drugs.
P—— J. A.....Lithographic Presses.
P—— N. O. & Co..............Oils.
P—— W. S...........Woodenware.
P—— G................Fireworks.
P—— M. H...................Oils.
P—— W. J..................Chemist.
P—— J. & Co............Gen'l Com'n.

P—— & C——........Mnfrs. Cigars.
P—— J....................Chairs.
P—— P. J....................Drugs.
P—— Bros...........Stock Brokers.
P—— B—— R—— Co.
P—— C—— S—— R—— & W—— Co.
P—— R—— T—— L—— Co.
P—— S—— A—— S—— Co.
P—— R. & Co...Shipping and Com'n.
P—— L. & Bro........Photo. Goods.
P—— C. G.................Operator.
P—— G T..............Bookbinder.
P—— H. A............Stock Broker.
P—— F. & Co....Druggists' Sundries, etc.
P—— K—— & Co............Foundry.
P—— F. C. & Co.....Billiard Saloon.
P—— I—— M—— Co.
P—— W. & Co..........Com'n Flour.
P—— G. W.......Jobber Dry Goods.
P—— L. M. & Co........Tea Dealers.
P—— P. L..........Ship Chandler.
P—— M. M..............Carriages.
P—— & B—— M——..Children's Carriages.
P—— C. H.................Banker.
P—— & M——..Mnfrs. Silk Ribbons.
P—— C...........Artificial Flowers.
P—— & P——..........Com'n Furs.
P—— Bros. & Co......Shipping and Com'n.
P—— & O——...Shipping and Com'n.
P—— & S——........R. R. Securities.
P—— J. A...........Gen'l Com'n.
P—— J. L............Music Pub'r.
P—— S. D.........Wheelwright.
P—— Bros............Imps. Cutlery.
P—— C. & E. J......Com'n Lumber.
P—— & Co..............Publishers.
P—— & O——....Wheelwrights, etc.
P—— J. T.................Tailor.
P—— L. A....Liq. and Canned Fruits.
P—— W. K...........Ret. D. G.
P—— T.....................Wines.
P—— J. & Co..........Paper Boxes.
P—— E.......Ret. Men's Furn'g.
P—— G. E....Mnfr. Billiard Tables.
P—— & E——.......Jobbers Fancy Goods.
P—— & G——...........Jewelry.
P—— & S——..........Mnfrs. Clo.
P—— J....................Tailor.
P—— A—— & Co........Publishers.
P—— J. B. & Son.....Shipping and Com'n.
P—— M—— Co....Camera Obscuras.
P—— & Co.....Gen'l Mdse. Brokers.
P—— F.............Insect Powders.
P—— E. S. & Co..............Feed.
P—— E—— Co.
P—— & D——.....Steam Governors.

P—— A...............Liquors.
P—— Bros. & Co...........Hops, etc.
P—— R. L............Fruit Broker.
P—— J. B.................Fwdg.
P—— B. Son.............Optician.
P—— H. II....Bookseller and Stat'y.
P—— & Co.........Gold and Specie.
P—— F. H. & Co.......Publishers.
P—— I..........Ret. Fancy Goods.
P—— G..........Machinery Agent.
P—— & Co.................Spices.
P—— M. A.........Stock Broker.
P—— H. R. & J. L .. ....Furniture.
P—— H.............Ret. Clothing.
P—— H. & Co.................Lye.
P—— J. & Bro.........Confec.
P—— & L——...Mnfrs. Ladies' Caps,
etc.
P—— & Co.................Store.
P—— E. D............Com'n Prod.
P—— E—— Co.
P—— & B——...........Founders.
P—— W. E...........Mnfg. Agent.
P—— B—— A—— Co.
P—— Bros............Cabinetmkrs.
P—— E ....Ret. Millinery.
P—— J.................Hardware.
P—— & S—— M—— Co.......Furn.
P—— Bros...Sewing Machine Attach-
ments.
P—— & M——.........R. E. Agents.
P—— D.................Chairs.
P—— P. F................Tailor.
P—— M—— & S——.......Printers.
P—— M. & Bro... .....Whol. Shirts.
P—— S. L.......Imp. Feathers and
Flowers.
P—— J. P.................Printer.
P—— R. M.............Ret. Shoes.
P—— Bros.................Cloaks.
P—— J. II.................Gro.
P—— & Sons.........Wines and Liq.
P—— W. I....Com'n Flour and Grain.
P—— Dr. C. T..........Patent Meds.
P—— D... ....Drugs.
P—— J. D.........Ret. Clothing, etc.
P—— J.................Books.
P—— J. & Son...........Japanners.
P—— D. H.............Printer.
P—— J. L.............Ret. Hats.
P—— J. D. & Co......Stock Brokers.
P—— & T——.......Mnfrs. Plated
Jewelry.
P—— M—— P—— Co.
P—— R........ ...Ret. Men's Furn'g.
P—— & P——......R. R. Supplies.
P—— J. B....Jobber Toys and Fancy
Goods.
P—— A—— & M——.........Mnfrs.
Ladies' Suits.
P—— C. J...............R. R. Iron.

P—— W. B.................Drugs.
P—— T. L......Mnfr. Piano H'ware.
P—— S—— & Co.......Mnfrs. Ladies'
Suits, etc.
P—— M—— Co.
Q—— F..................Publisher.
Q—— Mrs. G...........Hair Goods.
Q—— H................Mahogany.
Q—— J............Boots and Shoes.
Q—— H—— & Co.......Cut and En-
graved Glass.
Q—— E. A.................Coal.
Q—— O. C.................Safes.
R—— J. H.................Fish.
R—— & Bro.........Ship Brokers.
R—— S—— & Co....Mnfrs. Hats and
Caps.
R—— O—— Co.
R—— P—— Co.
R—— & K——...... ....Manures.
R—— M............W. I. Com'n.
R—— P—— I—— Co.
R—— J. R. & Co....Blasting Powder.
R—— & T——.........Bookbinders.
R—— O. A.............Printer.
R—— S............Confec.
R—— S. R.............Hardware
R—— I. C. B.............Crockery.
R—— W.................Gro.
R—— & S——. ....Ins. Brokers.
R—— M. L...:.....Mnfr. Umbrellas.
R—— G. H................Baker.
R—— & Son.............Jewellers.
R—— & Bro.........Woollen Rags.
R—— W. M. M—— Co...Burial Cases.
R—— G. W....Ginger Beer and Cider.
R—— J. A.................Banker.
R—— C. II........... ....Hotel.
R—— J. Jr.......Cider, Brandy, etc.
R—— W. J.................Printer.
R—— W. II.................Liquors.
R—— G. H...............Envelopes.
R—— S—— G—— Co.
R—— & Co.............Books, etc.
R—— & S——.............Tobacco.
R—— J. E......House Furn'g Goods.
R—— C. E................Jeweller.
R—— G. R.............Ret. Millinery.
R—— H. C. Jr...........Platedware.
R—— J. A.............Machinery.
R—— J. J.................Printer.
R—— P................Prod. Dealer.
R—— I. T.................Stables.
R—— A. M.............Men's Furn'g.
R—— J. T Jr.............Billiards.
R—— S — & Co....Confec. Supplies.
R—— F. A....Imp. Drugs, Paints, etc.
R—— J. J. & Son...Mnfrs. Furniture.
R—— & S——..... .....Varnishes.
R—— F...........Photo. Materials.
R—— C. B.................Feed.

R—— P............Ret. Jewelry.	R—— & B——......Mnfrs. Rufflings.
R—— E............Musical Insts.	R—— P. D. & Co......Com'n Cotton.
R—— S. J............Cloths.	R—— & Co.........Foreign Express.
R—— J........Ret. Boots and Shoes.	R—— M. C............Cuban Com'n.
R—— J............Builder.	R—— Bros.............Cigars.
R—— C. W.........Seeds and Grain.	R—— W. H. & Co......Patent Lined
R—— T. P............Com'n D. G.	Pails.
R—— R............Chemicals.	R—— J............Tailor.
R—— A............Cigars.	R—— H. H............Tailor.
R—— L. F........Mnfr. Grain Bags.	R—— & M——............Printers.
R—— & B——......Leather Varnish.	R—— A. & Co.........Jewelry, etc.
R—— R—— & Co........Gen'l Com'n.	R—— H. C. & Co......Fish & Com'n.
R—— A............Dyer.	R—— J. S. & Co....Teas, Coffees, etc.
R—— P—— Co........Mnfrs. Paint.	R—— & D——....Stock Brokers, etc.
R—— J. M............Fruit.	R—— J............Brewery.
R—— P. M............Ret. B. and S.	R—— C. V............Hats & Caps.
R—— F. F............Liquors.	R—— J. B............Steam Boilers.
R—— & N——............Restaurant.	R—— S............Com'n Cotton.
R—— W. M............Banker.	R—— S—— E—— Co.
R—— & H——......Com'n Alcohol.	R—— C—— E—— Co.
R—— J............Fruit Broker.	R—— C. J............Coal.
R—— M............Mnfr. Neckties.	R—— J. B. & Co....Patent Meds.
R—— A. K. & Co..Manfrs. Perfumery.	R—— & Co............Stationers.
R—— C............Manfr. Artificial	R—— J. M. & Co......Liquid Glue.
Flowers.	R—— & K——......Mnfrs. Neckties.
R—— J. J............Iron.	R—— & B——....Ret. Fancy Goods.
R—— W. J............Ruches.	R—— F............Fancy Goods.
R—— T. C. H—— Co.....Hardware.	R—— M........Jobber Fancy Goods.
R—— G. E............Ship Chandler.	R—— & Co............D. G. Brokers.
R—— B. & Son......Com'n Silk and	R—— & Co............Tobacco.
China Goods.	R—— & Co............Whol. Clothing.
R—— B............Mnfr. Neckties.	R—— & M——........Mnfrs. Shirts.
R—— M............Broker and Com'n.	R—— M............Ret. D. G.
R—— B—— & Co............Coal.	R—— & Co............Jobbers Fancy D. G.
R—— C—— Co.........Copper Ore.	R—— S............Hoopskirts,
R—— & Co......Imps. Curtains, etc.	R—— E............Ret. Fancy Goods.
R—— S—— & Co.....Looking-Glass	R—— A. & Co........Whol. Liquors.
Plates.	R—— A............Mnfr. Cloaks.
R—— I—— & Co............Patterns.	R—— J........Leather and Findings.
R—— A........Com'n Embroideries.	R—— Mrs. M............Fancy Goods.
R—— & Co............Com'n Prod.	R—— I. & A............Ret. D. G.
R—— T............Com'n Mer.	R—— S. D. & Co.........Neckwear.
R—— & M——............Painters.	R—— J............Liquors.
R—— & W——............Painters.	R—— J............Distiller.
R—— J. H............Com'n Lumber.	R—— & W——............Com'n Prov.
R—— C. & Co........Mdse. Brokers.	R—— J. O'D............Hotel.
R—— T............Drugs.	R—— W—— C—— Co....Toothpicks,
R—— & Co............Whol. Liquors.	etc.
R—— & R——............Liquors.	R—— W........Imp. Fancy Leather.
R—— E............Gro.	R——J............Billiard Tables.
R—— S. & Co............Com'n Prod.	R—— W......Leather and Findings.
R—— S............Leather.	R—— S., Jr........Mnfr. Lace Goods.
R—— M—— Co.........Mnfrs. Lace	R—— Bros....Mnfrs. Ladies' Under-
Goods.	garments.
R—— W. C............Lithographer.	R—— & F——.........Jobbers Clo.
R—— J............Brewer.	R—— J. F............Brewer.
R—— C. H. & Co.....Stock Brokers.	R—— C............Jobber Cloth.
R—— E. H. & Co....Brass Goods, etc.	R—— C............Mnfr. Feathers and
R—— G. B. & Co.......Com'n Flour.	Flowers.
R—— H............Gro.	R—— J. R......Shipping and Com'n
R—— M—— A——	Prov.

R—— T.................Linseed Oil.
R—— E. A...........Whol. Liquors.
R—— B—— & S—— M—— Co.
R—— T....Shipping and Com'n.
R—— & U——......Imps. Wines and
                           Liq.
R—— J. C...................Drugs.
R—— & Co...................Drugs.
R—— J. F...................Hotel.
R—— W., H.................Glass.
R—— & B.............Bookbinders.
R—— C—— & Co...Imps. and Jobbers
                     Men's Furn'g.
R—— D.....................Tailor.
R—— M. F................D. G.
S—— L...................Wagons.
S—— M.............Pipes, etc.
S—— & Co........... Whol. Cigars.
S—— & Co...Shirts and Men's Furn'g.
S—— J. A.............Job Printer.
S—— J. H......Druggists' Sundries.
S—— T. M.............R. E. Broker.
S—— E. W. & Bro....Stationers and
                          Printers.
S—— & M——........Ret. Clothing.
S—— D. & J.............Publishers.
St. J—— G.........Gen'l Com'n.
St. M—— R—— L—— Co.
S—— W. & Co.........Ship Brokers.
S—— S...................Tobacco.
S—— M. & E...........Tobacco.
S—— E. Y...................Com'n.
S—— M...........Ret. Fancy Goods.
S—— S. L.........Com'n Hardware.
S—— W...............Ret. D. G.
S—— T. & Co......Agents Ales.
S—— & S——............Whol. Clo.
S—— & B——Agent for H——'s Sons.
S—— J...............Hair Goods.
S—— D................Liquors.
S—— E...........Coffee Broker.
S—— S—— Co......Mineral Waters.
S—— J. B.............Guano.
S—— J. H.............Restaurant.
S——M.............Fancy Goods.
S—— W. E. Jr. & Co......Ret. Drugs.
S—— E...................Gro.
S—— E. & A.............Jewellers.
S—— P...................Brewer.
S—— J.........Builders' Hardware.
S—— D. & Co.......Whol. B. and S.
S—— & S——.......Bankers, etc.
S—— Bros..........Whol. Clothing.
S—— H...........Agent Stationery.
S—— F. X.............Restaurant.
S—— J...............A—— House.
S—— J. & Co......Mnfrs. Tinware.
S——J.......Importer Optical Goods.
S—— C. & Co........Cabinetmakers.
S—— R.................Speculator.
S—— E.............Auctioneer.

S—— C.........Com'n Fancy Goods.
S—— J. P...................Iron.
S—— H....Picture Frames, etc.
S—— G. & Son......Jobbers Clothing.
S—— S. & N——.........Whol. Gro.
S—— V.................Liquors.
S—— L.........Ret. Hats and Caps.
S—— M.........Ret. Fancy Goods.
S—— H. & Co.............Ret. Clo.
S—— L. & Co.........Ret. Clothing.
S—— J.............Fancy Goods.
S—— W. J.........Jobber Cloths.
S—— T.............Job Printer.
S—— H.................Plumber.
S—— L. & Co......Shipping Com'n.
S—— J.............Rhine Wine.
S—— J. & Co......Leaf Tobacco.
S—— & S——.............Furniture.
S—— E.........Mnf. Hair Goods.
S—— H.........Peddlers' Supplies.
S—— F.............Prov. Broker.
S—— J. M.........Ret. Fancy Goods.
S—— S—— & R—— Co....Solder and
                           Lead.
S—— G. H.................Hats.
S—— J. G...........Mnfg. Jeweller.
S—— W.................Furniture.
S——D. L.........Com'n R. R. Iron.
S—— & Co.............Maps, etc.
S—— H.............D. G. Auctioneer.
S—— J.........Fish and Oysters.
S—— & D.............Guns, etc.
S—— J. E.............Texan Com'n.
S—— L.........Brass Band Insts.
S—— & C——.........Showcases.
S—— J.............Stairbuilder.
S—— E.............Prov. Broker.
S—— H.................Pianos.
S—— & Co...Mnfrs. Cloth Hats, Caps,
                           etc.
S—— J. G.................Tailor.
S—— C. L.....Toys and Fancy Goods.
S——J. F.........J—— W——Park.
S—— & M——....Cement and Mineral
                          Waters.
S—— H. W.................Gro.
S—— P...........Ret. Fancy D. G.
S—— W.......Ret. Fancy Goods.
S—— F. H.............Specie Broker.
S—— F. C. & Co....Mnfg. Stationers.
S—— & Co.............Umbrellas.
S—— M. F. & Co.........Planing Mill.
S—— S.................Butcher.
S—— P—— M—— Co..Looking-Glass
                          Plates.
S—— R. K. & V. R........Whol. Gro.
S—— A.................Furniture.
S—— H. S. & Co...........Novelties.
S—— H.................Tailor.
S—— Mrs. J...........Mnfr. Tobacco.
S—— L.............Ret. Millinery.

S—— A. J................Stoves.	S—— J. Jr..............Hardware.
S—— G—— B—— Co.	S—— R............Boots and Shoes.
S——'G. W..Shipper Flour and Grain.	S—— E. S............Metal Broker.
S—— G. W. & Co..........Clothing.	S—— I. A................Trusses.
S—— J. & Co..Mnfrs. Horse Blankets.	S—— H—— & Co........Imps. White
S—— H. M.............D—— House.	Goods, Linen, etc.
S—— W. B...........Stock Broker.	S—— W. & Co..............Bankers.
S—— & C——.Soda Water Apparatus.	S—— C. W..................Gro.
S—— S. V. & F. P........Dyewoods.	S—— D...................Cooper.
S—— I................ ....Teas, etc.	S—— G..........Petroleum Broker.
S—— E....................Gro.	S—— M..................Tailor.
S—— Mrs. E............Restaurant.	S—— & E——...Mnfrs. Clothing and
S—— J. A...........Ship Chandler.	Shirts.
S—— L. I.............Com'n Prod.	S—— B................Brewer.
S—— C................Mirrors, etc.	S—— H. B.......Com'n Straw Goods.
S—— J.................Wagons.	S—— R. L.......Ret. Fancy Goods.
S—— I. M. Jr.............Jewelry.	S—— P—— Co.
S—— M. & Co....Com'n Fancy Goods.	S—— J. M.......Imp. Leaf Tobacco.
S—— U—— C—— B—— S——.	S—— I.........Jobber White Goods.
S—— Z.................Contractor.	S—— D. & Co....Masonic Goods.
S—— S. & Son.... ...Boilermakers.	S—— G.;..............Jeweller.
S—— S—— M—— Co.	S—— H. D............Jobber Toys.
S—— & K——..........Com'n Prod.	S—— A. & Co........Ret. Clothing.
S—— H........Imp. Foreign Fruits.	S—— J. J. & F.......Wines and Liq.
S—— & M——......Mnfrs. B. and S.	S—— & J......Sewing Machines.
S—— L. D............ ...Crockery.	S—— T..................Clothing.
S—— L. & W——...Jobbers Flowers.	S—— & G..............Ret. Clo.
S—— A.......Jobber White Goods.	S—— & H——....Ret. Hats, Caps,
S—— R.........Imp. German Linens.	Furs, etc.
S—— Z................Tobacco.	S—— Mrs. M. M........Ret. D. G.
S—— H.........German Prod., etc.	S—— C..... ....Jobber Fancy Goods.
S—— & F——....Mnfrs. Showcases.	S—— T.........Mnfr. Shirts.
S—— J. H................Optician.	S—— U................Real Estate.
S—— S...................Cigars.	S—— G. F. & Co......Mnfrs. Pocket-
S—— A. T. & Son.... ... Mouldings.	books.
S—— M—— E—— Co.	S—— M. & Bro............Clothing.
S—— C................Liquors.	S—— J. P.............Lithographer.
S—— E..................Pictures.	S—— C. D...........Ship Broker.
S—— W—— & Co...Mnfrs. Silk Hats.	S—— S. L...............Liquors.
S—— & K——....Satinets and Cotton-	S—— L. H. & Co....Lumber and Coal
ades.	S—— & Co.......Imps. Fancy Goods
S—— M—— Co.....Cordials, Bitters,	S—— W. Jr.............Books.
etc.	S—— & M——...Shipping and Com'n.
S—— & W——.........Com'n Meat.	S—— J. J.................Gro.
S—— S..............R. E. Operator.	S—— W. S............T—— House.
S—— J..................Liquors.	S—— & L——...Saddlery Hardware.
S—— & S——.........Note Brokers.	S—— E.....................Hats.
S—— S. I.......Men's Furn'g Goods.	S—— R...........Ret. Fancy Goods.
S—— W. F. & Co......Com'n H'ware.	S—— Bros ....Liquors.
S—— L...............Human Hair.	S—— M—— & Co......Sugar Brokers.
S—— J. G. & Co...Mnfrs. Blankbooks.	S—— J. C. & Son........Com'n Prod.
S—— M. & W. I. & Co.Com'n Carpets.	S—— G. C........Prov. Broker.
S—— & R—— L—— Co..Metal Pipes.	S—— J. H................Builder.
S—— C. C. & Co......Ret. H. and C.	S—— W—— & Co.....Mnfrs. Blank-
S—— D.................Tow Boats.	books.
S—— Bros................Carpets.	S—— & B——........Sugar Brokers.
S—— T.................Liquors.	S—— A...............Leaf Tobacco.
S—— S. W. & D ——..Agents Grocers'	S—— A. W.........Auctioneer, etc.
Sundries, etc.	S—— B. W..................Prod.
S—— J..................Liquors.	S—— C. M.............Lithographer.
S—— N. M..........Mdse. Broker.	S—— C. G...................Hats.

S—— D. M.................Builder.
S—— Mrs. E. J....Ret. Fancy Goods.
S—— F.......................Oils.
S—— F. H.........Gov't Contractor.
S—— G. P..............Contractor.
S—— H.......................Hotel.
S—— H. N.........Stock Operator.
S—— J. F.........Mnfr. Brushes.
S—— J. W.................Builder.
S—— N. W.................Builder.
S—— P. F............:.......Stationer.
S—— R....................Carpets.
S—— S. C.............F—— House.
S—— S. J.........Mnfg. Jeweller.
S—— S. W., Est. of.........Wooden
                          Horses.
S—— W. J.............Flour Broker.
S—— W. I...............Pottery.
S—— W. H.........Stairbuilder, etc.
S—— C. & Co ....,..Blacking.
S—— C—— & Co.....Com'n Lumber.
S—— J. A. & Co.............Lighters.
S—— J. M. & Co............Cotton.
S—— R. W. & Co.......Bookbinders.
S—— & B——................Coal.
S—— & Co., Agents........Carpets.
S—— & E——..........Com'n Prod.
S—— & G——..........Restaurant.
S—— & L——......Bronze Articles.
S—— & S—— M—— Co...Machinists.
S—— & B——..........Iron Railings.
S—— W. B............Job Printer.
S—— W. B............Ship Broker.
S—— J................Art Gallery.
S—— W...............Jobber D. G.
S—— E....................Builder.
S—— J....................Builder.
S—— & R——.....Shipping & Com'n.
S—— & Co.................Pianos.
S—— A. & Sons......Mnfrs. Ribbons.
S—— D.& Co.............Ret. D. G.
S—— L............Whol. Clothing.
S—— Bros......Mnfrs. Neckties, etc.
S—— R................Art Gallery.
S—— I...................Liquors.
S—— J. P...................Paper.
S—— I........Shipping and Com'n.
S—— J. & Co............Petroleum.
S—— H. & G. & Co..Mnfg. Jewellers.
S—— M...Imp. Watches and Jewelry.
S—— & Co................Lumber.
S—— J. P. & Son......Drug Brokers.
S—— L—— E—— & P—— Co.
S—— Mrs. S. E.............Honey.
S—— H.................Stationer.
S—— G. & Co.........Men's Furn'g.
S—— F................Gro., etc.
S—— & Co.........Mnfrs. Imitation
                      Champagnes.
S—— A. & Son.............Billiards.
S—— T. P. & Co.........,.Perfumers.

S—— T. C. & Co.....Western Com'n.
S—— E. M.........Real Estate, etc.
S—— H....................Cloths.
S—— L............Jobber Cloths.
S—— J..........Peddlers' Supplies.
S—— E. & Co............Tobacco.
S—— A...................Liquors.
S—— Bros. & Co....... Shipping and
                          Com'n.
S—— J. A........Fixed Ammunition.
S—— & N——....,.Jobbers Millinery
                          Goods.
S—— C.............Tobacco Broker.
S—— J. & Co............Gen'l Com'n.
S—— W. & Co............Gen'l Com'n.
S——J................C—— Hotel.
S—— & N——...............Hotel.
S—— J...............Human Hair.
S—— J. H....................Gro.
S—— S. S...Mnfr. Ink and Mucilage.
S—— S. W....................Teas.
S—— Mnfg. Co.......Stencil Plates.
S—— J.........Ret. Fancy Goods.
S—— P—— & S—— L—— Co.
S—— P—— Co.
S—— D. R. & Co.............Pianos.
S—— M. J. & Co...............Prod.
S—— L—— O—— Co.
S—— M—— Co.....Women's Under-
                          wear.
S—— A.........Shipping and Com'n.
S—— M. W..........Prod. Broker.
S—— & D——..............Liquors.
S—— R. H. & Co............Cigars.
S—— & C——....Bankers and Brokers.
S—— B........Mnfr. Trimmed Hats.
S—— J.....................Hotel.
S—— J...............Ship Chandler.
S—— E. P.................Lumber.
S—— J. J..........Jobber Jewelry.
S—— A. & Co...............Tobacco.
S—— & Bro...........Jewelry, etc.
S—— & S——.....Mnfrs. Suspenders.
S—— W. & Co.......Whol. Clothing.
S—— W. C...................Hops.
S—— T. & Co....S. Am. Shipping and
                          Com'n.
S—— & F——........Whol. Clothing.
S—— & P——...Jobbers Fancy Goods
                      and Hosiery.
S—— J.........Ret. Boots and Shoes.
S—— R. & Co................Jewelry.
S—— S...................Bonedust.
S—— A. F..........Mnfr. Cigars.
S—— P—— V—— Co..Mnfrs. Vices.
S—— J. & Co......Car Builders, etc.
S—— E.............Furs and Skins.
S—— & D—— ....Skin Brokers.
S—— J...........,......Peddler Cloth.
S—— S.................Pawnbroker
S—— M. & S.........,......Bankers.

S—— A. & Co....California Wines and Liq.
S—— F. & Co.....Imitation Jewelry.
S—— & H——..Jobbers White Goods.
S—— L., Jr.............Job. Jewelry.
S—— S. S.................Builder.
S—— W.............Paperhangings.
S—— A. T. & Co.....Paints, Oils, etc.
S—— M—— & L—— Co.
S—— & Co...............Jewelers.
S—— V. K., Jr......R. E. Broker, etc.
S—— G. H. & Co.:.....Hand Stamps.
S—— A...............Stock Broker.
S—— T.............Wines and Liq.
S—— W. D..................Pottery.
S—— R. & Co...Mnfrs. Shirt Bosoms.
S—— & M——....Ret. Fancy Goods.
S—— & W——........Mnfrs. B. & S.
S—— J. T....................Prod.
S—— & N——.Mnfrs. Hats and Caps.
S—— G. W., Jr.......Freight Broker.
S—— M—— & Co.....Jobbers Cloths.
S—— C.......................Baker.
S—— & U——.....Mnfrs. Woollens.
S—— L................Mnfr. Shoes.
S—— & Co.........Mnfrs. Vinegar.
S—— E. & Co....Ladies' Collars, etc.
S—— & G——..........Ret. Clothing.
S—— & W——.Jobbers Fancy Goods.
S—— T.....................Millinery.
S—— E.......................Cigars.
S—— E. & S——.........Cigars, etc.
S—— R. & Co.....Coffee, Spices, etc.
S—— J. W.................Pickles, etc.
S—— W. T.............Wireworker.
S—— H. D..............Machinery.
S—— M—— Co..........Machinery.
S—— B...................Stationer.
S—— & H—— Bros....Wool Brokers.
S—— E. W.............House Furn'g.
S—— E. M....................Coal.
S—— A...............Veneers, etc.
S—— S..............Mnfr. Cigars.
S—— S.............Mnfr. Neckties.
S—— S. & Co.......Imps. Watches.
S—— & S——......Com'n Flour and Grain.
S—— W. H.............Com'n Prod.
S—— L. V. & Co...............Soap.
S—— Mrs. M. H...........Ret. D. G.
S—— M. D....................Prod.
S—— J.........Carriage H'ware.
S—— D. H..............Shipstores.
S—— J. P...............Com'n Prod.
S—— J........Broker Window Glass.
S—— J.............Metal Broker.
S—— J. E..................Painter.
S—— Bros............Whol. B. & S.
S—— R—— & Co.Cotton, Shipping and Com'n.
S—— G. A..................Builder.

S—— Mrs. R.....Mnfr. Ladies' Scarfs.
S—— S. M. & Son.......Builders, etc.
S—— H.................Cabinetmkr.
S—— I. G.....Printing Presses, etc.
S—— J. G...........Mnfr. Clothing.
S—— J. D..................Peddler.
S—— M.....................Liquors.
S—— C.................Upholstery.
S—— Mrs. M. E...............Cigars.
S—— S. & Co.................Hats.
S—— E....................Repacker.
S—— J. P. & Son.....Drug Brokers.
S—— J. P.....................Oils.
S—— D. W...................Hotel.
S—— S. A............R. E. Agent.
S—— H. & Co.....Ship Brokers, etc.
S—— & D——.Com'n Bats and Twine.
S—— & W——.............Fertilizers.
S—— C. H. & Co.......Stock Brokers.
S—— S. & Co.................Cloths.
T—— & R——.........Cigar Dealers.
T—— J........Mnfr. Thermometers.
T—— G............Water Wheels.
T—— & Son....Saleratus, Spices, etc.
T—— C...................Jeweller.
T—— & Co............Gold Brokers.
T—— Bros. & Co............Shipping.
T—— M. E....Ret. Boots and Shoes.
T—— & H...............Confec.
T—— D....................Printer.
T—— E. W., Jr.......Mnfr. Ruffles.
T—— H. A.........Jobber Hosiery.
T—— H. H................Cutlery.
T—— J...................Restaurant.
T—— J..................Contractor.
T—— S. W.......Ret. Men's Furn'g.
T—— T................A—— House.
T—— T.....Printers' Materials.
T—— W. R.............Saw Mill.
T—— A. B. P—— P—— & M—— Co.
T—— F. B. & Co....Oil Shippers, etc.
T—— H. & J. A..Shipping and Com'n.
T—— I—— & Co.......Photographs.
T—— & Co.......Havana Lottery.
T—— & D——......Paper and Paper Stock.
T—— I....................Tobacco.
T—— E....................Coatmkr.
T—— E—— C. A...........Lighters.
T—— J. H. & Co.......Gen'l Com'n.
T—— A...................Ret. D. G.
T—— J......Mnfr. Window Shades.
T—— J. R....Ret. Hats and Caps.
T—— Bros...............Leather, etc.
T—— W.......................Gro.
T—— Bros.....Jobbers White Goods.
T—— H—— Co............Heaters.
T—— N. C.........Photo. Materials.
T—— M—— Co....Imitation Jewelry.
T—— W.................Restaurant.
T—— G....................Liquors.

T—— J. A...Broker, Prov. and Petroleum.
T—— A. J........Liq. and Diamonds.
T—— A. A............Com'n Flour.
T—— P. J............Stock Broker.
T—— W........Ret. Boots and Shoes.
T—— G. J. & Co..........Com'n Prod.
T—— & S——.............Printers.
T—— A. D..............Restaurant.
T—— L................Cotton Goods.
T—— Mrs. R..............Corsets.
T—— A. E. & Co...Com'n Paints, etc.
T—— L. & Co............Imps. D. G.
T—— & M——....Jobbers Millinery.
T—— & W——.............Tailors.
T—— & Son......Rubber and Leather Goods.
T—— C. E............Stock Broker.
T—— H. T. & Co................Coal.
T—— & Co......Agents Composition Coating.
T—— C. & Co............Stationers.
T—— W. & Co....Purchasing Agents.
T—— J. M. & E. A.........Masons.
T—— J. R. & Co..........Ret. Hats.
T—— J. V. & Co..............Prod.
T—— J...............Photographer.
T—— N. & Son.Books and Stationery.
T—— M—— Co..............Meters.
T—— O. M............Peddler.
T—— A. F. & Co.....Com'n Soap, etc.
T—— & Co................Chemists.
T—— Mme. N. & Co.........Artificial Flowers.
T—— Mrs. M. A..............Hotel.
T—— A. E. & C. E........Gen'l Mers.
T—— G. H..........Jobber Hosiery.
T—— A. & J.....Jewelry and Men's Furn'g.
T—— J. D. & Co....Jobbers Jewelry.
T—— R. M. & Co.......Jobbers Clo.
T—— W. S..............Polisher.
T—— P................Jeweller.
T—— R. & Son..........Liquors.
T—— D. C..............Mnfr. Ties.
T—— W........Mnfr. Plated Goods.
T—— L. & Co.Straw Goods, Caps, etc.
T—— A. L.............Packing Boxes.
T—— Bros................Printers.
T—— E. S. & J...Weather Strips, etc.
T—— G—— & Co.....Stationers, etc.
T—— W. H.............Ship Broker.
T—— W. A.............Publisher.
T—— W. H.........Com'n Oilcloths.
T—— J. B................Liquors.
T—— F. A..............Stationer.
T—— W..............Jewelry.
T—— I..............Jobber Millinery.
T—— M................Jewelry.
T—— W. R..............Stocks.
T—— J. F., Agent......Cotton Goods.

T—— Mrs. C. M.............Lumber.
T—— Bros. & Z——,Jobbers F'cy G'ds.
T—— M....................Tailor.
T—— C..................Lamps.
T—— J. & Son........Mahogany, etc.
T—— J..................Painter.
T—— Mrs. A. J....Ret. Men's Furn'g.
T—— E. B..............Stationer.
T—— J. E. & Son......Whol. Drugs.
T—— R. M. & Co....Jobbers Jewelry.
T—— R................Ret. D. G.
T—— J. F. & Son........Printers.
T—— Mrs. J. S........Ret. Millinery.
T—— & G——.............Stoneyard.
T—— & Co............Stock Brokers.
T—— & L——.........Fringes, etc.
T—— F. W...............Feed.
T—— H. W..............Printer.
T—— Bros...............Bankers.
T—— J. & Co........Oil, Soap, etc.
T—— & Co.................Prov.
T—— T..............Naval Stores.
T—— A..........Upholstery Goods.
T—— J. M..........Com'n Prod.
T—— H. A.....Ret. Boots and Shoes.
T—— C..................Oil.
T—— J............Whol. Liquors.
T—— M. C. & Co........Stationers.
T—— & Co............Iron and Steel.
U—— & Co.............Printers.
U—— S........Imp. Bronze Powder.
U—— W..........Artificial Flowers.
U—— J. C.......Sashes and Blinds.
U—— I................Tobacco.
U—— M. C....Stoves and Tinware.
U—— F—— Co.
U—— Capt. E.............Liquors.
U—— L,...Mnfr. and Jobber Trim'gs.
U—— S.........Ret. Hats and Caps.
U—— B—— Co.....Mineral Waters.
U—— C—— S—— Co.
U—— C—— A——.
U—— E—— W——.
U—— O—— W——.
U—— P—— C—— Co.
U—— S—— B—— C—— & G—— Co.
U—— P—— F—— O—— Co.
U—— S—— R—— W——.
U—— S—— C—— Co.
U—— S—— G—— Co.
U—— S—— I—— M—— Co.
U—— S—— P—— G—— Co.
U—— S—— P—— Co.
U—— S—— S—— P—— Co.
U—— S—— T—— Co.
U—— P—— Co.
U—— E. & Co........Imps. Hosiery.
U—— A. & Co..........Publishers.
U—— W. R............Stock Broker.
V—— T. C...........R. E. Broker.
V—— H. & J. A............Tailors.

V—— S—— & Co............Millers.	V—— R.........Ret. Men's Furn'g.
V—— G...............Cattle Dealer.	V—— J. A............Advg. Agents.
V—— H. M..........Cattle Broker.	V—— & U——.....Builders' H'ware.
V—— A—— S. M.....Jeweller, etc.	V—— M....................Gro.
V—— B—— & W——.Mnfrs. Satchels.	W—— F.......Watch Materials, etc.
V—— B—— C. A. Shipping and Com'n.	W—— & Co...............Bankers.
V—— B—— & Bro......Ship Brokers.	W—— R. J. & Co.....Glue and Sand-
V—— H. T....................Coal.	paper.
V—— & T——....Ret. Men's Furn'g.	W—— W.........Mnfr. Suspenders.
V—— R——W. G...Artificial Flowers.	W—— F. W............Optical Insts.
V—— J. W...............Furniture.	W—— F....................Hair.
V—— D—— M. M...........Hotel.	W—— W. E. & Co....Jobbers Fancy
V—— D—— & D——..Mnfrs. Sewing-	Goods.
Machine Tops.	W—— & H——....Com'n Cotton, etc.
V—— G—— Bros......Hat Leathers.	W—— T. H..........Stock Broker.
V—— H—— J. & Son....Willowware.	W—— E—— C—— Co.
V—— L—— H..................Gro.	W—— J..................Lumber.
V—— N—— & G——.Elastic Sponges.	W—— & F——......Com'n Candles.
V—— N—— & Co...........Confec.	W—— M. E.....Jobber Fancy Goods.
V—— O—— J. H..............Coal.	W—— A.....Ret. Fancy Goods.
V—— P—— J. J....Lumber and Saw	W—— M..........Mnfr. Neckties.
Mill.	W—— F. R..................Paper.
V—— P—— & Co. Shipping and Com'n.	W—— G....................Gro.
V—— R—— J.........Imp. Ales, etc.	W—— E. Sons..........Publishers.
V—— R—— J. P., Jr...Shipping and	W—— & W——............Builders.
Com'n.	W—— T. M................Paper.
V—— S—— & Co..........Chocolate.	W—— D. S.....Com'n Fancy Goods.
V—— M. L...................Prod.	W—— J........Hatters' Furs, etc.
V—— T—— A. P., Jr. Marble Works.	W—— F. B. & Co.....Stock Brokers.
V—— T—— M—— Co.....Founders'	W—— R.............Stock Broker.
Facings.	W—— F. & Co....Stock Brokers, etc.
V—— V—— A.........R. E. Broker.	W—— Mrs. M. E....Ret. F'cy Goods.
V—— W—— H. S. & Co...Com'n Prod.	W—— W.................Liquors.
V—— W—— A. & Son, Ship Chandlers.	W—— S—— & L——.........Drugs.
V—— W. E..........Photographer.	W—— G. B. & Sons....Brokers R. R.
V—— M—— & Bros....Imps. Cigars	Supplies.
and Tobacco.	W—— & W——.........Glassware.
V—— F—— Co.	W—— W. H................Fruit.
V—— D...................Jewelry.	W—— N.............Glassware.
V—— J. A............Whalebone.	W—— C. E. & Co............Oils.
V—— C. E...................Tea.	W—— H—— & Co......Glasscutters.
V—— & I——................Coal.	W—— J. E. & Co......Ship Brokers.
V—— A. H...........Fruit Broker.	W—— & W——.....Jobbers Cloths.
V—— & Co...............Bankers.	W—— M.......Ret. Millinery, etc.
V—— T. H. Son...........Tobacco.	W—— Bros. & Co...........Oil.
V—— J. P.................Flowers.	W—— R—— D—— Co.
V—— Sons.....Family Tea Dealers.	W—— Dr. J. M........Patent Meds.
V—— A. & M..........Dressmkrs.	W—— & W——...Pub'rs and Book-
V—— & B——.............Liquors.	sellers.
V—— F.........Imp. Human Hair.	W—— D....................Prov.
V—— C. R. & Co.....Weather Strips.	W—— M. B..........R. R. Supplies.
V—— C...................Printer.	W—— T—— M—— Co......Miners'
V—— C—— F—— W——.	Tools, etc.
V—— G...................Liquors.	W—— E.............Blue Stone.
V—— P.....................Cigars.	W—— A. G...........Drug Broker.
V—— B. & W...............Liquors.	W—— B....Ret. Men's Furn'g Goods.
V—— H...................Marble.	W—— W. H. & Co.............Coal.
V—— B—— C. M....Hatters' Trim'gs.	W—— H. & Son.........Pianofortes.
V—— C—— & Co.........Hardware.	W—— C. C.....Ret. Men's Furn'g.
V—— S—— W. & Son..Shipping and	W—— E. J. & Co.........Mnfrs. Silk.
Com'n.	W—— & D——.........Iron Works.

W—— J. S. ....Tinware.
W—— & G——. ....Wines, etc.
W—— G. B. ......Exchange Broker.
W—— J. A. ....Liquors.
W—— Mrs. M. F. .....House Furn'g.
W—— H. W. .....Mnfr. Trimmings.
W—— F. W. ....Wool Puller.
W—— P. ....Glass Shades.
W—— L—— & Co. ......Dealers and
                Smelters Lead.
W—— L—— Co.
W—— & McN——. ....Tobacco.
W—— Bros. ....Builders.
W—— & Co. ....Hotel.
W—— P. .....Paper Stock and Mnfr.
                Clothing.
W—— H. ....Glue, etc.
W—— L. ....Cigars, etc.
W—— Mrs. P. ....China.
W—— & R——. ......Canned Goods.
W—— H. & Son. ......Ret. B. and S.
W—— H. ....Mnfr. Hydrometers.
W—— H. ....Mnfr. Straw Goods.
W—— & Co. ....Jet Goods.
W—— W. ......Mnfr. Dress Trim'gs.
W—— & De G——. ....Guns and
                Pistols.
W—— W—— & Co. ....Hide Brokers.
W—— K—— & Co. ....Imps. Liquors.
W—— J. G. & Co. ....Publishers.
W—— J. C. & Co. ....Drugs, etc.
W—— J. ....Loan Broker.
W—— & Bro. ....Cotton Waste.
W—— B. ....Extension Tables.
W—— G. J. ....Ret. Drugs.
W—— & Co. ....Com'n Domestic D. G.
W—— H. ....Gro.
W—— J. ....Furs, etc.
W—— R. ....Mnfr. Ruffles.
W—— E. T. ......H'ware and House
                Furn'g.
W—— & S—— M—— Co. ....Picture
                Frames.
W—— P—— N—— M—— & P——
Co.
W—— C—— & Co. .....Shipping and
                Com'n.
W—— M. ....Coal.
W—— M. ...,..........Leather.
W—— J. ....Restaurant and Liq.
W—— N. ....Blinds and Doors.
W—— F. G. ....Mnfr. Presses.
W—— R. ....Wines.
W—— W. A. ....Gen'l Com'n.
W—— Bros. ......Imps. Fancy Goods.
W—— A., Jr. ....Com'n Flowers.
W—— A. D. ....Bookseller.
W—— R. C. ....Steamboats.
W—— & D. ....Com'n Prod.
W—— C. H. & Co. ......House Furn'g
                Goods.

W—— W. L., Jr. .....Whol. B. and S.
W—— M—— Co. ....Silversmiths.
W—— W. H. & Co. .Mnfg. Jewellers.
W—— S. V. ....Teas.
W—— W. M. ....Stock and Bond
                Broker.
W—— & W——. ......Stock Brokers.
W—— L—— A—— Co.
W—— S—— B—— A—— Co.
W—— & H—— H—— Co.
W—— M—— Co. ....Saddletrees.
W—— J. ....Drugs.
W—— R., Jr. ...Mnfr. Ladies' Cloth-
                ing.
W—— Mrs. R. ....Fancy Goods.
W—— & Van L——. .....Paints, etc.
W—— & H——. .....Com'n Lime, etc.
W—— H. R. ......Com'n and Broker.
W—— J. H. Co. ....Bedding.
W—— M. A., Son & Co. ....Lumber.
W—— T., Jr., & Co. ...Mnfrs. Solder.
W—— H. ....Shipping Broker.
W—— D. & Co. ....Mnfrs. Hatters'
                Goods.
W—— W. A. ....Looking-Glasses.
W—— J. S. M—— Co. ......Looking-
                Glasses.
W—— H. C. ......Ret. Men's Furn'g.
W—— H. S. ....House Furn'g.
W—— J. H. ....Cattle.
W—— A. P. & Co. ....Letter Holders.
W—— G. N. & N. A. ......Stoneyard.
W—— H. C. & Co. ....Stock and Bond
                Brokers.
W—— J. F. & Co. ....Jewelry.
W—— J. H. & Sons. ...Cattle Brokers.
W—— J. C. & Co. .....Stock Brokers.
W—— P. H. & W. ....Fringes.
W—— S—— & Co. Mnfrs.. and Jobbers
                Linen and Lace Goods.
W—— W—— & C——. .....Hardware.
W—— & G——. .Shipping and Com'n.
W—— J. ....Sashes.
W—— G—— & Co. ....Sugar Refiners.
W—— J. ......Agent Flour and Grain.
W—— A. ....Builder.
W—— G. ......Steam and Gas Fitter.
W—— I—— Co.
W—— J. J. .Cement and Slate Broker.
W—— T. ....Broker Flour and Grain.
W—— W. ....Liquors.
W—— W. H. ....Crockery.
W—— H. S. & Bro. ....Bankers.
W—— J. H. & Co. ....Auctioneers.
W—— & G——. Imps. Shawls, White
                Goods, etc.
W—— & L——. .Wines and Billiards.
W—— J. ....Ret. Clothing.
W—— T. D. ....Hotel.
W—— & Co. .....,....Patent Meds.
W—— H—— Co.

W—— & E——.......Chemicals, etc.
W—— & W——.......Com'n Wool, Blankets, etc.
W—— I............Shippers' Agent.
W—— & D——........Fruit Brokers.
W—— C..............Fancy Goods.
W—— C. A............Ret. Shoes.
W—— & McA——....Sign Painters.
W—— & B——..............Wool.
W—— A...................Neckties.
W—— C............Carriagemaker.
W—— C...................Colors.
W—— & M——.....Mnfg. Jewellers.
W—— J.........Mnfr. Underwear.
W—— & Q——.......Cotton Brokers.
W—— B...........Jobber Millinery.
W—— C.................Hats, etc.
W—— J.........Jobber Hosiery, etc.
W—— L............Ret. Clothing.
W—— M.... ....Storage.
W—— W............Jobber D. G.
W—— & Bro...Diamond Brokers, etc.
W—— S............Whol. Liquors.
W—— C. H.....Brushes and Bristles.
W—— G. R............Iron Broker.
W—— Mrs. J. H.................Coal.
W——P..............Oyster Saloon.
W—— W. A...................Oils.
W—— Bros. Co............Carriages.
W—— C—— & Co......Government Supplies.
W—— J.............Gro. and Liq.
W—— Mrs. S. A.........Stationery.
W—— & R——...Tobacco and Cigars.
W—— W. J.........Southern Com'n.
W—— S—— P—— M—— Co.
W—— D. A...........Ret. Stationer.
W—— S. & Co......Tailors' Trim'gs.
W—— & Co...............Feathers.
W—— & Co...........Artificial Stone.
W—— & N——......Stock Brokers.
W—— W. E.......Sewing Machines

W—— H. P...........Stock Broker.
W—— W. J....Ret. Boots and Shoes.
W—— J. G. & Co........Com'n Prod.
W—— W. P. & Co....Cotton Brokers.
W—— & M——....Jobbers Millinery.
W—— & S——......Gen'l Com'n, etc.
W—— F. & Co...............Hotel.
W—— A............Paper Box Mkr.
W—— J...................Gro.
W—— A. & Co..Imps. Insect Powder.
W—— J. E............Mdse. Broker.
W—— & Co............Mdse. Brokers.
Y—— W. A........Mnfr. Trimmings.
Y—— M...................Clothing.
Y—— T...................Clothing.
Y—— J. H. & Co.........Com'n Prod.
Y—— E. T...............Tea Broker.
Y—— G. G....Agt. U—— S—— E—— Co.
Y—— J. N...................Pianos.
Y—— L...'.....Jobber Hats, Caps, and Furs.
Y—— M. & Co.......Perfumery, etc.
Y—— T. S. & Co.....Whol. Clothing.
Y—— & McC——......Com'n Cotton.
Y—— & Co......Com'n Cuban Sugar.
Y—— H. A....Stock and Gold Broker.
Z—— A.........Ret. Boots and Shoes
Z—·· B.........Ret. Boots and Shoes.
Z—— G.........Ret. Boots and Shoes.
Z—— J............Ret. Fancy Goods.
Z—— D...........Mnfr. Hair Goods.
Z—— S. & F——....Jobbers Millinery.
Z—— M. A...............Furniture.
Z—— J. & Co.............Furniture.
Z—— D.............Optician, etc.
Z—— B. H............Cabinetmkr.
Z—— B. B......Ret. Boots and Shoes.
Z—— W.............Wood Turner.
Z—— F. & F——..Imps. Musical Insts.
Z—— P. & Co........Window Glass.
Z—— H...............Leaf Tobacco.

[TO BE CONTINUED.]

BROOKLYN N. Y.

A—— Mrs. H.....Tobacco and Cigars.	B—— Mrs. P..................Gro.
A—— J. & R.......Spring Mattresses.	B—— & H——...........Chromos.
A—— M...............Fancy Goods.	B—— M.............Wagonmkr.
A—— J. W................Machinist.	B—— J.............:.......Brewer.
A—— C.................Liquors.	B—— & Co.............Coopers.
A—— D.................Liquors.	B—— & S——.......Mnfrs. Carriages.
A—— J...............Men's Furn'g.	B—— M.................Scrap Iron.
American E—— & B—— G—— Co.	B—— P. H.................Liquors.
A—— T. W.................Gro.	B—— & S——.................Liquors.
A—— R.........Tailor and Clothing.	B—— B.................Liquors.
A—— & Co..............:...D. G.	B—— D...................Coal.
A—— J......................Baker.	B—— H.................Liquors.
A—— J. H............Coppersmith.	B—— J. N.............Charcoal.
B—— W. W.............Auctioneer.	B—— B. & Son............Tailors.
B—— E. H..............Carpets.	B—— T. P.........Boots and Shoes.
B—— J.............Fancy Goods.	B—— J...............Iron Railings.
B—— Bros.................Carpets.	B—— A. A.............Brewer.
B—— S.................D. G.	B—— D................Soap
B—— J. & J...............Painters.	B—— P................Tinsmith.
B—— P. J.............Men's Furn'g.	B—— J. & W.............Builders.
B—— L..............Lager Beer.	B—— W. G. & Co......Variety Store.
B—— W.................Drugs.	B—— A. C. & Co.Plumbers' Materials.
B—— G..................Painter.	B—— I. H.................Builder.
B—— W. J.................Jeweller.	B—— D...................Gro.
B—— & M——.....Billiards and Liq.	B—— T. H.................Builder.
B—— B...................Clothing.	B—— J. W.................Wood.
B—— S., Jr.............Crockery.	C—— W. H.................Builder.
B—— Mrs. J. H.................Shoes.	C—— H. A.................Drugs.
B—— K....................Baker.	C—— T.................Furniture.
B—— A..................D. G., etc.	C—— J. S.............Real Estate.
B—— & N——.................Gro.	C—— T. & Co...........Marble, etc.
B—— C. & Co..............Awnings.	C—— P.............Steam Engines.
B—— S. A............Hats and Caps.	C—— & B——.......Boots and Shoes.
B—— & C——..........Flour Mills.	C—— & Co.................Hair, etc.
B—— H. A....................Gro.	C—— J. D. & Son..........Jewellers.
B—— Mrs. W. G.......Fancy Goods.	C—— I.................Clothing.
B—— Mrs. A..........Millinery, etc.	C—— & Co.................Toys.
B—— Mrs. R....Women's Underwear.	C—— R................Hotel.
B—— Mrs. M...Hats, Caps, and Furs.	·C—— R. & Son.............Marble.
B—— C. H.......Mnfr. Straw Goods.	C—— C.................Liquors.
B—— T. J..........Boots and Shoes.	C—— T. H.....Artists' Materials, etc.
B—— S. C. & Co........Mnfrs. Dress	C—— Mrs. W.......Fancy Goods.
Trimmings.	C—— C.................Boilermkr.
B—— & L——..........Paper Stock.	C—— E. A.................Coal.
B—— & D——.......Brass Finishers.	C—— R. S..........Boots and Shoes.

C—— E. E...Mnfr. Oil-Can Stoppers.	F—— W. L.............Upholsterer.
C—— J. E................Presses, etc.	F—— J. F.............Pianomkr.
C—— W. H................Trunks.	F—— J. S......:.......Hats and Caps.
C—— W. P..........R. E. Agent.	F—— J. M..............Hotel.
C—— W. A..........Fancy Goods.	F—— S. W.......Boots and Shoes.
C—— T. A............Shipbuilder.	F—— B..............Brewer.
C—— J. H............Foundry.	G—— J..............Fancy Goods.
C—— J.............Fancy Goods.	G—— B..............Builder.
C—— C. H.....House Furn'g Goods.	G—— M. F. & E. J...Woollen Goods.
C—— J..........Teas, Coffees, etc.	G—— B..............Brewer.
C—— T. F. & Co............Fcy G.	G—— T..............Soap.
D—— E................Printer.	G—— O.............Liquors.
D—— W. H............Shirtmkr.	G—— P.............Liquors.
D—— H............Crockery, etc.	G—— M.............Gro.
D—— G............Tailor.	G—— & S——.........Crockery.
D—— T. W............Auctioneer.	G—— J.........Fancy and D. G.
D—— J. A............Rectifier.	G—— & Co..........Pianos.
D—— W. W........Hats and Caps.	G—— B. F...——...Washboards.
D—— J—— & Co......Iron Founders.	G—— P—— R—— Co.
D—— T. S............Builder.	G—— Mrs. P..........Fancy Goods.
D—— P................Gro.	G—— C. H..........Fancy Goods.
D—— S—— E. F....Books and Stat'y.	G—— F. C.............Tailor.
D—— R. B........Sewing Machines.	H—— H.........Fancy and D. G.
D—— E ....Soda Water.	H—— D. F...........Carpets.
D—— C ....Gro.	H—— T. A............Builder.
D—— A. W............Restaurant.	H—— H............Hardware.
D—— P................Wagons.	H—— Bros..........Brassworkers.
D—— J........Hats and Caps.	H—— J. M..........Books, etc.
D—— T. O. M............Builder.	H—— Mrs. R......Fancy Goods and
D—— W................Builder.	Millinery.
D—— W. F......Paints and H'ware.	H—— D............Clothing.
D—— D......Stat'r and Printer.	H—— H. A............Jeweller.
D—— J. C............Tailor.	H—— J................Saloon.
D—— & Co............Soaps.	H—— S...............D. G.
D—— J............Stairbuilder.	H—— R...............D. G.
D—— W. E............Mnfr. Hats.	H—— Mrs. G. F....Ret. Fancy Goods.
D—— D............Liquors.	H—— J..............Tailor.
D—— L............Painter.	H—— W. J.........Mnfr. Skirts.
D—— J. C. & Co............D. G.	H—— G. A..........Painter.
D—— J. W................Gro.	H—— G. H...Mnfr. Children's Shoes.
D—— Mrs. E............D. G.	H—— Mrs. C............Teas.
D—— A............Cloaks, etc.	H—— & B——.........Roofers.
D—— C............Carriagemkr.	H—— P.............Liquors.
D—— Mrs. A. A.......Dress Trim'gs.	H—— J............Tailor.
D—— C. H............Men's Furn'g.	H—— Mrs. E. A.......Hairdresser.
E—— & McK——............Stoves.	H—— H............Turner.
F—— J. P......Hoopskirts and F. G.	H—— H. P............Gro.
F—— J............Boots and Shoes.	H—— L............Tailor.
F—— J. & Co............Gro.	H—— J. & Co............Gro.
F—— A. S.....House Furn'g Goods.	H—— S............Gro.
F—— A............Wines and Liq.	H—— W. E. & Co..........Foundry.
F—— R................Gro.	H—— H.
F—— Bros............Liquors.	H—— & M——........Men's Furn'g.
F—— J. F. & Co...........Tobacco.	H—— P. & Co............D. G.
F—— L............Men's Furn'g.	H—— R. R. & Co............Mnfrs.
F—— J. W............Cooper.	H—— T. M............Upholstery.
F—— M. B............Drugs.	H—— J...........Sewing Machines.
F—— C.......Leather and Findings.	H—— J............Liquors.
F—— C. E............Bedding.	H—— J. C. & Co............Stoves.
F—— H............Storage.	H—— C. G.............Dressmkr.
F—— Mrs. S............D. G.	H—— T............Hats and Caps.

H—— H............Mnfr. Shoes.	L—— Bros............Fancy Goods.
H—— & V——.............Tailors.	L—— J.................Builder.
I—— C.................Brewer.	L—— S...........Slat Matting.
I—— E.................Gro.	L—— W. R.............Liquors.
I—— Bros..........Marble Works.	L—— J. & Co............D. G.
I—— C......Carpenter and Builder.	L—— & P——..........Plumbers.
I—— L. & M.............Livery.	L—— I. O...............Hotel.
J—— H.............Chemist.	L—— G. R.............Brewer.
J—— C. M.............Books.	L—— H.................Gro.
J—— W. E............Marble.	L—— L——— M——— Co.
J—— G. H.........Fancy Goods.	L—— I—— M—— Co.
J—— S., Jr., & Son.......Oil Works.	L—— P. & Co..........Painters.
J—— A. F.............Builder.	L—— T. C. & J. C..........Saloon.
J—— W. W........Hats and Caps.	L—— L............Clothing.
J—— T.................Liquors.	L—— M............Clothing.
J—— H. C.............Liquors.	L—— M.............Liquors.
K—— H. A.................Gro.	L—— S. B. & Co.............D. G.
K—— C..........Fancy D. G.	McB—— J. H.........Painter.
K—— M. J.........Boots and Shoes.	McC—— Mrs. P.........Glass, etc.
K—— Mrs. A. E.........Stoneyard.	McC—— M. C.........Restaurant.
K—— & M——.........Liquors.	McD—— M.............Liquors.
K—— L.........Stoneyard.	McE—— & Co......Boots and Shoes.
K—— Bros.................Gro.	McF—— J. Jr.........Boilermkr.
K—— T..........Coal and Wood.	McF—— T.........Hoopskirts.
K—— R.........Boots and Shoes.	McG—— A.............Plumber.
K—— F.................Gro.	McG—— S.........Fancy Goods.
K—— H.................Brewer.	McG—— W. A.......Ship Chandler.
K—— E. S.............Tailor.	McG—— M. J.........Jeweller.
K—— R. D.............Jeweller.	McG—— J.............Builder.
K—— J. S. & Co.......Fancy Goods.	McG—— J.............Clothing.
K—— & R——..........Builders.	McK—— J. H.............Hotel.
K—— A.............Liquors.	McK—— F. & W.............Liquors.
K—— M.............Plumber.	McK—— P.............Liquors.
K—— J. J............Auction.	McL—— J. S.............Builder.
K—— G.................Coal.	McM—— P. & Son.........Furniture.
K—— E.............Builder.	McM—— A.............D. G.
K—— P.................Drugs.	McM—— Mrs. S.............D. G.
K—— M. M............Millinery.	M—— Mrs. E.......Boots and Shoes.
K—— N.................Tailor.	M—— Mrs. J.............Liquors.
K—— Misses..........Fancy Goods.	M—— J. T.............Tailor.
K—— A.................D. G.	M—— & Bro.................Gro.
L—— W. M.............Carpets.	M—— E. H.............Plumber.
L—— P. W.............Builder.	M—— G. L.............Stairbuilder.
L—— F—— H. A.....Men's Furn'g.	M—— Mrs. R.............Hoops.
L—— Bros.................Gro.	M—— J. B.............Liquors.
L—— J...........Mnfr. Chemicals.	M—— & S——...........Furniture.
L—— J.................Mason.	M—— J. B..............Trusses.
L—— P.........Fancy Goods.	M—— R. T..........Crockery.
L—— H. S.............Builder.	M—— J. F.........Fishing Tackle.
L—— A.............Sashmkr.	M—— B.............Clocks.
L—— L.........Fancy Goods.	M—— J.........Fancy Goods.
L—— B. & Co......R. E. Brokers, etc.	M—— P.............Tailor.
L—— & Co...Mnfrs. Boots and Shoes.	M—— R.............Tassels.
L—— B.................Liquors.	M—— V.............Sewing M.
L—— A.................Clothing.	M—— G. & E. J.......Drugs and Liq.
L—— & S.................Coal.	M—— S. A.............Paints.
L—— H.................D. G.	M—— L.............Upholsterer.
L—— B.............Millinery.	M—— Mrs. E.........Fancy Goods.
L—— S.........Picture Frames.	M—— S.........Fancy Goods.
L—— S.........Boots and Shoes.	M—— & Co......Mnfrs. Oils.
L—— I.................Butcher.	M—— A.................Builder.

M—— Mrs. P..........Fancy Goods.	R—— C..............Cabinetmkr.
M—— & Co..........Iron Founders.	R—— H. F. & Co.....Paperhangings
M—— A..............Hardware.	and Paints.
M—— J..............Liquors.	R—— Mrs. I. II.....Boots and Shoes.
M—— C..............Mnfr. Tools.	R—— A. P..........Carpenter, etc.
M—— J..............Liquors.	R—— M..............D. G.
M—— T. J. & Co..........Foundry.	R—— J..............Tailor.
M—— D..............Bedding.	R—— Mrs. S. B....Skirts and Corsets.
M—— S..........Teas and Spices.	R—— C. D........Roofing Materials.
M—— M..............Fancy Goods.	R—— Bros..............Restaurant.
M—— R—— & Co.....Mnfrs. Braids.	R—— C. W..............Cigars, etc.
M—— H..............Fancy Goods.	R—— F..............Baker.
M—— L. M..........Fancy Goods.	R—— R..............Coppersmith.
M—— T..............Liquors.	R—— T..............Builder.
M—— C..............Builder.	R—— W..............Builder.
M—— W..............Liquors.	R—— J. F.....Fancy Toilet Articles.
M—— & L——........Cotton Dealers.	R—— J. B..............Painter.
M—— & R——..............Liquors.	R—— J. S..............Jeweller.
M—— J. II..............Planter.	R—— W. S..............Builder.
N—— R..............Printer.	R—— T. W..............Builder.
N—— A. A..............Liquors.	R—— J..............Liquors.
N—— A. D..............Liquors.	R—— J..............Fancy Goods.
N—— F..............Gro.	R—— M..........Boots and Shoes.
N—— & S——.......Mnfrs. Shoes.	R—— F.......Hats, Caps and Furs.
N—— W..........Fancy and D. G.	R—— P..............Gro.
N—— N. T..............Painter.	R—— J. & Co..........Furniture.
N—— I—— W——.	R—— J. H.....Men's Furn'g G.
N—— J. D..............Drugs.	S—— A. R..............Billiards.
N—— & F——.........Machinists.	S—— & Co.........Door Knobs.
N—— F. T..............Hatter.	S—— J..............Brewer.
O'D—— P.........Gro. and Liq.	S—— L—— & M——......Furniture.
O'N—— J. H..........Wireworker.	S—— E. A..............Drugs.
O—— J. W..........Hoopskirts.	S—— H..............Clothing.
O—— F. W..........Hats, etc.	S—— B..............Clothing.
O—— H. B..............D. G.	S—— J..........Mnfr. Brooms.
O—— R..............Builder.	S—— J..............Mouldings.
O—— R. R..............Baker.	S—— C..........Paperhangings.
P—— & S——.........Men's Furn'g.	S—— J........Carriages and Livery
P—— T..........Roasting Mills.	Stable.
P—— C..............Storage.	S—— & Co..............Brewers.
P—— M. C..............Builder.	S—— B..........Boots and Shoes.
P—— S—— F.	S—— S.....Boots and Shoes.
P—— W. S..........Photographer.	S—— J. P..............Brewer.
P—— A..............Hardware.	S—— H..............Contractor.
P—— J. D. & Son....Flour and Grain.	S—— I. S........Liq. and Billiards.
P—— C..............Tailor.	S—— M..............Clothing.
P—— & Son..............Pianos.	S—— J. H..............Builder.
P—— H..............Hotel.	S—— E..............Tailor.
P—— W..............Ales, etc.	S—— J..............Cutlery.
P—— L..............Painter.	S—— J. P..............Boxmaker.
P—— J..............Clothing.	S—— G..............Painter.
P—— & R——........Carriagemkrs.	S—— B..............Builder.
P—— J..............Teas.	S—— C. B..............Builder.
P—— E..............Shoes.	S—— Mrs. M. A......Hoopskirts, etc.
P—— F. T........Fancy and D. G.	S—— H. G..............Millwright.
P—— J. H..........Mnfr. Hats.	S—— B..........Boots and Shoes.
P—— D..........Window Shades.	S—— Bros....Rectifiers and Distillers.
P—— Mrs. T. H........Fancy Goods.	S—— P..........Boots and Shoes.
P—— & H——.........Mnfrs. Soap.	S—— J. E........Dry Dock Builder.
R—— W..............Carriages.	S—— A..............Sashes.
R—— & Co..............Fruits.	S—— E. E..............Gro.

S—— F. B.	D. G.
S—— G. H.	Teas.
S—— L. H.	Drugs.
S—— W.	Saw Mill.
S—— H. S. & E. H.	Trimmings.
S—— & A——.	Umbrellamkrs.
S—— J.	D. G.
S—— L.	Gro.
S—— J.	Planing Mill.
S—— B—— S—— D—— Co.	
S—— B—— S—— E—— W——	
S—— J.	Gro.
S—— F.	Painter.
S—— Bros.	Tailors' Trim'gs and Shoes.
S—— Bros.	Builders.
S—— T.	Shipbuilder.
S—— H. W...V—— R—— T—— Co.	
S—— L. D.	Tailor.
S—— N.	D. G.
S—— J. B.	D. G. Auctioneer.
S—— I.	Clothing.
S—— & Co.	Gro.
S—— J.	Liquors.
S—— H.	Jeweller.
S—— Mrs. D.	House Furn'g.
S—— J.	Liquors.
S—— T. W.	Builder.
T—— E. & Co.	D. G.
T—— M.	Painter.
T—— J. & Bro.	Furniture.
T—— J.	Boots and Shoes.
T—— C. H.	Hats.
T—— C. F.	Pianos.
T—— E. J.	Hats.
T—— F. J.	Wrought-Iron.
T—— Mrs. A. M.	Stoves.
T—— J.	Liquors.
T—— A. M.	Clothing.
T—— Mrs. M.	Fancy Goods.
T—— W. A.	Auctioneer.
T—— J.	Foundry.
T—— Miss M.	Children's Carriages.
T—— E. O.	Restaurant.
T—— S. H.	Dentist.
U—— J. G.	Drugs.
U—— J. S.	Boilers.
U—— S—— M—— Co.	Pumps.
U—— S—— S—— B—— Co.	
V—— S.	Hotel.
V—— N—— J. B.	Boots and Shoes.
V—— S—— J. B.	Liquors.
V—— W—— R. & Co.	Carpenters and Builders.
V—— T. S.	Hotel
V—— J., Jr.	Gro.
V—— Bros.	Gro.
V—— P.	Boot and Shoes.
V—— D—— B.	Confec.
V—— H.	Confec.
W—— & C——	Painters.
W—— R. & Co.	Fancy Goods.
W—— C. R. M.	Maltster.
W—— J.	Painter.
W—— & M——	Carriages.
W—— H.	Sashes and Blinds.
W—— J. & Co.	Mnfrs. Glass.
W—— T.	Coachmaker.
W—— T—— & Co.	Auctioneers.
W—— A. E.	Gro.
W—— A.	Tinsmith.
W—— Mrs. E. F.	Fancy Goods.
W—— W. H.	Hardware and House Furn'g.
W—— & P——	Lumber.
W—— C.	Tailor.
W—— J. E.	Plumber.
W—— J.	Boots and Shoes.
W—— H.	Liquors.
W—— E.	Flour and Feed.
W—— A.	Clothing.
W—— G.	D. G.
W—— H.	Tinware.
W—— M. L.	Fancy Goods.
W—— J.	Brewer.
W—— L. & Co.	Furniture.
W—— Mrs. M.	Hoopskirts.
W—— J. W. & Son.	D. G.
W—— J.	Crockery.
W—— C. F.	Fancy Goods.
W—— M—— & L—— Co.	
W—— W.	Books, Toys, etc.
W—— & N——	Machinists.
W—— W. & Co.	Mnfrs. Brass Hinges.
W—— I. F.	Fancy Goods.
W—— H. B. & Co.	Carriages.
W—— J. & Co.	Cigars.
W—— & N——	Whol. Gro.
W—— A. M.	Storage.
W—— C. R.	Baker.
W—— Mrs. E.	Fancy Goods.
W—— J. L.	Gro.
W—— D.	Boots and Shoes.
W—— M.	Cabinetmaker.
W—— Mrs. T.	Fancy Goods.
W—— L—— & Co.	Gro. and Prov.
Y—— Dr. W.	Mnfr. Sauces.
Y—— & Son.	Prov.
Z—— J, B.	R. E. Agent.

ALBANY, N. Y.

A—— & V——..Looking Glasses, etc.	L—— H. V. R., Jr.....Gents' Furn'g.
A—— C. W....................Grain.	L—— I...................Millinery.
B—— B......................Tailor.	L—— J. W..............Carpenter.
B—— S.............Crockery, etc.	McA—— C...................Tailor.
B—— & L——.........Crockery, etc.	McC—— F.............Eating-house.
B—— Son & Co.............Lumber.	McD—— H..............Carriages.
B—— R. S. & Co.............Gro.	McD—— Bros................D. Gds.
B—— & Co..........Whol. Liquors.	McK—— P. B. & Co.....Candles, etc.
B—— & P——...............Flour.	McK—— & Co.....Flour, Grain, etc.
B—— D. G...........Coal, Gro., etc.	M—— J. W.........Billiard Saloon.
B—— & D——...........Pk. Packers.	M—— Bros....................Gro.
B—— I..........Brkr. and Clothing.	M—— J....................Lqrs.
B—— A. M. & Co.............Gro.	M—— & T——..............Com'n.
B—— J....................Watches.	M—— B....................D. G.
C—— W...........Boots and Shoes.	O—— G.................Clothing.
C—— O......................Gro.	O—— E.................D. G., etc.
C—— C—— S—— B—— Co.	P—— J.................Contractor.
C—— W......................Coal.	P—— & McL——.............Coal.
C—— M. L...................Gro.	P—— J. A..................D. G.
C—— J..........Poultry, Fruit, etc.	S—— F. A..............Builder, etc.
C—— S—— & Co...........Lumber.	S—— P....................Tailor.
C—— Bros.............Bk'g Powder.	S—— R. H...............Guns, etc.
C—— J. & Son.............Pianos.	S—— Bros...........Cabinetmkrs.
C—— A. M...............Flour, etc.	S—— C—— & Co...........Lumber.
C—— P.....................Cooper.	S—— S—— & W..........Tobacco.
D—— & K——.............Lumber.	S—— & H............Paper, etc.
D—— R. C. & Co.............Clothing.	S—— R. & Co.....Silver-plated Ware.
D—— P—— & L——......Boots and	T—— Mrs. M............Fancy Gds.
Shoes.	T—— W....................Drugs.
D—— J. W. & Co....Paper-hangings.	T—— & W——.............Carpets.
E—— C. P. & Co............Lumber.	T—— C. H..............Physician.
E—— J.....................Gro., etc.	T—— L—— & Co...........Wheels.
F—— N. A....................Grain.	V—— C. C. & Co...........Drugs.
G—— J. & Co..........Carriages, etc.	W—— Mrs. J. M..........Dressmkr.
G—— R. J.....................Coal.	W—— S. F.......Flour, Grain, etc.
G—— P. H.............Coppersmith.	W—— C...................Carpets.
H—— W. & Co.....Oysters and Fruit.	W—— J.................Gro., etc.
H—— J...............Furniture, etc.	W—— P. H.............Doors, etc.
H—— & D——.............Hay, etc.	W—— W. M. & Co...............D. G.
H—— G....................Saloon.	W—— W. H. & Sons.......Watches.
H—— J. H............Music Store.	W—— A.................Whol. Gro.
H—— J. L. & C............Lumber.	W—— W. P.............Provisions.
J—— J......................Gro.	W—— H............Moulding Sand.

[TO BE CONTINUED.]

ATLANTA, GA.

A—— J. W.	Planter.	G—— W—— & Co. ...... Music, etc.
A—— J. W. & C. F.	Nursery.	H—— T. J. .... Gro., etc.
A—— W. J.	Planter.	H—— G. F. & A. F. ...... Com'n, etc.
A—— W. C.	Planter.	J—— M. W. .... Ag'l Implts., etc.
A—— J. S	Stoves, etc.	J—— M. W. & Bro. ...... Com'n, etc.
A—— H. W.	Planter.	J—— P. .... Liquors.
B—— B.	Gro.	L—— W. B. & Co. .... Clothing.
B—— J. W.	Planter.	L—— L. .... D. G.
B—— W. R.	Printer.	L—— H. .... Foundry.
B—— C. F.	Music.	L—— C. H. .... Planter.
B—— L. E.	Grocer.	McC—— R. P. .... Planter.
B—— Mrs. F. M.	Planter.	McN—— W. & Co. .... Mills.
B—— C. B. & Co.	Gro.	M—— & J——. .... Lumber.
B—— & G——.	Agts.	N—— D. .... Grocer.
B—— J. S.	Gen. Store.	O'N—— J. .... Grocer.
B—— J. E.	Gro.	O—— P. R. .... Planter.
B—— E.	Fancy Gds.	O—— E. .... Planter.
B—— G. A.	Gen. Store.	P—— & W——. ...... Restaurant.
B—— & D——.	Liquors, etc.	P—— F—— & Co. .... D. G.
C—— F. M.	Planter.	P—— W. R., Jr., & Co. .... Gro., etc.
C—— W. T.	Gro.	P—— P—— Co.
C—— G. W.	Planter.	R—— A. J. K. P. .... Planter.
D—— S.	Planter.	R—— G. C. .... Saddler.
D—— S. H.	Saddler.	R—— J. C. .... Gro.
E—— & F——.	D. G. etc.	S—— C. H. & Co. ...... Cotton Bkrs.
E—— H.	Gro.	S—— I. .... Planter.
F—— G. H. & A. W.	Boots and Shoes.	S—— J. M. .... Gro.
F—— W.	Planter.	S—— A. S. .... Planter.
F—— & E——.	Plumbers.	T—— & J——. .... Drugs.
F—— J.	Planter.	V—— E. .... Miller.
G—— S.	Planter.	W—— J. L. .... Furniture.
G—— W. R.	Planter.	W—— & C——. .... Stk. Yard.

[TO BE CONTINUED.]

AUBURN, N. Y.

A—— A. . .'. . . . . .Shoes.	P—— & H——. . . . . .D. G.
A—— S. H. . . . . .Stoves, etc.	P—— W—— & H——. . . . . .Coal.
B—— C. S., Sr. . . . . .Lqrs.	P—— & N——. . . . . .Clothing.
B—— Bros. & Co. . . . . .Machinists.	P—— H. R. & C. W. . . . . .Lumber.
B—— C. P. . . . .Miller.	Q—— I. W. . . . . .Machinist, etc.
B—— & Son. . . . . .Distillers.	R—— A. . . . . .Marble.
C—— M. . . . . :. . . . .,.Gro.	R—— W. H. . . . .,. . .D. G.
C—— & Bro. . . . . .H'dware.	R—— D. C. & G. W.,. . . . . .Cab't Ware.
C—— E. D. . . . . .H'dware.	S—— & Co. . . . . .Flour, etc.
D—— J. . . . . .Gro., etc.	S—— & P——. . . . . .Patents.
D—— G—— J. . . . .Gro.	S—— J. D. & Co. . . . .,. . . .D. G.
D—— & S—— M—— Co.	S—— B. B. & Co..Mnfrs. Cornshellers.
G—— D. C. . . . . .Lime.	S—— E. G. & Son. . . . . .Agents.
H—— A. B. . . . . .Printer.	T—— Mrs. Dr. M. A. . . . . . . .Milliner.
K—— W. H. . . . . .Bricks.	T—— D. . . . . .Gro.
M—— P—— Co.	T—— N. . . . . .Boots and Shoes.
M—— & Co. . . . . .Sashes, etc.	V—— V—— & L——,. . . . . .D. G.
O—— D. M. & Co. . . . . . . .Reapers, etc.	

[TO BE CONTINUED.]

BALTIMORE, MD.

A—— W. H. & Co....Oyster Packers.
A—— T—— & Co....Auctioneers, etc.
A—— E......................D. G.
American F—— I—— Co.
A—— & D——............Furniture.
B—— M................Notions.
B—— J. J.............Provisions.
B—— C.................Shoes.
B—— S............Wines, etc.
B—— G. W............Hardware.
B—— G................Brewery.
B—— J................Brewery.
B—— & H——....Gen'l Com'n.
B—— & B——........Furniture.
B—— J.................Shoes.
B—— J.................Shoes.
B—— D. G............Tobacco.
B—— & H——.........Tailors.
B—— H.............Liquors.
B—— W..........Foundry, etc.
B—— J................Books.
B—— R. & Sons.......Whol. Shoes.
B—— R. P.............Books, etc.
B—— J................Coaches.
B—— G. H........Paints, Oils, etc.
B—— C. H. & J........Silverplaters.
B—— W. C..............Grocer.
B—— & Bro............Shoes.
C—— L—— & Co.........Oysters.
C—— Bros. & Co.............Drugs.
C—— R.................Gro.
C—— & W............F'cy Gds.
C—— E. J..............Lumber.
C—— H—— & Co........Founders.
C—— P. H.............Broker.
C—— T. E. & Co.........Gents' Gds.
C—— R. B................Hotel.
C—— & T——............Boilers.
C—— G. W.......Mnfr. Cotton Bats
　　　　and Wadding.
C—— & Co..............Stoves.
C—— T. R..............Lqrs.
C—— G. W. M..........Shoes.
C—— J..............Periodicals.
C—— J........Whol. Lqrs., etc.
C—— & Co...........Books, etc.

C—— J. W................Hdware.
D—— J. F. W............Stencils.
D—— F. F. & Co. Druggists' Sundries.
D—— J. O...............D. G.
D—— C. L—— & Co..........Gro.
E—— & B——...........Saw Mill.
E—— J. R. & Co.....Boots, Hats, etc.
E—— S. A. & Co........Oysters, etc.
F—— J..............Millinery.
F—— S..................Stoves.
F—— H.................Baker.
F—— M. L..............Plumber.
F—— N...................Junk.
F—— & B——....Mirrors, etc.
G—— Sons & Co.......Cotton Duck.
G—— C—— C—— Co.
G—— S................Tavern.
G—— J..............Silverplater.
G—— H. T. & T——..........Com'n.
G—— Bros. & Co................Gro.
G—— H. C.............Distiller.
G—— J.....Imp. and Com'n Fruits.
G—— I................Clothing.
H—— A. G. & Co........Laces, etc.
H—— S. M.............Coal, etc.
H—— J. M..............Coal.
H—— B. F.............Flour, etc.
H—— C. & Co............Printers.
H—— J. H.....Whol. Notions.
H—— C. & Son.........Contractors.
H—— G. C.............Books, etc.
H—— J. & Co.............Clothing.
H—— J. G..........Tinware, etc.
H—— W. J.............Cabinetmkr.
H—— J., Jr.......Fertilizers, etc.
J—— S. M. & Co.......Coal Shippers.
K—— H.............Gro., etc.
K—— H. & Son..............D. G.
K—— Bros................Prov.
K—— W. H. & Co......Whol. Paints,
　　　　Oils, etc.
K—— Bros...........Chandlery, etc.
K—— J. H., Jr.............Lumber.
K—— J. & Co................Prov.
L—— H................Tobacco.
L—— S. S. & Son......Iron and Coal.

L—— A....................D. G.	R—— M—— R—— and O—— Co.
L—— S. C....................Hotel.	R—— G. H................Gasfitter.
L—— D....................Leather.	R—— G....................Brewer.
McC—— W................Carriages.	R—— J. L. & Bro............Fruit.
McC—— T. & Co............Lqrs.	R—— J. A. & Co............Shoes.
McC—— T..................Bakery.	S—— P. D. & Co..........Carriages.
McG—— O—— Co.	S—— M. L. & Co.........Books, etc.
McL—— S. R...................Gro.	S—— J.............Bookbinder, etc.
M—— G. W............Books, etc.	S—— E....................Hosiery.
M—— C. B. & Co..............Gro.	S—— C....................Gro.
M—— Bros..................Cigars.	S—— J. & Co................Broker.
M—— R. & Sons...........Crackers.	S—— C....................Brewer.
M—— J. H..............Furniture.	S—— Bros...............Regalias.
M—— J....................Gro., etc.	S—— & C——...............Bldrs.
M—— C—— & Co...........Tailors.	S—— S. J..................Oysters.
M—— M............Hoop Skirts, etc.	S—— H. & Co............Clothing.
M—— J. & Co..............Agency.	S—— S....................D. G.
M—— F....................Shoes.	S—— C. P..............Furniture.
M—— & Bro.........Paperhangings.	S—— J. D...........Livery Stables.
M—— R. & Bro.............Cloths.	S—— A. & Son............Turners.
N—— A. & Sons...........Gro., etc.	S—— V................Carpets.
N—— F. H................D. G., etc.	S—— D. S....................Ice.
N—— E................Shoes.	T—— S. G..............Machinist.
O'C—— H..............Carriages.	T—— W. H..............Preserves.
O—— & G—— Bros.........Mldgs.	T—— N. & Co.............Leather.
P—— G...................Brewery.	T—— L—— & Co...........Lumber.
P—— A. B. & Co......Stock Broker.	T—— J. E..................Hatter.
P—— A. & Co........Com'n Lumber.	W—— L....................D. G.
P—— G. G., Jr.........Capitalist.	W—— D——............Furniture.
P—— & H——.............Lumber.	W—— C....................Junk.
P—— W. G. & Co....Com. and Fruit.	W—— S. G.........Steel and Iron.
P—— H. B....................Gro.	W—— S................Clothing.
P—— G. P. & Co..Confec. and Fruits.	W—— W..............Clothing.
R—— A....................Tobacco.	W—— W. E. & Co....Steam Heaters.
R—— T....................Liquors.	W—— F................Brewery.
R—— & W——..........Carriages.	

[TO BE CONTINUED.]

BANGOR, ME.

A—— & S——............Boots, etc.	J—— T. & Son.............Hdware.
B—— P. M.................Broker.	J—— I. S. & Co............Medicines.
B—— M—— & Co..........Clothing.	K—— N....................Lumber.
B—— I. M................Lumber.	L—— G. W....................Gro.
C—— A. F................Clothing.	M—— & U——...........Shoes, etc..
C—— T—— Co.	N—— C. A........Gro. and Lumber.
C—— Bros. & D——.............Gro.	P—— & J——.................Lumber.
D—— C. H.................Lumber.	P—— W. T. & Co......Lumber, etc.
D—— C.....................Gro.	P—— A. E. & Co..........Fruit, etc.
F—— & S——.......Com'n and Flour.	P—— A. W.............Machinery.
G—— S. B. & Co...........Lumber.	P—— H. M.................Lumber.
G—— H. F...........Millinery, etc.	P—— & L.................Gro., etc.
G—— E. A....................Gro.	S—— O. M...................Hotel.
G—— B. W.............Prod., etc.	T—— & Co.................Lumber.
H—— & C——........Lumber, etc.	T—— W.............Navigation, etc.
H—— J. A. & C. P..........Lumber.	W—— D.............F'cy Gds., etc.

[TO BE CONTINUED.]

BINGHAMTON N. Y.

A—— S..............Speculator.
A —— C. D...............Hdware.
B—— O—— R—— Co.
B—— J. F...................Hotel.
B—— W.....................Gro.
B—— E...................Bitters.
B—— L. A..............Jeweller.
B—— J......................Wool.
B—— J. C.................Drugs.
C—— N—— O—— & Co......Paper.

D—— L............. ...Grist Mills.
D—— E. F................Gro.
L—— Bros. & Co....Boots and Shoes.
L—— E. L................Liquors.
M—— N. D.............Physician.
O—— H. B...........Builder, etc.
O—— W.............Builder, etc.
O—— B..........Shoes and Gro.
P—— S. D. & Co..........Hdware.
W—— C. H.................Drugs.

[TO BE CONTINUED.]

BOSTON, MASS.

A—— I...................Clothing.
A—— & Son..............Clothing.
A—— A. M. & Co.........Produce.
A—— A. H.............Furniture.
A—— C. F. & Co.............Shoes.
A—— J. S.................Shoes.
A—— S—— & Co.............Teas.
A—— J................Publisher.
A—— O—— C—— Co.
American S—— S—— Co.
A—— E. H.........Steam Gauges.
A—— W. W..............Cutlery.
B—— A. W..........Billiard Tables.
B—— F......................Salt.
B—— G. P................Leather.
B—— W—— & Co.......Doors, etc.
B—— W. H.................H'ware.
B—— P......................Gro.
B—— Mrs. A. M................Gro.
B—— C. L. & Co........Com'n Mers.
B—— J. R. & Co.........Com'n Oils.
B—— W. J. & Co.............Shoes.

B—— R................ ...Oils.
B—— M....................Mason.
B—— J.....................Shoes.
B—— & B——........Rubber Goods.
B—— & B——............Hats, etc.
B—— & H——...............Oils.
B—— B..............Shoe Fndgs.
B—— W. H. & Co............Spices.
B—— C. D.............Contractor.
B—— J. F...............Lumber.
B—— G—— & Co.......Storage, etc.
B—— J. E.............Japanner.
B—— J..................Clothing.
B—— L. D. & Son.........Clothing.
B—— & T——...........Curriers.
B—— T—— & W——.....Furniture.
B—— C—— & Co....Tailors' Trm'gs.
B—— J. L.............Clothing.
B—— & B——.........Cabinetmkrs.
Boston C—— S—— Co.
Boston D—— Co.......Fancy Goods.
Boston F—— Co.

Boston M—— R—— Co.
Boston R—— M——.
B—— B—— & Co.........Millinery.
B—— & L——...........Carpenters.
B—— J. & Co...............Shoes.
B—— G—— & Co........Paints, etc.
B—— T. C................ ...Liquors.
B—— T. B. & Co...........Trunks.
B—— O. L.........Billiard Tables.
B—— J. B. & Co............Com'n.
B—— R. & Co.............Clothing.
B—— C. M...............Stoves.
B—— H. T............Fancy Goods.
B—— T:................Liquors.
B—— B. & Sons............Brokers.
B—— J......................Shoes.
B—— F. & C............Smallwares.
B—— & B——.........Machinery.
B—— S—— & M—— A——.
B—— & S——..........Leather.
C—— M. S..........Shoe Blacking.
C—— J. B...........Glassware.
C—— F.... ....Liquors.
C—— J..............Bookseller.
C—— U. B.............Tin Cans.
C—— P..................Gro.
C—— N. D...............Calf Bts.
C—— C. & Co............Stoves.
C—— C. H. & Co...........Tobacco.
C—— R—— & Co..............Gro.
C—— I. M.............Plate Iron.
C—— J. S. & Co............Prod.
C—— Bros. & Co.......Hosiery, etc.
C—— & Sons.............Pianos.
C—— W. C.........Leather, etc.
C—— F—— & Co...Gas Fixtures, etc.
C—— H. A.............Apothecary.
C—— W. & Co............Threads.
C—— S. W...............Cordials.
C—— J. N. M. & Co...........D. G.
C—— H. F............W—— Mills.
C—— D.....................D. G.
C—— J. & Co.............Liquors.
C—— M. & Son..........Com'n Car.
C—— G. T................Furniture.
C—— Bros. & Co........Chairs.
C—— J. & Co..............Liquors.
C—— F..........Boots and Shoes.
C—— E. G............Tanner, etc.
C—— C—— & Co........Shoes.
C—— E. W. & Co..........Leather.
C—— H. & Co...........Glassware.
C—— J. K. & Co..........Clothing.
C—— J..................Hosiery.
C—— W..................Tailor.
C—— H. Sons............Coal, etc.
C—— L—— & M——......Boots and
                             Shoes.
C—— M. & Co...........Linseed Oil.
C——C. H. & Co..........Flour.
C—— N....................Pianos.

C—— B. P. & Co............Carpets.
C—— G. W. & Co.........Hats, etc.
C—— H. C.................Gloves.
C—— H—— & Co......Fancy Goods.
D—— S—— & Co.:...........Gro.
D—— C. B. & Son...........Liquors.
D—— D. H. & Co....Boots and Shoes.
D—— & C——.........Firebricks.
D—— G. B. & Co.............D. G.
D—— W. W.........Com'n Cigars.
D—— J.....................Mer.
D—— & Co.......Paper and Twine.
D—— E. P. & Co...Lamps and Fluid.
D—— M. & Co..........Liquors.
D—— C...................Tanner.
D—— P..................Publisher.
D—— E. L. & Co............Cotton.
D—— E. C................Mer.
D—— J. P. P..............:.Liquors.
D—— & W——.....Boots and Shoes.
D—— & W——.........Trunks, etc.
E—— W. W..............Brushes.
E—— A. & Co............Cotton.
F—— J. P...............Broker.
F—— W. A. & Co...........Shirts.
F—— W. D. & Co...........Boots.
F—— & R——..........:..Liquors.
F—— S—— & Co..........Curriers.
F—— O. L................Liquors.
F—— & Co..............Woollens.
F—— S—— & Co.......Navy Shirts.
F—— D. F. & Co..........Liquors.
F—— J. P. & Co.....Firebricks, etc.
F—— M. J................Hotel.
F—— O. & Co........Tallow, etc.
F—— R—— & Co......Smallwares.
F—— Mrs. J. G.........Corsets, etc.
F—— I. S................Tailor.
F—— & H——......Pat. Sponge Bed-
                             ding.
F—— K. & Co...............Fish.
F—— A. & Co........Crockery, etc.
F—— J. H.............Distiller.
G—— S. N................Baker.
G—— S. N. & Co..........Butter.
G—— A—— P—— Co.
G—— F—— & Co............Fish.
G—— & G——.....Chemical Engs.
G—— K—— & Co........Chandlers.
G—— A...............Shipwright.
G—— P—— & Co........Woollens.
G—— B. J........:Shoulder Braces.
G—— J. & Co.............Flour.
G—— W..................Wool.
G—— & Bros.........Crockery, etc.
H—— & Co.......Furniture, etc.
H—— F............Furniture, etc.
H—— R. W. & Co......Men's Furn'g.
H—— C. E. & Co........Com'n Wool.
H—— F—— & Co.........Shoes.
H—— M—— Co.

H—— A. & Co.............Doors, etc.	M—— B. C. & Co.............B'krs.
H—— B—— & Co.....Men's Furn'g.	M—— B—— & Co.........Millinery.
H—— Bros. & Co....Boots and Shoes.	M—— Bros. C—— & Co.....Lumber.
H—— F—— & Co..........Leather.	M—— F. W. & Co.........Produce.
H—— W. D................Wool.	M—— R. & Co.........S. M. Needles.
H—— C—— & Co........Chemicals.	M—— K—— & A——........Paper.
H—— & B——......Women's Collars.	M—— P—— & Co.........Millinery.
H—— P. B. & Son..........Lumber.	M—— R................Liquors.
H—— S. L. & Co.........Machinery.	M—— J—— & Co.........Clothing.
H—— S. S.............Boots, etc.	M—— L. B.............Coal, etc.
H—— M. C. & Co.......Fancy D. G.	M—— W. B............Liquors.
H—— E. & Co.............Watches.	N—— O—— & G—— Co.
H—— J. A...........Trim'gs, etc.	N—— J. J.............Flour.
H—— W—— & C—— Co.	N—— F—— & Co.........Hats, etc.
H—— Bros... .Buttonhole Machines.	N—— T. S. & Co.........Shoes.
H—— C. B. & Co..........Organs.	P—— & B——.......... ...Brushes.
J—— D—— & Co.........Bookbinders.	P—— Bro. & Co.............Steel.
J—— & M——........R. E. Brokers.	P—— C. H. & Co.......Iron Works.
J—— R—— & V——..........Hats.	P—— S. H. L..........Planing Mill.
J—— T. L.............Apothecary.	P—— G. & Son.............Leather.
J—— W. H. & Co...........Pianos.	P—— J. & Co.............Junk.
J—— C—— & Co........S. Machines.	P—— J................Chocolate.
J—— H. M. & Co..............Iron.	Q—— G—— Co.
J—— & R——.................Iron.	Q—— R—— Co.............Granite.
K—— J. G. Jr..............Gro.	R—— S—— & Co.......Grindstones.
K—— E. J.............Boots, etc.	R—— L. & Co.............Clothing.
K—— N................Liquors.	R—— & Co............Metals.
K—— & D——.............Leather.	R—— G. H.............Clothing.
K—— & J——.............Boots, etc.	S—— W. A ....Real Estate.
L—— J................Boilermkr.	S—— H—— & Co.........Lumber.
L—— J................Gro.	S—— J. P. & Co.........Provision.
L—— & H——.............Carpets.	S—— I—— & G—— P—— Co.
L—— W—— & Co.....Men's Furn'g.	S—— S...............Builder, etc.
L—— A. S. & W. G. & Co.......Mers.	S—— M—— Co.......Furniture, etc.
L—— A. K..........Lead Pipe, etc.	S—— G—— Co.........Glassware.
L—— G. W. & Co.....Stock Brokers.	T—— B. F. & Co...........Leather.
L—— D. & Co.............Books.	T—— B—— & Co...........Books.
L—— D—— & Co.............Com'n.	V—— Mrs. J.............Millinery.
McK—— H—— M—— A——	W—— Bros. & H——........Paints.
McP—— A. M. & Co.........Pianos.	W—— E. H. & Co..........Produce.
M—— & E——......Tailors' Trim'gs.	W—— E..............Clothing.
M—— C. B. & Bro.............Oils.	W—— & Co.......Com'n D. G.
M—— J. P. & Bro........Glassware.	W—— P—— & Son.........H'ware.
M—— N—— & W——........Paints.	W—— C. E..............Crockery.
M—— H. J. & Co.............Shoes.	W—— N............ I—— M—— Co.
M—— H—— & Co............Shoes.	W—— N. G. & Son.........Jewelry.
M—— S. W.............Carpenter.	W—— P—— & Co.........Liquors.
M—— C—— Co.	Y—— R. H.............Com'n Mer.

[TO BE CONTINUED.]

BUFFALO, N. Y.

A—— J.	Saddler.	
A—— & B——	Furniture.	
A—— & C——	Fertilizing.	
A—— F. A.	D. G., etc.	
A—— H.	Pharmacy.	
A—— & W——	Carriages.	
B—— D. E.	Contractor.	
B—— & B——	Lumber.	
B—— N. H.	Joiner.	
B—— P.	Marble.	
B—— D.	Locomotives.	
B—— F. & H.	Cab'tware.	
B—— & Bro.	Hats, etc.	
B—— & H——	Shirts.	
B—— A. A. & Co.	Com'n, etc.	
B—— Bros.	Whol. Jewelry.	
B—— N.	Clothier.	
B—— J.	Lumber.	
B—— A. Son & Co.	Hats, Boots and Shoes, etc.	
B—— Bros.	Saloon.	
B—— & Co.	Saloon.	
B—— W. C.	Hotel.	
B—— C. S. Bros.	Tobacco.	
B—— & F——	Clothing.	
B—— M. A.	Bricks.	
B—— M. W.	Sch. Furniture.	
C—— J.	Coal.	
C—— T.	Files.	
C—— W. A.	Tin, Copper, etc.	
C—— J. A. & Co.	G. S.	
C—— J. A. & Son.	Barrels.	
C—— S—— & Co.	Sashes, etc.	
C—— & Van A——	Iron Works.	
C—— J.	Coal, etc.	
C—— G.	——	
C—— & A——	Furs, Hats, etc.	
C—— J. Jr.	Real Estate.	
C—— B. C.	Stock Dealer.	
C—— L. L.	Cattle Dealer.	
C—— J. F.	Millinery.	
D—— & C——	Maltsters.	
D—— F—— & F——	Coal.	
D—— R.	Mach. Gauges.	
D—— C. Y.	Boilers.	
D—— H.	Gro. etc.	
D—— C.	Brewer.	
D—— H. & C.	Planing Mill.	
D—— & Co.	Fish Packers.	
D—— & H——	Foundry, etc.	
E—— C.	Shipping, etc.	
E—— E. W.	Contractor.	
E—— J.	Boots and Shoes.	
E—— & W—— T—— Co.		
E—— A.	Confec.	
F—— W. G.	———	
F—— & W——	Brewery.	
F—— S—— & Co.	Lumber.	
F—— F.	Variety, etc.	
F—— C. H. & Co.	Distillers.	
G—— C. W.	Maltster.	
G—— J.	Foundry.	
G—— F. H.	Lumber.	
G—— P.	Bricks.	
G—— L.	Cabinetmkr, etc.	
H—— D.	Brewer.	
H—— J. L.	Brewer.	
H—— C. J.	Capitalist.	
H—— F.	Lumber.	
H—— & G——	Stoves, etc.	
H—— A. G.	Spices.	
H—— R. R. & Co.	Frwdrs.	
H—— J. M. & Co.	Spices, etc.	
H—— & Co.	Furniture.	
H—— F. J.	Flour and Feed.	
H—— E. & B.	Planing Mill.	
K—— B—— Co.		
K—— S. & Co.	Clothing.	
K—— H. W.	Hammers.	
K—— & F——	Livery.	
L—— J. G.	Gro.	
L—— J.	Flour, Wood, etc.	
L—— B.	Boots.	
L—— M.	Gro.	
L—— S.	Tobacco.	
L—— C.	Contractor.	
McC—— & J——	Sailmkrs.	
McL—— J. B.	Coffees, etc.	
M—— M. T.	Shoes, etc.	
M—— J. B.	Maltster.	

M—— B—— & Co.........:..Seeds, etc.	S—— O. E....Jewelry and Silverware.
M—— W. T. & Co..............D. G.	S—— A......................Gro.
M—— Bros............Theatricals.	S—— H......................Gro.
M—— & C——..........Hog Brokers.	S—— & H——................Lqrs.
M—— N. & Co...............Boots.	S—— Dr. F. G.....Oculist and Aurist.
M—— Bros.................Tanners.	S—— J...............Broker, etc.
M—— Bros..................Lqrs.	S—— F. J.....................Gro.
N—— S. W.................Leather.	S—— J. E................Shipping.
N—— M. & Co..........Fcy. Goods.	S—— Mrs. M. & Son........Cabtmkrs.
O—— C. A. & Co............Pictures.	S—— J. N. & Co...........Clothing.
O—— R—— & Co.......Planing Mill.	S—— Bros..............Machinists.
O—— & Co.................Paper, etc.	T—— H..............Dining Sal.
O—— J.................R. E. Agt.	T—— G. H. & Son.............Coal.
P—— & G——.......Bolts and Nuts.	T—— J. K...................Hotel.
P—— J. & Co.............Rectifiers.	T—— E. D. & H..............Hotel.
P—— J. H...................D. G.	U—— C...................Variety.
P—— F—— P—— E—— Co.	U—— D—— D—— Co.
P—— S. G.............. Inspector.	V—— V——J...........Lumber.
Q—— C—— F—— S—— M—— Co.	V—— R—— & H........Variety.
R—— A......................Drugs.	W—— A.................Gro., etc.
R—— G. W................Hats, etc.	W—— J..................Jeweller.
R—— C......................Drugs.	W—— J. D. & Co............Posters.
S—— A............Brewery, etc.	W—— F................Butcher.
S—— & Co..........Fruit, Game, etc.	W—— & B——.......Engravers, etc.
S—— J. F. & Son............Leather.	W—— & T——................Gro.
S—— J..............Planing Mill.	W—— P.............Lounges. etc.
S—— F....................Builder.	W—— & G——.......Cattle Dealers.
S—— & Co.....Meds., Perfumery, etc.	

[TO BE CONTINUED.]

BURLINGTON, IOWA.

A—— & Co.................Grocers.	G—— N. P.................Painter.
B—— T. W. & Co.......Whol. Boots.	G—— S—— & Co..............D. G.
B—— A....................Brewer.	G—— C...................Hotel.
B—— I—— Co.	G—— H. & Co.........Bookbinders.
B—— C. J.............. Newspaper.	G—— W—— F—— W——.
B—— W.............Oil Broker.	H—— M..............Candy Mnfr.
B—— W. & Co...............Grain.	H—— & S——................D. G.
B—— D. B............Match Mnfr.	I—— T—— Co.
C—— J. M..............Coal, etc.	J—— W.................Stationery.
C—— W. E & Co..........Shingles.	K—— A.............Clothing, etc.
D—— J. S............Real Estate.	K—— G....................Stoves.
E—— Mrs. E. M..........Millinery.	L—— P...................Lqrs.
F——W.................Builder, etc.	M—— Bros...................Gro.
G—— H..................Cigars.	M—— & Sons.............Builders.
G—— G. & Co..................Lqrs.	M—— I—— W——.........Fndry.
G—— J. & Co...........Carr'g Fcty.	M—— D.....................Gro.

O—— J.....................Com'n.	S—— J...................Furniture.
O—— J.............Boots and Shoes.	S—— C...................Nursery.
P—— F...................Newspaper.	S—— & Son........School Furniture.
P—— J. H.......Mnfr. Bed Springs.	T—— H—— Co........Printers, etc.
P—— I...............Undertaker.	T—— J......................Lqrs.
R—— S. J...................Gro.	T—— L.......................Gro.
S—— H...................Brackets.	W—— J. C........Mnfr. Bed Springs.

[TO BE CONTINUED.]

CAMDEN, N. J.

B—— P...................Tailor.	H—— J...............Wines, etc.
B—— Mrs. J............Dry Goods.	H—— R. N........Window Shades.
C—— & P—— E—— Co.	J—— T.........Boots and Shoes.
C—— & M——...........Webbing.	K—— E...................Hotel.
C—— L...................Tobacco.	K—— P—— F—— Co.
D—— W. H...............Varieties.	L—— E. H...................Drugs.
E—— S—— P—— M—— Co.	P—— E. L.......Notions and Books.
F—— H. H...........Tobacco, etc.	P—— H.......................Gro.
G—— J. M. J..........Upholsterer.	R—— J. D...................Hides.
G—— S. B. & Co............Lumber.	S—— J. W. & Sons.............Iron.
H—— C. B.................Bottler.	

[TO BE CONTINUED.]

CHARLESTON, S. C.

A—— D.............Gro. and Feed.	C—— H. R. & Co.............Com'n.
A—— J..................D. G.	C—— C.......Whol. Liq. and Com'n.
B—— J...................Gro.	C—— J.............Com'n Cotton.
B—— P.........D. G., Gro., etc.	C—— P. M...................Drugs.
B—— J. H. & Co.........D. G.	C—— T. H...............Factor.
B—— Mrs. A...............Gro.	C—— M. H. & Co............Drugs.
B—— G...................Gro.	C—— & D——...............Com'n.
C—— & G——....Auction and Com'n.	C—— D. S.........Boots and Shoes.
C—— E. H...............Gro, etc.	D—— & J——.......Livery and Sale
C—— T. T. & Co.........Turpentine.	Stables.

D—— L..............Whol. Liquors.
E—— J. M. & Bro...Foundry and Machinists.
E—— J. A.&Co....Auction, Shipping and Com'n.
F—— N......Restaurant and Billiard Saloon.
F—— B..Shoes, Trunks and Clothing.
F—— J. D.....Ins. Agent and Com'n.
F—— J. M..........Com'n and Iron.
G—— D. & Son.....Boots and Shoes.
G—— H. E..............Wood, etc.
H—— J.................Liquors.
H—— W. S. & Son.....Stocks, Bonds, and Ins. Agents.
H—— G.........D. G. and Clothing.
I—— M.....,...............Broker.
J—— D. & Son................Com'n.
J—— & B——................Hats.
K—— W. A.........Cotton Factor.
K—— F., Jr...................Gro.
K—— & B——......Whol. Fruit, etc.
L—— E. & Co........Gen'l Com'n.
L—— & S——.........Gen'l Com'n.
L—— W. M. & Son....Com'n Cotton.
L—— E. J....................D. G.
L—— P. P.................Com'n.
McL—— A....Machinist and B'smith.
M—— & M——..... ....Gro.
N—— T. S.........Boots and Shoes.

P—— E...........Printer and Stat'r.
P—— R. A...................Com'n.
P—— J. R......Factor and Com'n.
Q—— P. & Co.......Steam Saw Mill.
Q—— M. J...........Mnfr. Cigars.
R—— H—— & Co....Whol. Gro. and Com'n.
R—— J. R. & Co.,..Laces, Embroideries, etc.
R—— & D——....Factors and Com'n.
R—— W. P. & Co.Builders' Materials.
S—— J. H. L...................Gro.
S—— C. W.....................Coal.
S—— W. W.....Com'n and Shipping.
S—— T. G.........Cotton Broker.
S—— J. H.................Lumber.
S—— & S——..........Lumber, etc.
S—— H. C....................D. G.
S—— A. O.........Ship Chandler.
S—— Bros. & Co:.............Com'n.
T—— & L——.......Ship Chandlers.
T—— W. J.............Upholsterer.
T—— & B——..........Mnfr. Soap.
V—— S—— F.........Fancy Goods.
W—— H—— & Co............Com'n.
W—— & Von K——....... ..Com'n.
W—— & R——.....Soap and Candle Factory.
Z—— Mrs. M. J............Millinery.

[TO BE CONTINUED.]

CHICAGO, ILL.

A—— E...................:Notions.
A—— & E——.............Live Stk.
A—— B—— & L—— P—— Co.
A—— H. & Sons............ Bricks.
A—— O. & Co....Stationery and Publishers.
A—— S. L................Clothing.
A—— C.................Furniture.
A—— M—— & Co.......Carpets, etc.
A—— & B——.............Builders.
A—— P. M. & Co....Artists' Gds., etc.
A—— S—— & Co....Whol. Hats and Straw Goods.
A—— J. H..................Wagons.
A—— B. L. Co............Lumber.

A—— & Co...........Whol. Paints.
A—— J. G..........Whol. Jeweller.
A—— & B——..........Iron Works.
A—— S—— S—— Co.
B—— E——................Gasfitter.
B—— J. C. W......:.Masonic Goods.
B—— & Bro.........Wood and Coal.
B—— L...................D. G.
B—— M. C. & Co......Loan Bkrs., etc.
B—— Bros...............Stoves, etc.
B—— D................Showcases.
B—— & J............Stoves, etc.
B—— J. S. & Co.........Hats, etc.
B—— Bros. & S——.....Type F'ndry.
B—— C—— & Co.....Carriage Goods.

B—— & P——........Flour and Feed.	F—— J. V. & Co..............D. G.
B—— A...................Lumber.	F—— C. C.................Lumber.
B—— & T——........Merch. Tailors.	F—— G.....................Banker.
B—— R. J...............Carriages.	F—— & H——......Contractors, etc.
B—— F.........Tobacco and Cigars.	F—— S. & Co..............Clothing.
B—— G. T. & Co..............Com'n.	G—— I—— Co.
B—— L. A. & Co...........H'dware.	G—— & P—— M—— Co..Sashes, etc.
B—— A. H.......Sashes and Doors.	G—— C. & Co................D. G.
B—— R. K. & Co......Lumber Bkrs.	G—— & S...............Tobacco.
B—— & B——.......Whol. Cloths.	H—— & P.........Brewery, etc.
B—— A. M......Gaslight and Coke.	H—— J. T.............Advertising.
B—— F....................Brewer.	H—— & R——........Card Stand.
B—— W..................Leather.	H—— W. E........R. E. Operator.
B—— J. G.................Lime.	H—— A. L. & Bro.........Furniture.
B—— G. W.............Carriages.	H—— D—— & Co..D. G. and Notions.
B—— Bros...........R. E. Owners.	H—— Bros..........Whol. Liquors.
B—— H............Cisterns, etc.	H—— J. F. & Co.......Bedding, etc.
B—— E. E.............Whol. Fish.	H—— J...........Boots and Shoes.
B—— H...................Drugs.	H—— P....................Gro.
B—— H. W..........Real Estate.	H—— & L—— Co..........Tannery.
B—— & H——.............D. G.	H—— J—— & F——....Paper-hang-
B—— & N——..........Confec.	ings, Bedding.
B—— E. & Co......Woollen Mnfrs.	H—— J. C.............Crockery, etc.
Supplies and Dye-Stuffs.	H—— R—— & D——..Mnfrs. Sashes,
B—— D. & Son.............Harness.	Doors, etc.
B—— & M——.............Lumber.	K—— G............Picture Frames.
B—— C..................Contractor.	K—— C. P. & Co...........Clothing.
B—— J. & Co.............Guns, etc.	K—— Bros................Lumber.
C—— W..................H'dware.	K—— A. E. & Co......Com'n Grain.
C—— Bros...........Real Estate.	K—— & S............Planing Mill.
C—— A. J. & Co...........Bricks.	K—— H. W. & Co.Whol. Clothing, etc.
C—— & R——............Com'n.	K—— A. J.........Brick Machines.
C—— L. R..............Loan Bkr.	K—— Bros..........Whol. Gro.
C—— F—— W——	L—— M—— & Co........Grain, etc.
C—— I —— B—— Co.	L—— H. N. F....Rural.
C—— & N—— R—— Co.	L—— J. & Co.....Cab't H'dware, etc.
C—— R—— C—— Co.	L—— P.............Whol. Tobacco.
C—— S—— Co.	L—— H...............Loan Bkr.
C—— S—— & D—— Co.	M—— A. B. & Co......Pig-Iron, etc.
C—— S., Jr................Clothing.	M—— J...........Boots and Shoes.
C—— S. D., Jr., & Co.....Engravers.	M—— W—— & Co..........Elevator.
C—— A. B. & Co.........Carriages.	N—— P—— M—— & L—— Co.
C—— L—— & Co........Real Estate.	N—— C—— R—— M—— Co.
C—— C..............Real Estate.	P—— P.........Capitalist and Hotel.
C—— E. A. & Co...........Printers.	P—— & Co...............Bakery.
C—— C. & G. & Co....Machinery, etc.	P—— A...................Banker.
C—— N.................Pig Lead.	P—— & C——.....Com'n Merchants.
C—— P—— H—— & Co...Stationers.	R—— W..........Grain, Flour, etc.
C—— & Co............Lumber.	R—— & Bro.....Woollen Rags.
C—— & H——.............Bankers.	R—— S—— & W——.........D. G.
D—— J. H. & Co..............D. G.	R—— C. R................Bricks.
D—— W. M.............Real Estate.	R—— S. J...Baskets and Rope Mould-
D—— J. W. & Co........Teas, etc.	ing.
D—— L—— & Co.............Com'n.	S—— G—— & Co......Mnfrs. Furn'g.
E—— E. E..............Guns, etc.	S—— & P——...........Pat. Meds.
E—— H—— & Co..........Lumber.	S—— M. & Co.Mnfrs. Boots and Shoes.
E—— P.........Boots and Shoes.	S—— F. B..............Real Estate.
E—— C. L. & Co.............Com'n.	S—— L. & Co.............Bankers.
E—— & H——.............Liquors.	S—— S. P. & Co. Whol. Fcy. Gro., etc.
F—— F—— & Co............Millers.	S—— A. & Son.............Bankers.

S—— H. O.................Real Estate.
S—— F. & Co............Tin Plate, Japanned Goods, etc.
T—— Mrs. K.................Saloon.
T—— Bros.........Filter Wells, etc.
T—— W. & Co......Wood and Coal.
T—— Bros. & W——.Dried Fruits, etc.
T—— & S——,.. ....Hotel.

V—— N—— & Co.........Elevators.
W—— S. J..............Real Estate.
W—— J. & Bro........Planing Mill.
W—— Y—— Co...............Yeast.
W—— D. & Co...Whol. and Ret. Millinery.
W—— T................Real Estate.
W—— T. & Co........Artificial Stone.

[TO BE CONTINUED.]

CINCINNATI, O.

A—— C. M.........Boots and Shoes.
A—— S..................Seeds, etc.
A—— N—— U——
A—— S. & Co..Watches, Jewelry, etc.
A—— M. T. & Co........Com'n D. G.
A—— J. C....Distiller and Essence of Coffee.
A—— H. F....................D. G.
B—— J. S. & Co.Hats, Caps and Furs.
B—— D. B. & Co....Stoves and House Furn'g Goods.
B—— II........Tinner, Roofing, etc.
B—— W. & Co.....Ladies' and Gents' Furn'g Goods.
B—— & Co..................Bankers.
B—— E. & Co.......Chemical Works.
B—— F...................Furniture.
B—— F. W. & Son...........Pianos.
B—— H. N. & Co......... ...Chairs.
B—— & L——..........Whol. D. G.
B—— II. & Co........Whol. Liquors.
B—— L. & Son.... ....Liquors.
B—— J. Sons..............Cordage.
B—— II..............Saddler.
B—— S. B.......... ....Pork.
B—— L ....Notions.
B—— P...................Wines, etc.
B—— II. H.......Whol. Wall-paper.
B—— F....Mnfr. Plush and Fringes.
B—— J. H. & Co................Gro.
B—— P. C......House Furn'g Goods.
B—— A. G. & Co...........Bankers.
B—— D..................Flour Mill.
B—— & B——...Cont'rs and Builders.
C—— J......Com'n Boots and Shoes.
C—— L.........Smokers' Materials.
C—— R. W..............Distillery.

C—— L—— & Co...Pork Packers and Com'n.
C—— Bros. & M——......Importing Agents Lace Goods.
C—— W. B. & Co.....Stationery, etc.
C—— R. W. & Co.........Publishers.
C—— T....................Wines.
C—— D. & Co.........Mnfrs. Shoes.
C—— B. & Son ....Gro.
C—— J. G..........Boots and Shoes.
C—— C—— Co.
C—— C—— F—— Co.
C—— C—— U——
C—— F—— A——
C—— S—— W——
C—— F. & Bro.........Queensware.
C—— P—— G—— W—— Co.
C—— J. S. & Co...Horticulturists, etc.
C—— E—— & Co......Mnfrs. Shoes.
C—— R. & Co..............Lumber.
C—— F. A....................Drugs.
D—— B—— P—— S—— & E—— Co.
D—— J. A. & Co....Oysters, Fish, etc.
D—— W. & Co...........Spice Mill.
D—— & N——........Whol. and Ret. Music, etc.
D—— R. M.........Gro. and Tobacco.
D—— G. T.......Whol. Jewelry, etc.
D—— R..................Books, etc.
D—— D. H..............Ranges, etc.
D—— J. T. & Co................Coal.
D—— W....................Gro.
E—— E. C..................Paint.
E—— & M——......Paperhangings.
F—— O. B. & Co..............Pork.
F—— R. & Co......Prod. and Com'n.
F—— A....................Drugs.

F—— A. G. W. & Co....Tob. and Cig.
F—— J. W. & Co.............Com'n.
F—— R. H. & Co.....Com'n and Coal Elevator.
F—— D.............Cracker Bakery.
F—— E. J. & Co....Boots and Shoes.
F—— J. F. & Co..Sheepskin Tanners.
F—— W. H. & Bro........Sheepskin Tanners.
F—— J.........Mnfr. Paper Collars.
F—— B. & W..............Clothing.
F—— I. C.....Saw Mill and Lumber.
G—— J......Fancy Goods and School Books.
G—— J.......................Coal.
G—— J. & W................Hotel.
G—— J. H. & Co....Pork Packers and Com'n.
G—— D..................Com'n Mer.
G—— H—— & Co....Com'n Mers., etc.
G—— H.........Tobacco and Cigars.
G—— & W——............Clothing.
G—— & Co.......Wines and Liq.
G—— J.........Gro., Feed, etc.
G—— C. C..........Com'n Lumber.
G—— M.............Cheap Notions.
G—— P.............Fancy Goods.
G—— W. & Co....Belting and Mnfrs. Brushes.
G—— M...............Iron Works.
G—— M. & Co.....Mnfrs. Hardware, etc.
G—— G. H. & F.....Undertakers and Livery Stable.
G—— H. & Co...........Com'n Mers.
H—— E. R...................Coal.
H—— A...........Boots and Shoes.
H—— J............D. G., Notions, etc.
H—— H. H.............:....Rectifier.
H—— A..................Clothing.
H—— S. B. & Co....Prod. and Com'n.
H—— H. F. & Co.....Pork and Beef Packers.
H—— J. A.......Roofing and Paving.
H—— M........Looking Glasses and Frames.
H—— S. W. & Bro.....Mnfrs. Cigars.
H—— B.............Woollen Rags.
H—— Bros...........Whol. Liquors.
H—— & M——............Furniture.
H—— A.......Mnfr. Window Blinds.
H—— G.............Gen'l Com'n.
H—— H. & F.........Mnfrs. Cigars.
H—— A.......Pictures and Frames.
H—— E..................Books, etc.
H—— G. & Co......Boots and Shoes.
H—— F. F.............Carriages.
I—— A., Jr..............Hides, etc.
J—— & A——.......Mnfrs. Bags and Sacks.
J—— B—— & Co......Prov. Brokers.

J—— N. S................Broker.
K—— & O—— C—— Co.
K—— S. & Sons......Cotton Brokers.
K—— S. & Co........Whol. Liquors.
K—— A. & Co.............Distillers.
K—— Bros........Books and Stat'y.
K—— Mrs. M................Hotel.
K—— J. F.............Coal Agent.
K—— E. & Co ....Com'n.
K—— T. R. & Co.........Seeds and Ag'l Implts.
K—— G. F., Jr................Gro.
K—— T. F. & Co..Step Ladders, etc.
K—— D. C. & Co....-Tar and Roofing Materials.
K—— E. & Son................G. S.
K—— F. G.........Mnfr. Silk Hats.
K—— G................Distiller.
L—— S—— & Co.....Stock Brokers.
L—— & N——...........Machinery.
L—— A. & Co.............Hops.
L—— G. N...........Real Estate.
L—— R........Gent's Furn'g Goods.
L—— S....Trunk Paper and Flags.
McC—— R......Hides, Leather, etc.
McF—— G. & H........Notions, etc.
McG—— J. J................Hotel.
McG—— W. W.............Jewelry.
McI—— M................Gasfitter.
M—— J. H....Boots and Shoes.
M—— T. T....O—— C—— H—— Co.
M—— & Bros....D. G. and Carpets.
M—— A. W.......Whol. Cigars, etc.
M—— W.............Hats and Caps.
M—— S.............Boots and Shoes.
M—— & Co.............Clothing.
M—— M—— & Co.......Whol. D. G.
M—— W. D.............Lumber.
M—— H......Mnf. Syrups and Soda Water.
M—— E........Map and Book Pub'r.
M—— J. F................Builder.
M—— A. B. & Co.....Whol. and Ret. Drugs.
M—— V—— & Co.......Mnfrs. Lead Pipe.
M—— W. & J. C.........Jewellers.
M—— & D——...........Whol. Gro.
M—— J. B.............Machinery.
M—— J. M. & Co......Whol. Paints.
M—— E. E.................Com'n.
M—— H. & Co......Whol. Liquors.
M—— M....................Leather.
M—— H......... ....Furniture.
M—— J. H. & Co........Printers and Stat'rs.
M—— A.............Stoves, Tin, etc.
M—— C. B....................Pub'r.
M—— T. J.............Fancy Goods.
M—— & Son.........Whol. and Ret. Clothing.

N—— H. G. & Co.........Publishing.
N—— E—— S—— M—— Co.
N—— C. A. & Co.......Whol. Drugs.
N—— H......................Pork.
N—— & H——.....Pork Packers and Com'n.
O—— F. J....................Hotel.
O—— J. & Son.............Liquors.
O—— G. P. & Co.....Mnfrs. Sealing Wax.
O—— W. & Co..............Jewelry.
P—— Bros. & Co.....Transfer Ornaments.
P—— J. H...................Pub'r.
P—— D—— S—— Co.
P—— L. & Co ....Flour and Com'n.
P—— Mrs. M. M............Notions.
P—— M—— Co...........Furniture.
P—— M....................Hotel.
P—— & S——........R. R. Supplies.
P—— W. & Co........Brass Works.
Q—— T. G. & Co.....Tin and Slate Roofing.
R—— A. A...........Whol. Liquors.
R—— J. M............Mnfr. Cigars.
R—— Bros. & Co...Whol. Fancy Gro.
R—— C. E...........Hats and Caps.
R—— F. J. & Bros.....Chair Factory.
R—— J. G.............Mer. Tailor.
R—— & P——.........T—— C——.
R—— B. H........Com'n, Tailor and D. G.
R—— W—— Co.
R—— G. I.......Lime, Cement, etc.
S—— L. H. & Co.....Salt, Grain, etc.
S—— J. F...................Printer.
S—— W. H. & Co........Whol. and Ret. Hats and Caps.
S—— C.....Fancy Goods and Paperhangings.
S—— C..............Whol. Liquors.
S—— & H——........Whol. Tin and Furn'g Goods.
S—— F—— & Co.....Whol. Liquors.
S—— A. & Co.........Maltsters' and Brewers' Supplies.
S—— & A——.................Gro.
S—— J. T. & Co....Hatters and Furriers.
S—— J. W. & Co........Iron Bridges.
S—— A.............Boots and Shoes.
S—— A. L....................Pub'r.
S—— L. D.................Printer.
S—— F. & Co..........Com'n Mers.
S—— J. & J. & Co........Whol. D. G.
S—— V......Whol. Boots and Shoes.

S—— J. A................. ...D. G.
S—— L. N. & Co......Whol. Candies.
S—— W. B. & Co...........Lottery.
S—— & Co................Com'n.
S—— E—— S—— Co.
S—— E. W. & Co.....Pub'rs Books.
S—— J. & Co...............Jewelry.
S—— C....................D. G.
S—— & N——....Saw Mill and Lumber.
S—— W. H....Carpenter and Builder.
S—— J.................Fertilizers.
S—— F. & Bro........Whol. Liquors.
S—— I. P. & Bro.....Whol. Clo., etc.
S—— T......Pork and Beef Packer.
S—— G.....................Liquors.
T—— H. J........Mnfr. Lace Collars.
T—— Bros............Mnfrs. Shoes.
T—— J. L. & Sons...Wool and Com'n.
T—— & A——...........Mnfrs. Plug and Twist Tobacco.
T—— W. H. & Co...Whol. Millinery, etc.
T—— J.......Whol. Hats and Caps.
T—— E. R. W......Whol. Leaf Tob.
T—— J.........Leather Belting, etc.
T—— & V——....Awnings, Tents, etc.
T—— M.................Mnfr. Caps.
T—— J. M. & Co.......R. E. Brokers.
T—— L—— & Co.............D. G.
U—— S—— M—— A—— Co.
W—— F.......Cutlery and Opticians' Goods.
W—— S.....................D. G.
W—— I—— Co.
W—— C. S. & Co..............D. G.
W—— A..............Mnfr. Cigars.
W—— G..........Boots and Shoes.
W—— S—— B—— Co.
W—— & J——.............Brewers.
W—— H..................Lumber.
W—— H. L. & Son........Furniture.
W—— & W——......Leaf Tobacco.
W—— & C—— P—— Co.
W—— E..................Furniture.
W—— F. Jr. & Co..........Bankers.
W—— M............Whol. Clothing.
W—— S....................Hides, etc.
W—— N. & Co...........Hides, etc.
W—— W. H..........Fancy Goods.
W—— & Co....Printers and Binders.
W—— C........:.Sealing Wax, etc.
W—— H——& Co...Com'n D. G. and Cotton Buyers.
Y—— T. W....... Com'n Iron Pipe.

[TO BE CONTINUED.]

CLEVELAND O.

A—— L—— Co.
A—— N.....................D. G.
A—— N...........Boots and Shoes.
A—— M—— Co.
A—— H—— & Co..Coal, Pig Iron, etc.
A—— & D——................Drugs.
A—— P—— Co.
B—— W—— & Co.............Agents.
B—— & C——........,Whol. Confec.
B—— C. S...................Coal.
B—— M.....................Brewer.
B—— I. L.....Whol. Fruits and Ret.
Gro.
B—— Mrs. M. C...Books and Notions.
B—— G. C. & Co......Pork Packers.
B—— & Co...........Woollen Mill.
B—— C. R. & Co........Clothing and
Furn'g Goods.
B—— M. & Co..........Cabinetmkrs.
B—— P. W....Printer and Publisher.
B—— W. E....Mnfr. Patent Sporting
Boats and Step-Ladders.
B—— M—— & B——......Foundry.
B—— F. L. & Co.............Fruits.
B—— J. M.............Fancy Goods.
B—— A.............Gro. and Saloon.
B—— C—— Co.
B—— W. & Co..............Brooms.
B—— H—— & Co....Hides, Pelts, etc.
B—— Bros..........Booksellers, etc.
B—— M. & Co......Whol. and Retail
Jewellers, etc.
C—— & R——.Whol. Gro. and Com'n.
C—— Bros...Plumbers and Gasfitters.
C—— J. H.......Whol. Millinery and
Straw Goods.
C—— C. B...........Prod. and Com'n.
C—— G—— & C—— Co.
C—— P—— Co.
C—— C....................Hotel.
C—— A. & Co.......Whol. and Retail
Booksellers and Stationers.
C—— E................Clothing.
C—— A. W.....Mnfr. Chewing Gum.
C—— O—— Co.
C—— & B——.Lamp Fixtures, Oils, etc.
C—— J..................Jeweller.
C—— W. V..Whol. Liq. and Vinegar.
C—— L. & Sons.........Whol. Coal.

C—— S—— & Co..............Coal.
C—— O..................Jeweller.
C—— H. A. & Co.'......Mnfrs. Stave
Jointing Machines.
C—— A.................Crockery.
D—— J. J................Broker.
D—— P.........Boot and Shoe Mkr.
D—— C. H. & Co......Stone Quarry.
D—— N—— & Co.........Ag'l Implts.
D—— J. & Co....Painting and Wall-
paper.
E—— & S——............Hardware.
E—— Bros..........Whol. Liquors.
E—— C—— Co.
E—— A......Printers and Pub'rs.
F—— G...................Saloon.
F—— M—— Co........Street Lamps.
F—— W. F. & Co.....Whol. Confec.
F—— & W——................Coal.
F—— J. P....Coal, Gro. and Saloon.
F—— S. H. & D. P....Whol. Liquors.
G—— T................Undertaker.
G—— J. H. & Co......Mnfrs. Ground
Coffees and Spices.
G—— A. H. & Co....Mnfg. Druggists.
G—— I—— W——........Machinists.
G—— J. H. & A. S......:Cracker and
Biscuit Bakers.
G—— J...................Roofer.
G—— J. & Co......D. G. and Notions.
G—— M.............Fancy Goods.
G—— J. W. & Son....Ship Chandlers.
H—— F. A. & Co............Printers.
H—— E. B. & Co............Bankers.
H—— G. E.........Marble Quarries.
H—— A.............Fancy Goods.
H—— & M——......Whol. Furniture.
H—— H. H. & Co.....Whol. Liquors.
H—— Bros.........Carriagemkrs.
H—— A. S. F—— Co.
H—— F—— I—— Co.
H—— J. N................Furniture.
H—— H...................Brewer.
H—— M. L.......Burning Fluid and
Lamps.
H—— H. R...............Dentist.
K—— E.....Musical Insts. and Fancy
Goods.
K—— C. S. & Co..Flavoring Extracts.

K—— Mrs. L. F. & Son.
K—— D. J. & Co....Mnfrs. Carriages.
K—— H. M. & Co............Printers.
K—— A. F.........Boots and Shoes.
K—— & C—— M—— Co.......Axles.
L—— S—— & Co....Mnfrs. Nut Bolts.
L—— I. & Co................Brewers.
L—— M....................Clothing.
L—— E.....Furniture and Crockery.
L—— W..........Boots and Shoes.
L—— G. H., Jr........Gro. and Fruit.
L—— I. M......Paper Stock and Old
                              Metals.
L—— D. W.........Wines and Liq.
L—— R. T. & Son....Com'n and Prod.
McC—— A. C.......Safes and Com'n.
McD—— F. G. & Co...Whole Coal and
                         Iron Ore.
McN —— & C—— M—— Co....Bridge
                    and Car Builders.
McN—— P..................Builder.
McN—— E. M....Tobacco and Cigars.
M—— J. & Co....Clothing and Furn'g.
M—— C—— Co.
M—— C—— & Co....Plumbing, Gas-
                    fitting and Furnaces.
M—— & A——..............Clothing.
M—— A. M................Marble.
M—— F.............Mnfr. Trusses.
M—— & S——.......Hats and Caps.
M—— A...........T—— C——.
M—— A. H. & Co.......Mnfrs. Files.
N—— E—— Co.
N—— O—— E—— A——.
N—— M...................Clothing.
O—— L—— I—— Co.
P—— F. H......Machinery Oils, etc.
P—— & L—— A—— I—— M—— Co.
P—— T—— & P—— Co.
P—— W. E............Claim Agent.
P—— H. O.................Saloon.
P—— H. O. & Co.....Billiard Saloon.
R—— J. J..............Cooperage.
R—— H—— & Co...Planing and Sash
                          Factory.

R—— A......................D. G.
R—— & A——..Iron and Gen'l Com'n.
R—— A.....................Gro.
R—— F—— I—— Co.
R—— A. & G...Whol. and Ret. Fancy
                    Goods and Notions.
R—— M. & Son.....Mnfrs. Cigars and
                          Tobacco.
R—— & W——.......Com'n Lumber.
R—— E. W.........Boots and Shoes.
R—— W. R.........Boots and Shoes.
R—— H. G. & Co....Boots and Shoes.
R—— J. P..............Pork Packer.
S—— J. W.....Mirrors, Frames, etc.
S—— A. M....................Drugs.
S—— A........... ....Clothing.
S—— S...........D. G. and Notions.
S—— Mrs. H. D.............Milliner.
S—— S. H. & Co............Lumber.
S—— P.................Contractor.
S—— C—— B—— Co.
S—— H. S...................Stages.
S—— B................ ...Dentist.
T—— & T——..Shingles, Roofing, etc.
T—— S. Sr.........Hides and Wool.
T—— & M——..........Planing Mill.
U—— I—— W—— Co.
V—— E. H., Sons & Co.....Whol. No-
                    tions, Gro., etc.
W—— J....................Clothing.
W—— A.....................Gro.
W—— T—— & Co.....Planing Mill.
W—— A. & Son................Gro.
W—— J......... ...Stoves and Tin.
W—— D. C...........Stock Broker.
W—— J. H........Boots and Shoes.
W—— J...Watchmaker and Jeweller.
W—— J...........Gro. and B'smith.
W—— J. A. & Co.......Mnfrs. Tob.
W—— H. & Co.............Bankers.
W—— W.....Plumber and Gasfitter.
W—— S—— M—— Co.
W—— G. & Co..............Paper.
Y—— C.....................Brewer.

[TO BE CONTINUED.]

'COLUMBUS, O.

A—— A........Jewelry and Clothing.
A—— D. P..................Drugs.
A—— S. & Co.............Clothing.
A—— &F——...........Clothing.
A—— J.................Slate Roofer.
A—— E. B. & Co....Cornices, Stoves, and Tin.
B—— L. M. & Co..........Millinery.
B—— J..............Mnfr. Cigars.
B—— E. &H. F........Carriagemkrs.
B—— & H——...Whol. Gro. and Liq.
C—— A..................Lumber.
C—— C. C................Furniture.
C—— H. H.......Mnfr. Iron Fences.
C—— E. B...........Coal and Coke.
C—— J. H.................Drugs.
D—— L. D....................Gro.
F—— J. A.Stoves, H'ware and Saloon.
F—— G. H. & Co...............Gro.
F—— & McC——............Coal.
F—— & P——.............Feed.
F—— Mrs. H...............Clothing.
G—— H. C....................Gro.
G—— J. L.....Mnfr. Ploughs, etc.
G—— J. A................Clothing.
G—— I....................Clothing.
H—— M..................Architect.
H—— H..................Clothing.
H—— J. F. & Co....Pianos and Music.
H—— C—— Co.
H——L.............Boots and Shoes.
H—— C...........Gro. and Saloon.
H—— F.........Tobacco and Cigars.
H—— C...............Mer. Tailor.
H—— G.............Boots and Shoes.
H—— & S——......Fancy D. G., etc.
J—— T. A..............Gro., etc.
J—— I...................Notions.
J—— Mrs. J. E......Picture Frames.
J—— J. T...............Furniture.
K—— L...................Clothing.
K—— & Bro.........Tin and Stoves.

K—— C. T..........Gro. and Saloon.
K—— H. R................Notions.
K—— & S——........Mnfrs. Brooms.
K—— A...................D. G.
L—— E. D. W............Books, etc.
L—— & F——................Mill.
L—— T. O—— B—— & W—— W——
L—— A. S................Varieties.
L—— M............Boots and Shoes.
L—— A. B................Scales.
M—— J....................Drugs.
M—— E. J...........Mnfr. Coffins.
M—— C. H.........Tob. and Cigars.
N—— N—— Co....Photo. Mat'ls, etc.
N—— W. P................Pumps.
O—— A—— A——
O—— O. & Co........Stationery, etc.
R—— R............Machine Works.
R—— D................Hoopskirts.
R—— J.....Paper and Paperhanger.
S—— & H——..Agents Fluting Irons.
S—— F—— W——
S—— P. & Co.............Brewers.
S—— M. & Son.....Stat'y and Paper.
S—— J. & Co......Pianos and Music.
S—— Mrs. I........Boots and Shoes.
S—— C. C....Com'n Leather and Oils.
S—— A...............Clothing.
S—— R....................Prod.
S—— J. H............R. E. Agent.
T—— H—— & C——..Com'n Agency.
T—— T.........Curtain Factory.
U—— S. L..................Hotel.
V—— W..................Builder.
W—— F............Gro. and Saloon.
W—— F.......Confec. and Saloon.
W—— G. J.........Boots and Shoes.
W—— A. A........China, Glass, etc.
W—— & D——.Leather and Findings.
Z—— & S——................Gro.
Z—— C. H............Mdse. Broker.

[TO BE CONTINUED.]

DAVENPORT, IOWA.

A—— J.................Fruits, etc.	K—— J. A........Sewing Machines.
A—— O. & Co..............Tobacco.	McH——J. C........Boots and Shoes.
B—— J. W. H.....:......Physician.	McW—— E................Builder.
B—— C...............Tobacco, etc.	M—— J. H. & Co..............D. G.
C—— J. N.........Photo. Materials.	M—— & Co................Com'n.
C—— J....... .....Boots and Shoes.	M—— C. W. F............Liquors.
C—— C........Gent's Furn'g Goods.	M—— J. M.........Flour and Feed.
C—— M. B.............Furniture.	M—— T. Y...........Ag'l Implts.
C—— & S—— ....Liquors.	O—— Bros.............Florists.
C—— J. & Son..............Gro.	P—— J. C...............Saloon.
D—— Mrs. R. E.........Hair Goods.	P—— E..................Ice.
E—— M—— Co.	P—— T..............Hats, etc.
F—— P....................Gro.	P—— J. F...............Gro.
G—— H............Boots and Shoes.	R—— & W——............Tobacco.
G—— C...........Boots and Shoes.	R—— A............Confectionery.
G—— P—— Co.	R—— B—— & Co...........Tailors.
G—— M. J..........Hats and Caps.	R—— E. & Bros..........Clothing.
G—— D.................Hotel.	S—— J..............Woollens.
G—— W..................Coal.	S—— H. M. G.............Gro.
H—— J............Boots and Shoes.	T—— J............Upholsterer.
H—— H...........Com'n Grain.	W—— C. & Co.............H'ware.
H—— H...............Hotel.	W—— C. S...............D. G.
K—— & L——........... Brewers.	W—— J. W.................Gro.
K—— G. A..............Grain.	W—— F.............Ag'l Implts.
K—— N...............Tobacco.	Z—— F.............Boots and Shoes.
K—— F.................Harness.	

[TO BE CONTINUED.]

DAYTON, O.

A—— F.....................Gro.	B—— A...............Brewery.
A—— & B——...............Gro.	B—— C.....Mnfr. Cigars and Saloon.
A—— W........Mnfr. Fire Kindler.	B—— A. & J..............Saw Mill.
A—— & M——.......Whol. B. and S.	B—— H. H...........Livery, etc.
A—— C......Confec. and Newsdealer.	B—— Mrs. A. M.........Millinery.
A—— J..................Brickmkr.	B—— D..................Saloon.
B—— J. L. & F. M........Carriages.	B—— C.............Gro. and Liq.
B—— C. H............ ....Trader.	B—— J................Confec.
B—— D. E.................D. G	B—— Mrs. H. E.......Fancy Goods.

B—— J...............Gro. and Liq.
B—— M...................Builder.
B—— & K——...........Mnfrs. Oils.
B—— W. G.............Mer. Tailor.
B—— H. ....Gro.
B—— H. L. & Co...Tin and Japanned Ware.
B—— J. H. & Co.........Boilermkrs.
B—— S. T..............Stoneyard.
B—— G............Boots and Shoes.
C—— J..................Livery.
C—— & P.......Mer. Tailors and Gent's Furn'g.
C—— J. M. & M....Fwdg and Com'n.
C—— Bros.........Mnfrs. Organs.
C—— G. P.................Books.
C—— J............Whol. Liquors.
C—— P...........Stoves and Tin.
C—— O. & Co....Mnfrs. and Pub'rs.
C—— J..............Gro. and R. E.
D—— W. L. & Son......Leather and Findings.
D—— C—— D—— & D—— Co.
D—— I—— Co.
D—— J. V. & Co...............D. G.
D—— B...............O—— L——.
D—— D................Brickyard.
D—— J. G..................Pub'r.
D—— & K....Mnfrs. Turbine Water Wheels.
D—— & M——.......Mnfrs. Tools.
E—— & H——..............Tailors.
E—— C. M. & Co....Mnfrs. Extension Tables.
E—— J. G.........Boots and Shoes.
F—— L...................D. G.
F—— R—— & Co...Woollen Factory.
F—— E..................Hats.
F—— J. & Bro.........Pub'rs Music.
F—— G. H.................Drugs.
F—— G. H................Saloon.
F—— F...........Boots and Shoes.
F—— & D——.....Builders and Carpenters.
F—— J. S. & Co.......Whol. Drugs.
G—— V.................Saloon, etc.
G—— & R——.............Livery.
G—— H. C. & Bro....Whol. Gro. and Liq.
G—— W. M...........Confec., etc.
G—— J................Wagonmkr.
G—— T.................Carpenter.
G—— Bros..... ....Whol. Millinery
G—— W. G................Gro.
G—— W. A................Agent.
G—— A. W.....Children's Carriages and Baskets.
H—— I......B. & S., Hats and Caps.
H—— J. R.....Saddles and Harness.
H—— G. P...................Gro.
H—— W...............Speculator.

H—— W...................Tailor.
H—— A. H..........Drugs, etc.
H—— Miss L...........Milliner.
H—— & H——..Mnfrs. Iron Railings.
H—— & H—— M—— Co.
H—— H...................Gro.
H—— W. H.........Clothing, etc.
H—— B. E.................Notions.
H—— Bros.............Lumber.
H—— R. S. & Co..........Lumber.
H—— Z. T...............Drugs.
H—— J...........Trunks, etc.
H—— W. S.....Auction, Com'n and D. G.
H—— W................D. G.
J—— J. T.................Hotel.
J—— L. B. & Son.......Leather and Findings.
J—— H. H...Whol. and Ret. Liquors.
K—— K. S..........Mer. Tailor.
K—— W. & Co... ......Ropemkrs.
K—— J............Boots and Shoes.
L—— J................Furniture.
L—— J. T.................Hotel.
L—— & R——...............Mill.
L—— C. P...........Gro., etc.
L—— W............Saddles, etc.
L—— B.................Clothing.
L—— H...... ....Tree Agent.
L—— A......... ....Stoves and Tin.
L—— Bros....Whol. Paints, Oils, etc.
L—— J. O..... ...Boots and Shoes.
L—— G. B. & Co...Mnfrs. Table Slides.
McC—— & W——...............Gro.
McD—— & F——......Marbleworkers.
McH—— A....Carpenter and Builder.
McS—— D. E. & Co.....Mnfrs. Grain Drills.
M—— & L——.......Whol. Liquors.
M—— J. J..Mnfr. Bagging, Miller, etc.
M—— B.......Mnfr. Brushes.
M—— G............Gro. and Saloon.
M—— S...................Gro.
M—— W.............Gro. and Liq.
M—— W................Broker.
M—— N............Money Lender.
M—— H. & Bro.......Mnfrs. Rakes.
N—— G....................Pub'r.
N—— E.............Gro., etc.
N—— A................Jeweller.
O'N—— & D——....Com'n Mers. and Leaf Tobacco.
O—— M.........Ret. Furniture.
O—— P..........B. and S., H. & C.
P—— P.........Machine Agent.
P—— H. F.....Flour and Feed.
P—— G. G. & Co............D. G.
R—— & Sons........Hides and Furs.
R—— F—— & Co.....Mnfrs. Cigars.
R—— J....Whol. and Ret. Books, etc.
R—— & D——......Photo. Materials.

R—— J.....Builder and Planing Mill.	T—— B. C.............Mnfr. Rakes.
S—— G..........Bakery and Saloon.	T—— I. N.............Stoves, etc.
S—— M......Flour Mill and Saloon.	W—— B. F..................D. G.
S—— B.......................Hotel.	W—— J. B...............Nursery.
S—— M...................Brewer.	W—— J. H................Marble.
S—— C....................Brewer.	W—— A..........Gro. and Saloon.
S—— & D——.............Drugs.	W——S.....................Gro.
S—— G.....B. and S., Hats and Caps.	Z—— A....................Drugs.
S—— Dr. W. B........Patent Meds.	

[TO BE CONTINUED.]

DENVER, COL.

A—— S. & Son............Clothing.	H——J. H. & Co...........Tailors.
A—— H. E........Com'n Eggs, etc.	K—— C. A. & Co..... Stationery, etc.
B—— J....................Butcher.	L—— & A——.............Cigars.
B—— & H——.....Carriage Painters.	M—— L. M......... ....Hotel.
C—— M. A........ .....Restaurant.	M—— A..........Paints, etc.
C—— W. J.........Carpenter, etc.	M—— J. M........Hubs and Felloes.
C—— W. D. & Bro.....Stock Dealers.	M—— J. W................Hotel.
C—— E....................Blksmth.	O—— J. B............Stairbuilder.
C—— C. S..................Gro.	P—— Mrs. E... ....Milliner.
C—— A...................Jeweller.	P—— W. H. & Co.........Transfer.
C—— F...................Builder.	R—— M. L.................Guns.
E—— Mrs. B............Millinery.	S—— J. W.............Jeweller.
F—— J............ ....Stock Dealer.	S—— P......... ......Stock Dealer.
F—— J.............Clothing, etc.	S—— C. M....,....Liq. and Tobacco.
F—— J. H..............Drugs.	S—— J............Confectioner, etc.
F—— & Bro..........Sporting Gds.	S—— T. H. & Co....Flour and Com'n.
G—— Bros....................Gro.	S—— E. K.................Paper.
G—— P. P..........Saw Mills.	S—— Mrs..............Hair Goods.
G—— J.............Pawnbroker.	W—— Bros......D. G., Clothing, etc.
H—— M....................Gro.	W—— & W——......Planing Mill.
H—— B....................Tailor.	W—— J. H.............Publisher.
H—— & B——....... ...Clothing.	W—— W. A.............Tobacco.
H—— Bros..............Soap, etc.	

[TO BE CONTINUED.]

DETROIT, MICH.

A—— & G——......................Com'n.	G—— S. B..................Vessels.
A—— S...................H'dware.	G—— C. K....................D. G.
A—— C...................Tobaccos.	H—— R. H..................Bricks.
A—— E. G.................Lumber.	H—— & S——.............Notions.
A—— & M——...........Lumber.	H—— A................Clothing.
B—— J. B...............Contractor.	H—— Bros. & Co........Teas.
B—— L.......................Hotel.	H—— & V.............Lumber.
B—— A............Boots and Shoes.	H—— J. L. & Co........Vessels, etc.
B—— & P——...........Grates, etc.	I—— I. W.............Builder.
B—— P. P.................Confec.	J—— C. B. & Co........H'dware.
B—— & G——.........Books, etc.	J—— E. Jr............H'dware.
B—— Bros.....................Gro.	J—— M. & Co...........Grain.
B—— & K——...........Trunks.	K—— J. L............Clothing.
B—— H. B................Drugs.	K—— P. & Co..........Brewers.
B—— P............Brewer, etc.	K—— A. & Co...........D. G.
B—— M.................Broker.	L—— H. S..........Furniture.
B—— N.................Notions.	L—— J. M.........Clothing.
C—— T. & Co................Gro.	L—— & Sons......... Com'n.
C—— C. & Sons..............D. G.	L—— & S——......Millinery.
C—— J. H.................Oysters.	M—— Mrs. J.........Furniture.
C—— Bros.................Boilers.	M—— F............Gro.
C—— G. C.............Shirts, etc.	M—— P............Auction.
C—— J. P.............Fish, etc.	M—— C. R.........Clothing.
C—— D....................Tailor.	M—— R. & Son.......Brewers.
C—— J..................Bakery.	M—— L—— & Co........Lumber.
C—— D. T. & Co........Lithograph.	M—— R. & Co...........Shoes.
C—— W. H. & Co...........Com'n.	M—— H. & P..........Saws.
C—— W. W.................Lumber.	M—— P. J...........Gro.
D—— J...................Brewer.	M—— F—— & E——....Lumber, etc.
D—— & N...............Brewery.	M—— J. & Co..........Mchnry.
D—— B—— & D—— Co.	M—— C—— R—— Co.
D—— B—— M—— Co.	M—— W. & R...........Gro., etc.
D—— C—— M——.	M—— H...............Brewer.
D—— & M—— R.R. Co.	M—— F—— & Co.........Gro.
D—— N—— W——.	N—— C. H. & Co.......Bkg Powder
E—— & R——..........Vinegar.	N—— G. & Co.........Cigars, etc.
E—— H. D. & Co.....Chandlers, etc.	O—— S—— M—— & M—— Co.
F—— W—— & Co...........Drugs.	P—— & C——............Lumber.
F—— C—— & Co.......Spices, etc.	P—— & C——..........Furniture.
F—— S—— & L—— Co.	P—— & B——.........Clothing.
F—— B—— & Co.........Bnkrs.	P—— J...........Vessels, etc.
F—— & Bros..........Furniture.	P—— & B——..........Drugs.
F—— G. H. & Co........Agl. Impts.	R—— D. M............Matches.
F—— H. A.................Drugs.	R—— F...........Jewelry, etc.
F—— D—— L—— & W—— W——.	R—— M.............D. G., etc.
F—— A......................Gro.	S—— J...............Tailor.
F—— F.................Spice Mills.	S—— & B——........Ship Bkrs.
G—— P ....Ropemkr.	S—— Bros............Builders.
G—— J..................Lqrs.	S—— T. W. & Son.......Wire Wks.
G—— H. A.................Coal.	S—— & B——.............Cigars.

S—— J. D., Sr.............Pine Lands.
S—— C..................Wood Yards.
S—— C. D....................H'dware.
S—— W. H....................Prod.
S—— J. W..............Woodenware.
T—— L. W. & Co................Gro.
T—— Bros.......Silver Platers, etc.
T—— W. E........Whol. Books, etc.
T—— & P——........Ret. Books, etc.
T—— H—— & C——........Gro., etc.

T—— & D——.................Gro.
T—— & R——.................Gro.
U—— J—— P—— Co.
W—— J. D. & Co........Bill Posters.
W—— S. W. & Co.............Coal.
W—— A. B. & Co.............Lqrs.
W—— F—— Co.
W—— C. M.............Theatricals.
W—— C. D. & Co.......Mldgs., etc.
W—— W. & Co.........Decorators.

[TO BE CONTINUED.]

DUBUQUE, IOWA.

B—— M........................Brewer.
B—— G. W. & Co..............Bkrs.
C—— M........................Baker.
C—— W—— & Co.....D. G. and Gro.
C—— & W——.........D. G., etc.
C—— R....................Real Estate.
D—— J. L. & Co............Foundry.
D—— S—— R—— Co.
D—— & W——.................Agts.
F—— J....................Flour, etc.
G—— E. A. & Co..........Jewelry.
G—— A.......................Lqrs.
H—— A........................Brewer.
H—— Mrs. M. A.............Hats.

M—— A......................Grain.
M—— G. H. & Co........Whol. D. G.
M—— J.....................Gro.
P—— S—— B——
P—— P. M..............Clothing.
R—— Bros. & H——.......Crockery.
R—— W.................Contractor.
R—— L. A.................Liquors.
R—— J. M..................Lumber.
R—— M. S............Agr'l Implts.
T—— & S——..............Brewers.
W—— J. & W................Lead.
W—— C—— & Co.............D. G.
W—— W. W.................Hotel.

[TO BE CONTINUED.]

ELMIRA, N. Y.

A—— P. A....................Gro.
A—— M. H................Speculator.
A—— S. T................Capitalist.
A—— S....................Jeweller.
B—— S—— & Co...............Oil.
B—— & D——.............Fcy Gds.
B—— W. A..............Boots, etc.
B—— & O——..............Com'n.
B—— T. & Co...........Brewers, etc.

B—— J. G...............H'dware.
B—— Mrs. E............Boots, etc.
E—— S—— Co.
E—— J....................Carriages.
F—— G. R. & Co....;........Gro.
F—— & H——........Boots & Shoes.
F—— D—— & Co.......Notions.
F—— Bros.......Buffalo Robes, etc.
G—— J....................Nursery.

H—— A......................Prod.
J—— R....................Lumber.
M—— J........................Gro.
M—— & W——....Mnfrs. Boots and
                              Shoes.
O—— Bros................Liquors.
R—— M. R...............Liquors.

R—— P......... ......Liquors, etc.
S—— & S——.............. ..——
S—— & H——............Bankers.
T—— & S——................Hotel.
T—— & P——............Foundry.
V—— A.....................Miller.

[TO BE CONTINUED.]

ERIE, PA.

A—— J..............Beer Garden.
B—— A....Builder and R. E. Dealer.
B—— P. A. & Co....:............Gro.
B—— I............Boots and Shoes.
B—— E. R.............Ins. Agent.
B—— J.......................Hotel.
B—— C..........Boots and Shoes.
C—— & Sons...................Gro.
C—— E...........Boots and Shoes.
C—— M...............Capitalist.
C—— S. E............Hair Goods.
D—— G..................D. G.
D—— J.........Boots and Shoes.
E—— G. & Co ....Gro.
E—— C—— S—— B——.
F—— P..................Harness.
F—— G..........Carriage Trimmer.
F—— J.........Coal and Wood.
F—— II................Clothing.
G—— M....Notions and Second-hand
                              Goods.
G—— J. & Co..................Gro.
G—— I—— Co.
G—— J....................Saloon.
H—— R. C..................Store.
II—— J. K.......Church, School, and
                      Hall Furniture.
II—— & M——...Phys'ns and Drugs.
H—— J.......................Hotel.
II—— & K——.............Tailors.

H—— C. N....Gro., Builder and Con-
                              tractor.
H—— R. O.................Hotel.
H—— W.............Bleachery, etc.
J—— H..................Builder.
J—— M. H................Hotel.
K—— A..................Maltster.
L—— L. & G....Hats, Gents' Furn'g,
                              etc.
L—— F.......................Hotel.
M—— T. & Co...........Hardware.
M—— T. P............Restaurant.
M—— W. T.............Drugs.
M—— & M——..........Clothing.
M—— C. H............Flour, etc.
M—— C. F........S—— M—— Agt.
N—— H..................:.......Gro.
N—— A..Sashes, Blinds and Builder.
Q—— & C——...............Junk.
R—— S. M...............Builder.
R—— J. B. & Co...........Billiards.
S—— Bros...,............D. G.
S—— F...................Brewer.
S—— W.............. ....Gro.
S—— J.................Clothing.
S—— A...................Notions.
S—— E. E.........Publisher, etc.
S—— J. B.................Jewelry.
T—— T—— & N——...........Coal.
V—— Mrs. S. A...........Millinery.

[TO BE CONTINUED.]

EVANSVILLE, IND.

A—— & Co........Sewing Machines.	G—— S.................Auctioneer.
A—— F. A....................Hotel.	G—— T. J...................Printer.
A—— J................Boots, etc.	R—— & G—.............Liquors.
A—— C. & Co............Furniture.	H—— G.....................Gro.
B—— G. I. & Co........Ag'l Impl'ts.	J—— H—— & Co..............D. G.
B—— H. O. & Co.......Ag'l Impl'ts.	L—— J. A..................Hotel.
B—— J. R. & Co.......Ag'l Impl'ts.	M—— & R—.........Bookbinders.
B—— H. V. & Bro.........Whol. Liq.	M—— & F........D. G. and Gro.
B—— A. & Co..........Ginger Ale.	M—— D...................Physician.
B—— B...............Glassware.	M—— J. & Bro..........Sashes, etc.
B—— II. & Co............Cloths.	N—— J....................Saloon.
C—— N. F. & Co...........Liquors.	R—— F.....................Gro.
C—— A. & W............Bakers.	S—— J. G..............Tobacconist.
D—— P. & Son......Soaps, Oils, etc.	S—— T. C. & Co........Commission.
E—— B................Jeweller.	S—— C...................Saloon.
E—— M—— C——	S—— J.........Pork, Liquors, etc.
F—— T..............Boots, etc.	S—— & Sons..........Livery Stable.
G—— J.................Sausages.	S—— M...................Brewery.
G—— J. C....... ....Insurance Agt.	W—— S..................Lumber.

[TO BE CONTINUED.]

FALL RIVER, MASS.

A—— J. W........Boots and Shoes.	H—— S. & Son...............Hotel.
B—— D. W...............Furniture.	H—— P. P..............D. G., etc.
B—— J. G. & Co....Whol. Fruits and	H—— E. M............Bricks, etc.
Gro.	H—— & W—..........Furniture.
B—— H...................Tailor.	L—— E......Mnfr. Waterproofs, etc.
B—— C—— M—..........Prints.	L—— M. & Co ....Clothing.
B—— L. & Sons.............Fish Oil.	L—— N. U......Mnfr. Blacking, etc.
C—— & B—.................Gro.	N—— J. F.........Roll Coverers.
C—— N—— & D—..........Mills.	R—— C. V. S...............Cotton.
C—— P. D............Sashes, etc.	R—— R. K..................Drugs.
D—— M........Miller and Bleacher.	R—— T.....................Gro.
E—— G......................D. G.	S—— M—................Cloths.
F—— M—— & Co...........Bakers.	T—— E.....................Gro.
F—— E..................Gro., etc.	W—— M—...............Cloths.
G—— P...........Sewing Machines.	

[TO BE CONTINUED.]

GALVESTON, TEXAS.

A—— & M——.......Cotton Factors.
A—— & Bro....Hats, Caps and Straw
    Goods.
A—— C....................Billiards.
B—— & D——................Com'n.
B—— S................Jeweller.
B—— Mrs. M ....Gro.
B—— T................Watchmkr.
B—— E................Watchmkr.
B—— H. J...........Soap Factory.
B—— J. & Son................Com'n.
B—— R................Restaurant.
B—— J. W................Pub'g.
B—— & K——..........Com'n Mers.
B—— & E——............Furniture.
C—— C...........D. G. and Notions.
C—— A. H..........R. E. Broker.
C—— H. A., Bros. & Co.Iron Foundry.
C—— & B——................Com'n.
D—— O. H................Pub'r.
D—— G. H.... ....Saloon.
D—— & B——.........Soap Factory.
E—— W. A. & Co...Hides and Wool.
F—— C——...................Teas.
F—— C. F...........Bookbinder.
F—— F..................Tailor.
G—— A——, H—— & I—— A——
G—— A. C. & Co...Cotton Buyers and
    Com'n.
G—— C................Saddler.
G—— Mrs. E...............Confec.
G—— T..................Liquors.
G—— T..................Jeweller.
G—— T...............Cotton Buyer.
G—— T..................Hotel.
H—— P. H..................Gro.
H—— J. H...........Publisher.
H—— J..........Gro. and Grist Mill.
H—— T. F............Builder, etc.
H—— I.................Books.
I—— J. B................Drugs.
J—— Mrs. H............Dressmkr.

K—— & R——.........Mer. Tailors.
K—— F. W.................Gro.
K—— & B——............Contractors.
K—— J. N....Mnfr. Boots and Shoes.
L—— J. J................Harness.
L—— S..............Watchmaker.
L—— J..................Ale.
L—— A...............Mnfr. Bitters.
L—— S.........D. G. and Notions.
L—— & S——........Whol. Notions.
M—— W. W. & Co...Cotton Factors.
M—— J. L..............Whol. Gro.
M—— S............Real Estate.
M—— Bros.............Clothing, etc.
M—— & R——.............Tailors.
M—— J. M. & Co...Com'n and Cotton.
M—— & B——....H'ware, Stoves and
    Tin.
P—— B. S......Com'n Lumber, etc.
P—— & M——..............Printers.
P—— W. D............Tinner.
P—— F.................Liquors.
P—— A. & Co................Hides.
R—— Sons.......Imps. Crockery, etc.
R—— H. T...........Ship Broker.
R—— M....................Tailor.
S—— S....................Florist.
S—— J. S. & Co..Shipping and Com'n.
S—— C. S..........Oils, Lamps, etc.
S—— F......Confec. and Soda Water.
S—— Mrs. L........Tob. and Cigars.
S—— M. K...................Hotel.
S—— W. S.........Ins. Agent.
T—— G—— & Co........Newspaper.
T—— Mrs. E.............Milliner.
W—— J..................Cotton.
W—— D...................D. G.
W—— N. C..................Slater.
W—— W..................Com'n.
W—— A....Com'n and Mdse. Broker.
W—— W..................Saloon.

[TO BE CONTINUED.]

GRAND RAPIDS, MICH.

A—— & K——..............Brewery.
A—— & K——.................Gro.
B—— S. S....................Stages.
B—— M. T.........Lightning Rods.
B—— J. W................F'cy Goods.
C—— J....................Gro., etc.
C—— J. H...................Hotel.
C—— W. H. & Co............Lime.
C—— Bros.....................Gro.
C—— H——............Cigars, etc.
D—— & C——..........Ag'l Impl'ts.
D—— F. & Sons................Gro.
D—— Bros. & Co...........Printers.
E—— E. G.................Jewelry.
E—— J. T............L. Rods, etc.
E—— J...............Wagons, etc.
F—— & Co................Lumber.
F—— & R——.......Wagons.
F—— D....................Lumber.
F—— & Co....................Glass.
G—— H. M. & Co...........Paints.
G—— E. L. & Co.............Brkrs.
G—— P. M. & Co...........H'dware.
G—— J. G....................Tools.
G—— W. S. & Co..........H'dware.

H—— Mrs. E.....Books and Stat'ry.
H—— E. B. & Co..............Beds.
H—— H. M.............Paper, etc.
K—— E. W...........Ag'l Impl'ts.
L—— A., Bros. & Co......Machinists.
L—— Bros......................Hats.
M—— R. G................Lumber.
M—— L. A.................Boots.
N—— & Co...........Planing Mill.
P—— J. W.............Machinery.
P—— E., Sons & Co........Teas, etc.
P—— E. R........Planing Mill, etc.
P—— W. T.......Water Power, etc.
P—— Mrs. T. A........News Depot.
P—— W. T. & Son.........Lumber.
Q—— I. L................Lumber.
S—— & H——..........Drugs, etc.
S—— B. C...................Hotel.
S—— & A..............D. G., etc.
W—— G—— & G——.....Safes, etc.
W—— J. L.................Saw Mill.
W—— E. W. & S. A......Furniture.
W—— & Co................Lumber.
W—— & L——..........Leather.
W—— J. S.............Ag'l Impl'ts.

[TO BE CONTINUED.]

HALIFAX N. S.

A—— A. B..................Com'n.
B—— J. B........Mnfr. Soda Water.
B—— & R——......Gro. and Com'n.
B—— J. S....................Com'n.
B—— W...................Com'n.
B—— H. P..................Drugs.
C—— Bros..........Express, etc.
C—— T. P..........Stationer, etc.
C—— F. D. & Co.....Com'n and Coal.

C—— J...................Merchant.
D—— P.............Gro. and Liq.
D—— R.....................Gro.
D—— T......................Gro.
D—— A.....................Com'n.
F—— F. W..................Express.
F—— J. W...................Hotel.
G—— P...................Liquors.
G—— B.....................Tailor.

H—— S. T....................Books.
H—— G. C. & Co..........Merchants.
H—— D......................D. G.
H—— J. & Son................Gro.
H—— D..............Livery Stable.
H—— L. & Co................D. G.
H—— W.....................Lumber.
H—— J............Gas Fitter, etc.
K—— E. & Co.............Stationers.
L—— D. J..........Gro. and Com'n.
M—— & Co................Furniture.
M—— A............ ....Machinist, etc.

M—— D. A...........Brass Founder.
M—— G. E. & Co....Drugs and Books.
M—— J. K.................Clothier.
M—— P. & J...............Brewers.
O—— W. D..............Contractor.
O—— E.......................Gro.
O—— & Co............Com'n Mers.
P—— M....................Liquors.
R—— D............Gro. and Liq.
S—— W...............Butcher, etc.
W—— T..........Boots and Shoes.

[TO BE CONTINUED.]

HAMILTON, ONT.

A—— A. T....................Gro.
A—— W......................Gro.
B—— R. M..............Books, etc.
B—— J. A...................Drugs.
B—— J. N. & Co...Wines and Spirits.
B—— & Co.................Vinegar.
B—— N. F....................Fwdg.
B—— S—— & M——..........Iron.
C—— H. G. & Co.........Carriages.
C—— T. & Co.........Founders, etc.
C—— J......................Shoes.
D—— J. H. & Co........Com'n Wool.
F—— C. J....................Hotel.
F—— T.......................D. G.
F—— R.............Lumber Com'n.
G—— W...........Boots and Shoes.

G—— G..........Steel Spring Mnfr.
H—— T...........Cabinetmkr.
H—— W. J..................D. G.
K—— W...................Clothing.
K—— J. & R......Music and Sewing
                        Machines.
M—— J............Lamps, etc.
M—— I...........Whip Lashes.
N—— T...........Speculator.
R—— J. W..............Physician.
T—— J...............Melodeons.
W—— T. C....................D. G.
W—— R..................Ice.
W—— L—— & Co..Sewing Machines.
W—— S............Boots and Shoes.
W—— J., Sr...............Gro., etc.

[TO BE CONTINUED.]

HARTFORD, CT.

B—— B. B.............Silversmith.	K—— F. W...............Pens'
B—— & Co...............Dyestuffs.	L—— L...................Hotel
B—— H. & S.............Masons.	L—— W. H.........Electrotyper.
B—— R. F. & Co..........Iron, etc.	M—— B...............Carriages.
B—— J. H.................Gro.	M—— Bros.............Builders.
B—— E...................Harness.	M—— T..................Tea.
B—— H. M.............Jeweller.	M—— R..................Banker.
B—— H. S............Confectioner.	M—— H. & Co........Upholsterers.
B—— A. E...........Restaurant.	M—— L. B. & Co........Sashes, etc.
B—— R., Sr.............Capitalist.	M—— S. M.............Marble.
B—— W..................Harness.	M—— C............Silversmith.
B—— P...................Gro.	N—— S—— Co.
B—— I. B. P—— Co.	N—— M. C..........Teas and Lqrs.
B—— E. W..............Fish.	N—— R.............Lqr. and Gro.
C—— A...............Clothing.	O—— J.................Lqrs.
C—— J...............Clothing.	P—— T. H...........Com'n Prod.
C—— S—— & W—— F—— M—— Co.	P—— Bros................Meat.
D—— L.................Miller.	P—— M.................Hotel.
D—— & R——.........Carriagemkrs.	P—— A. G..............Tobacco.
D—— A. B...............Clocks.	P—— M. M............Oysters.
D—— A. & Son............Wool.	P—— P—— & Co........Milliners.
E—— C—— P—— Co.	P—— S. S.........Boots and Shoes.
F—— T—— S—— M—— Co.	R—— S—— & Co....Ag'l Impl'ts, etc.
F—— & H——..............Gro.	R—— J. C. & Co......Packing Boxes.
G—— D..........Boots and Shoes.	S—— E. & Son.....Lime and Cement.
G—— H. & Co...............D. G.	S—— & D——..............Cigars.
G—— D. A...........Furniture.	S—— P. H. B.............Tailor.
G—— H. A., Est. of.........Drugs.	S—— C. L............Builder.
G—— & F——.....Soap and Candles.	S—— O. D.......R. E. Broker, etc.
H—— H. & Bro..........Jewellers.	S—— & Co.................Gro.
H—— P—— Co.	S—— F. C. & Co.......Whol. Meats.
H—— S—— Co.	S—— D.................Builder.
H—— & F——.............D. G.	S—— W. B...........Lumber.
H—— W. K........Flour and Feed.	T—— C—— & Co........Tripe, etc.
H—— N.............Leaf Tobacco.	T—— W...........Auctioneer.
H—— A. J.................Baker.	W—— S—— M—— Co.
H—— W. C................Printer.	W—— E. H. & W. S.....Stevedores.
K—— H. P................Gro.	W—— D. R................Coal.
K—— & F——..........Wines, etc.	W—— C.........Paints, Sashes, etc.
K—— R. & Son.......Carriagemkrs.	W—— & Co........Boots and Shoes.
K—— H. F................Gro.	W—— J. K.............Drugs.

[TO BE CONTINUED.]

HOUSTON, TEXAS.

A—— N.....................Prov.
A—— J. J....................Hotel.
B—— M. A................Tailor.
B—— J. C...................Gro.
C—— J. W. & Co.........Cigars, etc.
C—— Mrs. F.................G. S.
C—— E. H..........Books, etc.
C—— J. A.........Machinery, etc.
D—— T. W.............Banking.
D—— J. W....Carriage Trimmings.
D—— W—— & Co..............Mill.
D—— J. R.............F'cy·Goods.
D—— & Co.........Whol. Liquors.
D—— G ......Stoves and Hardware.
E—— I................D. G., etc.
E—— & V——..........Gen'l Com'n.
E—— E.................Gunsmith.
F—— P.....Confec., Banker, and Ex-
                          change.
F—— W....................D. G.
F—— T. R.............D. G., etc.

F—— C. J.........Carriage Trimmer.
G—— F.........Boot and Shoe Mkr.
H—— A. & F——........Whol. D. G.
H—— H. & Co....Whol. and Ret. Gro.
I—— & G——...Furniture and Uphol-
                          sterers.
L—— & Bro..................D. G.
M—— W. H..........Carriagemkr.
M—— S.....................Gro.
M—— S. S..........Lumber Dealer.
R—— Mrs. M. J..........Millinery.
S—— J......................Gro.
S—— F. A............Clocks, etc.
S—— & H——.............Pub'rs.
S—— C............Cabinetmkr.
S—— & S——.............Clothing.
S—— M....................G. S.
V—— W. B......Cotton and Com'n.
V—— & B——.................G. S.
Z—— L...............Fancy Goods.

[TO BE CONTINUED.]

INDIANAPOLIS, IND.

A—— D. M.................Broker.
A—— C...........Boots and Shoes.
A—— H. & Bro............Saddlers.
A—— & G——...............Wood.
A—— E. S ......Real Estate.
A—— D—— W—— Co.
B—— & Co...............Factory.
B—— & D——..........Real Estate.
B—— & Son.................Drugs.
B—— H. S.................Agent.
B—— W. P. & Co..........Jewelry.
B—— F. A....................Oils.
B—— J. C. & Co.......Whol. Lqrs.

B—— C. H.........Patent Medicines.
B—— & B——................Chairs.
C—— W. S..................Printer.
C—— & T——.........Engines, etc.
C—— J. H................Jeweller.
C—— R. P......Photographic Mtr'ls.
C—— P......Money Lender.
C—— R. & Co.................Coal.
D—— J.............Fruits, etc.
D—— R. M..............Millinery.
D—— H............Notions, etc.
D—— W. J. & Co.........H'dware.
D—— C....................Drugs.

D—— Bro. & Co............Cloth.n₀.
D—— W............Boots and Shoes.
D—— C. & Co..........Mnfrs. Sup.
D—— J. B.................Drugs.
D—— J.....................Shoes.
D—— M..................Tanner.
E—— & O——.......Carpenters, etc.
E—— S....................Stoves.
F—— I. L................Stoves.
F—— I. T..........Tobacco Broker.
G—— A............ ......Carpets.
G—— I—— R—— C—— Co.
G—— J. C..................Mill.
G—— J. W................Hotel.
G—— R. & Co.............Mill.
G—— G. O...............Lqrs.
H—— M. T.................Gro.
H—— A. N. & Co.........Machines.
H—— J. O..............Newspaper.
H—— & M——...........Drugs.
H—— J. C.............Saddler.
H—— R—— & H——....Undertakers.
H—— K—— & Co............D. G.
I—— J. W...............Cigars.
I—— S—— L—— S—— Co.
I—— C. D.................Hotel.
I—— C—— Co.
I—— P—— & P—— Co.
I—— W—— W——.
J—— A...................Candles.
J—— E. W.....Marble.
J—— J....................Marble.
K—— A................Jeweller.
K—— J. S.................Drugs.
K—— C.....................Gro.
K—— A....................Drugs.
L—— L. & Co........Notions, etc.
L—— Miss...............Millinery.
L—— & L——..........Iron Works.
M—— J. W................Chairs.

—— E...................Drugs.
M—— E....................D. G.
M—— S.................Liquor.
M—— H—— & O——........Agts.
M—— J. P..............Brewer.
M—— P—— & Co............Coal.
M—— C..................Chairs.
M—— W. L.......Sewing Machs.
M—— D..................Mnfr.
N—— H..............Fcy Gds.
N—— C................Plumber.
O—— J....................Ale.
P—— E. L...............Statnr.
P—— H..........Boots and Shoes.
P—— J. T...............Lumber.
P—— S—— P—— Co.
R—— Mrs. M.............Hotel.
R—— W.................Stoves.
R—— & P——..............Gro.
R—— & S——..........Furniture.
R—— & L——.........Coal, etc.
R—— R. R. & Co........Pumps, etc.
S—— C....................Gro.
S—— J..............Notions, etc.
S—— & Co............Lumber.
S—— Mrs. L. D.........Millinery.
S—— W....................Gro.
S—— M. H. & Co.......Notions, etc.
S—— J..........Boots and Shoes.
S—— J. B. & Co............Lqrs.
S—— Mrs. S. L........Millinery.
S—— J................Harness.
T—— & S——.............Factory.
V—— S. C.............Publisher.
W—— L. S............Chemicals.
W—— E. H..............Hotel.
W—— & S——............Drugs.
W—— B—— & Co.........Printers.
Y—— & P——.............Books.
Z—— T.................Jeweller.

[TO BE CONTINUED.]

JERSEY CITY, N. J.

A—— W—— & G—— P—— Co.
C—— A.................Lumber.
D—— S ....Hulling Mach.
F—— J. A............Shoes, etc.
G—— M................Stoves.
G—— R. L.......Dry Goods, etc.
G—— T.................Livery.

H—— A. & Co............Fcy Gds.
H—— W. C................Iron.
J—— C—— I—— W——
K—— W..................Drugs.
L—— T. T.............Tin, etc.
L—— L. D.............H'dware.
M—— B..............Real Estate.

M—— J. A.............Newspaper.	S—— J....................Boots.
M—— B—— Co.	S—— W. D............Books, etc.
M—— J. M. & Co...........Livery.	T—— H. A........Gents' Furn'g.
M—— B. H...............Drugs.	W—— & C...........Coal, etc.
N—— E. S. & Co.........Clothing.	W—— J. P.............Coal.
S—— C. G............Contractor.	W—— S. R.............Lqrs.
S—— & F——.........Brewers.	

[TO BE CONTINUED.]

KANSAS CITY, MO.

A—— I. H............Hardware.	H—— & C——...........D. G.
A—— H. W............Furniture.	H—— & D——..........Gro.
B—— A. A.........Genl. Com'n.	H—— W.......Prod. and Feed.
B—— & B——..........Agts.	J—— & Co.........Jewellers.
B—— & B——..........Lqrs.	K—— R. H. & Co....Coal, etc.
B—— E. D............Agent.	K—— J. L. & Co........H'dware.
B—— & Bro........D. G. and Gro.	K—— & T——......Furniture.
C—— & Co................Gro.	L—— A. S................Hotel.
C—— Bros............Pianos.	L—— & W——.....Publishers.
C—— W. E............Drugs.	M—— I. W..........Saddlery.
C—— J. H............News.	M—— J. E............Drugs.
D—— M................Hotel.	M—— & S——........Machinists.
D—— J. N............Leather.	M—— & Co......Cattle Dealers.
F—— W. B...........Builder.	R—— & Bro..........Vinegar.
F—— & D—— S—— B——.	R—— E. P........Boots and Shoes.
F—— N. R. & Son........Gro.	R—— & Co.............D. G.
F—— H. C. & Co........Hotel.	S—— J. C.............Hotel.
G—— M. B. & Bros.....Cattle Dealers.	T—— & Co.......Whol. Gro.
G—— W. C............Lqrs.	T—— H. & Bro......Whol. Tobacco.
H—— J. & Son.........Hotel.	T—— G...............Gro.
H—— I. P............Gro.	T—— & B——.......Agl. Implts.
H—— G. W...........H'dware.	W—— J. Q. & Co........Bankers.

[TO BE CONTINUED.]

LAWRENCE, MASS.

B—— J. R. ....Gro.
B—— M. ....Gro.
B—— Mrs. A. M. ....Fcy Gds.
B—— W. E. ....Jeweller.
B—— A. D. ....Books, etc.
B—— R. & Co. ....Newspaper.
C—— W. C. ....Boots and Shoes.
C—— B. D. ....Bobbin Mnfr.
C—— D. Jr. & Co. ....Gro.
C—— Mrs. J. ....Liquor.
D—— S. & Son. ....Contractors.
H—— T. W. ....Hotel.
H—— W. ....Millinery, etc.
H—— W. B. ....Waterproof Cloth.
J—— J. K. ....Pottery.

K—— W. A. ....Braid Mnfr.
L—— G. ....Boots and Shoes.
L—— C. H. ....Drugs.
L—— D— S— & B— Co.
M—— H. ....Jeweller.
N—— Miss R. ....Fcy Gds.
S—— W. ....Fcy Gds.
S—— M. A. ....Harness.
T—— D. ....Liquors.
T—— M. A. ....D. G.
T—— J. A. & Co. .....Painters' Sups.
W—— J. ....Sewing Mach.
W—— A. H. ....Gro.
W—— S. ....Gro.

[TO BE CONTINUED.]

LEAVENWORTH, KAN.

A—— S. ....Capitalist.
A—— E. B. ....Capitalist.
A—— J. M. ....Stationer.
A—— J. & Co. ....Lqrs.
B—— M ....Clothing.
B—— W. C. Jr. & Co. ....Boots.
B—— T. G. ....Prod.
B—— F. B. ....Furrier.
C—— T. ....Printer.
C—— E. ....Coal, Grain, etc.
C—— M. A. ....Gasoline.
C—— C. ....Agent.
C—— W. ....Gro., etc.
D—— M. E. ....Gro.
D—— O. ....Contractor, etc.
E—— L. ....Marble.
G—— T. C. ....Seeds.
H—— Miss A. ....Milliner.
H—— O. J. ....Ins. Agt.
H—— J. W ....Agent.
H—— A. A. ....Agent.
H—— S. E. ....Capitalist.

H—— I. P. ....Gen. Store.
I—— J. ....Lumber.
I—— S— & Co. ....Bankers.
K—— W— & C— Co.
K—— T— Co.
K—— W. D. ....Agt.
K—— & Co. ....Brewers.
K—— J. B. ....Contractor.
K—— A. T. & Co. ....Livery.
L—— L. .....Dry Goods and Clothing.
L—— B— Co.
L—— J. ....Boots and Shoes.
M—— & Co. ....Agl. Implts.
M—— H. L. S. ....Livery.
M—— W. ....Printer.
M—— J. W. ....Capitalist.
N—— B. ....D. G.
R—— J. S. & Co. ....Hotel.
R—— M. ....Packer.
S—— F. W. ....Gro.
W—— J. A. ....Lqrs., etc.

[TO BE CONTINUED.]

LOCKPORT, N. Y.

A—— M.....................Hotel.	H—— Mrs. A. C...........Clothing.
B—— S. M.....................Lime.	K—— P. & Bro............Fcy Gds.
B—— & G——...............Gro.	K—— J. P...............Sashes, etc.
B—— R.....................Miller.	L—— B—— A——.
B—— A. A.......Prod., Fwdg., etc.	M—— A. J.....................Glass.
B—— H.................Drugs, etc.	M—— J. P.....................Agt.
B—— J. L.............Carpets, etc.	P—— J. H...........Fwdg., etc.
C—— H. F.............Boatbuilder.	P—— & Co.................Wool.
E—— S. M.....................Gro.	P—— G.....................Dairy.
E—— G. B...............Miller.	R—— T...............Carriages.
F—— A.....................Agent.	U—— Mrs. E. S...........Clothing.
H—— & D——...............D. G.	W—— W. J....... ....Dyer.

[TO BE CONTINUED.]

LOUISVILLE, KY.

A—— A. J.............Lumber, etc.	C—— D—— & Co... ....Gro.
A—— H. C.............Physician.	C—— & Co...................Com'n.
A—— C.................Books, etc.	C—— F. H. & Co............Liquors.
A—— J. C.............Gro., etc.	C—— A.....................D. G.
A—— W. E.............Hotel.	C—— M.....................D. G.
A—— H—— & Co.............Pork.	C—— Mrs. A. H.........F'cy Goods.
B—— D. S.............Com'n Prod.	D—— M—— & Co.........Foundry.
B—— Bros. & Co...........Liquors.	D—— J.....................Gro.
B—— W.............Blacking, etc.	D—— D. & Co...........Hides, etc.
B—— & F——.............Foundry.	D—— F.....................Books.
B—— M. & Co.............Foundry.	E—— H—— & S——.......Hats, etc.
B—— M—— & Co.......Carpets, etc.	E—— J. V. & Son.......Pictures, etc.
B—— C. F.............Chairs.	F—— F.....................Lard, etc.
B—— R. R. & Co.........Stat'y, etc.	F—— J.............Parlor Furniture.
B—— J.............Capitalist.	F—— H.....................Books.
B—— R. L.........Com'n and Prod.	G—— J.............Fruits, etc.
B—— I.............Millinery.	G—— E. S.............Publisher.
B—— H. S. & Co...........Notions.	G—— Mrs. A. E...........Millinery.
C—— & T——.............Liquors.	G—— Mrs. W. F.............D. G.
C—— D—— & Co.............Stock.	H—— J.............Elevators, etc.
C—— & M——..... ....Com'n.	H—— K—— & Co.........Furniture.

H—— M—— & Co..........Clothing.
H—— J....................Builder.
H—— G.......................Gro.
H—— I...................Contractor.
H—— & A——.................Gro.
H—— & Son....................Gro.
H—— H. J...............Physician.
H—— & Bro..............Printers.
K——J...................Confec.
K——J.................Gro., etc.
K——J.......................Hats.
K—— J. & Co...........Newspaper.
L—— B. C................Agent.
L—— A. & Co...........Clothing.
L—— J. S..................Stoves.
L—— D..................Foundry.
L—— A. B................Confec.
L—— J.......................Nails.
M—— W—— M—— Co.
M—— W. H.............Carpets.
M—— T.......................D. G.
M—— W. H........Boots and Shoes.
M—— J..................Jewelry.
M—— & V——...............B'krs.
M—— J. W. & Co.........Saddlery.
N—— N—— & Co.........Florists.
N—— M.................Clothing.
N—— E. P. & Co.........Hardware.
O—— R. F...................Gro.

P—— D. G............Real Estate.
P—— E. & Co.............Cigars.
P—— M...................Brewer.
R—— M. C.............Jewelry.
R—— M. & Son........Wagons.
R—— M.............Carriages.
R—— L..................Saloon.
R—— J. H. & Sons.............Gro.
S—— F.................Trunks.
S—— C......................Gro.
S—— F.................Clothing.
S—— J......................Glue.
S—— A.................Machines.
S—— F............Flour Mill.
S—— A..................Brkr.
S—— M—— & Co.........Liquors.
S—— Mrs. L.........:....Brewery.
S—— G. M.........Hemp Dusters.
S—— B—— W——.
T—— Miss K.......Fancy Goods, etc.
T—— J. H..............Newspaper.
V—— C. J..................Drugs.
V—— P.............Real Estate.
W—— J. C.................Books.
W—— & B——.............Tobacco.
W—— J. S. & Co...........Tobacco.
W—— H—— A—— & Co.....Livery.
W—— J. H. H................Agent.
Y—— & Co................Roofers.

[TO BE CONTINUED.]

LOWELL, MASS.

A—— S............Dry Goods and
                Sewing Machines.
A—— W. & Son.............Flocks.
B—— A. & Co........Planing Mills.
B—— W......................Furs.
B—— E.......................Gro.
B—— M. A.....................Gro.
B—— M................Provisions.
B—— J. M............Fancy Goods.
B—— S. D...........Foreign Fruits.
B—— E. O................Notions.
B—— S..................Tinsmith.
C—— C. E...................Drugs.
C—— P. & Co...............Gro.
C—— S—— Co.

C—— & N——................Iron.
C—— E. G.................Tanner.
D—— T.....................Tailor.
D—— J. & Son..............Mnfrs.
D—— A.........Mnfr. Shoe Shanks.
F—— F....................Mason.
F—— O. D..................Drugs.
F—— G. R...........Ladies' Suits.
G—— J...........Boots and Shoes.
G—— J...........Boots and Shoes.
H—— M................Dry Goods.
H—— B. V..................Shoes.
H—— D. W...................Coal.
H—— J......Mnfr. Boots and Shoes.
H—— C................Newspaper.

K—— H. G................Teas, etc.
K—— R................Machinery.
I,—— J. H...........Hats, Caps, etc.
L—— F—— S—— Co.
L—— D. & Son.......Mnfrs. Knives.
L—— O—— C—— Co.
M—— J. A..................Mnfr.
M—— O................Furniture.
M—— D. J................Liquors.
P—— J. N.............Machinist.
R—— A. J.................Produce.

S—— J.........Mnfr. Shade Rollers.
S—— A. W....................Gro.
S—— S—— & Co.............Flour.
S—— T—— Co.
T—— T................Waters, etc.
T—— J. M. & Co.............Boxes.
T—— J...............Roll Coverer.
W—— G. H....................Mnfr.
W—— Bros. & K——........Gloves.
W—— W. H.................Builder.

[TO BE CONTINUED.]

.

LYNN, MASS.

A—— S. T ....Hotel.
A—— J. L.............Upholsterer.
B—— T. W................Shoes.
B—— S. J................Shoes.
B—— W. N. & Co.........Coal, etc.
B—— S. H.............Boots, etc.
B—— P. W. & Co.............Gro.
B—— B................Shoes.
B—— W. N.............Stitcher.
B—— H. H................Drugs.
C—— C. H..............Builder.
C—— H. R.....Boot and Shoe Mnfr.
C—— H. & N.............Morocco.
C—— B. F..............Carpenter.
D—— & D——............Shoes.
D—— B. & Co........ ....Shoes.
D—— H. T......Boot and Shoe Mnfr.
G—— W. H......Paster Inner Soles.
G—— S. A................Shoes.
G—— S., Jr................Shoes.
H—— J. W..............Cement.
H—— G. W............Stiffenings.
H—— P. C................Shoes.
H—— W. S.................Gro.

H—— & D——..............Shoes.
H—— P. H.............Builder.
J—— L. S.............Slippers.
K—— J...........Paints and Oils.
K—— J. P................Hotel.
L—— C₁ H..............Uppers.
L—— J. W................Shoes.
L—— J. P..............Shoewax.
M—— S. S.........Boots and Shoes.
M—— J......................Gro.
M—— G. W................Shoes.
M—— R..............Carpenter.
N—— & W——................Shoes.
P—— E..................Shoes.
P—— G..................Shoes.
P—— J..................Shoes.
P—— H. L................Shoes.
R—— J. R...........Stoves, etc.
S—— & P——..............Shoes.
S—— P. P................Shoes.
S—— A. F................Shoes.
S—— & M——..............Shoes
T—— W. S..............Operator.

[TO BE CONTINUED.]

MANCHESTER, N. H.

B—— G. F.................Auctioneer.	M—— S. T. & Co..........Druggists.
C—— J. B. & Co...........Leather.	M—— S—— & L—— Co.
C—— T.......... .....Provisions.	M—— & Co....................Gro.
C—— T....................Clothing.	N—— & H——...........Machinists.
C—— W.............Needle Mnfr.	R—— J.................Lqrs., etc.
C—— D.......................Gro.	S—— A. W. & Co.........Carriages.
E—— W. H................Jeweller.	S—— Bros................Stoves.
F—— S. C. & Co.........Machinists.	W—— G. W...........Millinery.
G—— F...........Boots and Shoes.	W—— A. C...............Lumber.
H—— P. W..................Hotel.	W—— A. H.............Clothing.
H—— A. D.................Tobacco.	W—— Mrs. J. L.......Fcy Gds., etc.
J—— C. H.............Fcy Gds.	

[TO BE CONTINUED.]

MEMPHIS, TENN

A—— B—— & Co.........Furniture.	B—— J. J. & Co..............Com'n.
A—— S. M.................Com'n.	C—— J. S...................Cotton.
A—— M. & Son.....Boots and Shoes.	C—— W. J. & Co.........Feedstore.
A—— J. L............Fancy Goods.	C—— E. L........Books and Stat'y.
A—— T. P. & Co...Cotton and Com'n.	C—— E. D. & Co...Cotton and Com'n.
B—— H. ....D. G.	C—— J.....................D. G.
B—— M. F....................Gro.	C—— J. W.............Contractor.
B—— & S——........Whol. H'dware.	D—— H. C. & Co...............Prov.
B—— E. P. & Co.....Cotton Factors.	D—— E.............Hats and Caps.
B—— B—— & Co ....Com'n.	D—— & S——..............Com'n.
B—— H...................D. G., etc.	D—— & B——....R. E. Agency, etc.
B—— M. M.......Sewing Machines.	D—— J. S..........Cotton Buyer.
B—— B. J....................Com'n.	F—— W. J.............Upholsterer.
B—— N. A. & Co................Gro.	F—— R—— & Co..Cotton and Com'n.
B—— H................Furniture.	F—— T. A............Stoneworker.
B—— J. T. & Co..........Com'n, etc.	F—— S......................D. G.
B—— & C——.....Books and Stat'y.	F—— & D——....Tobacco and Cigars.
B—— C. G. & Co....Prod. and Com'n.	F—— F.... ....Gro.
B—— J. M.................Cotton.	G—— S...........Boots and Shoes.
B—— W. M..........Stockyards, etc.	G—— Bros...........Cigars, etc.
B—— W...............Newspaper.	G—— W. B., Sr..........Capitalist.
B—— & P——.....Cotton and Com'n.	H—— G.................Furniture.

H—— J. S. & Co....Books and Stat'y.	M—— & S——......Boots and Shoes.
H—— J. E......................Gro.	M—— J. & A. P..........Carriages.
H—— R. C.............Newspaper.	M—— A. R..................Com'n.
H—— B. A......................Dyer.	M—— G..............Claim Agent.
H—— H. G.......Pianos and Music.	N—— J. A. & Co...Cotton and Com n.
H—— C—— & H——..Whol. Notions.	P—— J. C..............Speculator.
H—— G................Baker.	P—— & M——..........Cotton Shed.
H—— D. & Son...............Gro.	P—— G. W. & Co.Gin and Machinery.
H—— & S——............Printers.	P—— C—— & Co.....Com'n and Gro.
I——F. W. & Co...Cotton Factors and	R—— S. G.....................D. G.
Com'n.	R—— G. N................ ....Gro.
I—— D. C. & Co.........Publishers.	R—— B......................Confec.
J—— R—— & Co.Wagon Factory, etc.	S—— & C——.... ....Hotel.
J—— J. T... ....Whol. Gro.	S—— M—— & M—— R——.
J—— C.....................Builder.	S—— N....... ......Clothing, etc.
K—— S. D. & Co.............Com'n.	S—— J. B............Cotton Buyer.
K—— S.....................Brewer.	S—— & S——...............Cotton.
K—— & G——.........Florists, etc.	S—— C................Plumber.
L—— & Co.................Plumbers.	T—— J.........Paperhangings, etc.
L—— P.................Machinist.	T—— G. W. & Co............Com'n.
L—— L.....................D. G.	T—— J. M. & Co........Whol. Gro.
L—— C.........D. G. and Clothing.	T—— & Co......Auction and Com'n.
L—— L ....Clothing.	U——L.....................D. G.
L—— M. & Co....D. G. and Clothing.	V—— F. W..................Drugs.
L—— W......Newsdealer.	W—— & Co.................Storage.
L—— W................Plumber.	W—— Miss A. A..........Millinery.
M—— & Co.........Com'n and Prod.	W—— & G——............Carriages.
M—— P. J. & Co.......Plumbers, etc.	W—— C. C. & Bro......Whol. Drugs.
M—— R. M............Gas Machine.	W—— & Co..........Dental Depot.
M—— J................Stone Works.	W—— G. G. & Co........Gen'l Com'n.
M—— & Co.........Boots and Shoes.	W—— Z. H.................Hotel.
M—— & Co..........Whol. H'dware.	W—— E. & Co......... Publisher.
M—— T............Marble Works.	W—— T—— & Co...Rolling Mill, etc.
M—— & A—— P—— Co.	W—— G. J. & Co...........Lumber.
M—— A——	W—— A. N. & Co........Feedstore.
M—— L—— Co.	W—— J. M. & Co..Cotton and Com'n.
M—— & R—— R——	W—— & Co..........Mnfrs. Bitters.
M—— R——	W—— M.....................D. G.
M—— G. & Bro........Whol. Paper.	W—— & Co.................Drugs.
M—— V. B.............Com'n, etc.	

[TO BE CONTINUED.]

MILWAUKEE, WIS.

A—— G. A................Foundry.	A—— O. & Co...Bankers and Brokers.
A—— D.................Clothing.	A—— M—— & Co....Dry Docks, etc.
A—— P. N.............Blacksmith.	A—— J....................Marble.
A—— A.... ....Stages.	B—— Bros.........Whol. Saddlery.

B—— J. W. & E. J...........Com'n.	H—— & D——..........Ins. Agents.
B—— G...........Boots and Shoes.	H—— C. J.............Com'n Flour.
B—— & R——.........Whol. Drugs.	H—— J....................Gro.
B—— & M——.............Com'n.	H—— H ....Notions.
B—— H. M.........Wood and Coal.	H—— & V——........Com'n and Ins.
B—— F.......Com'n and Distillery.	H—— J. H...............Jeweller.
B—— F....................Mill.	H—— W....Composition Marble.
B—— & P——........Coal and Wood.	J—— J. & H............Furniture.
B—— P..........Boots and Shoes.	J—— P.............'.Blacksmith.
B—— A. W. & Co........Carpets and	K—— F.............Liquors.
Mnfrs. Woollen Goods.	K—— S......................D. G.
B—— Miss I................Milliner.	K—— F.............Type Foundry.
B—— F. & Son......Com'n and Prod.	K—— & C——.............Hotel.
B—— J........................Gro.	K—— I. & Co..........Notions, etc.
B—— J. B. & Co.............Pianos.	K—— A........Boots and Shoes.
B—— H. L...........Mdse. Broker.	K—— A....................D. G.
B—— K—— & K——.A——O—— Co.	K—— E.........Musical Insts., etc.
B—— H. S...........Photographer.	L—— C. C...........Saw Works.
B—— L. J. & Co.........Ag'l Implts.	M—— R. A. & Co.......Mnfrs. Soap.
B—— J. W. & Co.........Painters.	M—— A. D........Boots and Shoes.
C—— & B——.......Whol. Tobacco.	M—— J. S. & Co............Lumber.
C—— N—— Co........Printers and	M—— J. T. & Co......Musical Insts.
Pub'rs.	M—— & S——...........Foundry.
C—— & B——..........Newspaper.	M—— H.................Feed.
C—— T. P. & Co.......Painters and	M—— J...............Wagons.
Wallpaper.	M—— H—— & L—— Co.
C—— E. G................Com'n.	M—— U—— D—— Co.
C—— W. W.........Mdse. Broker.	M—— & N—— W—— S—— M——Co.
C—— L..................Lumber.	M—— F...................Cigars.
C—— L...................Roofer.	M—— M—— & Co........Flour Ma-
C—— J. H ....Whol. Gro.	chinery.
C—— & G——............Tanners.	N—— & D——.....Doors, Sashes, etc.
C—— W. J.................Wool.	O—— & B——.............Printers.
D—— T............Whol. Liquors.	O—— B. A.................Com'n.
E—— F............Hats and Caps.	P—— F.................Wines, etc.
E—— R. P. & Co.............Coal.	P—— E. B. & Co...........Com'n.
E—— T—— Co.	P—— A. P., Son & Co.......Soap, etc.
E—— J...............Wagons, etc.	P—— A....................Miller.
E—— F. & Bro....Flour and Woollen	P—— G........Sashes, Doors, etc.
Mills.	P—— D. G.........R. E. Agent and
E—— A. D.................Agent.	Trip Hammer.
E—— J. W...............Boilermkr.	R—— W. C............Ag'l Implts
F—— J. S. & Sons....Upholsterers.	R—— J............Fruit, etc.
F—— & S——....Mnfrs. Furniture.	R—— R. & Co..........Clothing.
F—— W. & Co.......Whol. and Ret.	R—— P. Jr.................Com'n.
Hardware.	R—— L.................Distiller.
F—— & B——.......Whol. Liquors.	R—— Bros..........Whol. Liquors.
G—— M....................Hotel.	R—— A. & Co...........Jewellers.
G—— S..............Dry Goods.	S—— R.........Wines and Liquors.
G—— & Co............Carpets, etc.	S—— J....................G. S.
G—— S.............Mnfr. Slippers.	S—— J. H.......R. E., Wood, etc.
G—— T................Fruit, etc.	S—— J. & Co........Bridge Builders.
G—— A..................Vinegar.	S—— C. A.............Furniture.
G—— F.......Whol. Hats and Caps.	S—— C............Wood and Coal.
H—— J ....Boots and Shoes.	S—— & P——.......Ales and Liquors.
H—— & S............Millinery.	S—— M—— & Co......Gent's Furn'g
H—— J. M..............Notions.	Goods.
H—— E. A............ ...Foundry.	S—— & Co.................Books.
H—— W...................Rags.	T—— & C——..........Pub'rs, etc.
H—— & S——.........Publishers.	T—— H.............Mnfr. Hats.
H—— E. C...............Jeweller.	T—— S—— & Co...........Lumber.

U—— A...................Com'n.
W—— J. P. & Co.............Com'n.
W—— J. W......Prod. and Com'n.
W—— W. A..............Billiards.
W—— E..........Boots and Shoes.

W—— R. J. C............,.....Fruit, etc.
W—— A.......Tobacco and Cigars.
W—— J. T.................Packer.
W—— & M——..........Ag'l Implts.
Z—— & R——............Jewellers.

[TO BE CONTINUED.]

MOBILE, ALA.

B—— T. S......Books and Stationery.
B—— W. A................Drugs.
B—— H—— & Co.......Drayage and Storage.
B—— J.....................Com'n.
C—— H. W................Drugs.
C—— Mrs. M. C................Hotel.
C—— P. Z.................Drugs.
C—— L. & Co...............Cigars.
C—— E. W. & Co...........Produce.
C—— J. & Co..........Cotton Com'n.
D—— J.......................D. G.
D—— & W——.................Gro.
D—— J. D ....Harness.
D—— J. A.................Furniture.
F—— S..................Gen. Store.
F—— L. G. & Co.........Com'n Prod.
G—— R. L. & Co............Tobacco.
G—— G..................Jeweller.
G—— C—— P—— Co. .
H—— I. L................ ...Drugs.
H—— E. F...........Cotton Com'n.
K—— S. N. & Co...........Dredgers.
L—— J. & Co..............Founders.
L—— B. R..........Boots and Shoes.
L—— Mrs. M........Boots and Shoes.

M—— M.............Cotton Factor.
M—— I. A. & Co..............Com'n.
M—— & Son..........Cotton Brokers.
M—— J...............Livery Stable.
M—— D.................Furniture.
M—— F—— & Co... ......D. G.
M—— G. H......Boots and Shoes.
M—— W. H..............Auction.
M—— A. J...................Safes.
M—— M.................Furniture.
N—— C. D......................Gro.
P—— & P——........Cotton Pickery.
P—— L. & Co.................Gro.
P—— A. A. & Co........Com'n Prod.
P—— W. D................Seeds, etc.
P——C..... ......Whol. Hardware.
R—— A. B. & Bro......Cotton Press.
S—— E. R.......R. E. and Ex. Bkr.
S—— J. F. & Co......Gro. and Com'n.
S—— I—— Co.
T—— R. E.............:.....Prod. Com'n.
T—— & C——...............Lumber.
W—— W. L..............Cotton Factor.
Y—— G. W.................Hotel.
Z—— G. & B.............Furniture.

[TO BE CONTINUED.]

MONTREAL, QUE.

A—— A. & E.	Imps. Leather.	L—— R.	Lumber.
A—— E.	Banker.	L—— L. H. & Co.	Whol. D. G'ds.
A—— & Co.	Fcy Gds.	L—— F.	Lumber.
B—— E. I. & Co.	Livery.	L—— A.	Carpenter.
B—— & S——.	Express.	L—— R.	Flour.
B—— W. H.	Crockery.	L—— T. & Co.	Boots and Shoes.
B—— W. P. & Co.	Founders.	L—— J... Whol. Jeweller, and Fancy
B—— B.	Contractor.		Goods.
B—— S. W. & Co.	Coal.	L—— M.	Hoopskirts, etc.
B—— A. R.	Liquors.	L—— D. E. & Co.	Drugs and Oils.
B—— E.	Coal Oil.	L—— W. F. & Co.	Wines.
B—— C.	Provisions.	L—— C. B. & Co.	Lumber.
B—— A. & Co.	Furs.	M—— L. & Son.	Brokers.
B—— J.	Butcher.	M—— P. P. & Co.	Whol. D. G'ds.
B—— & C——.	D. G.	M—— J.	Agent.
B—— D. & Co.	Com'n Merchants.	M—— D. I.	Gro.
C—— W. A. & Co.	Coffee and Spice	M—— W.	Straw Works.
	Mills.	M—— D.	Leather.
C—— S. & Co.	D. G.	M—— & Co.	Lumber.
C—— J. B.	D. G.	M—— & J——.	Forwarders.
C—— J. & Co.	Soda Water.	M—— W. M.	Iron Works.
C—— C. E.	Wines, etc.	M—— H. & Co.	Dry Goods.
C—— A.	Trader.	M—— G. W.	Com'n D. G.
D—— N. & Co.	Bkrs.	M—— M. & Co.	Lumber.
D—— & P——.	Cigars.	M—— P.	Wood and Coal.
D—— S. & Co.	Mnfrs. Cigars.	O—— J. & R.	Whol. Dry Goods.
D—— J.	Contractor.	P—— C. E.	Furniture.
D—— E.	Hotel.	P—— W.	Mills.
D—— & M——.	Gro.	P—— J.	Jeweller.
D—— J. N.	D. G.	P—— J.	Mnfr. Cider.
E—— D.	Com'n Teas.	P—— L. & Co.	Printers.
E—— H. & Co.	Imps. Cigars, etc.	R—— W. H. & Co.	Com'n.
F—— R.	Marble Works.	R—— T. & Co.	Paper and Stat'rs.
G—— & Co.	D. G.	R—— P. A.	Lumber.
G—— M—— & Co.	Gro.	R—— G. L. & Son.	Shoes.
G—— J. G.	Lithographer.	R—— P.	Dry Goods.
G—— E. E.	Machinist.	R—— & J——.	Oils, etc.
G—— S.	Tailor.	R—— B. & Co.	Fancy Goods.
G—— F.	Mnfr. Trusses.	R—— A.	Confec.
H—— & Co.	Lumber.	S—— O. & Co.	Whol. Gro.
H—— J. N. & Co.	Whol. Hardware.	S—— D. & J.	Books.
H—— D. A.	Fancy Goods.	S—— C. E.	Leather.
H—— T. W. & Bro.	Liquors.	S—— Bros. & C——.	Tanners.
H—— & S——.	Fwdrs.	S—— H. J. & Co.	Auctioneers.
H—— M. & Son.	Mnfrs. Hats.	T—— M. & Co.	Shoes.
H—— E. Fils & Co.	Dry Goods, etc.	T—— E. H. & Co.	Shoes.
H—— B.	Whol. Gro.	T—— M.	Dry Goods.
K—— & Co.	Machinists.	V—— N. & Co.	Iron Founders.
K—— W. L. & Co.	Engin'rs' Agts.	W—— & F——.	Shoe Findings.
K—— A.	Cooper.	Y—— J. M.	Prov.
L—— H. & Co.	Produce.		

[TO BE CONTINUED.]

NASHVILLE, TENN.

A—— R. F. . . . . .Hardware.
A—— F. M. . . . . .Carriages.
A—— & A——. . . . . .Jewellers.
A—— J. W. . . . . . . .Boots and Shoes.
B—— & Co. . . . . .Auction and Com'n.
B—— & J——. . . . . .Lumber.
B —— & P——. . . . . .Com'n.
B—— A. L. & Co. . . . . .Patent.
C—— A. W. .'. . . . . .Scales.
C—— J. . . . . .Clothing.
C—— Bros. . . . . .Lumber.
C—— W. . . . . .Gro.
C—— S. . . . . .Dry Goods.
C—— & Co. . . . . .Gro.
C—— J. O. & Co. . . . . .G. S.
C—— & Co. . . . . .Auction.
C—— B. R. . . . . .Shoes.
D—— D. D. . . . . .Mill.
E—— P—— & Co. . . . . .Drugs.
F—— E. H. . . . . .Cotton Broker.
F—— E. . . . . .Hotel.
F—— E. & Co. . . . . . .Boots and Shoes.
G—— R. I. . . . . .Drugs.
G—— M. C. & Co. . . . . .Saw Mill.
G—— H. . . . . .Clothing.
G—— J. P. & Co. . . . . . . .Fancy Goods.
H—— C. B. . . . . .Boots and Shoes, etc.
H—— & Son. . . . . .Com'n.
H—— G. W. . . . . .Drugs.
II—— W. T. . . . . . .Cotton and Com'n.
H—— & Son. . . . . . .Dental Depot, etc.
H—— S. . . . . .Clothing.
I—— Miss E. . . . . .Milliner.

K—— & W——. . . . . .Restaurant.
L—— C. . . . . .Printer.
L—— J. N. & Co. . . . . .Leather, etc.
L—— J. E. & Co. . . . . . . .Fancy Goods.
M—— J. A. & Bro. . . . . .Music.
M—— M. . . . . . .Dry Goods and Boots
                                                  and Shoes.
M—— H—— & Co. . . . . .Gro.
M—— J. & Sons. . . . . . . .Saddlery, etc.
N—— C—— T—— Co.
N—— C—— S—— O—— Co.
N—— & H——. . . . . . . .Clothing, etc.
O—— A. . . . . .Boots and Shoes.
P—— T. . . . . .Cotton Speculator.
P—— S. & Son. . . . . .Clothing.
R—— Mrs. E. F. . . . . . .Gents' Furn'g.
R—— G. & Co. . . . . .D. G.
R—— C. L. . . . . .Gro.
R—— J. A. J. . . . . .Clothing.
S—— T. F. . . . . .Photographer.
S—— H. G. . . . . .R. E. Agent.
S—— C—— & R—— Co.
S—— & P——. . . . . . . .Carpenters and
                                                  Builders.
S—— H. C. . . . . .Oils.
S—— N—— U——.
S—— & P——. . . . . .Brewery.
S—— S. & Co. . . . . .Leather, etc.
T—— & C——. . . . . .Boots and Shoes.
T—— I. & Co. . . . . .Jewellers.
T—— Mrs. E. . . . . .Millinery.
V—— J. . . . . .Mer. Tailor.
W—— W. E. . . . . .F—— S——.

[TO BE CONTINUED.]

NEWARK, N. J.

A—— F.................Fertilizers.	J—— M—— Co.
A—— H. B................Jewelry.	K—— J. H.................Wagons.
A—— & C——............Stoves.	M—— M.......................Prov.
A—— J. G................Oilcloth.	M—— P...................Liquors.
A—— & S——............Brewers.	M—— J.......................Hats.
A—— D...............Lumber, etc.	M—— L. B.............Mattresses.
B—— C—— & Co........Machinists.	M—— S—— & Co........Machinists.
B—— P................Contractor.	M—— J. & M. A.............Livery.
C—— H—— T—— Co.	N—— T—— T—— Co.
C—— M—— Co.	O—— M...............Spring Mnfr.
C—— M—— Co.	P—— C—— Co.
D—— W. J........Boots and Shoes.	R—— J. H..................Springs.
D—— S.................Morocco.	R—— & S——...............Junk.
E—— J..................Livery.	R—— W....................Bags.
E—— A. L........Undertaker, etc.	S—— U....................Brewer.
F—— J...................Soda.	S—— & S——.........Flour, etc.
G—— R. J...............Engines.	T—— & W——............Boots.
G—— A...............Imp. Wines.	T—— E—— Co.
G—— A,..............Books, etc.	V—— N...............Silverplater.
H—— C................Contractor.	W—— A..............Boots, etc.
H—— W. W.............Cooper.	W—— C. & B——.........Brewers.
H—— C. H..............Slater.	W—— J..............News Depot.
H—— W. A. & Co........Clothing.	Z—— & B——..........Plumbers.

[TO BE CONTINUED.]

NEW-HAVEN, CT.

A—— A.....................Lqrs.	B—— & D—— Bros....Gents' Furn'g·
A—— N—— L—— & T—— Co.	B—— W................ Builder.
A—— J..................Oysters.	B—— C. W.................Hotel.
A—— H.................Architect.	B—— F. S. & Co...........H'dware.
B—— G. M..........House Mover.	B—— I. M................Drugs.
B—— J..................Hotels.	B—— W. H. & Co....Mnfrs. Coaches.
B—— G. A.................Lqrs.	B—— M. P............Corset Mnfr.
B—— & W——.....Boots and Shoes.	B—— S....................D. G.
B—— W. A.........Daguerreian.	B—— F...........Boots and Shoes.
B—— T.....................Gro.	B—— B................Gen. Store.
B—— M—— Co.	B—— G................Cigars, etc.

B—— & S——............Stk Bkrs.	L—— A............Boots and Shoes.
B—— J.................Harnessmkr.	L—— W—— F—— Co.
B—— P....................Lqrs.	L—— J. T.........Perfumery Mnfr.
B—— C. L ....Cabtmkr.	M—— W.....................Gro.
B—— & Co..........H'dware Mnfrs.	M—— P.....................Gro.
C—— L. & Co.........India-Rubber.	M—— P........ ....Lqrs.
C—— & Co..............Publishers.	M—— & S——.........Iron Foundry.
C—— J. E.....Dry and Fcy Gds.	M—— M—— Co............Needles.
C—— R. T....................Hotel.	M—— C.............Tobacco.
C—— J. G..........Flour and Feed.	M—— E—— F—— Co.
C—— H. D. & Co.....Bldrs' Materials.	M—— F..................Oysters.
C—— E. A......Paperhangings, etc.	M—— F. O.......Wire Works.
C—— O—— F—— Co.	M—— E. P.....Window Springs.
C—— P.—— W—— P—— Co.	M—— F.................Leather.
C—— & S——..........Whol. Prod.	M—— C.....................Ins.
C—— & Co...............Carriages.	M—— W.............Billiards.
C—— F. A. & Co........Stoves, etc.	M—— M. & S.................D. G.
D—— C. C. & Co.............Shirts.	M—— F.................Saloon.
D—— B—— & Co............D. G.	M—— J. C. ....Tailor.
D—— W. J. & J. E.........Tinners.	N—— J. G. & Co............Ins.
D—— H. P.................Mnfr.	O—— & O——.............Tobacco.
D—— W. P..............Builder.	O—— W.....................Gro.
D—— T ....Harnessmkr.	P—— C. H......Mnfr. Coach Lace.
E—— C—— S—— Co.	P—— J. S............Fcy Gds, etc.
E—— H...................Gro.	P—— Bro. & Co.............Brass.
F—— & P——..........Machinery.	P—— J. H..............Pickles.
F—— E....................Hotel.	R—— I. J..........Real Estate.
F—— C. P..................Gro.	R—— D. F...........Gas Fixtures.
F—— P...................Brewery.	R—— S...............Broker.
G—— Bros.............Publishers.	R—— W. J..........Musical Insts.
G—— R. H...Printer and Steam Heat-	R—— B. N. & Co...........Oysters.
ing.	R—— H. J.........Boots and Shoes.
G—— J. L.............Harnessmkr.	S—— C. & C——.....Boots and Shoes.
H—— B.................Real Estate.	S—— H. B..................Gro.
H—— E.........Steel Shanks, etc.	S—— S....................Iron.
H—— C. F..............Auctioneer.	S—— J.....................Gro.
H—— A. J. & Co..........Builders.	T—— G....................Flour.
H—— D. M...................Hotel.	T—— J. E................Stoves.
J—— A. G..................Fruit.	T—— J. D.................Drugs.
L—— & B——............Lumber.	W—— H. N. & Co..........Crockery.
L—— H. H..........Gro. and Prov.	W—— R—— A—— Co.
L—— E..................Lumber.	W—— J. M.........Picture Frames.

[TO BE CONTINUED.]

NEW-ORLEANS, LA.

A—— J. F. ....Variety.	G—— R. ....Stoves.
A—— G. E. ....Lqrs.	G—— F. ... .Tailor.
A—— J. ....Drugs.	G—— M. & Son. ....Com'n.
A—— C. W. & Co ....Com'n.	G—— Bros. ....Hats.
A—— G. & Co. ....Brewery.	H—— J. G. ....Broker.
B—— & L——. ....Bakery.	H—— B. ....Gro.
B—— L. ....Tinsmith.	H—— R. ....Tailor.
B—— & N——. ......Whol. Boots and	H—— W. & Co.... ...Cotton Factors.
Shoes.	H—— J. F. & Co. ....Restaurant.
B—— J—— & Co. Whol. Boots, Shoes,	H—— A. F. ....Gro.
D. G., etc.	H—— P. ....Mill, etc.
B—— I. & Co. ....Whol. Gro.	H—— & G——. ....Cotton.
B—— L. & Co. ....Whol. Gro.	H—— & V——. ....Com'n.
B—— M. ....Whol. Millinery.	H—— J. M. ....Powder.
B—— P. ....Tailor.	H—— L. ....Coffee House and Wood-
B—— H. ....C. H. Broker.	yard.
B—— & C——. ....Whol. H'dware.	H—— & M——. ....Produce.
B—— J. ....Paints.	II—— A. W. ....Stationery.
B—— J. ....Exchange.	I—— G. B. & Co. ....Saloon.
B—— J. A. ....Lumber.	J—— J. W. ....Builder.
C—— F. ....Com'n.	K—— F. ....Books.
C—— C. W. ....Broker.	K—— & Co. ....Coal.
C—— & V——. ....Wines, etc.	K—— W. A. ....Oil and Lamps.
C—— R. Y. ....Bonded Warehouse.	L—— E. ....Fancy and D. G.
C—— O. ....Cotton Factor.	L—— G. H. W. ....Boots.
C—— & W——. ....Steam Cotton	L—— L. ....D. G.
Gunnery.	L—— S. ....D. G.
C—— J. ....Foundry.	L—— I. K. & Son. ....Notions, etc.
C—— M. ....Clothing.	L—— V. ....Gro.
C—— T. M. & Co. ....Com'n.	L—— J. G. ....Com'n Cotton.
C—— W. C. & Co.... .Whol. Grain.	L—— & B——. ....Ship Brokers.
C—— T. S. ......Planters' Agent and	L—— P. ....Cemetery Marble.
Com'n.	L—— C. ....Brewer.
C—— J. B. ....Saloon.	M—— T. ....Gro.
C—— B. & W. ....D. G.	M—— H. ....Fancy Goods.
C—— J. P. ....Oils and Lamps.	M—— D. ....Clothing, etc.
D—— T. & Sons. ....D. G.	M—— L. ....Gro.
D—— P. ....D. G.	M—— N. ....D. G.
D—— J. A. ....Hotel.	M—— G. F. ....Com'n Coal.
D—— P. ....Blksmith.	M—— J. ....Produce.
E—— M. ....Pianos.	M—— S. E. ....Crockery, etc.
E—— A. ....Gro. and Coffee.	P—— & R——. ....Gro.
F—— H. ....Ale Bottler.	P—— & T——. ....Hay and Feed.
F—— J. ....Gro.	P—— E. ....Cotton Brkr.
F—— P. H. ....Gro.	Q—— F. A. ....Nursery.
F—— C—— & Co. ....Com'n.	R—— Mrs. C. ....Millinery.
F—— & D——. ......Bldng Materials.	R—— J. ....Saloon.
F—— J. ....Saloon.	R—— J. ....Boots, etc.
F—— G. J. ....Builder, etc.	R—— F. L. ....Furniture.
G—— D. ....Sugar Broker.	R—— F. ....Gro.

R—— J....................Saloon.
R—— & Co................H'dware.
S—— J...................Crockery.
S—— J. A................Boots.
S—— & B——...............Gro.
S—— F...................Boots.
S—— T...................Leather.
S—— B...................Variety.
S—— M. & Co.........H'dware, etc.
S—— & K——..............Rice.
S—— D.................Stationery.
S—— J. B................Gro.
S—— J. G..............Gro., etc.
S—— M—— & Co..........Com'n.

S—— J...................Broker.
S—— & M——.............Crockery.
S—— G..................Marble.
T—— & A................Cotton.
T—— R. F................Gro.
T—— W. C...............D. G.
T—— & Co.........Mdse. Bkrs.
T—— M................Gro., etc.
V—— & B——..........Wines, etc.
V—— C..................Boots.
W—— J. J..............Brewery.
W—— M..................Paints.
W—— F. & Co.........Butchers.
W—— & M——..........Clothing.

[TO BE CONTINUED.]

NORFOLK, VA.

A—— J. S. B......Fancy Goods, etc.
B—— W. R. & Co...........Com'n.
B—— A. S. & Co.....Whol. Gro., etc.
B—— L.................D. G.
B—— W. & W——.......D. G., etc.
B—— S.............Gro. and Liq.
B—— D. B.........Carriage Mnfy.
B—— B. B..........Com'n.
C—— A—— & H——.....D. G., etc.
C—— & H——...........Com'n.
E—— H.........Oyster Packer.
E—— & P——........Crockery.
F—— S.............D. G., etc.
G—— J. O. Jr.....Lumber and Coal.
G—— J. R.........Stoves, etc.
G—— & C——.......Mnfrs. Funnels.
G—— M—— & Co........Furniture.
G—— J. W.............G. S.
H—— W. T. & Son.....Upholsterers.

H—— W. T. & Co........Whol. Gro.
H—— W. T...........Confec., etc.
K—— Mrs. B..........Liquors.
K—— F. L..............Drugs.
K—— J. H..............Tailor.
L—— W.....Shipping and Com'n.
M—— A. A.............Lumber.
M—— E. W., Son & Co....Hardware.
R—— Bros. & Co..........Com'n.
S—— L.............Furniture, etc.
S—— J—— & L——......Whol. Gro.
                        and Com'n.
S—— S. W.....Whol. Liquors.
T—— E—— & W——.Whol. Hdware.
V—— E. & Co...........Liquors.
V—— D—— Co.
W—— B. F.............Prod., etc.
W—— S..........Boots and Shoes.
W—— & H——............Gro.

[TO BE CONTINUED.]

OSWEGO, N. Y.

A—— G. W...................D. G.	J—— D...................Com'n.
A—— H.......D. G. and Notions.	K—— A.......................Gro.
A—— G...................Capitalist.	L—— B............ ....Liquors.
A—— A......................Hotel.	M—— P..............Upholsterer.
B—— F. E.....................Gro.	M—— A. M..................Hotel.
B—— B. D................Jeweller.	M—— J. J ....D. G.
B—— E..........Boots and Shoes.	M—— & M——.........Brokers, etc.
B—— P. O.............Clothing.	N—— M. P..............Clothing.
B—— C. W.................Tobacco.	O—— J. & Co..........Gasfittings.
C—— W. G............. ....Oil.	O—— M—— Co.
C—— T...................Painter.	O—— P—— Co.
C—— E..............Sashes, etc.	P—— J....................Tailor.
D—— & Sons..............Carriages.	P—— C....................Paints.
D—— A—— & Co............Millers.	P—— J. L........Paperhangings.
F—— J. & Co.................Gro.	R—— W................ .Gro.
F—— A. & H...............Clothing.	R—— I. & W——.............Gro.
G—— T......................Gro.	R—— L. B..............Jeweller.
G—— B—— & Co...........Lumber.	S—— R. E..................Tools.
H—— D.........Junk, etc.	T—— & B——.............Painters.
H—— J.............Fish and Fruit.	W—— A...........Picture Frames.
H—— E...................Lumber.	W—— C. H.............Builder.
H—— S. J.........Boots and Shoes.	

[TO BE CONTINUED.]

PATERSON, N. J.

A—— D...................Harness.	L—— J. H............ .....Painter.
A—— C. B. & Co.........Mufrs. Silk.	M—— S. C....................Miller.
B—— M...................Liquors.	M—— J................Cotton Mills.
B—— L. J., Jr............Silk Mills.	O—— C....................Coal.
C—— E............Lamps and Oil.	P—— Bros....................Silk.
C—— W.................Scrap Iron.	S—— J. G............Fancy Goods.
C—— & H——............Crockery.	S—— J....................Hotel.
D—— J.................Contractor.	V—— R—— M—— Co.
F—— T......................Gro.	W—— B—— C—— Co.
G—— O. V..................Drugs.	W—— M—— Co.........Machinists.
G—— & L——...............Dyers.	Y—— G............... Tinsmith.
H—— & Co.................Furniture.	Z—— J. P....................Hotel.
H—— W.............Cottons, etc.	

[TO BE CONTINUED.]

PHILADELPHIA, PA.

A—— J. K..................Clothing.
A—— J......................Coal.
A—— R. Jr..................Coal.
A—— T. M.........Flour and Feed.
A—— E...................Clothing.
A—— S....................Clothing.
A—— W. S. & Co.......Sashes, etc.
A—— & K——...........Lumber.
A—— A..................Liquors.
A—— P—— B—— Co.
A—— G. & Co.............Music.
A—— & Bro.................Coal.
A—— V. E,.................D. G.
A—— D....................Hatter.
A—— E. D...............Lumber.
A—— F—— & Co.......Queensware.
A—— H...............Grist Mill.
A—— W....................Shoes.
A—— H—— & Co.Mnfrs. Sewing Silk.
A—— H—— & L—— Co.
A—— S. W...........Tobacco.
B—— C. W., Jr.............Flour.
B—— J..................Furniture.
B—— T. W................Jeweller.
B—— J. J. & Co.Hosiery, Notions, etc.
B—— F. & Co.............Brandies.
B—— H. A...........R. E. Agent.
B—— S. M..................Tailor.
B—— E....................Hotel.
B—— J..............Mnfr. Shawls.
B—— J. P.........Gents' Furn'g.
B—— & S——.............Files.
B—— P............Stoves, etc.
B—— A. & J. B..............D. G.
B—— W. T.............Spar-yard.
B—— H...............Gro., etc.
B—— W....................Gro.
B—— Bros..............H'dware.
B—— & S——...........Clothing.
B—— T. & Bro...........Finishers.
B—— I...................Brewer.
B—— R——................D. G.
B—— E.................Notions.
B—— D. & Son.......Coppersmiths.
B—— A. & Bro.........Lumber.
B—— & G——...........Factors.
B—— J...................Wines.
B—— C....................Lqrs.
B—— R..........Machinists' Tools.

B—— E.............Mnfr. Carpets.
B—— D—— C—— & I—— Co.
B—— L. & Co..............Hatters.
B—— & F——...........Liquors.
B—— F. E...........Hom. Druggist.
B—— G. & Co......Japanned Ware.
B—— & G——............Chemists.
B—— Mrs. J............ ...Crockery.
B—— Bros..........Mnfrs. Paper.
B—— W. H. & Co...........Lumber.
B—— & Bros....Hosiery, Gloves, etc.
B—— E....................Coal.
B—— & Co..................Mnfrs.
B—— M—— Co..........Machinery.
B—— J. G. & Co............Cars.
B—— & Bros.......Whol. Dyestuffs.
B—— & Son...............Printers.
B—— D. & Bro............Lumber.
B—— M—— C—— Co.
B—— W. R. & Co........Iron Pipes.
B—— & M——............Liquors.
B—— P....................Coal.
B—— J...................Painter.
B—— P—— & W——.L—— Works.
B—— E.................Millinery.
C—— & K——.......Tin Plate, etc.
C—— S. S. & Co........Confectionery.
C—— & A——.......Sash Mill.
C—— W. P.................D. G.
C—— G. W. H—— & Co.......Whol.
                            Drugs.
C—— T—— Co.......Sleeping-Cars.
C—— M—— Co.
C—— E. W. & Co....... ...Brokers.
C—— J. S.......Ranges and Stoves.
C—— T.........Com'n Merchant.
C—— T. & W......... ....Liquors.
C—— M. Jr. B—— & N—— Co.
C—— J....................D. G.
C—— J....................Hotel.
C—— J...................H'dware.
C—— S. I. & Co.....Flour and Grain.
C—— & Bro.................Gro.
C—— S...........Whol. Linen Gds.
C—— F....................Soap.
C—— S. C...... ..Auction and Com'n.
C—— J. W. & Bro....Mnfrs. F'cy Cabinet Ware.
C—— W. & Sons..Ships and Engines.

C—— & Co................Carpets.
C—— G. & Sons............Wines.
C—— & K——.............Bankers.
C—— J...................Builder.
C—— E...............Catholic Bks.
D—— R....................Mnfr.
D—— L. & Co.. , Whol. Millinery Gd's.
D—— K................Flour, etc.
D—— J. F...............Millinery.
D—— J. & J.......Mnfrs. Woollens.
D—— T. & Co........Mnfrs. Hosiery.
D—— B. & Sons..............China.
D—— H. A.................Seeds.
D—— & Bro..................Liquors.
D—— I—— Co.
D—— Bros...............Bankers.
E—— J. S. & Sons.....Paintings and
          Looking Glasses.
E—— J. & Son...............Soap.
E—— F...................Toys, etc.
E—— C—— & Co..........Bankers.
E—— T—— Co.
F—— J. & Co..........Com'n D. G.
F—— D—— & H——......Notions.
F—— B. F.............Gen'l Com'n.
F—— R—— & Co......Whol. Drugs.
F—— Bros. & B——..Whol. Clothing.
G—— C—— P—— R—— Co.
G—— R—— & Co.............Coal.
G—— & C—— S—— P—— R—— Co.
G—— P..................Brewery.
H—— K—— & Co........Brickmkrs.
H—— W. W.......Mnfr. Bibles and
          Albums.
H—— & Co...................Oils.
H—— & H—— Co.
K—— H. W.................Hotel.
K—— & G——.......Mnfrs. Cottage
          Furniture.
L—— & S—— S—— P—— R—— Co.

M—— N—— & B——......Sugar Re-
          finers.
M—— W..................Stationer.
M—— T. J......Liquor and Distiller.
M—— S—— & Co....Cotton Brokers.
M—— & Bro...........Gen'l Com'n.
M—— W. C. & Co..........Brokers.
M—— H. G..............Machinist.
O—— J. S. & Son.............Grain.
P—— J. W. & Son.........Leather.
P—— R. & Co.........Com'n Cotton.
Philadelphia C—— Co.
Philadelphia P—— B—— M—— Co.
Philadelphia & S—— M—— Co.
P—— S. R. & Son.....Whol. and Ret.
          Saddlers.
P—— I—— Co.
P—— R. H...................Coal.
P—— C—— & I—— Co.
R—— H. R.............Whol. D. G.
R—— M. & Co.....Mnfrs. and Com'n.
R—— J....................Corks.
R—— H. W.............Tobacco.
R—— M. & Co...........Lumber.
R—— & B——........Gas Generator.
R—— D. E........Sewing Machines.
R—— J...............Imp. Drugs.
R—— S. T. & Son........Builders.
S—— P—— M—— Co.
S—— M—— & Co.....Iron Founders.
S—— & N—— P—— R—— Co.
S—— W—— & Co....Miners and Coal
          Shippers.
S—— W. Frames, Looking Glasses, etc.
S—— W. H...................Coal.
S—— W. & A. J...........Hardware.
S—— J, G................Carpets.
S—— M—— Co...............Paper.
S—— J. T. & Co.......Carpet Yarns.
S—— J....................Builder.

[TO BE CONTINUED.]

PITTSBURGH, PA.

A—— J.....................Jeweller.	D—— P—— Co.
A—— J.....................Lumber.	D—— J. H...........Brass Founder.
A—— V—— R—— Co.	D—— G—— Co....Dealers Glassware.
A—— B—— M—— Co.........Sash	D—— I—— Co.
Balances.	D—— H..............Mnfr. Bricks.
A—— D. D. & Co................Gro.	D—— J. H......Physic'n and Drugs.
A—— J. C...........Molasses Cans.	D—— A—— & Co.............Coal.
A—— C. H. & Son.....Coal and Coke.	D—— Bros............Gro. and Liq.
B—— S. H......................Gro.	D—— J. L.......Whol. Liquors.
B—— J. J. & Bro............Tobacco.	D—— W. C........Boots and Shoes.
B—— T......................Teas.	E—— J. D..................Books.
B—— W. A. & Bro..Boots and Shoes.	E—— D.............Whol. Tobacco.
B—— W. B............Contractor.	E—— C—— T—— Co.
B—— S............ ....Mer. Tailor.	F—— & G——.............. Hotel.
B—— C. C.....................Oil.	E—— G.............Scales, etc.
B—— & S——.........Mdse. Brokers.	E—— F—— Co.
B—— J....................Coal.	E—— I—— Co.
B—— T. L. & Co.......Mnfrs. Office	E—— D. W.................Variety.
Furniture, etc.	F—— W.................Jeweller.
B—— Mrs. M................Notions.	F—— C............. ....Hotel.
B—— N. N................Builder.	F—— J. S. & Co...........Distillery.
B—— A......... ....H'ware and Gro.	F—— & Bro.............Oil Dealers.
B—— J.................Wines, etc.	F—— Mrs. C.................Gro.
B—— J. M. & Son...........Boilers.	F—— D. H. & Son.............D. G.
B—— H. W. & Co....Mineral Water.	G—— B—— Co.......Mnfrs. Bricks.
B—— W. & Son.......Land Dealers.	G—— C..........Tailors' Trimmings.
C—— J. R...................Wigs.	G—— J. W. & Co...............D. G.
C—— A..................Liquors.	G—— & B——........Patent Agents.
C—— J. M. & Co......Whol. Liquors.	G—— S..................Agent.
C—— Bros.............Stained Glass.	G—— W. J.................Trunks.
C—— I—— Co.	G—— P...................Silks.
C—— T—— Co.......Glassware, etc.	G—— & M——............Nursery.
C—— O—— R—— Co.	G—— I. W.............Com'n Coal.
C—— J. W....................Hotel.	H—— H—— & C—— Co.
C—— A. J....................Hotel.	H—— W—— & Co..Grain, Flour, etc.
C—— C—— Co.	H—— M. & O——...Mnfrs. R. R. Iron.
C—— S. P...........Tobacco, etc.	H—— & M——............Rags, etc.
C—— I—— Co.	H—— O. C.................Drugs.
C—— J. M..........Boots and Shoes.	H—— A. & Co...... .Engine-builders.
C—— Bros. & Co.......Pianos and	H—— D. P...........R. E. Agent.
Musical Insts.	H—— E....................Brewer.
C—— & W——.................Coal.	H—— L....................Lumber.
C—— W. H......Clothing, Hats, etc.	H—— F. Jr. ....Gro.
C—— G. & Co.............Jewellers.	H—— W. & Co.........Com'n Whol.
C—— & P——.........R. E. Agents.	Tobacco.
C—— J. A.................Notions.	H—— W. A.....R. E. and Ins. Agent.
C—— J....................Bricks.	H—— J............Lumber, etc.
C—— J. R................Furniture.	H—— G. B. & Co...........Brokers.
C—— T................Mer. Tailor.	H—— W. & W——.............Coal.
C—— W................Mer. Tailor.	H—— H. M....................Coal.

H—— & H——....Belting and Rubber Goods.
H—— C. & Son...........Contractors.
H—— A—— & Co.......Mnfrs. Bolts.
H—— J. W...Whol. Lightning Rods.
I—— & Co.......   ....Saw Mill.
I—— P....................Clothing.
J—— & B——..............Teas, etc.
J—— D. M................Teas, etc.
J—— J. J. & Bro......Patent Rights.
K—— P.....................Liquors.
K—— J. W.................Jeweller.
K—— & Co...Prop's of G—— W——.
K—— G.........................Tin.
K—— D...................Harness.
K—— Mrs..................Variety.
L—— W. J....................Drugs.
L—— L.:......................Coal.
L—— O. F........H'ware and Mnfr. Hubs.
L—— H. A...............Com'n Iron.
L—— W. A. & Co............Pianos.
L—— R. T...............Oil Broker.
L—— W. H................Furniture.
L—— M.....................Trunks.
L—— G. W....................Tailor.
L—— & Co.....................Oil.
L—— & C——......Com'n Pig Metal.
L—— J............Boots and Shoes.
L—— C. H............R. E. Agent.
L—— & B————.......Ins. Agents.
L—— J. B. & Co...Mnfrs. Flint Glass.
L—— S—— & Co.............Iron.
L—— Mrs. S. W....Fancy Goods and Millinery.
M—— A. A............Stock Broker.
M—— H. R. & Co.....Mnfrs. Brooms.
M—— J. J.............Whol. Teas.
M—— D. A....................Coal.
M—— J. S.....................Coal.
M—— & D——.........Whol. D. G.
M—— P................Linen Goods.
M—— Bros..............Scrap Iron.
M—— D. & Co................Iron.
M—— P—— & Co..........Furnace.
M—— T. K. & Bro..........Variety.
M—— W. F................Leather.
M—— M. K.........Tobacco Broker.
M—— & Co..................Hotel.
M—— M. L..............Carpenter.
M—— C.....................Tailor.
M—— R. S..................Tailor.
M—— J....................Variety.
M—— M....................Clothing.
M—— W—— & Co.........Tanners.
M—— B—— of P——.
M—— C....................Marble.
M—— D. & Co.....Mnfrs. Patent Tin Cans.
M—— S. & Son............Furniture.
M—— H—— & Co....Whol. Liquors.

M—— P. H............Gro. and Liq.
M—— C. & Bro........Cabinetmkrs.
M—— J. M. & Co...........Jewellers.
M—— D——D——& Co....Springs and Axles.
M—— & N——.........Job Printers.
M—— C. W.................Confec.
M—— L. & A..............Saw Mill.
M—— P.......................Gro.
M—— S........Tin and Woodenware.
N—— J................Carriagemkr.
N—— C—— H—— Co.
N—— F. C. & Co.............Coal.
N—— W....Mnfr. Colored Glass and Painter.
P—— F. G.........Burning Fluid.
P—— C. H..........Hats and Caps.
P—— M—— Co....Patent for Steam Boilers.
P—— & V——...............Liquors.
P—— T. F..................D. G.
Pittsburgh & C—— S—— R—— Co.
Pittsburgh & St. L—— I—— I—— Co.
P—— C. T....................Oil.
P—— & J——......Scenic and Fresco Artists.
P—— J. B...................Lumber.
P—— H......Wagons and Carriages.
P—— J.....Clothing, Hats and Caps.
P—— W. G. Sr.............Foundry.
R—— J. S. & Co.................Oil.
R—— & R——....Coal and Lumber.
R—— J...............Com'n Iron.
R—— J. W. & Co. ....Coal.
R—— A.......Mnfr. Corrugated Iron.
R—— C......................Pianos.
R—— J....................Brewery.
R—— T. R........Boots and Shoes.
R—— W. W. & Co......Lumber and Planing Mill.
R—— J. D....................Coal.
R—— R. J........Analytical Chemist.
R—— & W——...............Coal.
R—— H. G................Carpenter.
R—— L......................Hotel.
R—— M......................Hotel.
R—— F......Woodenware, etc.
S—— & H——............Physicians.
S—— & H——..............Clothing.
S—— F. W. & Bro........Carriages.
S—— J. J. & Bro.....Printers, Books, etc.
S—— P....................Furniture.
S—— J. A...................Tailor.
S—— C........Tin and House Furn'g.
S—— T—— Co.
S—— C. A..................Tobacco.
S—— L. B.............Fancy Goods.
S—— T...................Clothing.
S—— G. E.........Boots and Shoes.
S—— N ....D. G.

S—— T. A.................Editor.
S—— W. J. & Co.....Fruit and Prod.
S—— A..................Liquors.
S—— & Co............Coal and Coke.
S—— & G—— B—— Co.
S—— J. I.................Jeweller.
S—— C....................Liquors.
S—— L—— Co.
S—— & B——...........Firebricks.
T—— Bros.............Oil Brokers.
T—— L..........Boots and Shoes.
T—— W—— L—— T——.

T—— O—— Co.
U—— S—— I—— & T—— P—— Co.
W—— W. W....Marble and Machine
                                    Works.
W—— S. B..............Builder, etc.
W—— Bros. & Co............Iron.
W—— II. ....Brewer.
W—— J. W....Mnfr. Gaspipe Tongs,
                                    etc.
W—— J. W. & Sons......Furniture.
W—— J. T.............Contractor.
Y—— S. M. ....Gro.

[TO BE CONTINUED]

PORTLAND, ME.

A—— E. C..................Books.
A—— B. & Sons...........Furniture.
B—— & W—— Misses.......Fcy Gds.
B—— G. W. II................Baker.
C—— W—— & Co..........Brushes.
C—— J. J.................Gro., etc.
C—— D. W. & Co...............Ice.
C—— F. W.................Bricks.
C—— D. W......•.....Com'n Flour.
C—— L—— & W——......Lumber.
D—— G. R...........R. E. Bkrs, etc.
D—— J. & Co.............Gro., etc.
D—— A. L..............Mow'g Mach.
E—— A..................Furniture.
F—— J. B. & Co....Painters' Oils, etc.
F—— C. H.................Tanner.
F—— C. R. & L. E......Builders, etc.
F—— A. P.............Varnish.
G—— M. S. & Co............Hotel.
G—— G. G.........Boots and Shoes.
G—— W—— & Co...Boots and Shoes.
H—— S. B.............Carriages.
H—— & M——.........Millinery, etc.
H—— W. P............Organ Mnfr.
II—— H. H.............Drugs.
II—— J. & Co.................Gro.
II—— W. F...................Hotel.
I—— C. L. & Co..........Clothing.
J—— & W——....Coal and Wood.
K—— G—— & Co.........Flour.
I—— & Co..............Plumbers.
I—— J...............Apothecary.

L—— W—— & Co.......Ship Stores.
L—— J. F..................Stabler.
L—— & W..................Flour.
L—— T. & Co...........Whol. Gro.
M—— P.......................Lqrs.
M—— G. II.............Periodicals.
M—— E................Druggist.
M—— C—— & B——.......Lumber.
P—— M. G..................Boots.
P—— N. M. & Co..........II'dware.
P—— & Co............Machines.
P—— M—— W——
P—— S—— Co.
Q—— W. A............Bookbinder.
R—— C. D.................Hotel.
R—— A...................Books.
R—— & M—....... Wood, etc.
R—— & C——...........Lumber.
R—— G. C. & Co......Fcy and D. G.
R—— & Bro............Spruce Gum.
R—— J............,........Carriages.
S—— Bros.............Pictures, etc.
S—— O. P........Razor-Strap Mnfr.
S—— G—— & Co.......Shoes, etc.
S—— G. W. & Co............Spices.
S—— G—— & Co..........Flour, etc.
S—— E. L ....Drugs.
S—— A. B...............Chandler.
S—— J..............Iron Founder.
S—— L. D..................D. G.
T—— E. N...............D. G., etc.
T—— & C——...........Findings.

W—— B—— Co.	W—— & C——................Lumber.
W—— T. H.............Gen'l Com'n.	W—— M—— W——
W—— W. W. & Co..........Drugs.	W—— P. E.................Hotel.

[TO BE CONTINUED.]

PORTLAND, OR.

A—— G.....................Com'n.
A—— & H——......Saw and Planing Mills.
A—— Mrs. L.............D. G., etc.
B—— P. G....... ....Contractor.
B—— C. C.........Books and Stat'y.
B—— W. & Son......Gunsmiths, etc.
B—— J........B. & S., Clothing, etc.
B—— M—— & Co....D. G., Gro., etc.
B—— E. J....Builder and Contractor.
C—— & G——......Boots and Shoes.
C—— I......................Painter.
C—— H. H...............Crockery.
C—— A....................Saloon.
C—— W. & Son......Mer. Tailors and Sewing Machine Agents.
C—— & M——...........Whol. Gro.
D—— R...............Money Broker.
D—— T.........Tobacco and Cigars.
D—— A. J...................Agent.
F—— & D——..................Gro.
F—— A. & Co..........Boilermkrs.
F—— M. & Bro............D. G., etc.
G—— W.............Prod. Dealer.
G—— J. W.............Builder.
G—— J. & Co............Drugs.
G—— & C——.......Contractors and Builders.
H—— J. L.............Contractor.
H—— R. S.................Hotel.
H—— S—— & L—— T—— Co.
H—— E. B.............Gro., etc.
H—— B....Steamboats and Railroads.
H—— P.......... ....Locksmith.

J—— & S——.............Butchers.
K—— J...................Clothing.
K—— J. & Co.......Boots and Shoes.
L—— J. & Co................Com'n.
L—— J. R......Stoves and Tinware.
L—— H. R.............Contractor.
M—— S. J.........Books and Stat'y.
M—— M...........Boots and Shoes.
M—— J...Whol. D. G., Millinery, etc.
M—— & F............D. G., etc.
M—— A. L................Clothing.
M—— D......Glue and Curled Hair.
M—— J. B......... R. R. Contractor.
M—— C. H.......Plumbing and Gas-fixtures.
N—— & U——..............Tailors.
N—— S—— S—— and C——
O—— S—— Co
S—— L.................Pub'r.
S—— W. T....'.......Agent S. M.
S—— S. F..Carriagemkr and B'smith.
S—— D.................Clothing.
S—— J...Doors, Sashes, and Window-Glass.
S—— B. F........Lime and Cement.
S—— Bros. & Co...........Lumber.
S—— B. L.............Jewelry, etc.
V—— C..........Books and Stat'y.
W—— & M——..........Saddlery.
W—— I—— W——
W—— R—— T—— Co.
W—— & M——............Gro., etc.
W—— R.................D. G., etc.

[TO BE CONTINUED.]

POUGHKEEPSIE, N. Y.

A—— S. B. & Son.........Boots, etc.
A—— & M——...........Drugs, etc.
C—— J ....Boots and Shoes.
C—— E.........................D. G.
C—— W. H................Tailor.
C—— A. F.........Boots and Shoes.
D—— G. L............Stoves, etc.
D—— R......... ....Builder.
E—— & L——.........Tobacco, etc.
H—— F. & Son..............Stoves.
II—— E..................Crockery.

H—— L. E.................Crockery.
H—— P. M.................Drugs.
H—— J. C......................D. G.
M—— W. R.............Fcy Gds.
M—— F. Jr..............Stoves, etc.
M—— A............Boots and Shoes.
M—— Mrs. J..........Woodenware.
P—— J. J.............Coffees, etc.
R—— A.....................B'smith.
S—— D. Sons............Soap, etc.
V—— M. & Co.............Brewers.

[TO BE CONTINUED.]

PROVIDENCE, R. I.

A—— T..............Cotton Dealer.
A—— E. & Co.........Carriages, etc.
A—— S...............Mnfr. Cotton.
A—— T....................Hotel.
A—— W—— W—— Co.
A—— G. O...Periodicals and Fcy Gds.
A—— D—— Co..Mnfrs. Woollen Gds, etc.
B—— A. O.................Jewelry.
B—— J. M............Patternmkr.
B—— S. W...Mnfr. Prints and Horse Blankets.
B—— W. & Co...Steam and Gas-Pipe Fitters.
B—— J. H...................Pianos.
B—— W. H..................D. G.
B—— F. L............Harness, etc.
B—— J.............Boots and Shoes.
B—— G...............Tea and Gro.
B—— E. W.......Fcy Gds, Toys, etc.
B—— C. E. & Co.....Mnfrs. Ladders.
B—— & B——......Mnfg. Jewellers.
B—— J. B. & Co.....Mnfg. Jewellers.
B—— H.............Brass Founder.

B—— C—— H—— Co.
B—— G. W. B...................Gro.
B—— Bros....Flour, Grain, Hay, etc.
B—— J.................Pile Driver.
B—— & H——...............Books.
B—— E. S................Fcy Gds.
B—— H. A. & Co..Mnfrs. Comforters.
B—— H. T...Jewelry and Fcy Gds.
B—— D. Jr.............Apothecary.
B—— S. W. & Co.....Fruit and Prod.
B—— & G——......Lumber Dealers.
B—— D. B. & Son..........Hay, etc.
B—— C. B..............Drugs, etc.
B—— C. G. & Co.....Mnfrs. Kaleidoscopes.
B—— C.........Pig Iron and Stoves.
C—— G. M..............Gas Pipes.
C—— B. B................Painter.
C—— T—— & Co.........Furniture.
C—— J.................Paints, etc.
C—— S. B. & Son...Mnfg. Jewellers.
C—— E. P.........Silk Ribbons.
C—— J. H.............Apothecary.
C—— E. S.......Mnfr. Straw Goods.

C—— W—— Co.
C—— J. M. & Son...............D. G.
C—— & W——.....Carriage Il'dware.
C—— A. Fancy Goods and Periodicals.
C—— J. B., Jr.........D. G. and Gro.
C—— L. & Co........Boots and Shoes
C—— J. M....................Gro.
C—— C. E................Teas, etc.
C—— & S——.........Gro. and Liq.
C—— P. C.................Lqrs.
C—— J. E. & Co....Mnfrs. Carriages.
C—— J. H.......Pickles, Fruit, etc.
C—— & R——..Mnfrs. Spiral Springs.
D—— W—— & Co......Whol. Drugs.
D—— & M——...........Gasfixtures.
D—— S—— M—— Co.
D—— L....................D. G.
D—— M—— Co. Mnfrs. Wringers and
          Tools.
D—— C. T................Com'n.
D—— C. & Co.......Mnfg. Jewellers.
D—— M...............Gro. and Liq.
D—— J. F.................Broker.
D—— W. H................Nursery.
E—— & P——...............Express.
E—— C. F. & Co........Cotton Goods.
E—— H. W........Mnfr. Carriages.
E—— J—— & E—— Co.
F—— G. E. B................Drugs.
F—— J...Lace Goods and Underwear.
F—— N. B......Composition Roofing.
F—— D—— Co.
F—— M. F. & Co.......Apothecaries.
F—— J...................Gro., etc.
F—— P—— O——
F—— A................Mnfr. Shirts.
F—— N. L. & Co............Cotton.
F—— T....................Lqrs.
G—— J. & Co....Brokers Drugs, etc.
G—— S. C. & Co....Fancy Goods and
          Periodicals.
G—— H. & Co...Gro., Liq., and Prov.
G—— Bros..................Lqrs.
G—— N. G..........Cotton Broker.
H—— D. G..........Gro. and Liq.
H—— C. W.......Sewing Machines.
H—— W. A.....Steam Engines, etc.
H—— G. & Sons.....Whol. Prod. and
          Fruit.
H—— & W——...Laces and Fcy Gds.
H—— & Co..............Machinists.
H—— E. A..........Coal and Grain.
H—— I. M.........Mnfg. Jeweller.
H—— G. L.........Flour and Grain.
J—— & C——................Agents.
J—— C. W. & Bro......Mnfrs. Paper
          Boxes.
K—— J..................Liquors.
K—— D. H.....Whol. Gro. and Fruit.
K—— P.............Wool Waste.
K—— & Co...........House Furn'g.

K—— & P——......Boots and Shoes.
L—— H—— & Co..............Gro.
L—— W. H....Gro., Flour and Grain.
L—— W......Tob., Periodicals, etc.
L—— O. E. & Co......House Furn'g.
L—— D......Whol. Teas and Spices.
L—— M—— Co...............Soap.
L—— C. R.................Jeweller.
L—— T. J..........Mnfg. Jeweller.
M—— W................Gro., etc.
M—— M..................Saloon.
M—— J.................Liquors.
M—— J....................D. G.
M—— J. H.................D. G.
M—— E....................D. G.
M—— W. S..................Wool.
M—— S. M................Printer.
M—— A.......Mnfr. Hoopskirts, etc.
M—— T. L..........Cotton Dealer.
M—— J. A..Mnfr. Foundry Facings.
N—— B—— Co.
N—— C—— Co.
N—— R—— Co.
N—— G. H...................Coal.
O—— A. G............Fire Supplies.
O—— C. J..................Coal.
O—— M—— & Co....Mnfrs. Wire.
P—— E. A..................Wool.
P—— J. B. & M...........H'dware.
P—— A. & Co. Wool and Wool Waste.
P—— H. C..................Hotel.
P—— & H——................Gro.
P—— M. V..................Hotel.
P—— C. F....Mnfr. Woollen Yarns.
P—— E. B........Boots and Shoes.
P—— J. L. & Co.....Starch and Oil.
P—— F. C........Advg. Agent.
P—— J. C.................Jeweller.
P—— J—— Co...........Japanners.
P—— M—— G—— & P—— M—— Co.
Q—— Co.............Print Cloths.
R—— T. A. & Co...........Cotton.
R—— O...........Mnfr. Carriages.
R—— T. C.........Hats, Caps, etc.
R—— G.........Mnfr. Woollen Goods.
R—— S. E................Stationer.
R—— I—— B—— F—— M——
R—— I—— D—— Co.
R—— I—— F—— S—— Co.
R—— I—— N—— Co.
R—— Bros...........Cotton Brokers.
R—— J...............Fancy Goods.
R—— M—— V—— P—— Co.
R—— W—— I—— Co.
R—— Bros...................D. G.
R—— C........Boots and Shoes.
S—— J. A. & D. S......Woollens.
          Furn'g and D. G.
S—— E. A................H'dware.
S—— G. M.......Auction and Com'n.
S—— G. W.........Liquors.

S—— J. R.........Mnfr. Chandeliers.
S—— S. W. Cotton and Cotton Waste.
S—— W. S..................Cotton.
S—— Bros............Men's Furn'g.
S—— A. J..............Apothecary.
S—— B. S.........Hair Goods, etc.
S—— G. J.......Mnfr. Caps and Clo.
S—— A. & W. M—— Co.
S—— J. L...............Carpenter.
S—— & M—— M—— Co.
S—— B. F............Woodenware.
S—— B—— D—— & C—— Co.
T—— O. A., Jr., & Co....Mnfrs. Starch and Gums.
T—— C. F...Mnfr. Patent Cop. Tubes.
T—— J. F................Hotel.
T—— L........Mnfr. Horn Jewelry.
T—— L. H. & Co....Plumbers' Materials.

T—— & M—— N—— Co.
T—— G. & Co.................D. G.
T—— R. W. & Co.............D. G.
U—— A—— L—— Co.
V—— A—— & Co........Books. etc.
W—— S—— & Co...Genl. Com'n and Oil Mers.
W—— N..........Boots and Shoes.
W—— R. M. & Co...Boots and Shoes.
W—— O. B..................Coal.
W—— J. H...........Steam Heaters.
W—— W. H............Stoves, etc.
W—— S. B..........Fruit and Prod.
W—— B. W.........Stock Broker.
W—— G. R...........Hats and Caps.
W—— J ....Mnfr. Woollens.
W—— A. & Co......Fruit and Com'n.
W—— J. S.........Harness Weaver.

[TO BE CONTINUED.]

RALEIGH, N. C.

A—— P. & W——.............Gro.
A—— Mrs.................Milliner.
B—— J. C......................G. S.
B—— S.............Gro. and Liq.
B—— R. W..................Gro.
B—— Dr. G. W.................Hotel.
B—— J. M...................Hotel.
B—— L...............Books, etc.
B—— T. B.............Speculator.
B—— C. S...............Hotel.
B—— N. L..............Confec.
C—— J. R. H..............Drugs.
E—— J. H...............Books.
H—— J..................Editor.
H—— S. D..................Gro.
H—— J......................Gro.

K—— J. L..........Patent Pumps.
K—— Mrs. & Son....:Gunsmiths, etc.
L—— J. S...........Whol. Liquors.
L—— A. G. & Sons.......Com'n, etc.
L—— J. C. S...............Tinner.
N—— P—— Co.
N—— C—— L—— Co.
"R—— S——."
R—— & H——.............Liquors.
S—— W.............Drugs, etc.
T—— J. M.......Auction and Com'n.
U—— A. N...........Gro. and Liq.
W—— J. W.........Photographer.
W—— B—— & Co........Com'n and Cotton Factors.

[TO BE CONTINUED.]

RICHMOND, VA.

A—— R.............Baker.	K—— J...............Trunks.
A——A.............Confec.	L—— J. A., Jr...............Gro.
——R——...Imp. Tobacco.	L—— F...............Undertaker.
——D., Jr...............Tobacco.	L—— P...............Clothing.
B—— B...............Books.	L—— S...........D. G. & Shoes.
B—— & Co...........Whol. Liquors.	L—— & Bro...R. E. and Auctioneers.
B—— P...............Clothing.	M—— W. M...............Com'n Liq.
B—— M...............Clothing.	M—— J...............Auctioneer.
B—— W. W. & Co...........Editors.	M—— J. V. L...............Hardware.
B—— I...............Clothing, etc.	M—— C...............Fertilizers.
B—— J. N...............Gro.	M—— J. H...............Coal Oil, etc.
B—— E. J...............Ropemkr.	M—— C...............Restaurant.
B—— M...............Liquors.	M—— Mrs. T......Fancy Goods, etc.
B—— Mrs. E. V...........Millinery.	M—— R. H. & Co...........Com'n.
C—— J. I...............Hotel	M—— D. C. & Co............Tobacco.
C—— S—— & Co............Com'n.	M—— A. M...............D. G.
C—— & O—— R—— Co.	M—— W. H...............Baker, etc.
C—— A. D. & Co.........Com'n Tob.	M—— J...............Whol. Gro.
C—— A. & Co...........Fancy Goods.	M—— M...............Clothing.
C—— C. A...............Hats.	M—— M.'& Bro.........Clothing, etc.
C—— J. F...............Coal.	N—— O...............Gro.
C—— E...............House Furn'g.	N—— & Bro...............Hardware.
D—— J...............Brewery, etc.	O—— R. W...........Mnfr. Tobacco.
D—— R. H...............Com'n.	P—— H. T...............Gro.
D—— J. P...............Drugs.	P—— Mrs. W. T...............T——
E—— G. W. & Co.....Carpenters, etc.	P—— P—— Co.
F—— R. J. & Co...........Fertilizers.	P—— G. S...............Tobacco.
F—— J...........D. G. and Clothing.	R—— F. J.........Wines and Liq.
F—— W. L...............Confec.	R—— D—— P—— & C—— M——
F—— S. G...........Planing Mill.	R—— R. F. & Co...............Coal.
F—— L. H. & Co........Tobacco, etc.	R—— D...............D. G.
G—— J...............Liquors.	R—— M. J...........Mnfr. Cigars.
G—— C...............Tobacco, etc.	S—— J. W...........Cabinetmkr.
G—— & B——,...........Printers.	S—— J. G...........Cabinetmkr.
G—— J. H...............Tobacco.	S—— J...............D. G., etc.
G—— O. P. & Co............Tobacco.	S—— & Co.......Smoking Tobacco.
G—— J...........Tob. Boxes, etc.	S—— E. J...........Gro. and Liq.
H—— G. C. & Co...............Mills.	S—— & Co...............Shoes.
H—— R...............Contractor.	S—— J............Gro. and Tobacco.
H—— C. H...........Paper Boxes.	S—— S...............Guns, etc.
H—— & P——...........Publishers.	S—— W. H...........Livery Stable.
H—— G. I...............Whol. Gro.	S—— J. F......D. G. and Notions.
H—— M...............Com'n D. G.	S—— H...........D. G. and Clothing.
H—— S. D...............Com'n.	T—— S. C. & Co.....Whol. Gro. and Com'n.
H—— I...............Notions.	T—— C. F. & Co...........Whol. Gro.
J—— J. F...........Mdse. Broker.	T—— W...............D. G.
J—— Mrs. L. P...........Milliner.	T—— P.......Leather and Findings.
J—— W. M...............Speculator.	T—— & Bro...............Tobacco.
K—— M...............Shoes.	U—— M—— Co............Tobacco.
K—— W. T...............Mills.	

W—— & Co.............Publishers.
W—— A.................Restaurant.
W—— & L——.Mnfrs. Tobacco Boxes.

W—— Mrs. E. E...........Gro., etc.
W—— & W——...........Clothing.
W—— J. F..............Liquors.

[TO BE CONTINUED.]

ROCHESTER, N. Y.

A—— D......................Gro.
A—— O. E..................Hotel.
A—— E. R..................Printer.
B—— J...................Carpenter.
B—— P—— & S——......Lumber.
B—— Bros.................Tailors.
B—— A......................Meat.
B—— T....................Pictures.
B—— J. M...................Gro.
B—— I...................Capitalist
C—— W. & Son...........Leather.
C—— W................Mason, etc.
C—— R—— & Co..Covering Machines.
C—— B. H..............Staves, etc.
C—— H.............Cooper, etc.
C—— M............Bookseller, etc.
D—— & L——......Millinery Goods.
D—— D. M............Books, etc.
E—— W. & Co.......Cotton Batting.
F—— J—— & M——.......Bankers.
F—— W. S..............Printer.
F—— J......................Gro.
F—— T.............Tanner, etc.
F—— J....................Hatter.
F—— & Co...............Nursery.
G—— G. W.................Turner.
G—— & Son..............Soap.
G—— A—— & Co......Furnaces, etc.
G—— & Son..............Shoes.
G—— Bros. & Co..........Bankers.
G—— M.............Edge Tools.
G—— J...................Shoes.
G—— S....................Hats.
H—— Mrs. J.....Ladies' Underwear.
H—— V.................Tailor.
H—— B—— M—— Co.
H—— H. J. & Co.........Scales, etc.
H—— Bros...........Stairbuilders.
H—— C....   ......Boots and Shoes.
K—— & C——.............Bankers.

K—— M....................Confec.
M—— C......................Gro.
M—— J......................Gro.
M—— J......................Gro.
M—— & Co................Lumber.
M—— J....................Cooper.
M—— J. W. & Bro..........Pianos.
M—— S. G..............Furniture.
M—— S..................Clothing.
M—— E. P............Machinist.
M—— L. W............Flour, etc.
M—— C. & Co................Gro.
M—— & H——............Vinegar.
M—— P.............Blacksmith.
M—— S.............Chandler, etc.
M—— M.................Jeweller.
O—— D.................Clothing.
P—— & D——...........Hay, etc.
P—— & C——..........Stoves, etc.
P—— H. S.............Capitalist.
R—— J............Ag'l Implts.
R—— F—— S—— Co.
R—— F—— & C—— Co.
R—— I—— M—— Co.
S—— P...................Gro.
S—— F. & Co...........Hardware.
S—— B....................Gro.
S—— & M——.............Stoves.
S—— S.........Showcases, etc.
S—— E................Clothing.
S—— F....................Gro.
S—— S....................Gro.
S—— Bros............Filecutters.
S—— G. L. & Co........Stationery.
S—— J. H..................D. G.
S—— Mrs. E. M..............Gro.
T—— & C——..........Machinists.
W—— & S——............Lumber.
W—— R. & T............Tobacco.
Z—— M.............Blacksmith.

[TO BE CONTINUED.]

SACRAMENTO, CAL.

A—— & K——...............Brewers.
B—— R.......................Wool.
B—— H. M..............,...Carriages.
B—— J..................Restaurant.
B—— J...................Furniture.
B—— R. T. & Co...........Clothing.
C—— J. L..........Paints, Oils, etc.
C—— G. W. & Co. Whol. Gro., Liq., etc.
C—— E. & Co.....Sashes and Blinds.
C—— W. E.................Saloon.
C—— C. S...............Ins. Agent.
C—— P......................Hotel.
C—— A., Sr...............Harness.
C—— J. F..................Music.
C—— A. H. & Co.....Fruit and Prod.
D—— J. G...............Furniture.
D—— B. & Co..............Crockery.
D—— S. C.........Boots and Shoes.
E—— L. & Co....Whol. Clothing and
                    Boots and Shoes.
E—— W. P..................Hotel.
F—— N. G. & Co............D. G.
F—— & Co............Bookbinders.
F—— G...............Furn'g Goods.
G—— M. & Co..Stoves, Hardware, etc.
G—— Bros...................D. G.
G—— S...........Coffee and Spices.
G—— J.....................Saloon.
G—— W. & Co...........Foundry.
H—— A. & Co..............D. G.
H—— T...........Boots and Shoes.
H—— W. A. & Co......Carriage and
                    Wagon Materials.
H—— & A——...,,..Boots and Shoes.

H—— J................Carriagemkr.
H—— F. A..................Hotel.
H—— W. H.....Tinner and Plumber.
H—— & A——........Steam Saw and
                    Planing Mills.
K—— L...Stoves, Tin and Hardware.
K—— M....Wagons and Blacksmith.
K—— M...................Fcy Gds.
L—— A.....................Hatter.
M—— J........................Gro.
M—— A. N. H............Varieties.
M—— J........................Gro.
M—— & R——..........Liquors, etc.
M—— W.....................Wagons.
M—— A..................Toys, etc.
M—— H...........Boots and Shoes.
M—— S.....Dry and Fcy Gds.
N—— A..................Cigars, etc.
N—— S. J....Clothing and B. and S.
N—— C. P. & Co...........Clothing.
O—— R...........Boots and Shoes.
P—— W. M..............Clothing.
P—— Mrs. J. L................Drugs.
P—— L. & Co........Whol. Liquors.
R—— W. B...........Blacksmith.
S—— S—— W——
S—— Mrs. C. H............Milliner.
S—— W. A.................Produce.
S—— S.....................Tobacco.
T—— & K——................Saloon.
T—— L............Boots and Shoes.
W—— H..................Jeweller.
W—— D.................Stoves, etc.
W—— J. B................Tinware.

[TO BE CONTINUED.]

SAN FRANCISCO, CAL.

A—— L.................Clothing.
A—— & Bro...........Variety Store.
A—— B. & Co..............Lumber.
A—— B.................Clothing.
A—— J. & Co........ Imps. Clothing.
A—— S..............Hats and Caps.
A—— S. O. & Co... ..Imps. Clothing.
A—— J.................Hardware.
A—— & H——........Whol. Liquors.
A—— T—— Co.
A—— T....................Coal.
A—— & I——.........Gents' Furn'g.
A—— A.................Jeweller.
A—— & D——,.......Woodware, etc.
A—— S. S...............Varieties.
B—— & H——.......Ag'l Implts, etc.
B—— S. M. & Co....Com'n and Whol.
                                Prov.
B—— M. M. & Co..........Jewelry.
B—— A. L. & Co.........Stationers.
B—— Bros................Clothing.
B—— I. D.......Real Estate Agent.
B—— E. I...........Cigars and Liq.
B—— C. P. & Co..........Produce.
B—— S. & Co..........Whol. Furn'g.
B—— H. D................Banker.
B—— J...................Tanner.
B—— J. C................Carpets.
B—— & P——.............Com'n.
B—— P. & Bro.......Hats and Caps.
B—— M..............Mnfr. Soap.
B—— N....................Coal.
B—— S................Fancy Goods.
B—— & Co.................Gro.
B—— R. M............Gents' Furn'g.
B—— L.........Boots and Shoes.
B—— Mrs. N.............Millinery.
B—— & T——......Hom. Medicines.
B—— & B——...........Livery, etc.
B—— T..............Advg Agent.
B—— G. F. & Co.............Com'n.
B—— & Bro.....Imps. Leaf Tobacco
                and Mnfrs. Cigars.
B—— M.................Contractor.
B—— C. O. & Co........Com'n Prod.
B—— G.................Marble.
B—— A.............Hay and Grain.
B—— J. L................Tailor.
B—— M.................Com'n.
B—— & Co.................Drugs.

B—— A. J. & Co................Ins.
B—— M. C.........Stoves and Tin.
B—— J. W. & Co..........Carpets.
B—— A....................Drugs.
B—— J................Warehouse.
C—— C. A................Printer.
C—— F—— M—— Co.
C—— B—— M—— Co.
C—— F. & P. J.......Whol. Liquors.
C—— P—— Co.
C—— J. & Co.......Imps. Crockery.
C—— T—— W——.
C—— W. S................Speculator.
C—— H. A..........Mnfg. Jeweller.
C—— T. R.................Clothing.
C—— & B——.........Newspaper.
C—— J. P...............Brickmkr.
C—— C. & Co......Com'n Prod., etc.
C—— & M——...............Cigars.
C—— & H——.......Ship Chandlers.
C—— G. & Co.........Whol. Cigars.
C—— C. J...............Hatter.
C—— D...................Fruit.
C—— F. D. & Son.......Flour Mills.
C—— M. G....Saddlery and Harness.
C—— I. & Bro.....Whol. Dry Goods.
C—— A. O..................Coal.
C—— W. B. & Co........Blankbooks.
C—— U—— A——.
D—— & W——.......Whol. Liquors.
D—— Bros............Fancy Goods.
D—— C. M. & Co.....Whol. Wines.
D—— B—— & Co.....Boys' Clothing.
D—— A. C. & Co..:..Oils, Lamps, etc.
D—— B—— & Co..Leaf Tobacco, etc.
D—— F...............Gents' Furn'g.
D—— A.................Jewelry.
D—— T..............Mnfr. Soap.
D—— J. & Co......Distillers and Rec-
                                tifiers.
D—— M............Lamps and Oils.
D—— R. & Co.....California Wines.
E—— J. M. & Co........Wire Works.
E—— Bros. & Co....Boots and Shoes.
E—— H. & Co...............Bitters.
E—— & B——.........Tobacco, etc.
F—— & Co...........Ship Chandlers.
F—— H., Sr............Com'n Prod.
F—— B. P. & Co.....Packers, Wool
                                Dealers, etc.

F—— M.................Bookseller.	M—— P......................Salt.
F—— Bros..........Imps. and Com'n.	M—— S. L. & Co........Lumber, etc.
F—— & Co.............Stationery.	M—— Mrs. C. H.............Candy.
F—— I..............Speculator, etc.	M—— D...........Money Lender.
F—— & Co..............Tanners.	M—— & W——..........Bags.
G—— H..................Wines.	M—— H...............Clothing.
G—— & H——.............Brewery.	M—— P. & Son.......Millinery G'ds.
G—— Bros. & Co.Imps. Fancy G'ds. etc.	M—— D. C. & Co.....Ship Chandlers.
G—— S—— & Co.....Sugar Refinery.	M—— & F——......Com'n Hides, etc.
G—— N.............Undertaker.	M—— & Co..................Oysters.
G—— M............Boots and Shoes.	M—— J. C., Jr.............Liquors.
H—— & Co...............Foundry.	M—— F. P. & Co.............Furs.
H—— G. S.................Gro.	N—— J. P...............Com'n.
H—— C. C. & Co..........Clothing.	N—— & Y——....Lumber, Tools, etc.
H—— T. H. & Co.......Butter, etc.	N—— M. D.........Looking Glasses
H—— M. C. & Co......Hardware, etc.	and Picture Frames.
H—— Bros. & Co........Millinery.	O—— E. F...Jeweller, Ship Chandler,
H—— & L——..........Pianos, etc.	etc.
H—— W. & Co..........Cigars, etc.	P—— O—— & L—— W——.
H—— & Co................Corks.	P—— R—— M—— Co.
H—— A........R. E. and Broker.	P—— I. & N..............Clothing.
H—— P—— & Co..........Saw and	P—— & C—— M—— Co.Carriages, etc.
Planing Mills.	P—— P. J...........Gro. and Liq.
H—— B.............Transportation.	P—— G. W. & Co...........Lumber.
H—— B. & Co........Contractors.	P—— J. K....Imp. Gas Fixtures, etc.
H—— H. T........Lime and Cement.	R—— ....Saw and Planing Mills.
H—— M—— I—— Co.	R—— H—— & Co...R. E. B'krs, etc.
H—— & Co...............Hardware.	R—— M. R......Shipping and R. E.
H—— Bros...............Clothing.	R—— C—— & Co.......Shipping, etc.
I—— & G——............Clothing.	R—— A. & Co.............Books, etc.
I—— J. & Co.......Fruits and Nuts.	R—— F—— & Co....Boots and Shoes.
J—— M. I. & Co..........Bonds, etc.	S—— D................Dry Goods.
J—— C. J.................Salt.	S—— & P—— S—— R——.
J—— W. H. & Co.........Matches.	S—— & Co.................Clothing.
K—— & S...........Gro. and Com'n.	S—— & V——.......Whol. Liquors.
K—— E. C...........Imps. Carpets.	S—— H ....Cigars, etc.
K—— J. & Co...........Lumber.	S—— W. & Co.........Clothing, etc.
K—— B. & Co............D. G'ds.	S—— I...............Hides and Wool.
K—— C. J. & Co.....Sealed Goods.	S—— A. M. & Bro.........Lumber.
K—— R. C. & Co.........Leather.	S—— & B..............Foundry.
K—— C—— & Co......Toys, etc.	S—— & H——.....Carriage Materials.
K—— Bros................Dry Goods.	T—— C. L. & Co.....Com'n Shipping.
K—— & Co...............Furniture.	T—— F. B. & Co...Oil and Lamp St'k.
L—— & Co...............Sheep, etc.	T—— & Co..............Com'n.
L—— O. & Co...........Crockery.	T—— & Co..Hardware, Machinery, etc.
L—— B. H................D. G'ds.	V—— & D...........Iron, Steel, etc.
L—— S. & H..............D. G'ds.	W—— H. P.................Drugs.
L—— & B——..........Hides, etc.	W—— M. S.........Wines and Liq.
L—— & P——..........Billiards, etc.	W—— F................Stones.
L—— H. & Co.............Furs.	W—— H. & Co............Wines.
L—— & B——......Tobacco, etc.	W—— P. & Co..........Merchants.
L—— K—— & Co.........Hardware.	W—— & F——......Wines, etc.
L—— H...............Com'n.	W—— W. H...........Drugs.
M—— F—— & M——........D. G.	W—— W. & Co............Liquors.
M—— & H——.........Real Estate.	W—— S—— & Co.........Pianos.
M—— G. O. & Co..............Gro.	W—— H. & Co...Jobbers F'cy Goods.
M—— D. A. & Co.....Saw Mills, etc.	W—— Bros.........Cloaks, etc.
M—— & W——.........Lumber.	W—— L—— & Co...........D. G.
M—— I—— & H——........Com'n.	Z—— J. & Co.........Com'n Prod.

[TO BE CONTINUED.]

SAVANNAH, GA.

A—— J. E. . . . . .Gro.
A—— M—— Co. . . . . .Cotton, etc.
B—— J. H. . . . . .Liquors.
B—— & K——. . . . . .Gro., etc.
D—— & D——. .Brokers and Auction.
B—— P. M. . . . . .Fancy Store.
B—— R. & Son. . . . . .Lumber, etc.
B—— E. . . . . .Clothing.
B—— L. E. . . . . .Furniture.
C—— P. . . . . .Gro.
C—— J. D. . . . . .Beer Mnfr.
C—— E. W. . . . .Pictures and Frames.
C—— J. . . . . .D. G.
D—— J. Y. & Co. . . . . .D. G.
D—— A. & Co. . . . . .Lumber.
E—— J. & Bro. . . . . .D. G. etc.
F—— M. & Co. . . . . .Lqrs., etc.
F—— C. F. . . . . .Stencils.
F—— G. J. . . . . .Printer.
F—— G. . . . . .Furniture.
F—— & E——. . . . . .D. G.
F—— L. . . . . .D. G.
G—— A. S. & Co. . . . . .Com'n.
G—— S. . . . . .Flour and Grain.
G—— A., Jr. . . . . .Clothing.
G—— C. . . . . .Tailor.
H—— A. E. . . . . .Gro.
H—— G. W. . . . . .Lumber.
H—— W. . . . . .Liquors.
I—— S—— & Co. . . . . .Com'n.
K—— S. L. . . . . .Lumber.
L—— J. . . . . .Gro., Liq., etc.

L—— J. & Co. . . . . .D. G.
L—— M. . . . . .Gro.
L—— H—— & Co. . . . . .Cotton, etc.
L—— J. . . . . .Clothing.
L—— J. & Bro. . . . . .Drugs, etc.
M—— A. . . . . .Marble.
M—— J. J. . . . . .Lumber.
M—— J. W. & C. A. . . . . . .Gen. Store.
M—— & B——. . . . . .Carriages.
M—— J. & Son. . . . . .Auctioneers.
M—— Mrs. E. . . . . .Toys, etc.
M—— C—— & Co. . . . .Boots and Shoes.
M—— A. J. & Co. . . . . .Furniture.
M—— H. T., Jr. . . . . .Com'n, etc.
M—— P—— & Co. . . . . .Foundry.
M—— G. H. . . . . .Drugs.
M—— R. W. . . . . .Drugs.
P—— D. G. . . . . .Printer.
P—— S. N. & Co. . . . . .Hotel.
P—— J. . . . . .D. G., etc.
P—— K. . . . . .Fcy Gds.
R—— D. J. . . . . .Photo. Gds.
S—— J. W. . . . . .Jeweller.
S—— E. D. . . . . .Crockery, etc.
S—— J. A. . . . . .Boots, etc.
T—— G. T. . . . . .Coal.
T—— F. E. . . . . .Founder.
W—— D. . . . . .Clothing.
W—— J. M. . . . . .Contractor.
W—— H. M. . . . . .Com'n, etc.
W—— A. N. . . . . .Com'n.

[TO BE CONTINUED.]

SCRANTON, PA.

A—— M. L.............Picture Frames.
A—— & J——........Paperhangings.
B—— F...................Furniture.
B—— J........Carpenter and Builder.
B—— A. & Co.....Wagonmkrs' Mate-
rials.
B—— M..........Furn'g Goods, etc.
B—— J..........Books and Notions.
C—— C—— Co.
C—— C...................Hatter.
C—— J. A....................Lime.
C—— M. D............Mnfr. Soap.
C—— P. H....................Hotel.
C—— J....................Clothing.
C—— & G——...........Clothing.
C—— Mrs. C. C...........Milliner.
D—— & E——................Gro.
D—— J. H..................Liquors.
D—— & G——............B. and S.
D—— T. J.................Harness.
F—— E....................Liquors.
F—— A. L....................Hotel.
F—— C. W.................Jeweller.
G—— & S——................Tailors.
G—— C—— Co.
G—— & Co............Cabinetmkrs.
G—— P..................Furniture.
H—— N..................Limekiln.
H—— A. R.....Millinery and F'cy G.
H—— A...............Painter, etc.
H—— E...................Carpenter.
H—— A.................. Livery.
H—— & G——..Hats, F'ng Goods, etc.
H—— C—— & I—— Co.
H—— J................·.......Hotel.
H—— & B——.............Furniture.
J—— C. J.....................Gro.
K——M. M...Brewer and Whol. Liq.
K—— W—— & Co.............Prod.
L—— N. Y..................Physician.
L—— J..................Gro., etc.

L—— I....................D. G.
L—— P...........Butcher and Gro.
M—— J..................Contractor.
M—— J., Jr....Fruit and Vegetables.
M—— J. J. & Co...........Gro., etc.
M—— P...............Gro., etc.
M—— M..................Clothing.
M—— A. J. & Co.............Tailors.
M—— H....................G. S.
M—— B. G...................Drugs.
M—— G....................Brewer.
M—— T.....................Hotel.
M—— H......Boots and Shoes.
N—— J.....................Gro.
N—— M—— & E—— Co.
O—— F. J. & Co............ ...G. S.
O—— C.....................Hotel.
P—— J. W....................Florist.
P—— A. S................Ins. Agent.
Q—— & D——.Leather and Findings.
R—— J.........Gro. and D. G.
R—— M. & Co............D. G., etc.
R—— H ....Hotel.
R—— C. & Co.........Whol. Liqs.
R—— G. J..................G. S.
S—— A. B...............Contractor.
S—— A....................Coachmkr.
S—— F...........Baker and Saloon.
S—— S. B.................Physician.
S—— & P——....Lumber and Com'n
Mers.
T—— C—— S——
T—— B. H................Physician.
W—— & H——................Gro.
W—— T....................G. S.
W—— Bros.......D. G. and Carpets.
W—— F. W......Gro. and B. and S.
W—— J......Carpenter, Builder, etc.
Z—— J...........Baker, Confec. etc.
Z—— & B——..................Hall.

[TO BE CONTINUED.]

SPRINGFIELD, MASS.

A—— J. F.............Varnish Mnfr.	H—— J. & Co.............Carriages.
A—— J. C. & E. A.........Doeskins.	H—— C. T.................Gro., etc.
B—— & W——..............Hotel.	H—— & S——........Furniture.
B—— M—— Co.....Soda Apparatus.	J—— & B——........Furniture.
B—— S. & Co.................Flour	J—— A. H...........Confec., etc.
B—— A. L.........Boots and Shoes.	K—— T. Jr..............Furniture.
B—— S. S.................Coal, etc.	L—— G. M............Lamps, etc.
B—— G.....................Hotel.	L—— C. M.......Hats, Caps, etc.
B—— W. S..............Carpenter.	L—— C. D....Mnfr. Cartridge Shells.
C—— G...........Batting Mnfr.	L—— J. L................Builder.
C—— G. E.........Paper Stock.	M—— J. D.............Carpets.
C—— H...............Tool Mnfr.	M—— N—— & H——.........D. G.
C—— H. M.........Paper Stock.	M—— W. P. & Co..........Shoes.
C—— A. W. & Co............Agts.	M—— A.............Contractor.
C—— C. H. & Co.............Mnfr.	M—— & F——.....Curriers, etc.
C—— & K——.................Gro.	M—— A. D. & Son...........Soap.
C—— H. M. & Co.......Boxes, etc.	M—— D. B. & Co.........Tinware.
C—— Miss S. J...........Books, etc.	M—— A. T..........Soap, etc.
F—— B. F.........Builder, etc.	N—— Y—— W—— Co.
F—— & W——.............D. G.	N—— P—— C—— Co.
F—— H. C...............Tobacco.	R—— & B——..........Lumber.
G—— I. N.................Drugs.	S—— C. H. & Co ....Lumber.
G—— C. M. & Co............Paper.	S—— C—— Co.
G—— & B——.............Pipes.	S—— M—— M——
H—— & S——...............Gro.	T—— C. C.................Boxes.
H—— S..........Coal Sifter.	V—— C..............Electrotyper.
H—— & B——............Bridges.	V—— & P——...........Clothing.
H—— T.....................Hotel.	W—— & E——..........Founders.

[TO BE CONTINUED.]

ST. JOHN, N. B.

A—— J. & Co............Dry Goods.	C—— C—— J..........Shipbuilder.
A—— Bros.................Foundry.	C—— J. B.............Cotton Mill.
A—— H. T. & Co.........Ropewalk.	C—— H. & Son......Fancy G'ds. etc.
A—— A...................Com'n.	C—— C................Liquors.
B—— G. R.........Musical Inst'ts.	D—— M.................Gro.
B—— T.............Gro. and Liq.	D—— J...........Boots and Shoes.
B—— C. E. & Co..........Furniture.	D—— R. R..............Com'n.
B—— T. B...........Gro. and Liqs.	E—— & G——.............Com'n.

E—— W. E. ....Stoves.
F—— E. ....Lumber.
F—— C. K. ....Dentist.
F—— Mrs. ....Clothing.
G—— J. ....Hotel.
H—— J. & Co....Mnfrs. and Founders.
H—— H ....Saddle and Harness.
J—— E. & C. D ......Hats, Caps, etc.
L—— E. ....Junk, etc.
L—— T. & Co. ....Clothing.
M—— J. T. & Co. ....Tinware.
M—— F. B. ....Drugs.
M—— & P——. ....Victuallers.
M—— T. ....Gro.
M—— W—— & Co.. ....D. G.
M—— J. D ....Shipping and Coal.

M—— E. ....Millinery.
M—— J. ....Boots and Shoes.
M—— J. ....Liquors.
N—— P—— M—— Co.
P—— G. R. ....Com'n.
R—— T. M. ....Apothecary.
R—— A. & Co. ....Mnfrs. Saws.
R—— C. E. ....Shipping.
S—— R. S. & Co. ....D. G.
S—— & M——. ....Gro. and Flour.
S—— S. ....Flour and Fish.
W—— J. & Co. ....Naval Stores.
W—— L. H. ....Salt, etc.
W—— W. I. ....Flour.
Y—— A. ....Stoves.

[TO BE CONTINUED.]

ST. JOSEPH, MO.

A—— J. ....Hotel.
B—— F. & Co. ....Clothing.
B—— F. ....Gro.
B—— J. C. ....Agent.
B—— W. ....Gro.
B—— & H——. ....G. S.
B—— C—— & R—— ....Foundry.
C—— M. I. ....Feed, etc.
C—— W. L. ....Livery.
C—— M. ....Books.
D—— J. T. ....Hotel.
D—— W. ....Livery, etc.
D—— W. ....Factory.
E—— J. ....Gro.
F—— D. ....News Depot.
F—— S. : ....Blacksmith.
F—— W. ....Painter.
G—— & A——. ....Hotel.
H—— J. G. ....Tailor.

H—— A. ....Capitalist.
H—— B. & Co. ....Liquors.
H—— P. A. ....Hotel.
K—— A. ....Tobacco.
L—— J. C. ....Saddlery H'ware.
L—— F. .....Blacksmith.
M—— Mrs. ....Hotel.
M—— & J——. ....G. S.
R—— & H——. ....Jewelry, etc.
S—— J. W. ....Scales.
S—— C. C. ....Newspaper.
S—— C. L. ....Drugs.
S—— B—— & S—— ....Lumber.
S—— W. P. ....Feed Mills.
S—— & D——. ....D. G.
T—— J. M. ....Hotel.
T—— & Co. ....G. S.
U—— F—— Co.
W—— & W——. ....Wagons.

[TO BE CONTINUED.

ST. LOUIS, MO.

A—— D.	Books, etc.
A—— W. H. & Co.	Notions.
B—— & Bro.	Safes.
B—— W. & Co.	Plug Tobacco.
B—— R. & Co.	Soap.
B—— W. S.	Books.
B—— Bros. & R——.	Tobacco.
B—— Bro. & Co.	Hats, etc.
B—— L. & Co.	Com'n.
B—— J.	Corks.
C—— B——.	Newspaper.
C—— W—— L—— Co.	
C—— I. & Co.	Clothing.
C—— U—— Co.	D. G., etc.
D—— B—— & Co.	D. G.
D—— W.	Gro.
D—— G.	Tobacco.
F—— J. D. & Co.	Gasfitters.
F—— S. G. & Co.	Com'n.
F—— J. H. & Co.	Liquors.
F—— J. B.	Ales, etc.
F—— E. & Co.	Wool, etc.
G—— Bros.	Glass.
G—— C. H. L.	Hotel.
H—— W. H.	Auction, etc.
H—— Bros.	Medicines.
H—— & S——.	Clothing.
H—— R—— & Co.	Railway Supplies.
H—— & G——.	Lumber.
H—— L. W. & Co.	Stoves, etc.
H—— C—— & Co.	Books.
H—— J.	Gro.
H—— E. F. & Co.	Books, etc.
H—— & Co.	Clay.
H—— J.	Machines.
H—— L. J.	Tob. and Cig.
H—— S—— B——.	
H—— R—— P—— Co.	
J—— & Y——.	Carriages.
J—— I—— W——.	
K—— H. A.	Tobacco.
K—— & B——.	Clothing.
K—— W.	Clothing.
K—— J.	Wagons.
K—— E. C. & Co.	Painters.
K—— J.	Brewery.
L—— T—— Co.	
L—— P. & Co.	Live Stock.
L—— G.	Boots and Shoes.
M—— M—— Co.	
M—— J.	Carpenter.
M—— H.	Pictures, etc.
M—— & M——.	Gasfitters.
M—— E. & Co.	Jewelry.
M—— S—— P—— Co.	
M—— J.	Shirts, etc.
M—— A. W. & Co.	Bankers.
M—— & T——.	Transfer.
M—— C.	Pictures.
M—— & B——.	Saw Mill.
O—— J.	Saloon.
O—— D. M. & Co.	Ag'l Impl'ts.
P—— R. C.	Restaurant.
P—— C. H. & J. W.	Planing Mill.
P—— C.	Tobacco.
P—— L.	Confectioner.
Q—— O.	R. E. Agent.
R—— T. & Co.	Tobacco.
R—— & C——.	Tools.
R—— B—— & Co.	Fruits.
R—— B.	Gro.
S—— B—— & N—— Co.	
S—— P—— M—— Co.	
S—— W—— G—— M—— Co.	
S—— M. & L.	Clothing.
S—— R. F.	F. Agent.
S—— F. H.	Tobacco.
S—— H. M.	Broker.
S—— Dr. G. H. & Co.	Pat. Meds.
S—— L.	G. S.
S—— V.	Mills.
S—— C. P.	Liquors.
T—— F. & Co	Vinegar.
V—— B—— B—— & T——.	Blank-books.
V—— I—— W——.	
W—— B.	Jewelry, etc.
W—— M.	Maltster.
W—— T. B. & Co.	Publishers.
W—— J. G.	Books.
W—— W.	Mnfr. Spring Bed Bottoms.
W—— G.	Organs.
W—— H.	Books.
W—— A.	Mnfr. Brooms.
W—— E.	Books.
W—— J.	Ink Mnfr.
W—— F.	Dry Goods.
W—— T.	Iron Railings.
W—— J. & Co.	Brewery.
W—— E. K.	Books.
Y—— & C——.	Plumbers.
Z—— & C——.	Wines, etc.

[TO BE CONTINUED.]

ST. PAUL, MINN.

A—— G...............Stoves, etc.	L—— N.....................Hotel.
A—— L—— Co.	L—— & S——...........Carpenters
B—— H................Coppersmith.	L—— Mrs. J. B............Milliner.
B—— G. M..............Ranges, etc.	M—— L. B..................Grain.
B—— E. C................Scales.	M—— P—— M—— Co.
C—— & P——............Com'n.	N—— W—— T—— Co.
C—— & M——............Com'n.	O—— D..................Books.
D—— H. & Co............Gro.	P—— H................Tobacco.
E—— R................Clothing.	P—— N..................Hotel.
F—— J............Boots and Shoes.	R—— E. D. K.............Notions.
G—— J............Supply Store.	R—— C............Periodicals.
G—— E. R. & Co............Hotel.	R—— H. W................Drugs.
G—— H. C. & Co........Stationery.	S—— A..................Books.
G—— & B——........Speculators.	S—— P—— A—— & M—— Co.
H—— H. P............Newspaper.	S—— & K——........Leather, etc.
H—— P. R. L.............Leather.	S—— R. O. & Co...........Carpets.
J—— & M——..........Boots, etc.	T—— H. J. & Co..........Lumber.
K—— T. J................Teas.	T—— F. A............News Agt.
K—— J. M.............Lumber.	V—— W. A. & Co..........Com'n.
K—— D—— & Co...........Lqrs.	W—— I. N...............Livery.
L—— R. A. & Co..........Hats, etc.	

[TO BE CONTINUED.]

SYRACUSE, N. Y.

A—— J. & Sons..........Flour, etc.	H—— P....................Gro.
B—— W. S.........Sporting Mat'ls.	H—— F.............Saloon, etc.
B—— M—— Co....Mowing Machines.	H—— Bros..................Oil.
B—— B. & Co.....Millinery Gds, etc.	H—— E............Carriages.
B—— R................Livery.	H—— S. E. & Co...............Gro.
C—— N. M......D. G., H'dware, etc.	J—— W. & Sons............Shoes.
C—— M................Salt.	J—— & B——...........Fcy Gds.
D—— J. P..............Saloon.	L—— E.................Gro.
E—— T. C................Cigars.	L—— & B——.........Sashes.
F—— J............Contractor, etc.	M—— J............Speculator.
F—— & Son.............Carriages.	M—— & G——...........H'dware.
F—— M. N..............Notions.	M—— & Co.............Clothing.
G—— D.................Boilers'	M—— P. R................Gro.
H—— B.................Brewer.	N—— & N——.........Plumbers.

P—— A. F. & Co..............Lqrs.
P—— G. A. & Co..............Salt.
P—— & L——..............Foundry.
P—— M. S..................D. G.
R—— A. & Bro...........Clothing.
R—— R. & Son.............Trunks.

S—— J..............Planing Mill.
S—— D. R..............H'dware.
S—— & B——...........Clothing.
W—— E. L........Boots and Shoes.
W—— C...................Gro.
W—— J. M......Ladies' Furn'g Gds.

[TO BE CONTINUED.]

TOLEDO, O.

A—— W. W..............Jeweller.
A—— A. A..................Hotel.
A—— D.........Gro. and Saloon.
A—— H—— & W——.......Brass.
A—— H—— M—— Co.
A—— S—— & S——.....Sewing Machines.
A—— J...................G. S.
B—— C......Millinery and Fcy Gds.
B—— E.................Malt.
B—— J.............Ship Timber.
B—— L. C................Shoes.
B—— & C——..........Ins. Agents.
B—— W. H. & Co.. Whol. Carpets, etc.
C—— L. A. & Co.......Lumber, etc.
C—— J. W...............Jeweller.
C—— C. W................Com'n.
C—— H. E........Teas and Coffees.
C—— G—— & Co ....Com'n.
C—— J. D......Auctioneer Fcy Gds.
C—— J. C. & Son.....Fire Apparatus.
D——M. S...........Hats and Caps.
D—— S—— M—— Co.
D—— C. E.........Clothing.
F—— Dr. D. G.............Drugs.
F—— J...................Gro.
G—— & B.................Prod.
G—— M.................Clothing.
G—— V. W. & Co.......Mer. Tailors.
G—— J.............Ins. Agent, etc.
H—— & W——............Com'n.
H—— P. T................Com'n.
H—— & B——..........Drugs, etc.
H—— & W——....Sashes and Blinds.
H—— & N——.....Paints, Glass, etc.
H—— J...................Brewer.
H—— M. W............Real Estate.

H—— L. J. H..........Box Factory.
K—— T. L. & Co............Com'n.
K—— P. W.................Gro.
K—— Bros.........R. E. Agents.
K—— J. & Co.............Com'n.
K—— L.................Saloon.
K—— C..........Boots and Shoes.
K—— F..........Boots and Shoes.
L—— & C——.............D. G.
L—— J.............D. G., etc.
L—— & W——...........Staves.
L—— G......Stoneyard.
L—— I............Clothing.
L—— F..................Boxes.
M—— G...................Gro.
M—— W. H..........Gro., etc.
M—— & Y——....B. & S. and H. & C.
N—— J............Boots and Shoes.
O—— J.........Marble, etc.
O—— J.........Teas, etc.
O—— P—— Co.
O—— & S——..........Lime, etc.
P—— J. S...........Mill Supplies.
R—— G. H........Sewing Machines.
R—— G. W. & Co..........Millers.
R—— B................Harness.
R—— & T——.........N—— Works.
S—— J. V.........Planing Mill, etc.
S—— S...........Boarding House.
S—— & H——......Fwdg and Com'n.
S—— & Co................Brewers.
S—— T N. & Co..Mnfrs. Tinware, etc.
S—— J. L............'Furniture.
S—— J...................Hotel.
S—— J...............Mer. Tailor.
T—— A. B....Ag'l Impl'ts and Seeds.
T—— J. L................Jewelry.

T—— M—— Co.
U—— B—— Co.............Brewers.
U—— & D——.................Coal.
W—— & W——.............Tobacco.

W—— L...................Builder.
W—— C. A.........Boots and Shoes.
W—— & F——...Saddlery Hardware.
W—— H—— & Co....Mnfrs. Tobacco.

[TO BE CONTINUED.]

TORONTO, ONT.

A—— & Co...................Brewers.
A—— J. R................Foundry.
A—— D. & Co..........Whol. D. G.
B—— N.....................Miller.
B—— J.......................Shoes.
B—— B......................Saloon.
B—— E. O.....................Iron.
B—— J. & J. L............Milk, etc.
B—— R.........Flour, Grain, etc.
B—— W....................Builder.
B—— M—— & Co.........Fcy D. G.
B—— & Co...............H'dware.
C—— C—— Co.
C—— R.....................Books.
C—— S—— & Co..............D. G.
C—— P. G. & Co ....Whol. Gro.
C—— A....................Fcy Gds.
D—— N—— & Co...........Foundry.
D—— W. E.................Cigars.
D—— W................Blksmith.
D—— F....................Cigars.
F—— A. & Son.............——Hall.
F—— A. & Co............Wine Mers.
G—— J....................Plaster.
G—— M. J............Jobber Cloths.
G—— R. C. & Son.....Printers' Mtrls.
H—— G...................Plumber.
H—— B—— & Co....Whol. Millinery
        and Straw Gds.
H—— W.............Whol. Confec.
H—— H.................Restaurant.
H—— J......................Shoes.
H—— Bros.............Whol. D. G.
J—— & C ....Builder, etc.
J—— J. B..................Shoes.
K—— J.....................Hotel.
K—— W....................Hotel.
K—— S. P................Watches.

L—— S—— N—— Co.
L—— T—— & L——...........G. S.
L—— E......................Gro.
L—— E....................Drover.
L—— G. & Sons...........Nursery.
L—— Bros................Printers.
M—— R....................Saddler.
M—— A.....................Prod.
M—— H.............Patent Rights.
M—— T...................Produce.
M—— & H——.................D. G.
M—— D. Estate of.......Steamboat.
M—— Mrs. A............D. G., etc.
M—— W. A. & Co............D. G.
M—— W. & Son..............Coal.
O—— D—— & Co..........Lumber.
O—— J....................Lumber.
P—— J. S................House Agt.
R—— A....................Drover.
R—— J. H................Hats, etc.
R—— T. & Son............Watches.
R—— M......................Gro.
S—— & F——...........Machinist.
S—— H. T................Plumber.
S—— J. B..Lumber and Planing Mill.
S—— J. W..............Chemicals.
S—— J.....................Tailor.
S—— Bros.........Tavern, Gro., etc.
T—— R......................Prov.
T—— T. & Son.......D. G. and Shoes.
T—— T...................Saddler.
T—— P—— & Co..........Leather.
V—— P......................Gro.
W—— C. & W.......Mer. Tailors.
W—— & Co..................Prov.
W—— Mrs..............Millinery.
W—— A. B. & Co............Lqrs.

[TO BE CONTINUED.]

TRENTON, N. J.

A—— H. G..............Flour Mills.	L—— J.....................Shoes.
B—— G....................Hotel.	L—— A. R..................Hotel.
B—— C. E............Fancy Goods.	M—— L. H. & Co........Furniture.
B—— S. T....Coal and Wood.	M—— & E——...........D. G.
B—— A. J. & Co..............Candy.	M—— & A——.............Pottery.
C—— & N——........Liquors.	M—— I...................Miller.
C—— & C——.........Hats.	M—— J. W..............Newspaper.
D—— & V——.......Undertakers.	N—— D—— & N——........Pubr's.
D—— D. O.........Liquors, etc.	P—— G. A...............Capitalist.
F—— L.................Furniture.	P—— E. & Co.............Crackers.
F—— D. P. & Co..........Pork, etc.	R—— J. W..................Gro.
F—— & Sons..............Brkrs.	R—— J. A. Sons..............Rope.
G—— I. C...................Gro.	S—— H. G..................G. S.
G—— W. E..................Baker.	S—— A. D. ....H'dware.
H—— R—— Co...........Rubber.	T—— J...........Boots and Shoes.
H—— P.....................Gro.	T—— J.................Packer.
H—— E................Blacksmith.	T—— J. L............Physician.
H—— E. M................Hotel.	T—— H—— & B—— A——
J—— J. T..............Tobacconist.	W—— B..............Carpet Mnfr.

[TO BE CONTINUED.]

TROY ¡N. Y.

A—— M.....................Hotel.	C—— L. & De W.. ....Mnfrs. Paper.
A—— S. & Son................Gro.	Collars, etc.
A—— H. & Co..Agts. N—— S—— Co.	C—— J. W............Com'n Mer.
A—— J................,..Furniture.	C—— Mrs. K..............Brewer.
B—— G. H ....Liquors.	C—— T. A...................Roofer.
B—— P. & Son........Flour and Gro.	C—— & Co.............Gro., etc.
B—— J. L..........Tinware, etc.	C—— W. S. & Son.........Tailors.
B—— J. W....Undertaker and Livery	C—— R. F..................Books.
Stable.	D—— F. & Co.................Gro.
B—— H. K...................Hotel.	D—— M................Furniture.
C—— E.........H'dware, Tools, etc.	D—— W. H. & L. L...........Stone.
C—— & F——........Wooden Ware.	E—— J.....................Drugs.
C—— Mrs. S. A ....Milliner.	E—— W...........Boots and Shoes.
C—— H. & H. S..............Stoves.	E—— L. D..............Engineer.
C—— G................Mnfr. Shirts.	E—— J....Billiard Saloon and Cigars.

E—— E.	Clothing.	
F—— J. S.	Clothing.	
F—— & P——.	Clothing, etc.	
F—— W. W.	Ins. Agt.	
F—— T. B. & Co.	Liquors.	
F—— & L——.	Fish.	
F—— M.	Jeweller, etc.	
G—— A. G.	Laundry.	
G—— & Co.	Boots and Shoes.	
G—— S. O.	Drugs.	
G—— L.	Cotton Mill.	
G—— T—— & S——.	Jewellers, etc.	
H—— A. M.	Fruit.	
H—— A. E.	Printer.	
H—— W. J.	Builder.	
H—— T. J.	Job Printer.	
H—— E. W.	R. E. Operator.	
J—— W. H.	Gents' Furn'g.	
J—— & B——.	Clo. and Tailor.	
J—— O.	Foundry.	
K—— & Co.	Shoddy Material.	
K—— C.	Upholsterer.	
K—— R.	Gro.	
K—— & M——.	Liquors.	
K—— J.	Clothing.	
L—— W. H.	Clothing.	
L—— W.	Clothier.	
L—— H. L.	Feed.	
L—— Mrs. J.	D. G.	
L—— E. C.	Varieties.	
M—— L. J.	Hotel and Livery.	
M—— & C——	Boots and Shoes.	
M—— M.	D. G. and Notions.	
M—— T.	Fwdg.	
M—— Mrs. E.	Fancy Goods.	
M—— & P——.	Mnfrs. Paper.	
M—— & A——.	Hotel.	
M—— & Co.	Gro. and Com'n.	
M—— T.	Carpet Weaver.	
N—— W. A.	Claim Agent.	
N—— H. E. & Co.	Gro., Prov., etc.	

N—— & B——.	Ins. Agents.
O—— J.	Junk.
P—— F. T.	Fancy Goods.
P—— J. B.	Publisher.
P—— G. D. & J. W.	Gro. and Liq.
R—— J. H.	House Furn'g.
R—— G. N.	Hats and Caps.
R—— C. W.	Candies.
R—— D.	Boots and Shoes.
R—— J. H.	Jeweller.
S—— J.	Clothing.
S—— M.	Tinware.
S—— G. W.	Shoes.
S—— & H——.	Stoves.
S—— & Co.	Fish, Salt, etc.
S—— M.	D. G.
S—— E. & M.	Milliners.
S—— A. H.	Drugs.
S—— Bros.	Gro. and Liq.
S—— & Co.	Plumbers and Gasfitters.
S—— H—— & Co.	Furniture, etc.
S—— J. E. & Co.	Lumber.
S—— J.	Upholsterer.
S—— R. H.	Druggist.
S—— J. F.	Brewer.
S—— E. L. & Co.	Ins. Agents.
S—— T. S.	Mnfr. Boilers.
T—— J. S. & Co.	Clothing.
T—— W. H.	Machinist.
T—— D. D.	Mnfr. Paper.
T—— B—— C—— Co.	
U—— N.	Coffee and Spice.
V—— & S——.	Boots and Shoes.
V—— A—— & Co.	Coal.
V—— N. S.	Patternmkr.
W—— & T——.	Ag'l Implts.
W—— E. & Sons.	Boats.
W—— J. B. & Co.	Clothing.
W—— D. M.	Fancy Goods.
W—— C. H. & Co.	Boots and Shoes.
W—— J. F.	Musical Insts.

[TO BE CONTINUED.]

UTICA, N. Y.

A—— & G——.	Boots and Shoes.
B—— F. W.	Gro. and Saloon.
B—— J.	Builder.
B—— C.	Brewer.
B—— F. W.	Florist.
B—— W.	Builder.

B—— H. C.	Boots and Shoes.
C—— H. N.	Stoves, Tin, etc.
C—— Mrs. S. A.	Hotel.
C—— N—— & P——.	Mnfrs. Caps.
C—— & C——.	Whol. Clothing.
C—— A. E.	Transportation.

D—— C. P. & Sons........Glass, etc.
D—— J.......................Gro.
D—— S....Lumber and Planing Mill.
D—— R. C....................Marble.
D—— J. E....Flour, Feed, and Grain.
D—— G. & Co...............Crockery.
D—— M—— Co............Hoes, etc.
E—— B. G. & Co.....Whol. Jewelry.
F—— F. D..................Roofing.
F—— H. D. & Co....Boots and Shoes.
G—— H. & W. K..............Coal.
G—— E. B. & Co.......Mnfrs. Paper.
G—— J. P................Physician.
G—— T. J..................Printer.
H—— J. B.....Mnfr. Boots and Shoes.
H—— G. W...............Jeweller.
H—— & L——......Mnfrs. Boots and
                                Shoes.
H—— G. T.................Factory.
H—— A........R. E. and Speculator.
J—— J.....................Builder.
J—— P.......................Hotel.
J—— F—— & Co.........Stoves, etc.
J—— & H——...............Pipes.
J—— W....................Harness.
K—— C.....................Drugs.

L—— E...........Oysters and Fruit.
L—— C. A. & Co..............Hotel.
L—— S......................Hotel.
M—— & Co..........Picture Frames.
M—— H. C...........Gro. and Prov.
M—— E. C......Window Shades, etc.
M—— & H——...Whol. Tob. and Cig.
N—— N. C. & Son........Paints, etc.
O—— T............Boots and Shoes.
O—— W......Mnfr. Boots and Shoes.
P—— J. Sons....Whol. and Ret. Gro.
P—— & C——.......Boots and Shoes.
P—— W. B.............Tobacconist.
P—— F.......................Gro.
P—— L.....................Builder.
R—— R. W.....Printer and Bookb'dr.
S—— L...............Gro. and D. G.
S—— J......................Hotel.
S—— A. H. & Co........Mnfrs. Saws.
S—— N. F.................Hotel.
S—— W. B. & Co.Mnfrs. Spring Beds.
S—— C. F..........Mnfr. B. and S.
T—— W. S...............Jeweller.
T—— & P——.............Fdwg.
T—— H. H.................Paints.
U—— S—— E—— Co.

[TO BE CONTINUED.]

WASHINGTON, D. C.

A—— J. H......Stoves and Tinware.
A—— L......................Cigars.
A—— I..............Watches, etc.
A—— J.............Paperhangings.
A—— A. M..........Paperhangings.
B—— L.......................Agent.
B—— P. L....................Gro.
B—— J. C....................Gro.
B—— G. W...................Prod.
B—— & S——........Feed and Lqrs.
B—— J.........Books and Stat'y.
B—— A..................Undertaker.
B—— L. C...................Drugs.
B—— B.................Millinery.
B—— H..................Liquors.
C—— J. T.........B'ldng Materials
C—— C. R... ....Drugs.
C—— E. T. & Co...........Lumber.

C—— T. A.......Books and Stat'ry.
C—— J. H. & Co................Gro.
C—— C...................Boots, etc.
C—— R. & Co................Shoes.
C—— J. C....................Gro.
D—— S. E...................Cigars.
D—— L.....................Tailor.
D—— A. W...........Com'n Paper.
D—— A................Hats, etc.
D—— T. G...................Prod.
D—— E......................Tailor.
E—— C. M...................D. G.
E—— S—— N—— Co.
E—— F.................Cabinetmkr.
E—— H. M...............Tinware.
F—— & S——.......Bldng Materials.
H—— J. C................Architect.
H—— G. M. & Co.........Stoves, etc.

H—— V.	Baker.	M—— C.	Restaurant.
II—— G. C.	Clothing.	M—— J. T.	D. G.
H—— H.	Jeweller.	M—— F. & Son.	Lumber.
H—— F.	Whol. Gro.	M—— W. J.	Newspaper.
J—— H. S.	Saddler.	R—— W.	Paints, etc.
K—— N.	Clothing.	S—— A.	Foundry.
K—— G. E.	Gro.	S—— & S——.	Gro.
K—— W. E.	Drugs.	S—— J. H. & Co..	Clothing.
L—— & Bro.	D. G.	S—— & W——.	Lumber.
L—— J. & J. E.	Lumber.	S—— C. & Co.	Apothecaries.
L—— H—— & T——.	Gents' Furn'g.	W—— & D——.	Hotel.
M—— C.	Hotel.	W—— J.	Hotel.

[TO BE CONTINUED.]

WILMINGTON, DEL.

A—— J. A.	Stoves and Ranges.	H—— J.	Hotel.
A—— J. P.	Gro. and Prov.	H—— A. L. & Co.	Machinists.
B—— & H——.	Mnfrs.	H—— W. M.	Jeweller.
B—— D—— & Co.	Builders.	H—— P.	Liq. and Gro.
B—— G. W.	Agt. Sewing Machs.	H—— G. W.	Trimmings.
B—— J.	Paints, etc.	J—— H. S.	Silverplater.
B—— J.	China, etc.	J—— R. H.	Leather.
C—— W. H.	Hotel, etc.	J—— & W——.	Printers and Stat'rs.
C—— T. C.	Iron Railings.	L—— J.	Operator.
C—— I. T.	Currier.	L—— E.	D. G.
C—— J. A. & Co.	Harness.	L—— R.	Picture Frames.
C—— E.	Com'n.	L—— N.	Clothing.
D—— S—— I—— Co.		M—— O.	Shoes, etc.
D—— S—— S—— W——		M—— O. C.	Queensware.
D—— T. Sr.	Gro.	M—— J.	Prov.
D—— F. C.	Physician.	M—— P. C. & Co.	Gro.
E—— L. M.	Drugs.	M—— J.	Gro.
E—— G. W.	Com'n.	M—— Miss M. J.	Milliner.
E—— J. K.	Boots and Shoes.	M—— A. B.	Drugs.
F—— J.	Boots and Shoes.	M—— W.	Painter.
F—— W.	Physician.	M—— W.	Carpenter.
F—— C.	Druggist.	M—— L.	Greengro.
F—— R. H.	Gro.	N—— W. H.	Auctioneer.
G—— A.	D. G., etc.	P—— S. & Son.	Morocco.
G—— S. E.	Trimmings.	S—— R.	Marble.
G—— & E——.	Printers.	S—— L.	Baker.
G—— E.	Flour and Feed.	S—— M—— & G——.	Hubs, etc.
G—— Mrs. C.	D. G.	S—— M. B. & Co.	Bolts, etc.
G—— W. H.	Gro.	T—— & Co.	Florists.
G—— P.	Weaver.	W—— J. M. & Son.	Gents' Furn'g.
G—— J. B.	Hotel.	W—— & G——.	Gents' Furn'g.
G—— H. N. & Co.	Cotton Gds.	Z—— J.	Cooper.
G—— & B——.	Coachmkrs.		

[TO BE CONTINUED.]

WORCESTER, MASS.

A—— J. C. W......Boots and Shoes.	L—— V. A.................Gro., etc.
A—— J...... Co............ Tobacco.	M—— P.................. ....Gro.
A—— W. G. & Co.......Cabinetmkrs.	M—— O—— R—— Co.
B—— C. & Co............,....Lumber.	M—— E. A. & Co.............Shoes.
B—— R. & Co..........,....Machnry.	N—— S—— Co.
B—— H—— & Co.............Boots.	P—— F. H.............Dry Goods.
B—— & W——.............H'dware.	P—— P............. ....Satinets.
B—— W. C.................Soapmkr.	P—— & C——.............Stoves.
B—— J. J...... ...Fancy Dry Goods.	P—— P—— Co.
B—— F.............,....Mnfr. Slippers.	P—— D. W................Tools.
C—— J. S. & Co.....Leather Varnish.	P—— L. W................Tools.
C—— J. W.............F'cy Goods.	P—— O. N. & Co..............Agts.
C—— J........................Gro.	S—— & Bro..............Cards, etc.
C—— J.................. ......Brass.	S—— D. & Co.........Apothecaries.
C—— J. & Co..............Gro., etc.	S—— T. S. Sons.........Boots and S.
C—— G. H................Paints.	T—— J. C...............Boot Mnfr.
C—— W. S........ ....Wool.	U—— C. A......,....F'cy Gds.
C—— C. & J. A......... ......Fndry.	W—— S—— W——
E—— B....................Gro.	W—— W................Boots and S.
E—— D. H. & Co...........Clothing.	W—— E. B.............Contractor.
E—— H. W..............Carpenter.	W—— P—— & Co..........Clothing.
F—— A.............Clothing, etc.	W—— G. W..............Brewery.
G—— G................Hats, etc.	W—— & Co................. Bakers.
H—— J.......................Gro.	W—— & L—— G—— & P—— Co.
H—— C. C ....Mnfr. Paper Bags.	W—— T.............Rubber Goods.
H—— W. P.............Crockery, etc.	W—— S. J. & Co........... Dry Gds.
L—— J.................Boots, etc.	W—— M—— S—— Co.

[TO BE CONTINUED.]

www.ingramcontent.com/pod-product-compliance
Lightning Source LLC
Chambersburg PA
CBHW031359270326
41929CB00010BA/1251